LIVERPOOL

Player by Player

IVAN PONTING

LIVERPOOL
Player by Player

IVAN PONTING

DEDICATION

To Leila and Pete, dear friends in *almost* every respect . . .

ACKNOWLEDGMENTS

Pat, Rosie and Joe Ponting; Andy Cowie of Colorsport; designer Trevor Hartley; Roger Hunt; Adrian Killen; Steve Small; Alan Kennedy; Ian Callaghan; David Johnson; Tommy Smith; Phil Thompson; Tony Lyons, Gareth Stringer, Richard Roper and Simon Lowe of Know The Score.

ILLUSTRATIONS

Almost all pictures have been supplied by Colorsport. Every effort has been made to trace the copyright holders of all photographs used in this book. We apologise for any omissions, which are unintentional, and would be pleased to include appropriate acknowledgement in any subsequent edition.

First published in 1990 by The Crowood Press
Second, third and fourth editions published by Hamlyn in 1996, 1997 and 1998.
Fifth edition published by The Bluecoat Press in 2006.

Published in 2009 by Know The Score Books

Design by Trevor Hartley
Printed by Gutenberg Press of Malta

COPYRIGHT

ISBN 978-1-84818-306-3

INTRODUCTION

Liverpool are back. In 2008/09 they announced their quality comprehensively and paid their dues, narrowly missing out on the Premiership crown as future champions tend to do, but laying down an irresistible marker for the future. Now, with Liverpool football at its strongest and most compelling for all of 20 years, it feels right to look anew at the men who have graced the red shirt down the decades.

This is the sixth edition of *Liverpool Player by Player*, which has been expanded in two directions since the book was first published in 1990. Naturally the latest generation of heroes – Fernando Torres, Steven Gerrard, Javier Mascherano and company – are featured in depth, while all the previous favourites, from the dawn of the epoch-making reign of Bill Shankly through to the pomp of Robbie Fowler, Michael Owen and the rest are included again, many of them comprehensively revised and updated.

But now there is an extra historical dimension, not only introducing profiles of the first post-war champions – Albert Stubbins *et al* – but also an entry on every man who ever kicked a ball for Liverpool in senior competition, stretching all the way back to 15 October 1892, the day of the club's first FA Cup tie at Nantwich.

In the 19 seasons since *Player by Player* first reached the shelves, the Reds have experienced a rollercoaster of footballing fortune, the serial disappointment in the Premiership balanced by the most joyous of cup triumphs, included the astounding treble of 2001 and the tumultuous fifth capture of the European Cup four years later.

Writing about the men who starred in those unforgettable campaigns, as well as the lesser lights who garnered no medals but still wore the Liver Bird on their chests and therefore attained their own niche in the Reds' history, has been pure pleasure.

I have attempted to capture in words the essence of every player who has served under the Anfield banner since the messianic arrival of Shanks in December 1959, and also of many earlier contributors to the cause.

My objective assessments have been put together after far-reaching research, including countless fascinating hours in the company of Liverpool legends such as the late Billy Liddell, Roger Hunt, Ian Callaghan, Tommy Smith, Phil Thompson, Alan Kennedy and David Johnson, and to them I am eternally grateful. Also I have been privileged to draw on the recollections of a lively cross-section of candid Kopites past and present, a crucially important ingredient as the book is intended not merely as a souvenir but as a realistic record, with room for a little sentiment here and there but essentially down-to-earth and honest.

Alongside the profiles, *Liverpool Player by Player* features a photograph of every man to represent the club in the Premiership, Football League, FA Cup, League Cup (in all its guises), Charity and Community Shield, and European competition since the above-mentioned starting point.

In general I have tried to keep statistics to a minimum, though I have included all the basic facts, such as games played (with substitute appearances in brackets), goals scored etc, at the end of each profile. The Liverpool figures refer to all matches (a breakdown for each competition begins on page 332), but under the heading of 'Other Clubs', the games and goals are in the League only. The dates in large type refer to the seasons in which the player appeared in the first team, not when he joined or left the club. Under 'Honours' I have included only those won as a Red, except in the case of international caps, the figures for which cover each individual's complete career to date. All records are complete to 31 May 2009. Transfer fees mentioned are those favoured in the press as clubs do not always reveal official details.

When *Liverpool Player by Player* made its debut back in the long-ago, Kenny Dalglish had just guided the Reds to an 18th title triumph, easily a record, and Steven Gerrard was still playing with the presents received on his tenth birthday.

Come the outset of 2009/10, the Reds' seemingly unassailable mark had been equalled by Manchester United, but there was a genuine feeling abroad in the land that Rafa Benitez's vibrant team was capable of lifting Liverpool's first League crown at last, thus putting daylight once again between Merseyside's finest and their nearest challengers as England's champion of champions.

Meanwhile, having graduated from short trousers and matured into one of the most exciting players in the world, Gerrard was at the vanguard of that impassioned title tilt. The 2009 Footballer of the Year has gone on record as saying that if he wins only one more prize in his career, he would choose for it to be the Premier League trophy. Might this just be his season? It's rash, I know, and we've been here before, but this time, somehow, I wouldn't bet against it . . .

Ivan Ponting,
Chewton Mendip,
September 2009

6

FOREWORD
BY ROGER HUNT

I have always looked on it as a rare and precious privilege to have played for Liverpool and I treasure unperishable memories of the golden era under the incomparable Bill Shankly in the 1960s when we won the League title twice and the FA Cup for the first time in the club's history, as well as going agonisingly close to becoming the first Britons to claim the European crown.

But even that wonderful team in which I spent my decade in the Anfield sun represents only a fraction, albeit a glorious one, of all the footballers who have played their hearts out for the Reds. That much is strikingly evident from even the most cursory of glances between the covers of this book. Among the men profiled here by Ivan Ponting are some of the greatest the game has ever known, but the wonderful thing is that *Liverpool Player by Player* doesn't deal only with thoroughbreds such as Billy Liddell, Kenny Dalglish, Steven Gerrard and the rest. There is also a place here for every last one of the lads who ever pulled on the famous red shirt, no matter that they might have appeared for no more than five minutes after rising from the bench. They all did their bit for the club we love, and they deserve to be remembered for it.

I grew up supporting my local team, Bolton Wanderers, but when I came to make my way in the world it was to Merseyside that I gravitated, thus beginning a lifelong love affair with Anfield.

I was fortunate enough to make an early impact under Phil Taylor, but it was the arrival of Bill Shankly halfway through season 1959/60 that set the club on its pathway to the football heavens. I had been a late starter due to my National Service and it all seemed something of a dream for me. I was happy enough just to be a professional, and to find myself so quickly contesting the game's biggest prizes was mind-boggling.

It appeared to me that I was blessed to find myself under the guidance of such an inspirational manager and playing alongside so many exceptional footballers who were also really good lads. We got on well on the pitch, but also we were friends when the action stopped, and we have remained so to this day.

And then there were the fans, the endlessly enthusiastic, warm, funny, loyal people who followed us in every match. I like to think I enjoyed a certain rapport with them – they even bestowed on me an unofficial knighthood! – and I just feel so pleased and humble that so many of them still remember me.

Of course, Liverpool have never stopped being one of the world's top clubs and those marvellous supporters will always be there. They have witnessed enormous changes over the last half a century or more, and that is reflected by the cavalcade of contrasting characters to be found in these pages.

As for Rafa Benitez and his current squad, I think they are doing a magnificent job and that they are making huge progress. I don't think it's being too extravagant to suggest that, after just missing out on the Premiership title in 2008/09, they will go one better in the near future.

Meanwhile, I'm going to dip into this volume to refresh a few of those memories, pretty confident that by the time the next edition of *Liverpool Player by Player* appears on the bookshelves, there will be another Championship to celebrate.

Roger Hunt,
September 2009.

CONTENTS

PLAYER BY PLAYER

NEWCOMERS

STATISTICS

BILL SHANKLY

MANAGER 1959 → 1974

Liverpool and Bill Shankly were made for each other. When they joined forces in December 1959, the club was a slumbering mass of unfulfilled potential, while the passionately enthusiastic Scot was a soccer boss of only moderate success. But Shankly had a vision, and when he set eyes on Anfield he knew he had found the setting for his life's definitive work. The stadium was a mess and the training ground a wasteland, the team mediocre and the board complacent. But those fans, their spirit and that all-consuming thirst for a football team worthy of the name . . . ah, now they were really something.

The story of Shankly's transformation of the Reds has passed into folklore, but what was his secret? How did he do it? Well, to begin with, he was a motivator and psychologist supreme. His players respected him utterly, and some of them might even have feared him a little bit. Eventually, most of them loved him. Above all, no one wanted to let him down. Often outrageous, eternally indomitable, the Ayrshire miner's son built up his men until they felt like giants. Before the 1965 FA Cup Final he told them: 'You are the best. Leeds are honoured to be on the same pitch.' And after watching his side be annihilated 5-1 by Ajax in the first leg of a 1966 European Cup tie, he rasped: 'We've got their measure now. We can still beat them.' Those who played under Shankly swear that most of his lurid statements were not made for mere effect; he actually believed them!

Then there was his knowledge of the game and his obsessional attention to detail. His brain was an encyclopedia of footballers, their strengths and weaknesses, likes and dislikes – any scrap of information which might one day further the Liverpool cause. His long career as an abrasive wing-half for Carlisle, Preston and Scotland, and his management experience at Carlisle, Grimsby, Workington and Huddersfield inspired his creed for playing the game, which was deceptively simple: 'Get the ball, pass it to the nearest red shirt, and then move into space. It all comes down to give and take.' Bill possessed strong socialist ideals and carried them into his football; the work was shared by everyone in the team and there was no room for prima donnas, though be always resented the description of his side as mechanical, seeing this as an unjust slur.

As he put it in later years: 'No one was asked to do more than anyone else . . . we were a team. We shared the ball, we shared the game, we shared the worries. No one had to do it on his own. As for being mechanical or predictable, well aye, we were predictable all right – we always won!'

The Shankly wit, of course, was synonymous with the man, as the Liverpool directors had quickly discovered when they asked him if he wanted to take over the best club in the country. 'Why, is Matt Busby packing up?' was his quickfire reply. Having accepted the Anfield job, though, Bill knew that he would need more than jokes to resurrect the Reds. He began by retaining the backroom staff, insisting on scrupulous honesty and loyalty, to each other and, ultimately, to the club. The likes of trainer Bob Paisley, coach Reuben Bennett and reserve team boss Joe Fagan were told: 'I don't want anybody to carry stories about anybody else . . . if anybody tells me a story about someone else, the man with the story will get the sack. I don't care if he has been here for 50 years.'

Next he set to work on the players. A chosen few stayed, but over the next couple of seasons most of the men who had struggled unavailingly to lift the club out of the Second Division departed. Attempts to prise Jack Charlton from Leeds United and Dave Mackay from Hearts – soon the Scottish dreadnought was destined for legendary deeds at Tottenham – foundered on the board's ingrained parsimony. It's difficult to credit in the light of what was to follow, but there were even moments when the new Liverpool manager contemplated leaving on principle.

Long and heartfelt discussions with an old friend and fellow Scot, the aforementioned Matt Busby of Manchester United, went a long way towards convincing him to stay, a delicious irony in view of the pair's subsequent battles to occupy the loftiest pinnacles of the English game. There was also his own natural aversion to quitting any task that he had started, and those who knew him best were not surprised that Shankly persisted. Duly, in came the likes of Ian St John and Ron Yeats, and the playing foundations of the most successful soccer dynasty in the history of the British game were laid.

Promotion was secured in 1961/62 and was followed swiftly by unprecedented glories as the rest of the decade unfolded. The Reds' first FA Cup triumph was sandwiched by two League Championships and there was a series of enthralling European adventures to fire the imagination of the most committed supporters in the land. Shanks was placed on a pedestal from which not even a barren patch towards the end of the 1960s could remove him. He went on to build a second fine side, registering the memorable double of League title and UEFA Cup success in 1972/73, before stunning the soccer world with his retirement immediately after lifting his second FA Cup in 1974.

His subsequent relations with the club he had turned into an international institution were tainted with misunderstandings, and perhaps a little more tact might have been exercised on both sides. Bill died of a heart attack in 1981, and both the Shankly Gates – inscribed with the legend 'You'll Never Walk Alone' – and an imposing bronze statue stand as appropriate tributes at his beloved Anfield. But his ultimate memorial is something grander, more all-embracing than either of them – no less than Liverpool FC itself, the club that Bill Shankly built.

BOB PAISLEY

MANAGER 1974 → 1983

When Bob Paisley moved into the manager's chair unexpectedly vacated by Bill Shankly in the summer of 1974, most pundits saw the modest north-easterner as a two-way loser. If the Reds continued in their winning ways, it would be a case of yet more triumphs for the team that Shanks had created; if, on the other hand, the flow of trophies dried up, then poor old Bob would take the blame. But it didn't happen quite like that.

After one barren campaign, the man who had served Liverpool as player, coach and assistant manager since 1939 began putting his own stamp on the side. Six Championships, three European Cups, one UEFA Cup and three League Cups later, he retired as the most successful boss in English football history. And no one could seriously suggest that his incredible record was the result of anyone's efforts but his own.

Of course, Bob was the first to acknowledge that Bill had laid the foundations, although as number two in the Anfield hierarchy he had undeniably put in much of the spadework himself. With characteristic diffidence, he was reluctant to take the job when it was thrust upon him, even urging his predecessor to change his mind about stepping down. In the end, he said he'd do his best . . .

Paisley started with the complete respect of his players, though there may have been traces of resentment in some quarters as a result of tough decisions he had been called on to implement as first lieutenant during the Shankly regime. Probably he suffered some early embarrassment, too, when Bill, on appearing at the training ground, was addressed as 'Boss' by some of his former charges. Undaunted, he soldiered on, sensibly deciding not to compete with the wisecracking Scot for the fans' affections. He was no extrovert and had no intention of pretending to be one. 'I'll let the players on the pitch do my talking for me,' he said at the time, and over the seasons that followed their statements were eloquent indeed. To begin with, however, they were not quite so communicative, with no silverware being added to the Anfield collection in 1974/75. The prophets of doom had a field day, predicting that the new manager would prove little more than a caretaker and that some top 'name' was being lined up as his successor.

The Paisley way was not to panic. He responded by quietly enhancing his legacy of players, adding the likes of Phil Neal and Terry McDermott to his squad and – a master stroke, this – converting Ray Kennedy from a struggling striker into a vastly influential left-sided midfielder. In 1975/76 he began to enjoy the fruits, with a title and UEFA Cup double to match Bill's identical achievement of three years earlier. Thereafter he began to break new ground, the subsequent campaign yielding the ultimate prize which had perpetually eluded Shanks – the European Cup. As his confidence grew, Paisley even began to unbend a little in public, and when asked for his views before that greatest ever British football triumph on Italian soil, he revealed his own brand of wry humour: 'The last time I was in Rome was 33 years ago. I helped to capture it!'

As the honours mounted, the extent of Bob's soccer expertise became ever more apparent. He preached a gospel of control and movement, and made sure that he had the right men to put it into practice, bringing such exceptional talents as Kenny Dalglish, Graeme Souness and Alan Hansen to the club. A meticulous planner, shrewd tactician and canny judge of a player's strengths and weaknesses, also he was an authority on football injuries, often able to diagnose problems before they became serious. Refreshingly, he was willing also to own up to his rare mistakes, for instance taking the blame for changing his formation from 4-4-2 to 4-3-3 for the 1979 FA Cup semi-final replay against Manchester United, a switch which he believed cost the Reds the match.

Paisley retired in 1983 after nine years in charge, coming back two years later to advise Kenny Dalglish, and eventually taking a seat on the board. In summing up the Paisley career, some years before Bob's death in 1996, Brian Clough said it all: 'He is a great man, and has once and for all broken the myth that nice guys don't win anything.'

JOE FAGAN

MANAGER 1983 → 1985

Joe Fagan was faced with the seemingly impossible task of following not one, but two legends as boss of the Reds. How did he react? Why, by instantly outdoing them, how else? In his first campaign, Joe achieved what neither Bill Shankly nor Bob Paisley had managed: he led Liverpool to three major honours, the European Cup, the League Championship and the League Cup. It was the perfect riposte to critics who had said that not even the all-conquering Anfield outfit could promote from within for a second time and maintain success.

To people who knew the club, though, Fagan's triumphs came as no surprise. Joe, whose son Chris made one senior appearance for the Reds in 1971, had been a Liverpool coach since 1958 and had moved up to become Paisley's assistant after Shankly's retirement. As such, he was imbued with all things Liverpool and was already a vital part of the set-up, albeit a publicly silent one. He had the golden knack of getting the best out of the players in his charge and, in many cases, he was a mixture of friend and adviser to them.

It was from this position of strength that his reign began, inauspiciously as it turned out, with a Charity Shield defeat by Manchester United. But when the real business got under way, the status quo of Liverpool dominance was soon restored, and a glorious 1983/84 came to a climax with a nerve-tingling penalty shoot-out to decide the European Cup Final against AS Roma in Rome. And when Alan Kennedy slotted home the winner, Joe's familiar cheeky grin dominated the celebrations as the enormity of his triple triumph began to sink in.

But there were clouds on the horizon. With his imperious skipper Graeme Souness leaving for Italy, Fagan was always going to face a more demanding term in 1984/85, and so it proved. His early years in the game – when he had been an enthusiastic, if moderate performer for Manchester City and Bradford – had taught him the virtues of pragmatism, and he declared: 'Souness has gone; forget about him, we've got a job to do without him.' That, however, was easier said than done.

John Wark and Paul Walsh were added to the squad but, partly through injuries, neither player had the hoped-for impact. An appalling League start saw the Reds drop into the bottom three by October, and although they recovered to finish as runners-up, the title slipped across Stanley Park to Everton. There was an early League Cup exit at the hands of Tottenham Hotspur, and when progress towards the FA Cup Final was halted by Manchester United in a semi-final replay, all that was left was the European Cup. That Liverpool eventually lost the final to Juventus counted for nothing; that lives were lost when a wall collapsed during crowd trouble at the Heysel Stadium cast a blight over the football world.

Fagan, who had decided already to retire, shed tears of despair on that grievous night as he confirmed his intention to step down. So honest, knowledgeable and respected throughout the game, he did not deserve such a dire departure. But despite the trauma of Heysel, Joe could look back with pride on his two years in charge at Anfield. One former Liverpool star described him as the top coach in Europe, perhaps the world; another called him a gentleman and a gentle man. Few managers have left their desks with warmer, more heartfelt tributes, and when Joe Fagan died in 2001 he was mourned universally throughout the game to which he had given a lifetime of selfless and frequently inspirational endeavour.

KENNY DALGLISH

MANAGER 1985 → 1991

It had to happen, sooner or later. Someone in the mad, mad world of professional soccer was bound to crack. Unreal expectations fuelled by the spiralling financial stakes, the constant tension endured in the media's unforgiving glare, the consequent pressure on family and friends . . . they combined to make it inevitable. Thus, when it finally came to pass in February 1991, the only surprise was the identity of the victim: Kenny Dalglish.

At the time Liverpool were reigning champions, they were top of the League yet again and among the favourites for the FA Cup. Their manager was perceived universally as impregnably self-sufficient, his strength of character and *sang-froid* not in doubt after more than two decades of top-class competition. If his communication skills left something to be desired and his barbs of arid humour, aimed mainly at pressmen, were becoming ever more venomous, then what of it? Kenny was the master, Kenny had done it all, Kenny could cope . . .

What everyone overlooked, however, was a factor which, in retrospect, seems blindingly obvious, but not until Dalglish chose eventually to reveal the true story of his departure from Anfield did the pieces fit together. He had lived through the traumas of Heysel and, even more drainingly, of Hillsborough, and the cumulative toll on his wellbeing was utterly devastating. True, for his compassion, dignity and selflessness in the aftermath of the Sheffield tragedy he had earned widespread respect and affection, and he was praised for his immense strength. Yet somehow, in the wider world, all that was taken for granted. Nobody knew the depths of his personal debilitation, that he had felt like resigning by June 1990, that his health and family life were suffering, that soon he would fear for his very sanity.

Understanding that now, it puts a poignant perspective on the increasingly distracted Dalglish demeanour during the fateful months leading to his dramatic departure. Though the Reds continued to ride high, they were not as convincing as in recent years, and their boss had been the butt of steady criticism. At various times Kenny was slammed for negative tactics, peculiar selections, bizarre purchases and, most persistently, for his periodic dropping of Peter Beardsley.

It must be remembered that throughout a dazzling career with Celtic and Liverpool, just about everything had gone right for the multi-gifted Glaswegian. Now, with flak beginning to fly in his direction, he faced unfamiliar circumstances and, in his anguished state, he was not equipped to deal with them.

Weighed down by the cares of high office – and there were stories of some almighty behind-the-scenes rows at the club – he became increasingly tetchy and defensive in public, until the day he could take no more. Despite Kenny's subdued but emotional protestations that there was no ulterior motive behind his decision to quit as the season approached its climax – indeed, an FA Cup tie with Everton was still unresolved, his bombshell being dropped the morning after a 4-4 draw at Goodison – speculation was rife and conspiracy theories abounded. How hurtful that must have been to a fellow at the end of his tether, like so many in the unforgiving modern world; in essence, he was just another man whose job had become too much for him, but who was in an enviable position of security which enabled him to walk away.

Whatever the ins and outs of his exit, what remains indisputable is the eminence of his record at the Anfield helm. The vultures had gathered when he was appointed player-manager in the summer of 1985, succeeding Joe Fagan. A popular reaction was that after successfully replacing Shankly and Paisley by promoting long-time loyal servants, the board should have chosen another graduate from the legendary bootroom, probably Ronnie Moran. How could a man with no management experience possibly cope with one of the most demanding positions in football? The directors, however, knew a thing or two about Kenny Dalglish. They had perceived the leadership potential which was to make him comprehensively worthy of following his illustrious predecessors.

Dalglish's subsequent progress speaks for itself. In 1985/86 his side claimed the League and FA Cup double, something even Liverpool had never done before; season 1986/87 brought only League Cup Final defeat, though it moved the manager to create, by means of John Barnes and company, one of the most exciting combinations in Anfield history. That team won the League and lost the FA Cup Final in 1987/88, then missed the title by the narrowest margin but won the FA Cup in 1988/89. The following term they were champions again, albeit a little less stylishly, and then came that final harrowing campaign.

Kenny had never been afraid to back his judgement and for a long time his transfer acquisitions – the likes of McMahon, Barnes, Beardsley and Aldridge – bore the hallmark of inspiration. Only later, when such names as Speedie and Carter appeared on the Anfield roster, were questions raised, and by then the boss wasn't quite himself.

What cannot be contradicted is that, by his managerial deeds alone, he attained soccer greatness. Indeed, if the enormity of his sudden farewell had been allowed to sink in gradually, had there been no return to hugely lucrative employment with Blackburn Rovers some nine months later, then his god-like status on Merseyside would have remained undiminished. That's certainly the case in view of his subsequent revelation that, had Liverpool offered reinstatement in the summer of 1991, he would have accepted joyfully.

Astonishingly, his tenure at Ewood Park produced a similar tale of fabulous achievement (the League title) followed by controversial withdrawal, albeit in different circumstances. For his next trick, he succeeded Kevin Keegan as Newcastle boss and experienced initial success before leaving with accusations of dullness ringing in his ears. It seemed a sadly inappropriate end to the long and winding career of Kenny Dalglish, one of the truly great football men of this or any other age. But in July 2009 he returned to Anfield to take on a senior role at the youth academy, also acting as a sounding board to Rafa Benitez, and the Liverpool faithful rejoiced.

GRAEME SOUNESS

MANAGER 1991 → 1994

There were extenuating circumstances, but nothing can alter the unadorned truth that, as Liverpool managers go, Graeme Souness was a rank failure. He spent a fortune on new players, yet not since pre-Shankly days – and perhaps not even then – had such empty, frustrating, downright upsetting seasons been endured at Anfield.

Worse still, the man who had skippered the Reds to untold glory, whose midfield mastery and uplifting leadership had been hailed throughout the soccer world, became widely despised, partly on non-footballing grounds, by many of the very people who had once revered him.

Alienated supporters and discontented players, embarrassingly public wrangles and perceived weakness in the boardroom, 'Souness must stay' T-shirts selling merrily outside Old Trafford . . . a nightmare scenario had developed since the jubilant press conference in April 1991 at which Graeme was announced as the successor to Kenny Dalglish.

Fresh from an avalanche of domestic trophies with Glasgow Rangers, he brought charisma, pride and exceptional strength of character with him, but how relevant were the Scottish achievements to the task at hand? At Ibrox he had comprehensively revived a once-great club, backing his judgement with massive outlay in the transfer market, but there were lingering doubts. Was the competition much to shout about? Why had a significant number of his acquisitions been dumped so soon? Why had Rangers nosedived in Europe?

Souness, the first Liverpool boss since Shankly with previous managerial experience, reckoned that he was also the first new Anfield incumbent since the great man with a major job to do, and he declared that fresh faces were needed. Accordingly the merry-go-round cranked up: in came Wright, Saunders, Walters and the splendid Rob Jones, out went Beardsley, Staunton and Gillespie in short order. However, such changes could not lift the Reds above sixth place in the League and although the FA Cup was won, the side left much to be desired.

Shortly before the final, however, all that was overshadowed by the startling news that Graeme was entering hospital for a triple-bypass heart operation at the age of 38. Incredibly he turned up at Wembley flanked by two anxious medicos, and every twist and turn of the game was mirrored on his strained features. Foolhardy maybe, but characteristically courageous, and he vowed to be back on the training ground in time for 1992/93.

He was, too, but what a tumultuous term awaited. Before it began he dispensed with Houghton, Venison and Saunders, drafting in Stewart, James and more, but the blend was wrong, individuals under-performed and Premier League non-achievement was compounded by FA Cup defeat at Bolton.

True, there was a chronic injury crisis, though some observers apportioned much of the blame for that on Souness-inspired changes to the training regime, alterations which he has subsequently denied making. What could not be gainsaid, though, was the disharmony within the camp. The manager adopted a confrontational style and became involved in well-publicised differences with several senior players. Indiscipline occurred both on and off the field to a degree hitherto unthinkable at Anfield and, most telling of all, the fans' resentment was smouldering dangerously.

In fact, the roots of increasingly rampant public discontent lay in Graeme's close relationship with *The Sun* newspaper, a publication reviled on Merseyside for its controversial treatment of the Hillsborough disaster. Following one ill-judged series of paid-for articles, he apologised and made a donation to a children's hospital, but by then offence had been given.

Not surprisingly in the spring of 1993, the board decided that the situation was out of hand and that Souness should be sacked. But then, amidst confusion over compensation and doubt about the succession, there was a humiliating U-turn. Souness would stay but with Roy Evans promoted as his assistant.

Granted another new start, Graeme signed Clough, Ruddock and Dicks, but indifferent League form followed by FA Cup calamity against Bristol City presaged the end of the sad second liaison between Graeme Souness and Liverpool FC. At last he was forced to admit defeat, resigning ahead of the inevitable axe, and many thousands of Reds supporters emitted a huge sigh of collective relief.

Of course, the svelte Scot had not been all bad. He had been brave beyond measure and both his desire for success and his dedication had been immense. He had espoused an attractive passing game and blooded some brilliant youngsters who went on to become household names. Undoubtedly he felt let down by certain of his charges, whom he believed to be mercenary and less professional than himself. But, in the final reckoning, he was paid to get the best from his footballers and he did not make a good job of it.

During his 33 months of power, he handed over £21.25 million for 15 players, recouping some £12 million through sales. By the time compensation had been paid by the club at each end of his contract, he had proved astronomically expensive, and with precious little glory to show for it.

Did Souness buy badly? Or did he buy wisely and manage badly? After all, there was nothing intrinsically wrong with the people he brought in. To a lesser or greater degree, they had all succeeded elsewhere and several of them blossomed anew at Anfield after a change of boss. Did he sell rashly, dispensing with high-quality performers unnecessarily? Was the root of the problem that he had to do everything his way? Was he simply the victim of his own ego?

Whatever the answers, he arrived as a hero and departed as a villain. Some years earlier he had written that being successful was more important than being popular. Unfortunately by the time he left Anfield, Graeme Souness was neither.

Later, he was big enough to admit that he had made mistakes, while adding, perhaps with only partial irony, that he should have adopted an even tougher approach. Still a young man, he continued his career with Galatasaray, Southampton, Torino, Benfica and Blackburn Rovers, whom he led back to the Premiership and on to League Cup glory, before a torrid interlude at the helm of Newcastle United.

ROY EVANS

. . . .

MANAGER 1994 → 1998

Fourth, third, fourth, third - not some obscure marching chant but a chronological list of Liverpool's Premiership finishing positions during the four full seasons of Roy Evans' managerial reign. To the followers of most clubs it would make eminently satisfactory reading and equate with comfortable security of tenure for the man in charge; for Reds fans weaned on a surfeit of trophies, it represented nothing less than a damning indictment.

The upshot was that this agreeable, unassuming, wholly decent man departed, by mutual consent and movingly close to tears, in November 1998, leaving the field clear for Gerard Houllier, his co-boss since the previous summer, to assume sole command. In view of the serial frustrations of recent campaigns, and the predictable unworkability of blurred demarcation of responsibility with the Frenchman, the Evans exit was poignant but inevitable.

Whatever else could be levelled at Bootle-born Roy, none could question his commitment to the cause. He enjoyed a modest career as a full-back with the Reds before being convinced by Bob Paisley that his future lay in coaching; then, after much heart-searching, the 25-year-old ditched his playing ambitions in 1974 and embarked on the road that was to lead to management. At the time, with attention focused on the retirement of Shankly and the accession of Paisley, little heed was paid to Evans' appointment as reserve team trainer. Yet no less canny a judge of character than Sir John Smith, then the club chairman, predicted that one day the young man would boss Liverpool.

First, though, there were dues to pay and Roy did so comprehensively, presiding over a succession of Central League title triumphs before being promoted to help Ronnie Moran with the first team in 1983. His name was mentioned in dispatches when the Reds needed a new manager in 1985, and again in 1991, and when he was passed over both times he must have wondered if the Smith prophecy would ever be fulfilled.

However, with Souness' momentum faltering, Evans became assistant manager in spring 1993, some nine months before inheriting the top job. Inevitably, he was placed under minute media scrutiny and a picture emerged of an engaging, bloke-next-door type, an amiable fellow but one blessed with inner strength aplenty. It was an appealing image which contrasted vividly with the popular perception of his more showy predecessor and which gave him a head start with Liverpool fans who yearned for the old values. Crucially, Evans didn't have to earn the respect of his charges – he already had it. Practically overnight he restored morale among the players, removed the fear of failure, and made training more stimulating. Suddenly, Anfield and Melwood were happier places.

After taking over in February '94, he used the rest of that campaign to give everyone a fair chance, but having decided on drastic surgery, he didn't shrink from wielding the scalpel. Evans bought boldly, acquiring expensive defenders Scales and Babb, and had the courage to opt for a new 3-5-2 formation. There were hiccups, but in general the system was positive and frequently exhilarating, providing a fluid framework for the uplifting talents of McManaman, Redknapp, Fowler *et al*, although one frequent criticism was that the team 'passed itself to death'. Whatever, in autumn 1997 Evans reverted to 4-4-2, but with no improvement in results.

On a personal level, he demonstrated that he could handle a disparate collection of strong personalities. Indeed, when Mark Wright and Julian Dicks displeased him by their attitude and fitness respectively, he simply dropped them, making it abundantly clear that no one was indispensable. Later, when others allowed their egos too much rein, he was equally resolute, asserting his authority quietly and privately, but absolutely.

However, Evans remained acutely aware that his Reds needed to improve dramatically. The way the team fell away in the latter months of 1994/95 following the League Cup Final victory over Bolton and the mortifying fade-outs when their League challenges withered in each of the next three campaigns suggested a lack of backbone and concentration that was unacceptable. He was able to spend lavishly and yet, in general, his acquisitions proved only adequately or partially successful. Indeed, he found the club's flourishing youth system to be far more productive.

In summer 1997, after he added the midfield steel of Paul Ince to what was a potentially exceptional attacking line-up, it

RONNIE MORAN

CARETAKER MANAGER 1991 AND 1994

After the disruptive, disorientating departure of Kenny Dalglish, and the rather more predictable but hardly less traumatic exit of Graeme Souness, Liverpool could not have wished for a steadier hand on the Anfield tiller than that of Ronnie Moran.

Having spent his entire working life as a Red, Moran had become the high priest of Shanklyism, an ineffably wise sergeant-major cum soccer sage whom many pundits believe should have been offered the boss's chair when Joe Fagan retired in 1985. Intense and hard to satisfy but essentially golden-hearted, Ronnie was a shrewd coach and an ego-deflater supreme whose creed both for football and life was based on collective effort.

Throughout Liverpool's great years, as he moved from player to youth coach (1966), then took over the reserves (1971), began working with the first team (1976) and finally became chief coach (1983), he preached that the most important game was the next one. Everyone received the same down-to-earth treatment from Moran, who dispensed his level-headed philosophy to the exuberant class of '95 as they partied in the dressing room after beating Crystal Palace in the League Cup semi-final. He called them to order, pointing out simply: 'You've won nothing yet.'

When he stepped into the breach created by Dalglish, he began by presiding over three successive defeats but, typically refusing to panic, restored equilibrium to revive realistic title hopes, although Arsenal were to prove uncatchable. In 1994 his spell in control was too short to do any more than keep things ticking over until Roy Evans was appointed.

Would Moran have been a success as top man? Probably. But maybe his forte was in a supporting role, creating a bridge between players and management, busying himself with the minutiae of everyday football life. The Reds' final link with the 1950s, he served the club under nine managers – Don Welsh, Phil Taylor, Bill Shankly, Bob Paisley, Joe Fagan, Kenny Dalglish, Graeme Souness, Roy Evans and Gerard Houllier – and he was utterly loyal to each one, whether he agreed with him or not. On the summer's day in 1999 when Ronnie Moran discovered that he was no longer wanted at Anfield, Liverpool lost more than words can express.

was predicted widely that the Reds had reached their turning point, that 1997/98 would see them overhaul their bitterest rivals, Manchester United. The Anfield boss, so endearingly honest, cranked up the pressure on himself by declaring that this was the term in which he had to deliver. Well, United did not win the title for once, but it was Arsenal who supplanted them as champions, while Liverpool were barely in the hunt.

Why? Was Evans, for all his firmness, simply too nice to handle a bunch of hugely-paid young men, some of whom were perceived by the public – rightly or wrongly – to be so preoccupied with non-footballing matters that they were dubbed the Spice Boys? Was Roy, who had never worked for anyone but Liverpool FC and had been at Anfield since the Shankly days, a relic of a bygone age?

None would deny that he made mistakes, yet despite the disappointments, nothing should detract from his sterling achievement in launching the Reds' renaissance in the aftermath of the traumatic Souness regime. Equally, though, nothing could disguise the truth that in 1998 the Reds were lagging behind not only United but also the imaginatively reconstructed Arsenal.

Thus his fate was unavoidable, but it remains a telling tribute that, even with Liverpool at such a low ebb, most of the attacks on his record by long-time supporters contained more regret than venom. Indeed, they turned on the players before the manager felt their wrath, because they knew in their hearts that Roy Evans understood and shared their raging frustration. It was just that he had proved powerless to end the agony.

GERARD HOULLIER

JOINT MANAGER: JULY 1998 → NOVEMBER 1998
MANAGER: NOVEMBER 1998 → MAY 2004

The bare facts are brutal: after six seasons of vast expenditure, much of it on embarrassingly flawed performers, Gerard Houllier failed to lift Liverpool into genuine contention to be England's best. He had made an upliftingly positive contribution to the Reds' history, notably with his unique cup treble of 2000/01, but never during his troubled reign did his side look remotely capable of landing the Premiership title or the European crown. Worse still in the eyes of many Kopites, there were spells when he offered up football that was one-dimensional, unadventurous, just plain dull. Inevitably he was sacked, becoming the first Anfield boss since Don Welsh nearly half a century earlier to be shown the door.

No Liverpool manager since Bill Shankly had aroused more passionate emotions among the fans than Houllier; but unlike the gravel-voiced miracle-worker from Glenbuck, the erudite Frenchman split the camp asunder. On one hand there were those who acclaimed his restoration of the club's pride, his zeal for much-needed reform, his signing and nurturing of some terrific individuals, and his significant collection of silverware. Weighing in on the other was a stridently vociferous faction bemoaning the tedious style of play so deeply at odds with the Reds' glorious tradition, and the inability to challenge the relentless domination of Manchester United and Arsenal despite a net transfer deficit of more than £80 million.

Meanwhile, running parallel to this tempestuous debate was the consciousness that here was a man who went perilously close to giving his life in the service of Liverpool, after falling ill during the 1-1 draw with Leeds United in October 2001. His subsequent return to work five months on from open-heart surgery, with his commitment to the cause still raging as fiercely as ever, rendered him an uncomfortable target for some critics, though others proved rather less squeamish.

Unconventionally for a top football manager, Gerard Houllier never played the game professionally. Instead he taught English – spending a student year in Liverpool, during which he fell in love with the city and the Anfield club – before becoming a coach, leading Lens into the UEFA Cup, then guiding Paris St Germain to the French championship in 1986.

Though he never repeated that domestic success, he forged a reputation as one of the continent's most thoughtful operators, joining the French national side's staff in 1988, becoming assistant to boss Michel Platini and graduating to technical director in 1990. In that key role, he presided over the emergence of a new generation of precocious talent – Thierry Henry and Nicolas Anelka were among his proteges – and two years later he took charge of his country's team.

Failure to qualify for the World Cup prompted Houllier's resignation, but he resumed as technical director, then refused his first opportunity to become Liverpool boss when Graeme Souness departed in 1994, and went on to exert immense influence as France became world champions in 1998.

After that the lure of the club scene proved irresistible and, having been wooed unsuccessfully by Celtic, that July he accepted the curious appointment of joint Reds boss, working in tandem with Roy Evans. It seemed unlikely that blurred responsibility would prove an antidote to Anfield's ills and so it proved, with Roy leaving in November and Gerard assuming sole charge. Now the Frenchman, outwardly so genial and avuncular, showed that he possessed a core of steel and that in his own way he was just as driven, equally as obsessed with his work, as his friend and Old Trafford counterpart Sir Alex Ferguson.

Houllier made a dispassionately unsentimental appraisal of his footballing inheritance and resolved that radical changes were urgently required. He faced up to the so-called Spice Boys culture, waging war on arrogance and placing the accent on humility, making it clear that mere talent was not enough to be a Liverpool player, and setting out the four principles by which he would run the club.

He insisted on respect, for the job, opponents and team-mates alike; his men had to be winners to the depth of their being; the team ethos was paramount; and utter professionalism was demanded at all times. It was an admirable credo but not one for the short term, and 1998/99 ended with the Reds placed seventh in the Premiership table.

That summer Houllier made the first of many major excursions into the transfer market, recruiting £25 million worth of overseas talent, including the relatively low-profile but hugely effective centre-back pairing of Sami Hyypia and Stephane Henchoz, and he presided over several significant exits. That of the sumptuously gifted Steve McManaman to Real Madrid he might (or might not) have regretted, but that of his skipper, England star Paul Ince, fell into a different category. The ageing but still effective Ince, who liked to be called 'The Guv'nor', exercised vast influence over the Liverpool team and he was keen to stay. But Houllier wanted him out, and so he went, to be replaced by the less flamboyant, more composed German international Dietmar Hamann.

Now no one at Anfield doubted who was in charge and during 1999/2000 the side began to develop encouragingly. It retained ample flair and inspiration, in the shape of scintillating youngsters such as Michael Owen and Steven Gerrard, but also there was a new defensive solidity, a more convincing tactical organisation and, crucially, a sterner mental resolve.

Still the Reds were far from the finished article as they proved by collapsing dismally over the last five matches, failing narrowly to qualify for the Champions League, but gigantic steps in the right direction had been taken. Devastated by that abysmal finale, Houllier resolved that it should never be repeated and his spending continued to soar.

When it became clear during the early months of 2000/01 that, yet again, Liverpool would trail Manchester United in the championship race, brickbats were rained on the manager's head, many of them emanating from former Anfield heroes, a source of criticism which he resented deeply and which revealed a markedly thin skin. But as the campaign wore on, it became evident that Houllier's Reds were on the brink of something special. Though their football was infuriatingly cautious at times, they displayed

PHIL THOMPSON

ACTING MANAGER: NOVEMBER 2001 – APRIL 2002

Phil Thompson proved plenty of people wrong with his hugely impressive stewardship of the Reds during Gerard Houllier's five-month absence with heart trouble.

There were those who laughed when the assistant manager took over, not disputing his passion for the club – he had proved that conclusively down the years as both footballer and coach at his beloved Anfield – but questioning his man-management skills, especially in the light of a recent much-publicised spat with Robbie Fowler.

Thompson was portrayed as a one-dimensional ranter whose touchline antics sometimes verged on the comical, but although it was true that initially he was employed by Houllier primarily as a motivator, the man to put the boot back into the Boot Room, there was always far more to him than that.

Those who mocked would have done well to recall that, as a player, Phil was a great organiser with a deep understanding of the game, and now he showed his full mettle.

Growing rapidly into the job, he displayed sound judgement, commendable restraint, even subtle diplomacy, refusing to engage in slanging matches with opponents no matter how sorely he was tempted. Most importantly of all, he had Liverpool playing in a progressive and attractive style.

Thompson's tenure commenced with a string of invigorating victories, and although momentum was lost at the turn of the year, the team bounced back so strongly in the spring that at the end of March a League and FA Cup double was not out of the question. Even as Houllier resumed the reins, his deputy was being suggested in some quarters, and not fancifully at that point, as a contender for the manager of the year accolade, and he did receive two monthly awards.

The man himself, who had always insisted that he was merely minding the shop for the Frenchman, with whom he had remained in touch throughout his illness, reacted with typical modesty. He claimed no bouquets for himself, though he knew his own worth, making the point: 'If I didn't know what I was talking about (as a coach) then I wouldn't stand up and embarrass myself.'

All Phil Thompson asked for was respect; and that was the very least he deserved.

remarkable mettle in winning all the major cup competitions they had entered, first the League Cup, then the FA Cup and finally the UEFA Cup. This time, too, buoyed by their knockout exploits, they finished strongly in the Premiership, qualifying for the Champions League on the last day. The hard-edged nous and single-minded perseverance of Houllier had paid handsome dividends and the red half of Merseyside partied all summer.

Still, though, he saw that magnificent treble as merely a platform, a statement of his credibility as he sought to capture even more glittering prizes. He understood completely that Kopites demanded nothing less than the usurping of the Mancunians as Premiership kingpins and for Liverpool to be crowned once again as champions of Europe.

To that end Houllier continued to tinker with his combination, including the ruthless ditching of Dutch goalkeeper Sander Westerveld in favour of the Pole, Jerzy Dudek, and he remained immovably firm in dealing with his collection of hugely paid stars, notably the dazzlingly brilliant but occasionally recalcitrant Robbie Fowler.

The pressure of expectation, though, was never-ending and eventually, perhaps, it told. After engineering an acceptable, if not exceptional, start to the 2001/02 season, Houllier suffered chest pains at half-time when Leeds visited Anfield. An 11-hour heart operation followed and it seemed possible that he would never resume control of his Anfield empire but, as he pointed out, football was his life so how could he give it up?

Thus, despite a terrifying brush with death ascribed to overwork, he was back at pitchside in late March, and resumed the reins from Phil Thompson in April. Indeed, from the early days of his absence he had remained in close touch with his admirable stand-in, and later he would admit that perhaps he should have taken a longer break. In the circumstances, Liverpool's runners-up spot in

the Premiership and progress to the last eight of the Champions League was deemed to be acceptable, but 2002/03 brought more pressure than ever before.

After spending some £20 million on the unsatisfactory likes of El-Hadji Diouf, Salif Diao and Bruno Cheyrou, and pledging that his team would play with more fluency and vision, Houllier's Liverpool topped the table by seven points in November, but then sank into a morass of negativity. Now, as the Reds spluttered through their most depressing sequence of results for half a century, the Frenchman came under the most serious and protracted fire of his Anfield sojourn to date.

Though the side was not short of superb individual performers, too often it appeared hidebound by the fear of failure, and it was slammed repeatedly for lacking boldness, invention, precision, width . . . so many of the attributes for which Liverpool had earned worldwide renown. Their football wasn't beautiful and, the League Cup Final triumph over Manchester United notwithstanding, it didn't look like winning the silverware that mattered most, and it didn't even qualify for the Champions League.

After that, 2003/04 became a make-or-break campaign, but although they squeezed into the top competition with a fourth-place finish, in terms of points Liverpool were closer to the bottom of the table than the top. An aura of staleness emanated from Anfield, and now, at last, the Frenchman had to go.

Gerard Houllier, the first manager since Shankly not to hail from the Reds 'family', deserved colossal credit for his 'cleaning-up' operation, and for his cup exploits. But having created such vast expectations, he had to take his team to the next level and that proved beyond him. Happily, this courageous and honourable man moved on to further demonstrate his worth in his native land, leading Lyon to the last eight of the European Cup in 2006 and to serial domestic triumphs

RAFAEL BENITEZ

MANAGER 2004 →

In his first half-decade at the Anfield helm, Rafa Benitez has worked wonders, certainly in comparison to his three immediate predecessors in the job. Not only did he deliver the Champions League crown so unexpectedly in just his first campaign as Liverpool boss, but by the summer of 2009 he appeared to have constructed a thrilling team capable of scaling the ultimate pinnacle as far as most Reds fans were concerned, that of ending the demoralising 20-year wait for a domestic League title.

Win that and Benitez rubs shoulders with the truly great Liverpool bosses, the last of which was Kenny Dalglish. But let the opportunity slip away, especially if that enables Alex Ferguson's Manchester United to outstrip the Reds' historic total of 18 championships, and posterity's judgement would not be so kind.

In 2008/09 Rafa's runners-up pushed United very close, finishing as the only side in Premiership history to lose just two games without being top of the pile. In addition, they scored the most goals, boasted the best goal difference, did the double over both chief rivals United and Chelsea and accumulated their highest total of points since the new League structure was launched in 1992. Not since their last success in 1990 had they sustained a genuine title challenge into the closing weeks of the campaign, and certainly not since the pomp of the Dalglish era had Liverpool boasted so many footballers of such exceptional quality as Torres, Gerrard, Mascherano, Alonso, Carragher and Reina.

All this Benitez had achieved despite the question-marks over the club raised by the tetchy triangle of American owners Tom Hicks and George Gillett and the now-departed chief executive Rick Parry, which threatened on occasion to negate the manager's exhilarating progress on the field.

Also, for all his vast expenditure on new players compared to most of his competitors, Liverpool were never in the same financial ball-park as mega-bucks United and Chelsea, and when plans to build a much-needed new and bigger stadium were halted by the economic recession, it dealt a telling blow to the Reds' immediate silverware prospects.

Soft of voice, pale of face and distinctly portly of figure, Benitez did not seem, at first glance, the stuff of which inspirational sporting heroes were made when he arrived at Anfield as successor to Gerard Houllier in the summer of 2004. In truth few English football fans had monitored the progress of the 44-year-old former Real Madrid junior through his unremarkable playing days which had been terminated prematurely by injury, a stint as a coach at the Bernabeu which had included a fleeting shift as assistant to Real boss Vincente del Bosque, and an initially patchy managerial career.

Even after the astonishing feat of guiding hitherto unfashionable Valencia to two *La Liga* crowns and UEFA Cup glory, Benitez was hardly a household name beyond the borders of Spain, but his emulation of Alex Ferguson at Aberdeen in overthrowing a pair of reigning super-powers – for Celtic and Rangers read Real Madrid and Barcelona – through a stirring mixture of imagination, commitment and exceptionally meticulous organisation, earned him his Anfield opportunity.

On arrival, the relentlessly ambitious Benitez faced a challenge which, in its way, was on a par with the one which had confronted Bill Shankly nearly half a century earlier. True, the founding father of modern Liverpool had started from a much lower base, as the club he took over was struggling to rise from the Second Division. But both men were charged with satisfying a seething multitude of fans frustrated by a descent from earlier eminence, and Shankly had not been burdened by the intense expectations engendered by recent decades of unparalleled success.

Benitez set about his task quietly, realistically, effectively. There was criticism for shipping out Englishmen Owen and Murphy early on and building an extensive Spanish enclave, but Rafa was hardly to blame for Michael's defection to Madrid, and certainly the sheer quality of Xabi Alonso soon had the knowledgeable Liverpool fans drooling. Although early results were variable, there was a perception that the team was playing more fluently, and was less grimly predictable and hidebound by fear than in the dark final days under Houllier.

As season 2004/05 progressed, there was widespread puzzlement among Anfielders at the gulf between Premiership and European performances. How was it that frequently the Reds appeared to swing between the wretched and the brilliant, looking diabolical on a Saturday but assured on a Wednesday? Benitez, too, must have been perplexed, but he adhered to his sound principles of seeking to remain solid at the back, retaining possession of the ball patiently, and counter-attacking at pace, conceding that his squad was far from complete but plotting all the while to improve it.

Tactically he was canny, never more so than at half-time in the 2005 European Cup Final, with Liverpool three goals down to AC Milan and humiliation beckoning. Now he switched to a three-man rearguard and drafted in Didi Hamann as an extra midfielder, thus starving the Milan danger-men of possession. True, luck played its part in the stupendous victory that ensued, but Benitez deserved colossal credit for galvanising a side which finished 37 points behind domestic champions Chelsea, losing no fewer than 14 League games in the process, so that they lifted the most valued club prize in world football. That bought him time, and instilled the belief into players and fans alike that the Reds could prevail, no matter what the odds against them.

Now there might have been a danger of believing that his team was the finished article, that everything in the Anfield garden was rosy, but Benitez was far too shrewd an operator for that. Thus there was another flurry of major signings in the summer. Crouch, Reina and Sissoko were not obvious targets dripping in stardust, but they all addressed key areas where the squad needed to be strengthened, even if two of them were destined to fall by the wayside.

Unquestionably the side which finished third in the Premiership and closed the gap on Chelsea to nine points, then beat West Ham in the FA Cup Final, was far superior to the heroic combination which he took beyond the supposed limits of its ability to rewrite history in Istanbul. As a group the players radiated more assurance than any Anfield vintage since Dalglish's managerial heyday. Cliques which had grown up under Houllier had been

abolished; the paramount importance of team ethos and collective responsibility was preached with a passion reminiscent of Shankly at his most fervent.

In the space of two campaigns the modest Spaniard had secured the European Cup and the FA Cup, and seemingly built a platform for sustained success. As Carragher put it on the eve of the Millennium triumph over plucky West Ham, it would have been virtually impossible for any new boss to have made a better start and at that point it would have taken a confirmed pessimist to predict that the next three seasons would not yield a single trophy.

But so it was. Despite more heavy expenditure, Liverpool finished 21 points adrift of champions United in 2006/07, then 11 behind the Old Trafford brigade in 2007/08, while failing to pick up a cup in either term. That might have been a recipe for managerial doom . . . except that to this dismal cloud there was a lining of the most luminously incandescent silver. Fernando Torres arrived, scoring 33 goals in his first season and demonstrating, beyond the merest scintilla of doubt, that the Reds had finally acquired a player which made them the envy of the footballing world.

Certainly Alex Ferguson would have cherished Torres, but he didn't have him. He was all Liverpool's and, with the worthy likes of Mascherano and Kuyt having also bedded in, the Reds went into 2008/09 with genuine title aspirations instead of the wildly unrealistic hopes which had become all too customary.

True, ultimately the campaign produced bitter disappointment, but the improvement, and the sense of progress, were thrilling. Unarguably the hugely expensive signing of Robbie Keane was ill-judged, for which Benitez had to bear some of the blame, but with

the Irishman dispatched back to White Hart Lane in January, the team began to blossom convincingly.

The Spaniard's much-criticised, periodically perverse, occasionally downright injudicious squad rotation was rationalised, the caution and uncertainty which had marred the middle terms of his reign was replaced by a more adventurous approach, and an unbreakable team spirit burgeoned, so that rousing late comebacks became more glorious habit than occasional novelty.

This time Liverpool finished only four points off the crown, a gulf which might have been spanned had Torres and Gerrard not suffered injuries at key junctures. At last, Liverpool had a tremendous new team, bursting with talent, vitality and, most crucially of all, belief in its ability to capture the game's premier prizes. For this, no matter what the future brings, due accolades must go to Benitez.

It might be argued that he is unwise to be drawn into tedious and petty spats with his opposite number at Old Trafford – indeed, it can be imagined that Sir Alex Ferguson derives devilish satisfaction every time he elicits a plaintive response from a major rival – but if Rafa's touchline demeanour often tends towards that of some eccentric puppetmaster, it is understandable considering the constant pressure under which he operates. After all, he deals daily with the overweening desire of the fans for sustained Championship success, hardly assisted by the fractious relationships of those above his head who hold his destiny in their hands.

Despite all of that, Rafa Benitez has been so passionately committed to the Liverpool cause that he has spurned advances to take over at Real Madrid, his earliest footballing love. Already he has moved mountains, but come the autumn of 2009, even loftier peaks were beckoning. All things being equal . . .

THE EARLY YEARS

It's not easy to imagine now, but Liverpool FC did exist before the Shankly revolution. Somewhat bizarrely in view of subsequent rivalry, the club was formed as an offshoot of neighbouring Everton in 1892 and, with an almost exclusively Scottish side, topped the Second Division in 1893/94, their first Football League season.

However, after winning a 'test' match to establish their right to promotion, they could not hold their own in the top flight, being relegated straight away. A gradual advance was made, though, and another promotion in 1896 was consolidated, culminating in the Reds' first League Championship in 1900/01.

Now came switchback progress through the early years of the 20th century. Relegation in 1904 was followed immediately by a Second Division title triumph and another League Championship in 1905/06. Thus the Reds became the first club to win back-to-back Second and First Division crowns, and but for FA Cup semi-final defeat at the hands of Everton, they might have lifted the much-coveted double.

In the seasons leading up to the Great War, Liverpool's League fortunes continued to fluctuate, but much more mildly than in earlier days and, apart from an FA Cup Final reverse against Burnley in 1914, there were no more major alarms or excursions before military hostilities closed down top-class soccer for four years.

The Reds began life after the conflict in enterprising fashion, finishing fourth in the First Division in the two opening peacetime campaigns. That excitement proved a prelude to more concrete achievement, the Championship being secured convincingly in both 1921/22 and 1922/23, each time by six points.

Thereafter Liverpool entered a lengthy period of League mediocrity, their final placings during the remainder of the 1920s and '30s varying from 4th to 19th. Broadly speaking, it could be perceived as a steady decline, which was especially irksome to Kopites when Everton, inspired by the prolific Dixie Dean, were ascendant.

Between the wars there was no consolation to be found in the FA Cup, though the appointment of George Kay as the club's first full-time manager in 1935 spoke of ambition for the future. However, the fruits of his labour were not to become apparent until after World War Two.

Here follows a list of the men who represented Liverpool between 1893/94 and 1939/40, the latter campaign being abandoned after three matches when Hitler invaded Poland.

NOTE: Players who appeared on both sides of the Second World War are to be found in Before The Revolution, which begins on page 38.

ANDREW AITKEN 1930/31
Goalkeeper: 1 game, 0 goals

GEORGE ALLAN
1895/96 → 1896/97 and 1898/99
Centre-forward: 97 games, 60 goals

MESSINA ALLMAN 1908/09
Wing-half: 1 game, 0 goals

TOM ARMSTRONG 1919/20
Goalkeeper: 1 game, 0 goals

JACK BAMBER 1919/20 → 1923/24
Wing-half: 80 games, 2 goals

WILLIE BANKS 1913/14 → 1914/15
Inside-forward: 26 games, 6 goals

NED BARKAS 1930/31 → 1931/32
Centre-forward: 5 games, 0 goals

FRED BARON 1924/25 → 1926/27
Forward: 20 games, 7 goals

HAROLD BARTON 1929/30 → 1933/34
Winger: 106 games, 29 goals

WILF BARTROP 1914/15
Winger: 3 games, 0 goals

BARNEY BATTLES 1895/96 → 1897/98
Full-back or wing-half: 6 games, 0 goals

HARRY BEADLES 1921/22 → 1923/24
Inside-forward: 18 games, 6 goals

FRANK BECTON 1894/95 → 1897/98
Inside-forward: 86 games, 41 goals

AUGUSTUS BEEBY
1909/10 → 1910/11
Goalkeeper: 16 games, 0 goals

TOMMY BENNETT 1919/20
Inside-forward: 1 game, 0 goals

ARTHUR BERRY 1907/08 → 1912/13
Forward: 4 games, 0 goals

BOB BLANTHORNE 1906/07
Forward: 2 games, 0 goals

ERNIE BLENKINSOP
1933/34 → 1937/38
Full-back: 71 games, 0 goals

JOHN BOVILL 1911/12 → 1913/14
Inside-forward: 29 games, 7 goals

GEORGE BOWEN 1901/02
Winger: 2 games, 0 goals

SAM BOWYER 1907/08 → 1911/12
Forward: 48 games, 16 goals

JIM BRADLEY 1905/06 → 1910/11
Wing-half: 184 games, 8 goals

HARRY BRADSHAW
1893/94 → 1897/98
Winger: 138 games, 54 goals

TOM 'TINY' BRADSHAW
1929/30 → 1937/38
Centre-half: 291 games, 4 goals
Big 'Tiny' was a commanding centre-half blessed with a surprisingly deft touch. The fourth most expensive player ever when signed from Bury for £8,000, he won his sole Scotland cap as one of the 'Wembley Wizards' who crushed England in 1928.

TOM BROMILOW 1919/20 → 1929/30
Wing-half: 375 games, 11 goals
Small, slim and stylish Liverpudlian who flourished as midfield creator in the Reds' Championship teams of 1922 and '23. A beautiful passer and a canny tactician who also packed a sharp tackle, Tom was capped five times by England.

MATT BUSBY 1935/36 → 1939/40
Wing-half: 125 games, 3 goals
Scotland international acquired from Manchester City for £8,000 in 1936. An immaculate user of the ball and a natural leader, he rejected a coaching job at Anfield after the war to become manager of Manchester United, for whom he fared tolerably well.

PHILIP BRATLEY 1914/15
Centre-half: 13 games, 0 goals

JOE BROUGH 1910/11
Inside-forward: 10 games, 3 goals

JOHN BROWNING 1934/35 → 1938/39
Wing-half: 19 games, 0 goals

LES BRUTON 1931/32 → 1932/33
Inside-forward: 9 games, 1 goal

FRED BUCK 1903/04
Inside-forward: 13 games, 1 goal

BEN BULL 1895/96
Winger: 1 game, 1 goal

J CAMERON 1894/95
Full-back or half-back: 4 games, 0 goals

KEN CAMPBELL 1911/12 → 1919/20
Goalkeeper: 142 games, 0 goals

JOHN CARLIN 1902/03 → 1906/07
Inside-forward: 34 games, 8 goals

LANCE CARR 1933/34 → 1935/36
Winger: 33 games, 8 goals

JOHN CHADBURN 1903/04
Full-back: 2 games, 0 goals

HARRY CHAMBERS
1919/20 → 1927/28
Forward: 339 games, 151 goals
'Smiler' topped the Reds' goal charts for four consecutive seasons after the First World War, including two title campaigns. An England man whose bandy gait and generous build belied a savage shot, he joined West Bromwich Albion in 1928.

EDGAR CHADWICK
1902/03 → 1903/04
Inside-forward: 45 games, 7 goals

BILLY CHALMERS 1924/25
Winger: 2 games, 0 goals

JOHN CHARLTON 1931/32
Full-back: 3 games, 0 goals

FRANK CHECKLAND 1921/22
Wing-half: 5 games, 0 goals

TOM CHORLTON 1904/05 → 1910/11
Utility: 122 games, 8 goals

BOB CLARK 1927/28 → 1930/31
Forward: 43 games, 11 goals

TOM CLEGHORN 1895/96 → 1898/99
Wing-half: 70 games, 1 goal

JIMMY CLELAND 1894/95
Inside-forward: 1 game, 0 goals

BILL COCKBURN 1924/25 → 1926/27
Centre-half: 67 games, 0 goals

JIMMY COLLINS 1935/36 → 1936/37
Forward: 7 games, 0 goals

BOBBY COLVIN 1897/98
Winger: 3 games, 0 goals

TOMMY COOPER 1934/35 → 1938/39
Full-back: 160 games, 0 goals

CHARLIE COTTON 1903/04
Goalkeeper: 12 games, 0 goals

JACK COX 1897/98 → 1908/09
Winger: 360 games, 80 goals

H CRAIK 1903/04
Wing-half: 1 game, 0 goals

BOB CRAWFORD 1908/09 → 1914/15
Full-back: 114 games, 1 goal

TED CRAWFORD 1932/33
Forward: 7 games, 4 goals

SAM HARDY

1905/06 → 1911/12

Sam Hardy was the most eminent of all English goalkeepers throughout the first quarter of the 20th century, but his fame owed nothing to flamboyance. Instead he was a master of positioning, an almost metronomically consistent performer who scorned unnecessary embellishments and invariably made potentially difficult saves look easy.

No matter how hectic the action which swirled around him, Sam remained unflustered, a veritable pillar of serenity who breathed confidence into his entire defence, and such was the speed of his footwork that only rarely would he launch himself into a full-length dive.

Hardy, a teenage centre-forward who swapped roles only after excelling between the posts in a friendly kickabout, began his professional career with Chesterfield, for whom his exceptional quality shone through even on afternoons of unremitting adversity. Indeed, it was during his heroic display while the Spireites were being hammered 6-1 at Anfield in January 1905 that Liverpool secretary-manager Tom Watson identified Hardy as his preferred long-term replacement for the veteran Ned Doig.

Duly the slim, 5ft 9in 21-year-old was signed for £500 at season's end by the new Second Division Champions and, after making an impressive top-flight debut in a 4-1 home victory over Nottingham Forest in October, he went on to earn lavish plaudits as the Reds claimed that term's First Division crown.

An international call-up followed in 1907 and soon he became a leading light for his country, his final cap total being limited to 21 only by the outbreak of war. Hardy was the first man to record three successive clean sheets for England, and his 13-year international career was longer than any until he was overhauled by Stanley Matthews in 1947.

In 1912 he left Liverpool, rather unexpectedly, for Aston Villa, with whom he earned FA Cup winner's medals in 1913 and 1920. After guesting for Nottingham Forest during the war, Hardy joined the City Ground club in 1921, helping to lift the Second Division title in his first campaign. He was in his 42nd year when injury forced retirement in 1925 after some 600 senior appearances for his four clubs.

Subsequently he ran a hotel in Chesterfield and lived just long enough to glory in the achievements of another of his home-town's renowned custodians, Gordon Banks, for England in the 1966 World Cup.

But let's leave the final word to one of Hardy's shrewdest contemporaries, the Sunderland and Arsenal star Charlie Buchan, who went on to become a ground-breaking soccer journalist and made this unequivocal assessment towards the end of his long life in the game. He asserted: 'Sam Hardy was, quite simply, the finest goalkeeper I have ever seen.'

SAMUEL HARDY	
BORN	Chesterfield, Derbyshire, 26 August 1883.
HONOURS	League Championship 05/06. 21 England caps (07-20).
OTHER CLUBS	Chesterfield 02/03-04/05 (71, 0); Aston Villa 12/13-20/1 (159, 0); Nottingham Forest 21/2-24/5 (102, 0).
DIED	24 October 1966.

GAMES	239
GOALS	0

ELISHA SCOTT

1912/13 → 1933/34

Elisha Scott enjoyed a reputation for invincibility between Liverpool's posts which might, in later years, have qualified him for Melchester Rovers, the most famous of all comic-strip football clubs.

Certainly the long-serving Irish international, whose Anfield tenure spanned 22 years and took in two title triumphs, was revered above all his contemporaries by Reds supporters, who revelled in a story, presumably apocryphal, which had Elisha and the Everton goal machine Dixie Dean bumping into each other in the street. The yarn goes that when Dean nodded in greeting, Scott dived headlong into the gutter with his arms outstretched!

The irony was that the two great Merseyside heroes would have been team-mates if the Goodison management had paid heed to an earnest recommendation from their own regular custodian, Scott's brother Billy, who had urged them to sign the rookie Elisha.

However, Billy's words fell on deaf ears so he advised his gifted younger sibling to try his luck across Stanley Park, where he was enlisted with alacrity and set out on the pathway to stardom. For Elisha the Liverpool contract was a heaven-sent reprieve, having been already rejected by Linfield, one of his homeland's leading clubs, for being 'too small' at 5ft 9ins.

Soon he was called into first-team action, achieving a clean sheet on debut at Newcastle on New Year's Day 1913, having been told before the match that the Magpies had bid £1,000 for his services. Personally he was not averse to the move, believing that he might struggle to unseat regular Reds 'keeper Ken Campbell, but Liverpool realised Elisha's vast potential and vetoed the deal.

Duly the lithe Ulsterman justified their confidence, becoming first choice during 1914/15, then proving hugely instrumental in winning back-to-back League Championships in 1922 and '23. Despite his lack of inches he commanded his penalty box through a mixture of instinctive anticipation, catlike reflexes, unflinching bravery and, not least, a non-stop stream of roared instructions to his fellow defenders.

Scott retained his berth unopposed until 1926/27 after which he continued to appear more frequently than not, despite competition from the classy young South African Arthur Riley.

In 1934 Everton offered £250 to acquire the veteran at long last, but such was the heat of Liverpool fans' fury at the prospect of Scott joining their sworn rivals that instead he re-crossed the Irish Sea to become player-boss of Belfast Celtic.

Elisha laid aside his boots in 1936 but continued as manager until the club folded in 1949. Even then he remained *in situ* as caretaker of the ground, joking: 'I'm the only boss in the game who doesn't worry about next Saturday!' It was an eccentric exit for a passionate football man and one of the best 'keepers ever to emerge from Ulster.

	ELISHA SCOTT	
BORN	Belfast, 24 August 1894.	
HONOURS	League Championship 21/2, 22/3. 31 Ireland caps (20-36).	
OTHER CLUBS	Linfield, Belfast Celtic, both Ireland.	
DIED	16 May 1959.	

GAMES	467
GOALS	0

DAN CUNLIFFE 1897/98
  Centre-forward: 18 games, 7 goals
WILLIE CUNNINGHAM
  1920/21 → 1921/22
  Utility: 3 games, 0 goals
JOHN CURRAN 1894/95 → 1895/96
  Full-back: 24 games, 0 goals
BEN DABBS 1933/34 → 1937/38
  Full-back: 56 games, 0 goals
DAVID DAVIDSON 1928/29 → 1929/30
  Centre-half: 62 games, 2 goals
JOHN DAVIES 1900/01 → 1902/03
  Forward: 10 games, 0 goals
JIMMY DAWSON 1913/14
  Inside-forward: 14 games, 3 goals
BILL DEVLIN 1926/27 → 1927/28
  Centre-forward: 19 games, 15 goals
GERALD DEWHURST 1893/94
  Centre-forward: 1 game, 0 goals
DOUGLAS DICK 1893/94
  Forward: 10 games, 2 goals
JOE DINES 1912/13
  Wing-half: 1 game, 0 goals
NED DOIG 1904/05 → 1907/08
  Goalkeeper: 53 games, 0 goals
BOB DONE 1926/27 → 1934/35
  Full-back: 155 games, 13 goals
WILLIAM DONNELLY 1896/97
  Goalkeeper: 8 games, 0 goals
JOHN DRUMMOND 1894/95
  Winger: 18 games, 1 goal
BILLY DUNLOP 1894/95 → 1908/09
  Full-back: 358 games, 2 goals
DICK EDMED 1926/27 → 1930/31
  Winger: 170 games, 46 goals
SAM ENGLISH 1933/34 → 1934/35
  Centre-forward: 50 games, 27 goals
TOM FAIRFOUL 1913/14 → 1914/15
  Wing-half: 71 games, 0 goals
BOB FERGUSON 1912/13 → 1914/15
  Half-back: 103 games, 3 goals
PAT FINNERHAN 1897/98
  Centre-forward: 8 games, 1 goal
HARRY FITZPATRICK 1907/08
  Inside-forward: 4 games, 2 goals
MATT FITZSIMMONS 1938/39
  Centre-half: 1 game, 0 goals
GEORGE FLEMING 1901/02 → 1905/06
  Wing-half: 83 games, 6 goals
DICK FORSHAW 1919/20 → 1926/27
  Inside-forward: 288 games, 124 goals
ABE FOXALL 1899/1900
  Centre-forward: 1 game, 0 goals
TOMMY GARDNER 1929/30
  Wing-half: 5 games, 0 goals
JIM GARNER 1924/25 → 1925/26
  Full-back: 5 games, 0 goals

JIMMY GARSIDE 1904/05 → 1905/06
  Winger: 5 games, 0 goals
FRED GEARY 1895/96 → 1898/99
  Forward: 45 games, 14 goals
CYRIL GILHESPY 1921/22 → 1924/25
  Winger: 19 games, 3 goals
SAM GILLIGAN 1910/11 → 1912/13
  Inside-forward: 41 games, 16 goals
J GIVENS 1893/94 → 1894/95
  Forward: 10 games, 3 goals
BOB GLASSEY 1935/36 → 1936/37
  Inside-forward: 9 games, 4 goals
JOHN GLOVER 1900/01 → 1902/03
  Full-back: 60 games, 0 goals
ARCHIE GOLDIE 1895/96 → 1899/1900
  Full-back: 150 games, 1 goal
BILL GOLDIE 1897/98 → 1902/03
  Wing-half: 174 games, 6 goals

BERT GOODE 1908/09 → 1909/10
  Inside-forward: 7 games, 1 goal
PADDY GORDON 1893/94 → 1894/95
  Winger: 30 games, 8 goals
JIMMY GORMAN 1905/06 → 1907/08
  Centre-half: 23 games, 1 goal
TOMMY GRACIE 1911/12 → 1913/14
  Forward: 33 games, 5 goals
JIMMY GRAY 1928/29
  Full-back: 1 game, 0 goals
FRANK GRAYER 1913/14
  Full-back: 1 game, 0 goals
TOMMY GREEN 1901/02 → 1902/03
  Inside-forward: 7 games, 1 goal
MICK GRIFFIN 1907/08 → 1908/09
  Forward: 4 games, 0 goals
HARRY GRIFFITHS 1905/06 → 1907/08
  Full-back: 6 games, 0 goals

ARTHUR GODDARD 1901/02 → 1913/14
  Winger: 415 games, 80 goals
  Dubbed 'Graceful Arthur' for his flowing style, Goddard patrolled the Reds' right flank with admirable consistency and flair for a dozen years at the outset of the 20th century, pocketing Second and First Division title gongs for his pains.

GORDON GUNSON
1929/30 → 1932/33
Winger: 87 games, 26 goals

CHARLIE HAFEKOST 1914/15
Wing-half: 1 game, 0 goals

TED HANCOCK 1931/32
Inside-forward: 9 games, 2 goals

ANDREW HANNAH
1893/94 → 1894/95
Full-back: 44 games, 1 goal

DAVY HANNAH 1894/95 → 1896/97
Inside-forward: 33 games, 13 goals

ALF HANSON 1932/33 → 1937/38
Winger: 177 games, 52 goals

SAM HARDY 1905/06 → 1911/12
Goalkeeper: 239 games, 0 goals
See page 28

CHRIS HARRINGTON 1920/21
Winger: 4 games, 0 goals

JIMMY HARROP 1907/08 → 1911/12
Centre-half: 139 games, 4 goals

TED HARSTON 1937/38
Centre-forward: 5 games, 3 goals

BILL HARTILL 1935/36
Centre-forward: 5 games, 0 goals

ABE HARTLEY 1897/98
Forward: 12 games, 1 goals

ALASTAIR HENDERSON 1931/32
Wing-half: 5 games, 0 goals

DAVID HENDERSON
1893/94 → 1894/95
Centre-forward: 26 games, 12 goals

JAMES HENDERSON 1893/94
Centre-forward: 3 games, 0 goals

CHARLIE HEWITT 1907/08
Inside-forward: 16 games, 6 goals

JOE HEWITT 1903/04 → 1909/10
Forward: 164 games, 69 goals

ALAN HIGNETT 1907/08
Wing-half: 1 game, 0 goals

JOE HOARE 1903/04
Full-back: 7 games, 0 goals

GORDON HODGSON
1925/26 → 1935/36
Inside-forward: 378 games, 240 goals
See page 34

RALPH HOLDEN 1912/13 → 1913/14
Wing-half: 2 games, 0 goals

JOHN HOLMES 1895/96 → 1897/98
Wing-half: 44 games, 0 goals

BILL HOOD 1937/38
Full-back: 3 games, 0 goals

FRED HOWE 1934/35 → 1937/38
Forward: 94 games, 36 goals

RABBI HOWELL 1897/98 → 1900/01
Wing-half: 68 games, 0 goals

ABEL HUGHES 1893/94
Full-back: 1 game, 0 goals

FRED HOPKIN 1921/22 → 1930/31
Winger: 360 games, 11 goals
Inventive, industrious winger renowned for his paltry goal tally but who laid on loads for Harry Chambers and company during two Championship seasons. Cost £2,800 from Manchester United and later rejoined his first club, Darlington.

JIM HUGHES 1904/05 → 1908/09
Wing-half: 15 games, 0 goals

JOHN HUGHES 1903/04
Wing-half: 32 games, 2 goals

JOHN HUNTER
1899/1900 → 1901/02
Forward: 44 games, 13 goals

THOMAS HUNTER
1899/1900 → 1901/02
Centre-half: 5 games, 0 goals

WILLIAM HUNTER 1908/09
Inside-forward: 1 game, 0 goals

BOB IRELAND 1930/31
Wing-half: 1 game, 0 goals

JIMMY JACKSON 1925/26 → 1932/33
Half-back: 224 games, 2 goals

NORMAN JAMES 1930/31 → 1932/33
Centre-half: 8 games, 0 goals

BILL JENKINSON 1919/20
Full-back: 13 games, 0 goals

DICK JOHNSON 1919/20 → 1924/25
Centre-forward: 78 games, 28 goals

TOSH JOHNSON 1933/34 → 1935/36
Forward: 39 games, 8 goals

JOHN JONES 1924/25
Goalkeeper: 4 games, 0 goals

RON JONES 1937/38 → 1938/39
Forward: 5 games, 1 goal

CHARLIE JOWITT 1896/97
Goalkeeper: 1 game, 0 goals

STAN KANE 1934/35 → 1935/36
Goalkeeper: 6 games, 0 goals

BILL KEECH 1895/96
Half-back: 6 games, 0 goals

JOE KEETLEY 1923/24
Forward: 9 games, 3 goals

DIRK KEMP 1936/37 → 1939/40
Goalkeeper: 33 games, 0 goals

NEIL KERR 1894/95
Winger: 12 games, 3 goals

BILL KINGHORN 1938/39
Winger: 19 games, 4 goals

PETER KYLE 1899/1900
Inside-forward: 5 games, 0 goals

BILLY LACEY 1911/12 → 1923/24
Half-back or forward: 258 games, 29 goals

GEORGE LATHOM 1904/05 → 1907/08
Half-back: 19 games, 0 goals

HECTOR LAWSON 1923/24 → 1924/25
Winger: 16 games, 0 goals

BERT LEAVY 1910/11
Forward: 5 games, 0 goals

HARRY LESTER 1911/12 → 1912/13
Winger: 2 games, 0 goals

HARRY LEWIS 1919/20 → 1921/22
Forward: 70 games, 12 goals

JOHN LINDSAY 1928/29 → 1929/30
Half-back or forward: 16 games, 3 goals

JOHN LIPSHAM 1906/07
Winger: 3 games, 0 goals

GEORGE LIVINGSTON 1902/03
Inside-forward: 32 games, 4 goals

NORMAN LOW 1934/35 → 1936/37
Centre-half: 13 games, 0 goals

HARRY LOWE 1911/12 → 1919/20
Half-back: 135 games, 2 goals

TOMMY LUCAS 1919/20 → 1932/33
Full-back: 366 games, 3 goals

JOE LUMSDEN 1897/98
Winger: 8 games, 2 goals

NEIL McBAIN 1927/28 → 1928/29
Full-back or wing-half: 12 games, 0 goals

JAMES McBRIDE 1893/94 → 1894/95
Wing-half: 32 games, 3 goals

DONALD McCALLUM 1902/03
Full-back: 2 games, 0 goals

WILLIAM McCANN 1894/95
Goalkeeper: 17 games, 0 goals

McCARTHY 1893/94
Full-back: 1 game, 0 goals

JOHN McCARTNEY
1893/94 → 1897/98
Wing-half: 144 games, 5 goals

JOHN McCONNELL
1909/10 → 1911/12
Wing-half: 53 games, 1 goal

ANDY McCOWIE 1896/97 → 1898/99
Inside-forward: 35 games, 11 goals

BILLY McDEVITT 1923/24 → 1924/25
Centre-half: 4 games, 0 goals

JOHN McDONALD 1909/10 → 1911/12
Winger: 78 games, 4 goals

JIMMY McDOUGALL
1928/29 – 1937/38
Wing-half: 357 games, 12 goals

ROBERT McDOUGALL
1913/14 → 1914/15
Winger: 8 games, 1 goal

JOHN McFARLANE 1928/29 → 1929/30
Forward: 2 games, 0 goals

ANDY McGUIGAN 1900/01 → 1901/02
Inside-forward: 35 games, 14 goals

JIMMY McINNES 1937/38 → 1939/40
Wing-half: 51 games, 2 goals

JOHN McKENNA 1906/07
Winger: 1 game, 0 goals

PETER McKINNEY 1920/21
Forward: 3 games, 1 goal

DUNCAN McLEAN 1893/94 → 1894/95
Full-back: 58 games, 5 goals

JIMMY McLEAN 1903/04
Full-back: 4 games, 0 goals

JOHN McLEAN
1894/95 → 1895/96
Wing-half: 29 games, 0 goals

DAVID McMULLAN
1925/26 → 1927/28
Wing-half: 35 games, 0 goals

JOCK McNAB 1919/20 → 1927/28
Wing-half: 222 games, 6 goals

HAROLD McNAUGHTON 1920/21
Goalkeeper: 1 game, 0 goals

EPHRAIM LONGWORTH 1910/11 → 1927/28
Full-back: 371 games, 0 goals
Longworth was a thoroughbred defender who captained both Liverpool and England. Having joined the Reds from Bolton, he helped to win two titles in an 18-year Anfield playing career which was prolonged significantly by his shrewd reading of the game.

DON McKINLAY 1909/10 → 1928/29
Utility: 434 games, 34 goals
A left-back when he skippered Liverpool to title glory in consecutive seasons, McKinlay was fiercely combative and an attacking overlapper ahead of his time. A Scotland international, he was versatile enough to turn out in most positions.

BILLY McOWEN 1893/94
Goalkeeper: 26 games, 0 goals

ARCHIE McPHERSON
1929/30 → 1934/35
Inside-forward: 133 games, 19 goals

BILLY McPHERSON
1906/07 → 1907/08
Inside-forward: 55 games, 17 goals

JOE McQUE 1893/94 → 1897/98
Centre-half: 122 games, 12 goals

HUGH McQUEEN 1893/94 → 1894/95
Winger: 44 games, 14 goals

MATT McQUEEN 1893/94 → 1898/99
Utility: 87 games, 1 goal

DANNY McRORIE 1930/31 → 1932/33
Winger: 35 games, 6 goals

MALCOLM McVEAN
1893/94 → 1896/97
Forward: 102 games, 28 goals

W MARSHALL 1901/02
Goalkeeper: 1 game, 0 goals

BOBBY MARSHALL
1897/98 → 1898/99
Winger: 21 games, 2 goals

BILL MATTHEWS
1919/20 → 1921/22
Centre-forward: 9 games, 4 goals

ARTHUR METCALFE
1912/13 – 1914/15
Inside-forward: 63 games, 28 goals

BILL MICHAEL 1896/97
Inside-forward: 23 games, 4 goals

BILLY MILLAR 1928/29
Forward: 3 games, 2 goals

JOHN MILLER 1919/20
Forward: 8 games, 0 goals

TOM MILLER 1911/12 → 1920/21
Forward: 146 games, 58 goals

FRANK MITCHELL
1920/21 → 1921/22
Goalkeeper: 18 games, 0 goals

HUGH MORGAN
1897/98 → 1899/1900
Inside-forward: 69 games, 18 goals

DICK MORRIS 1901/02 → 1904/05
Inside-forward: 39 games, 5 goals

TOM MORRISON 1927/28 → 1934/35
Wing-half: 254 games, 4 goals

BILL MURRAY 1927/28 → 1929/30
Centre-forward or centre-half: 4 games,
1 goal

DAVID MURRAY 1904/05 → 1905/06
Full-back: 15 games, 0 goals

BOBBY NEILL 1894/95 → 1896/96
Centre-half: 27 games, 3 goals

JIMMY NICHOLL 1913/14 → 1914/15
Winger or inside-forward: 59 games,
14 goals

RONALD ORR 1907/08 → 1911/12
Inside-forward: 112 games, 38 goals

CYRIL OXLEY 1925/26
Winger: 34 games, 6 goals

FRED PAGNAM 1914/15 → 1919/20
Forward: 39 games, 30 goals

JACK PARKINSON
1899/1900 → 1913/14
Forward: 222 games, 128 goals

TED PARRY 1920/21 → 1924/25
Full-back: 13 games, 0 goals

MAURICE PARRY 1900/01 → 1908/09
Wing-half: 221 games, 3 goals

GEORGE PATERSON 1938/39
Winger: 3 games, 1 goal

ERNIE PEAKE 1908/09 → 1913/14
Half-back: 55 games, 6 goals

BERT PEARSON 1919/20 → 1920/21
Winger: 52 games, 4 goals

JAMES PENMAN 1920/21
Full-back: 1 game, 0 goals

BILL PERKINS 1898/99 → 1902/03
Goalkeeper: 116 games, 0 goals

KEITH PETERS 1938/39
Full-back: 1 game, 0 goals

GEORGE PITHER
1926/27 → 1927/28
Winger: 12 games, 1 goal

PETER PLATT 1902/03 → 1903/04
Goalkeeper: 45 games, 0 goals

DAVID PRATT 1922/23 → 1926/27
Half-back: 85 games, 1 goal

GORDON HODGSON

1925/26 → 1935/36

Gordon Hodgson was Liverpool's marksman-in-chief between the wars, setting club records which would not be broken until Roger Hunt exploded on to the Anfield scene a quarter of a century later.

A burly six-footer brimming with rumbustious zest, Hodgson adopted a shoot-on-sight policy and was not averse to charging through defenders if other avenues to goal were barred, although he was capable of subtlety when the situation demanded it.

A boilermaker by trade and a superb all-round sportsman – he was to bowl fast for Lancashire (1928 to '33) and was mightily effective with a baseball bat – the spirited Springbok arrived in England with a touring party from South Africa in 1925, and his 15 goals for his countrymen persuaded Liverpool boss Matt McQueen to proffer a contract.

Soon Hodgson was netting so bountifully for the Reds that the popular and prolific Dick Forshaw was allowed to join Everton in March 1927, a sensational event at the time, especially as Forshaw helped the Toffees to avoid relegation that term, then lift the title a year later.

Happily the Hodgson strike-rate remained formidable, especially in 1928/29 when he rattled in 30 League goals, including a first-half hat-trick in a 4-4 draw at Highbury, and in 1930/31, when his 36 First Division hits constituted a seasonal high for Liverpool.

Born of English parents, Gordon was eligible to represent his adopted nation, which sent for him three times during his pomp, and also he played twice for the Football League. Understandably, though, with celebrated Evertonian Dixie Dean rampant, he was unable to claim a regular place at a higher level.

On the club scene he continued to do well, but surely would have been even more effective had he linked up with a long-term front-running partner.

Having entered his thirties, Hodgson was transferred to Aston Villa for £4,000 just after Christmas 1935, but not before totalling 232 League goals, easily the most in Anfield history until Sir Roger came along.

Subsequently the resilient South African served Leeds United, demonstrating his contempt for the aging process by scoring five times against Leicester in 1938. During the war he guested for Hartlepools United and coached youngsters at Elland Road, then entered management with Port Vale in 1946.

GORDON HODGSON		
BORN	Johannesburg, South Africa, 16 April 1904.	
HONOURS	3 England caps (30-31).	
OTHER CLUBS	Transvaal, South Africa; Aston Villa 35/6-36/7 (28, 11); Leeds United 37/8-38/9 (82, 51).	GAMES **378**
MANAGER	Port Vale (46-51).	GOALS **240**
DIED	Stoke, Staffordshire, 14 June 1951.	

JACK BALMER

1935/36 → 1951/52

Jack Balmer was a thoroughbred footballer, a prolific maker and taker of goals, and captain of the Reds as they confounded the majority of pundits to lift the first League Championship of the post-war era.

Perversely, though, the slim, thoughtful Liverpudlian did not always receive the acclaim his skill, flair and high-velocity shooting deserved. A particularly vociferous section of the Anfield support denigrated him for a supposed lack of spirit, but that was manifestly unfair; fiery he wasn't, but no shrinking violet would have totalled more than a century of goals in English football.

It has been suggested that some fans' churlish attitude was coloured by a perception of Balmer as a middle-class boy in a working-class game, a fatuous concept which should have been outmoded even in the 1930s and '40s.

The nephew of William and Robert Balmer, two Everton full-backs in the early 1900s, Jack first sprang to the attention of both the Reds and the Blues as a free-scoring centre-forward for the locally based Collegiate Old Boys. After a short stint as an amateur at Goodison, he enlisted at Anfield in 1935 and lost little time in cementing a regular place.

Much of his prime was lost to the war, and his sole England recognition was an unofficial cap for England against Wales in 1939, but he continued to display magnificent form in 1946/47, netting 24 times on the title trail. Lining up at inside-right, he combined potently with spearhead Albert Stubbins and left-winger Billy Liddell as Liverpool pipped Manchester United, Wolves and Stoke to the crown. Jack delighted in tricking his way past one or more markers before striking, and though he continued to be dogged by scepticism, he was beloved of football connoisseurs.

The Balmer contribution proved particularly compelling during one tumultuous spell in the autumn when he became the first man in League history to register hat-tricks in three consecutive games, his victims being Portsmouth, Derby County and Arsenal.

He remained an integral part of George Kay's side over the next two terms before suffering an injury which cost him his place in the 1950 FA Cup Final, although after he returned to fitness ahead of the Wembley clash with Arsenal, there was some dissent over the manager's preference for Kevin Baron.

By then, however, Jack Balmer was approaching the veteran stage and he retired, aged 36, in the summer of 1952.

JOHN BALMER		
BORN	Liverpool, 6 February 1916.	
HONOURS	League Championship 46/7.	
DIED	25 December 1984.	

GAMES	313
GOALS	111

BOB PURSELL 1911/12 → 1919/20
Full-back: 112 games, 0 goals

HARRY RACE 1927/28 → 1929/30
Inside-forward: 43 games, 18 goals

ARCHIE RAWLINGS
1923/24 → 1925/26
Winger: 67 games, 10 goals

SAM RAYBOULD
1899/1900 → 1906/07
Centre-forward: 224 games, 127 goals

TOMMY REID 1925/26 → 1928/29
Centre-forward: 55 games, 31 goals

ARTHUR RILEY 1925/26 → 1938/39
Goalkeeper: 338 games, 0 goals

JOHN ROBERTS 1933/34
Centre-forward: 1 game, 0 goals

SYD ROBERTS 1931/32 → 1936/37
Inside-forward: 61 games, 13 goals

JACK ROBERTSON
1900/01 → 1901/02
Full-back: 46 games, 1 goal

TOM ROBERTSON 1897/98 → 1901/02
Winger: 141 games, 37 goals

ROBBIE ROBINSON
1903/04 → 1911/12
Forward: 271 games, 65 goals

FRED ROGERS 1934/35 → 1938/39
Half-back: 75 games, 0 goals

TOM ROGERS 1906/07 → 1910/11
Full-back: 40 games, 0 goals

BILL SALISBURY 1928/29
Centre-forward: 17 games, 3 goals

JACK SAMBROOK 1922/23
Centre-forward: 2 games, 0 goals

CHARLIE SATTERTHWAITE
1899/1900 → 1901/02
Inside-forward: 46 games, 12 goals

PERCY SAUL 1906/07 → 1908/09
Full-back: 83 games, 2 goals

TED SAVAGE 1931/32 → 1937/38
Wing-half: 105 games, 2 goals

ALAN SCOTT 1929/30 → 1930/31
Centre-forward: 4 games, 2 goals

ELISHA SCOTT 1912/13 → 1933/34
Goalkeeper: 468 games, 0 goals
See page 29

JAMES SCOTT 1911/12 → 1912/13
Wing-half: 10 games, 0 goals

TOM SCOTT 1924/25 → 1927/28
Inside-forward: 18 games, 4 goals

JOHN SHAFTO 1937/38 → 1938/39
Centre-forward: 20 games, 7 goals

BERT SHEARS 1925/26 → 1928/29
Centre-half: 16 games, 0 goals

JACKIE SHELDON
1913/14 → 1920/21
Winger: 147 games, 20 goals

JOHN SHIELD 1935/36
Wing-half: 1 game, 0 goals

DANNY SHONE 1921/22 → 1925/26
Forward: 81 games, 26 goals

DONALD SLOAN 1908/09
Goalkeeper: 6 games, 0 goals

ARTHUR SMITH 1937/38
Centre-forward: 1 game, 0 goals

JIM SMITH 1929/30 → 1931/32
Centre-forward: 62 games, 38 goals

SYD SMITH 1903/04
Centre-forward: 2 games, 1 goal

JAMES SPEAKMAN 1909/10 → 1912/13
Winger: 8 games, 1 goal

SAM SPEAKMAN 1912/13 → 1919/20
Full-back: 26 games, 1 goal

FRED STANIFORTH 1913/14
Winger: 3 games, 0 goals

WILLIE STEEL 1931/32 → 1934/35
Full-back: 128 games, 0 goals

GENERAL STEVENSON
1898/99 → 1899/1900
Full-back: 23 games, 0 goals

JAMES STEWART 1909/10 → 1913/14
Inside-forward: 68 games, 27 goals

HARRY STORER 1895/96 → 1899/1900
Goalkeeper: 121 games, 0 goals

JIMMY STOTT 1893/94
Inside-forward: 18 games, 14 goals

HAROLD TAYLOR 1932/33 → 1936/37
Utility: 71 games, 6 goals

JACK TENNANT 1933/34 → 1934/35
Full-back: 42 games, 0 goals

ALEX RAISBECK 1898/99 → 1908/09
Centre-half: 340 games, 21 goals
The most prominent Liverpool footballer of his era, intelligent, aggressive and remarkably consistent. Once of Hibs, he was signed from Stoke and was the key man as the Reds won promotion and lifted two titles. Capped eight times by Scotland.

JIMMY ROSS 1894/95 → 1896/97
 Inside-forward: 85 games, 40 goals
 A dazzling ball-player whose goals-to-games ratio would have modern bosses drooling, Ross was one of the Preston North End 'Invincibles' who won the first League and FA Cup double in 1889. Later he served Burnley and Manchester City.

CHARLIE THOMPSON
 1929/30 – 1930/31
 Wing-half: 6 games, 0 goals

JOHN TOSSWILL 1912/13
 Inside-forward: 11 games, 1 goal

HAROLD UREN 1907/08 → 1911/12
 Winger: 46 games, 2 goals

HARMAN VAN DEN BERG
 1937/38 → 1939/40
 Winger: 22 games, 4 goals

HAROLD WADSWORTH
 1919/20 → 1923/24
 Winger: 54 games, 3 goals

WALTER WADSWORTH
 1914/15 → 1925/26
 Centre-half: 241 games, 8 goals

JOHN WALKER 1897/98 → 1901/02
 Inside-forward: 133 games, 31 goals

JIMMY WALSH 1923/24 → 1927/28
 Forward: 76 games, 27 goals

HARRY WELFARE 1912/13
 Winger: 4 games, 1 goal

ALF WEST 1903/04 → 1910/11
 Full-back: 140 games, 6 goals

BILL WHITE 1901/02
 Inside-forward: 6 games, 1 goal

JOHN WHITEHEAD
 1894/95 → 1895/96
 Goalkeeper: 3 games, 0 goals

BERT WHITEHURST 1928/29
 Centre-forward: 8 games, 2 goals

TOM WILKIE 1895/96 → 1898/99
 Full-back: 65 games, 2 goals

CHARLIE WILSON 1897/98 → 1904/05
 Wing-half: 90 games, 3 goals

D WILSON 1899/1900
 Winger: 2 games, 0 goals

A WORGAN 1893/94 → 1894/95
 Forward: 2 games, 2 goals

DAVID WRIGHT 1929/30 → 1933/34
 Forward: 100 games, 35 goals

VIC WRIGHT 1933/34 → 1936/37
 Forward: 85 games, 33 goals

BEFORE THE
REVOLUTION

Once again, Liverpool FC emerged from years of earth-shaking conflict in fine fettle. Indeed, the first post-war season saw the Reds pip Manchester United – led by distinguished Anfield old-boy Matt Busby – for the League Championship, and in 1950 they reached Wembley, where they were beaten by Arsenal in the FA Cup Final.

That mid-20th century team boasted outstanding individuals such as Billy Liddell, Albert Stubbins and Jack Balmer, and was a credit to manager George Kay, who was to retire through ill health in 1951.

He was replaced by Don Welsh, who introduced new blood to the side, but it was not enough to stop a gradual slide which culminated in relegation in 1953/54. Despite missing out only narrowly on promotion in 1955/56 Welsh was dismissed and the job of putting Liverpool back among the elite was handed to the club's former skipper, Phil Taylor. He held the reins for three Second Division campaigns, finishing third, fourth and fourth again before bowing to the strain and stepping down in November 1959.

Then came Shankly – and life at Anfield was never the same again.

Listed here are the players responsible for Liverpool's mixed fortunes between season 1945/46 and 14 December 1959, when the footballing messiah arrived. Omitted from the roster are individuals for whom a full profile appears in the pages that follow.

ERIC ANDERSON 1952/53 → 1956/57
Inside-forward: 76 games, 21 goals

CHARLIE ASHCROFT
1946/47 → 1954/55
Goalkeeper: 89 games, 0 goals

KEVIN BARON 1945/46 → 1953/54
Inside-forward: 152 games, 33 goals
The diminutive blond Lancastrian was not a heavy scorer but created plenty of openings for team-mates through clever dribbling and ceaseless foraging. He played in the 1950 FA Cup Final, then peaked before joining Southend in 1954.

REG BLORE 1959/60
Winger: 1 game, 0 goals

KEN BRIERLEY 1947/48 → 1952/53
Forward: 59 games, 8 goals

KEITH BURKINSHAW 1954/55
Centre-half: 1 game, 0 goals

TOM BUSH 1933/34 → 1946/47
Half-back: 72 games, 1 goal

JOE CADDEN 1950/51 → 1951/52
Centre-half: 5 games, 0 goals

DON CAMPBELL 1953/54 → 1958/59
Wing-half: 58 games, 3 goals

WILLIE CARLIN 1959/60
Inside-forward: 1 game, 0 goals

LEN CARNEY 1946/47 → 1947/48
Inside-forward: 6 games, 1 goal

ALBERT CHILDS 1953/54
Full-back: 2 games, 0 goals

FRANK CHRISTIE 1949/50
Wing-half: 4 games, 0 goals

RUSSELL CROSSLEY
1950/51 → 1953/54
Goalkeeper: 73 games, 0 goals

JOE DICKSON 1955/56
Inside-forward: 6 games, 3 goals

JOHN EASDALE 1946/47
Centre-half: 2 games, 0 goals

HARRY EASTHAM 1936/37 → 1946/47
Forward: 69 games, 4 goals

JOHN EVANS 1953/54 → 1956/57
Inside-forward: 106 games, 53 goals
After signing from Charlton, Evans made his debut on Christmas Day 1953 but delayed most of his gifts to Reds fans until the following term, when he scored 33 times, including a five-goal haul against Bristol Rovers. Joined Colchester in 1957.

WILLIE FAGAN 1937/38 → 1951/52
Inside-forward: 185 games, 57 goals
A Scottish redhead recruited from Preston North End, Willie was versatile enough to fill any attacking role and served Liverpool ably before the war, then contributed seven goals to the 1946/47 title campaign. An FA Cup finalist in 1950.

FINNEY 1945/46
Wing-half: 2 games

HUGH GERHARDI 1952/53
Inside-forward: 6 games, 0 goals

JACK HAIGH 1950/51 → 1951/52
Inside-forward: 11 games, 3 goals

JIM HARLEY 1935/36 → 1947/48
Full-back: 133 games, 0 goals

JACK HEYDON 1950/51 → 1952/53
Half-back: 67 games, 0 goals

ALF HOBSON 1936/37 → 1945/46
Goalkeeper: 28 games, 0 goals

BRIAN JACKSON 1951/52 → 1957/58
Winger: 131 games, 12 goals
The Reds invested £7,000 to sign
18-year-old Jackson from Leyton

Orient, but
successive bosses
did not persist
with the clever,
pacy flankman
during times of
travail. Sold to
Port Vale in 1958
and soon earned
a Division Four
title medal.

HAROLD JONES 1953/54
  Inside-forward: 1 game, 0 goals
MERVYN JONES 1951/52 → 1952/53
  Forward: 5 games, 0 goals
GEORGE KAYE 1945/46 → 1946/47
  Wing-half: 2 games, 0 goals
PETER KIPPAX 1948/49
  Winger: 1 game, 0 goals
FRANK LOCK 1953/54 → 1954/55
  Full-back: 42 games, 0 goals
DOUG McAVOY 1947/48 → 1948/49
  Inside-forward: 2 games, 0 goals
TOMMY McLEOD 1946/47 → 1948/49
  Inside-forward: 7 games, 0 goals
TONY McNAMARA 1957/58
  Winger: 11 games, 3 goals
TOM McNULTY 1953/54 → 1957/58
  Full-back: 36 games, 0 goals
JOE MALONEY 1952/53 → 1953/54
  Wing-half or inside-forward: 12 games,
  0 goals
RAY MINSHULL 1946/47 → 1949/50
  Goalkeeper: 31 games, 0 goals
ALEX MUIR 1947/48
  Winger: 4 games, 0 goals
BOBBY MURDOCH 1957/58 → 1958/59
  Inside-forward: 19 games, 7 goals
JOHN NICHOLSON 1959/60
  Centre-half: 1 game, 0 goals
FRED NICKSON 1945/46
  Goalkeeper: 3 games, 0 goals
STEVE PARR 1951/52 → 1952/53
  Full-back: 20 games, 0 goals

BERRY NIEUWENHUYS
1933/34 → 1946/47
Winger: 260 games, 79 goals
Tall, slender 'Nivvy' was a dynamic
crowd-pleaser endowed with a
spectacularly fierce shot. He played
the majority
of his football
before the war,
but made enough
appearances to
pocket a title
medal in 1946/47
before going home
to South Africa.

FRED PERRY 1955/56
  Full-back: 1 game, 0 goals
STAN POLK 1946/47 → 1947/48
  Inside-forward: 13 games, 0 goals
JOHN PRICE 1955/56
  Full-back: 1 game, 0 goals
BOB PRIDAY 1945/46 → 1948/49
  Winger: 39 games, 7 goals
BERNARD RAMSDEN
1937/38 → 1947/48
  Full-back: 66 games, 0 goals
ARTHUR ROWLEY 1952/53 → 1953/54
  Inside-forward: 13 games, 1 goal

TONY ROWLEY 1954/55 → 1957/58
Inside-forward: 61 games, 38 goals
Lofty, angular marksman who nabbed

a hat-trick on his Reds
debut against Doncaster.
Though he netted 16
times in 24 League games
during 1957/58, come
the spring he was sold to
Tranmere, with whom he
won a lone Welsh cap.

DOUG RUDHAM 1954/55 → 1959/60
Goalkeeper: 66 games, 0 goals
South African six-footer who agreed
terms with the Reds while touring
Britain with his national team. He
vied with Dave Underwood for
recognition, then languished behind
Tommy Younger and Bert Slater before
returning home in 1954.

ROY SAUNDERS 1952/53 → 1958/59
Wing-half: 144 games, 1 goal
Small, quick and courageous, Saunders
was a reliable but rarely dominant
performer who peaked in the mid-
1950s and was given his chance
following the retirement of Bob Paisley
and Phil Taylor. Joined Swansea in
1959. Father of Dean.

LES SHANNON 1947/48 → 1948/49
  Centre-forward: 11 games, 1 goal
BILL SHEPHERD 1948/49 → 1951/52
  Full-back: 57 games, 0 goals
SAM SHIELDS 1949/50
  Inside-forward: 1 game, 0 goals
JACK SMITH 1951/52 → 1953/54
  Centre-forward: 59 games, 14 goals
SAMMY SMYTH 1952/53 → 1953/54
  Forward: 45 games, 20 goals
ALEX SOUTH 1954/55
  Centre-half: 7 games, 1 goal
FRED TOMLEY 1954/55
  Centre-half: 2 games, 0 goals
DAVE UNDERWOOD
1953/54 → 1955/56
  Goalkeeper: 50 games, 0 goals
BILLY WATKINSON 1946/47 → 1949/50
  Winger: 24 games, 2 goals
GEORGE WHITWORTH 1951/52
  Wing-half: 9 games, 0 goals

BARRY WILKINSON
1953/54 → 1959/60
Wing-half: 79 games, 0 goals
Left or right, it made little difference
to the adaptable, constructive

midfielder, who began
his career with Bishop
Auckland. He couldn't
claim a regular Reds
berth, though, and
joined Bangor City,
whom he helped to
win the Welsh Cup.

BRYAN WILLIAMS 1948/49 → 1952/53
  Utility: 34 games, 5 goals
DON WOAN 1950/51
  Winger: 2 games, 0 goals

Now turn over to begin meeting the footballers who launched Liverpool's post-war silverware collection by winning the League title in 1946/47. Then, commencing with Billy Liddell on page 46, begins a cavalcade of all the Reds who have served under Bill Shankly and his successors, right through to Rafael Benitez. Every man, whether a household name or a rookie who flashed only fleetingly across the Anfield firmament, played his part in the most astonishing long-term success story in the annals of English soccer.

Appended to the profiles which follow are statistics covering the Football League and Premiership; the FA Cup; the Football League Cup in all its guises; the European Cup and UEFA Champions League; the European Cup Winners' Cup; the European Fairs Cup and UEFA Cup; the European Super Cup; the World Club Championship; and the FA Charity (now Community) Shield.

CYRIL SIDLOW

1946/47 → 1950/51

Big Cyril Sidlow was a goalkeeper who provoked extreme emotions among Liverpool supporters.

Sometimes they loved him, as they did when he performed near-miracles against his former club, Wolves, during the last-day triumph at Molineux which clinched the 1946/47 League title.

But on other occasions they would castigate him luridly, such as when he conceded four goals in a ten-minute spell either side of half-time at home to Newcastle in 1950, in what proved to be his farewell appearance.

Occasional lapses of concentration gave rise to accusations of casualness but they were wide of the mark. Cyril was a safer-than-average custodian, bulky enough to withstand fierce buffetings, and renowned as one of the first to launch attacks by throwing the ball instead of kicking it.

CYRIL SIDLOW
BORN: Colwyn Bay, Denbighshire, 26 November 1915.
HONOURS: League Championship 46/7. 7 Wales caps (47-50).
OTHER CLUBS: Wolverhampton Wanderers 37/8-38/9 (4, 0).
DIED: 12 April 2005.

GAMES	165
GOALS	0

PHIL TAYLOR

1935/36 → 1953/54

Phil Taylor was a key figure in Liverpool's history during the middle years of the 20th century. His most memorable role was as a stylishly creative wing-half in the title-winning campaign of 1946/47 and for several years afterwards. A lovely passer, a clever assessor of play and a man of impeccable integrity, he was the natural choice to succeed Jack Balmer as captain in 1949/50.

Also there was a useful pre-war stint as a goal-scoring inside-forward following his £5,000 acquisition from Bristol Rovers, and finally he spent three and a half seasons as manager of the Reds, leading them to third, fourth and fourth again in the Second Division before bowing to the strain of the job. A comprehensively talented all-round sportsman, Taylor played county cricket for Gloucestershire in 1938.

PHILIP HENRY TAYLOR
BORN: Bristol, 18 September 1917.
HONOURS: League Championship 46/7. 3 England caps (47).
OTHER CLUBS: Bristol Rovers 35/6 (21, 2).
MANAGER: Liverpool (56-59).

GAMES	345
GOALS	34

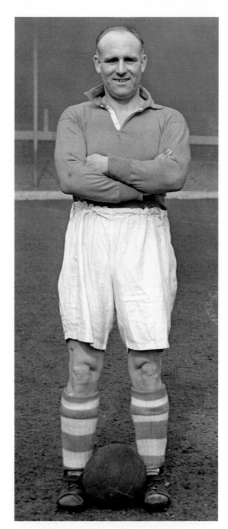

RAY LAMBERT

1945/46 → 1955/56

The balding head of Ray Lambert stood out like a beacon of reassuring calmness and solidity in the Liverpool rearguard throughout times of triumph and turbulence alike.

The sturdy Welsh international defender became Liverpool's youngest ever footballer when he enlisted as a 13-year-old amateur centre-half in 1936. After the war had claimed his early prime, Lambert slotted into the senior side as a full-back, and there he remained for the next decade, operating with equal expertise on either flank, his strength and courage matched by his canny positional play.

He was rewarded by a handful of Welsh caps, and was prevented from accumulating many more only by the stalwart international combination of Wally Barnes and Alf Sherwood. Ray Lambert deserved better than to wind down his League career in a struggling team.

RAYMOND LAMBERT
BORN: Bagillt, Flintshire, 18 July 1922.
HONOURS: League Championship 46/7.
5 Wales caps (47-49).

GAMES	341
GOALS	2

EDDIE SPICER

1945/46 → 1953/54

The quality that springs to mind at the mere mention of Eddie Spicer is raw courage. Bemedalled for his valour as a Royal Marine during the Second World War, the chunky full-back showed similar mettle on the football field, ever ready to risk his all for the team's sake.

Sadly, he paid the formidable price of two broken legs. From the first, sustained on a tour of Sweden in the summer of 1951, he recovered; but the second, suffered in a sickening collision with Manchester United's Tommy Taylor at Old Trafford in December 1953, signalled a poignantly premature end to the Spicer career.

An England schoolboy international, Eddie made ten appearances as a wing-half as the Reds lifted the title in 1946/47, but he was more effective on either of the defensive flanks, particularly the left, where he became established in 1949/50.

EDWIN SPICER
BORN: Liverpool, 20 September 1922.
DIED: Rhyl, Denbighshire, 25 December 2004.

GAMES	168
GOALS	2

CYRIL DONE

1939/40 → 1951/52

When Cyril Done kicked a football it was advisable not to stand in its path. Though he was slammed mercilessly by some critics for his indelicacy on the ball, this valiant if undeniably limited spearhead packed a howitzer of a left foot, and it brought him plenty of goals.

For instance, in only 17 outings on the 1946/47 title trail, there were ten Done strikes, including two hat-tricks, and a run of eight hits in seven games during1948/49, yet still he couldn't claim a regular berth.

What endeared him to many was his cheerful reaction to being panned, allied to boundless enthusiasm and energy which kept opponents under relentless pressure. After leaving Anfield, Done excelled at lower levels, and gleefully netted all four goals in Port Vale's 4-3 win over Liverpool in 1955.

CYRIL CHARLES DONE
BORN: Bootle, Liverpool, 21 October 1920.
HONOURS: League Championship 46/7.
OTHER CLUBS: Tranmere Rovers 52/3-54/5 (87, 61);
Port Vale 54/5-56/7 (52, 34).
DIED: Liverpool, 24 February 1993.

GAMES	109
GOALS	37

BOB PAISLEY

1945/46 → 1953/54

When Bob Paisley missed out to Bill Jones on a place in the side to face Arsenal in the 1950 FA Cup Final, there were lifelong fans who vowed they would never watch Liverpool again. That was a telling measure of the quiet north-easterner's popularity as a flintily indomitable wing-half whose industry and tenacity compensated amply for a slight shortfall in craft.

Paisley was devastated by his omission, especially after featuring in every previous round and netting a rare goal against Everton in the semi-final, and he was missed, as Scottish schemer Jimmy Logie was hugely influential in the Gunners' victory. Typically, though, the man who had helped Bishop Auckland to win the FA Amateur Cup in 1939 buckled down to regain his slot, then went on to become arguably the greatest manager of all time.

ROBERT PAISLEY
BORN: Hetton-le-Hole, County Durham, 23 January 1919.
HONOURS: League Championship 46/7.
MANAGER: Liverpool (74-83).
DIED: Liverpool, 14 February 1996.

GAMES	278
GOALS	13

ALBERT STUBBINS

1946/47 → 1952/53

Many footballers are admired, plenty are respected, some are even revered; but only a chosen few are taken into the collective heart of a community and cherished in the manner of Liverpool's Albert Stubbins.

The flame-haired north-easterner was adored on Merseyside for his unfailing good nature as much as for his lethal marksmanship, and his niche in English folklore was underlined by his presence on the sleeve of one of the best-selling pop music albums of all time.

Albert was chosen by the Beatles as one of 63 famous faces to adorn the artwork of their ground-breaking *Sergeant Pepper's Lonely Hearts Club Band* in 1967. Beaming broadly, he is wedged cosily among the likes of Marlene Dietrich, Lewis Carroll and Karl Marx, and it is a tribute to his charismatic stature that he doesn't seem remotely out of place.

A ball-playing centre-forward, endowed with subtle skills, searing pace and a scorching shot in both of his size-11 boots – though he was quite tall, the immensity of his feet was rather incongruous in such a slender fellow – Stubbins was not merely a scorer, but also a creator of goals. He led his forward line intelligently, constantly seeking to bring colleagues into play with his perceptive passing, and for all his dead-eyed menace it was clear that he enjoyed his work, his nickname of 'The Smiling Assassin' being singularly apt.

Albert made his debut for Second Division Newcastle United while still a teenager in 1938 and it was his ill fortune to find himself on the threshold of a richly promising career just as war broke out. Nevertheless, in emergency competitions over the next six years he scored 245 times in 199 appearances, more than anyone else in the land.

When peace was declared, the 26-year-old, who had won unofficial wartime caps for England but would never play in a full international, reviewed his options and decided that he needed to join the top flight to make the most of his potential. Accordingly he asked for a transfer, which was granted, and it is a mark of his prowess that only two First Division clubs failed to register an interest.

Eventually it came down to a straight contest between Liverpool and Everton, and he tossed up to decide which Merseyside institution to meet first. The coin came down in favour of the Reds, who quickly clinched a £12,500 deal by promising to secure him a regular column in the *Liverpool Echo*, something on which he was keen, having learned shorthand in his teens (one day he would become a full-time journalist).

The Anfield newcomer was an instant success, netting with a brilliant individual effort in a victorious debut at Bolton and going on to total 24 League strikes in his first campaign, including the winner against Wolves at Molineux which clinched the 1946/47 Championship crown.

The following term Stubbins was equally effective, one four-goal demolition of Huddersfield being especially spectacular, but the summer of 1948 brought discord when the club rejected his request to live and train on Tyneside, where most of his family lived. Initially he refused to re-sign, but although he relented after two months and spent another five seasons at Anfield, he was never quite the same force again, falling prey to serial injuries.

However, Albert played a major part in the Reds' progress to the FA Cup Final in 1950, in which they lost 2-0 to Arsenal and might have prevailed had he not been narrowly off target with several scoring attempts. That same year, though by then in his thirties, he demonstrated eloquently that he was far from finished, netting five times in the Football League's annihilation of the Irish League.

Tellingly, throughout his twilight years as a player the engagingly modest and humorous Stubbins remained wildly popular with the fans even when team performances were disappointing, a remarkable tribute to his enduringly warm and gentlemanly persona.

He always relished his link with the Beatles so it was appropriate that Paul McCartney sent him a copy of the record on release, accompanied by the message: 'Well done, Albert, for all those glorious years of football. Long may you bob and weave.'

	ALBERT STUBBINS		
BORN	Wallsend, Northumberland, 13 July 1919.		
HONOURS	League Championship 46/7		
OTHER CLUBS	Newcastle United 37/8-46/7 (27, 5).		
DIED	Cullercoats, Northumberland, 28 December 2002.	GAMES	180
		GOALS	83

BILL JONES

1946/47 → 1953/54

Bill Jones was a magnificently adaptable utility player who served Liverpool in no less than six positions as they lifted the League crown in 1946/47. He featured in all three half-back berths, left-back, inside-left and centre-forward, and would have been more than competent in any of the others, too.

His best position? England saw him as the natural successor to Neil Franklin as a footballing centre-half, a role he could not make his own, but perhaps Jones was at his most effective as a probing wing-half whose imaginative passing opened many a defence.

Sadly, after being selected at number-six ahead of Bob Paisley for the 1950 FA Cup Final, he did not do himself justice in the Wembley defeat by Arsenal, but thereafter he performed doughtily in a declining team.

Bill is Rob Jones' grandfather.

WILLIAM HENRY JONES
BORN: Whaley Bridge, Derbyshire, 13 May 1921.
HONOURS: League Championship 46/7.
2 England caps (50).

GAMES	278
GOALS	17

JIMMY PAYNE

1948/49 → 1955/56

When the teenage Jimmy Payne was dubbed 'The Merseyside Matthews' it was hardly helpful in terms of unrealistically raised expectations, yet such was the diminutive right-winger's dazzling array of natural skills that the glib tag became inevitable.

Payne was a breathtaking dribbler with a sharp football brain, and brave into the bargain, a combination of assets which earned him England 'B' recognition and early adulation from his home crowd.

Sadly, as he failed to maintain his impetus, the mood on the terraces began to change and so-called supporters got on his back. Not surprisingly, his confidence ebbed away almost visibly, especially after he suffered a string of niggling injuries. A switch to inside-left did not work, and neither did a £5,000 transfer to Everton, leaving Payne to retire with the bulk of that immense potential infuriatingly unfulfilled.

JAMES BOLCHERSON PAYNE
BORN: Bootle, Liverpool, 10 March 1926.
OTHER CLUBS: Everton 55/6-56/7 (5, 2).

GAMES	245
GOALS	42

LAURIE HUGHES

1945/46 → 1957/58

Though he shared the ignominy of England's darkest footballing hour – losing to the United States during the 1950 World Cup Finals – centre-half Laurie Hughes was one of his country's few successes during the tournament and was unlucky that subsequent injuries should retard his international opportunities.

The tall, slim Liverpudlian, who began as a teenage amateur with Tranmere, was a talented all-rounder, assured on the ball, a clever anticipator of unfolding attacks, and combative both in the air and on the deck. Occasionally he would reduce Kopites to near-apoplexy by his apparent nonchalance, but only rarely was he caught in possession and he remained a consistent bastion of the Reds' backline through 11 seasons.

Hughes, who suffered several serious knee problems but showed commendable resilience in bouncing back from them, was replaced by Dick White in 1957.

LAWRENCE HUGHES
BORN: Liverpool, 2 March 1924.
HONOURS: League Championship 46/7.
3 England caps (50).

GAMES	326
GOALS	1

LOUIS BIMPSON

. . . .

1952/53 → 1959/60

Louis Bimpson might have been Cyril Done Mk II, a big, strapping centre-forward whose commitment and industry could never be questioned but who was markedly short of subtlety and craft.

Still, his strike-rate was healthy, especially in 1953/54, when he was the relegation-bound Reds' joint top-scorer with Sammy Smyth, notching 13 goals, including four first-half strikes against Burnley at the Kop end.

Then, having languished on the fringe of the side during mid-decade, Louis stormed back with 11 goals in 15 appearances in 1958/59, only to be ousted a season later by the high-profile arrival of Dave Hickson.

After that there was no future for Bimpson at Anfield and a £6,500 deal took him to Blackburn, for whom he figured on the wing in the 1960 FA Cup Final.

JAMES LOUIS BIMPSON
BORN: Rainford, Lancashire, 14 May 1929.
OTHER CLUBS: Blackburn Rovers 59/60-60/1 (22, 5); Bournemouth 60/1 (11, 1); Rochdale 61/2-62/3 (54, 16).

GAMES	100
GOALS	40

GEOFF TWENTYMAN

. . . .

1953/54 → 1959/60

Only a lack of outright pace prevented Geoff Twentyman from being a truly exceptional performer. As it was, the £10,000 acquisition from Carlisle was converted successfully from centre-half into an inventive wing-half whose excellence in possession was matched by a keen soccer intelligence and indefatigable fighting spirit.

Twentyman – nicknamed 'Trapper' for a supposed resemblance to Fess Parker, the actor who played frontiersman Davy Crockett – was enlisted to bolster a shaky defence, but also he proved a potent attacking weapon, thanks in no small measure to his dead-ball expertise. Probably he peaked in 1955/56, when he was ever-present and contributed seven goals to the Reds' unavailing promotion bid. After retiring as a player, Twentyman served Liverpool as chief scout for some 20 years, from 1967. His son, also Geoff, was a stalwart defender for Bristol Rovers in the late 1980s and early '90s.

GEOFFREY TWENTYMAN
BORN: Brampton, Cumberland, 19 January 1930.
OTHER CLUBS: Carlisle United 46/7-53/4 (149, 2); Ballymena United, Northern Ireland, 58/9-62/3; Carlisle United 63/4 (10, 0).
MANAGER: Ballymena United 1959-63, Hartlepools United 1965.
DIED: Southport, Lancashire, 16 February 2004.

GAMES	184
GOALS	19

TOMMY YOUNGER

. . . .

1956/57 → 1958/59

Tommy Younger arrived at Anfield from Easter Road with an impeccable pedigree, being the current Scottish international goalkeeper and having twice tasted title glory with Hibernian.

Now the task facing the ebullient, larger-than life custodian was to inject confidence into a rearguard which had not exactly been creaking with Doug Rudham or Dave Underwood between the posts, but which needed a tad more consistency if promotion was to be achieved.

In the event he did pretty well, demanding and usually achieving command of his area, but when he re-crossed the border after three seasons – moving to Falkirk as player-boss in exchange for Bert Slater – the Reds remained in the second flight, so Younger's mission had not quite been accomplished.

THOMAS YOUNGER
BORN: Edinburgh, 10 April 1930.
HONOURS: 24 Scotland caps (55-58).
OTHER CLUBS: Hibernian 49/50-55/6 (177, 0); Falkirk 59/60 (6, 0); Stoke City 59/60 (10, 0); Leeds United 61/2-62/3 (37, 0).
MANAGER: Falkirk (59-60).
DIED: 13 January 1984.

GAMES	127
GOALS	0

BILLY LIDDELL

1945/46 → 1960/61

It is scarcely possible to exaggerate the stature of Billy Liddell in the history of Liverpool FC. As a footballer he thrilled the Anfield faithful; as a man he warmed their hearts; as a symbol of all that was fine in the field of sporting endeavour, he was unmatchable.

For nearly 15 years the self-effacing Scottish winger cum centre-forward was the outstanding player for a club which experienced fleeting moments of glory but which, in general, was a frustrated hotbed of unfulfilled potential.

Had he been born two, three or four decades later and played under Shankly or Paisley, Fagan or Dalglish, he would have been knee-deep in honours. As it was he had to be content with a solitary League Championship medal and the knowledge that the team he graced was known widely as 'Liddellpool'. True, the surname lent itself conveniently to such glib wordplay, but undeniably it expressed a sentiment which contained more than a little truth.

The oldest of a coalminer's six children, Billy grew up on salt porridge, kail (that's Scotch broth in the parlance of Sassenachs) and plenty of bread, a diet that did nothing to arrest a sturdy physical development which stood him in admirable stead in the boyhood football games in which he both revelled and excelled.

He graduated through his own village side to the enchantingly named Lochgelly Violet, with whom he caught the eye of a countryman, one Matt Busby, then playing for Liverpool and who recommended him to the Anfield regime.

Liddell signed for the Reds as a promising flankman in 1939 and then saw the first six years of his career lost to the war. During the conflict he served as an RAF navigator but his soccer talents were not entirely redundant. He played almost 150 times for his new club in emergency competitions, as well as guesting for Chelsea, Dunfermline Athletic and Linfield of Northern Ireland, and served notice that here was something special.

In January 1946, with life returning gradually to something approaching normality, he made his official Liverpool debut five days short of his 24th birthday, scoring at Chester in the FA Cup. But it was in the following campaign that Billy Liddell really set sail on the course that was to earn him sporting immortality on Merseyside.

Playing 35 games as the Reds took the title, he revealed the pace and power which were to become his hallmarks. Liddell was particularly dangerous running at defenders and cutting inside from the left wing – tackling him was akin to tangling with a runaway tank – and although he found the net only seven times that season he demonstrated effectively the dashing style which was to make him one of Liverpool's most prolific goal-scorers.

As he grew in experience his influence on the team burgeoned. He was muscular and skilful, blessed with a sprinter's speed and a fearsome shot, combative in the air and unfailingly courageous. He took the eye whether lining up on the left, the right or in the centre, a veritable one-man forward line. Sadly the side did not progress at the same rate and Liddell – by then a Scotland regular whose international standing and durability were recognised by selection for Great Britain against the Rest of Europe in both 1947 and 1955 – was in the unfortunate position of being a star in a team which plunged first to mid-table mediocrity and ultimately, in 1953/54, to relegation.

He reacted with characteristic determination and in his first four seasons in the lower grade notched 101 goals in 156 League matches. He was the Reds' leading scorer in eight out of nine seasons in the 1950s, but it was not enough to secure promotion.

As his pace waned with age, Billy lost that stirring ability to run past defenders but compensated with a more mature passing game from a deep-lying position. The devotion of the supporters never wavered and when he returned at the age of 37, after one of several spells on the sidelines, he scored two spectacular goals against Bristol City in August 1959. The acclaim was rapturous, and deservedly so.

By that time managerial and coaching offers had started to arrive, but Liddell had mapped out a future in accountancy and, after staying to play a few times under new boss Bill Shankly, he retired in 1961.

To fully appreciate Billy's radiant public image, it is essential to understand that there was much more to the darkly handsome Fifer than his athletic attributes. A chivalrous, loyal man who was not too proud to stud the boots for his team-mates when left out of the side in 1959, he was always ready to help youngsters and went on to become a youth worker, lay preacher and Justice of the Peace. If ever a footballer deserved to be called a hero, then it was Billy Liddell. He will be revered forever on Merseyside and beyond.

WILLIAM BEVERIDGE LIDDELL

BORN	Townhill, Fife, 10 January 1922.
HONOURS	League Championship 46/7. 28 Scotland caps (47-56).
DIED	Liverpool, 3 July 2001.

GAMES	537
GOALS	229

DICK WHITE

1955/56 → 1961/62

For four seasons, as Liverpool knocked in vain on the door of the First Division, Dick White was the calm and valiant kingpin of a generally resolute defence.

The first link in the Reds' illustrious Scunthorpe connection, which was to lead the likes of Ray Clemence and Kevin Keegan to Anfield, White was a part-timer at the Old Showground when he was signed by 'Pool boss Don Welsh in November 1955 as a prospective long-term replacement for stalwart stopper Laurie Hughes.

The veteran responded with spirit to the challenge of youth and White was allowed only sporadic opportunities during his initial 18 months on Merseyside. He made the most of his time, though, helping his new club take the Central League title in his first full season, and when Hughes bowed finally to the inevitable, White appropriated the number-five shirt with relish, missing only two League matches between 1957/58 and 1960/61.

He built a reputation as a dependable, unspectacular centre-half who was willing to assume responsibility and carry it well. As befitted a six-footer, he excelled in aerial combat but, as with so many of his ilk, distribution was not his strong point.

White rarely suffered a chasing but when pressurised – Tommy Johnston of an excellent, underrated Leyton Orient side and Graham Moore of Cardiff City were two opponents of the late 1950s who had the ability to stretch him to the limit – he stuck to his task with admirable tenacity.

Attack was never the White forte and he scored only one goal in more than 200 Liverpool appearances, though he is remembered for one surging sortie which took him past three Orient defenders to lay on an injury-time winner for Roger Hunt in the FA Cup at Anfield in January 1960.

White's tenure in central defence ended, as did a spell as captain, with the advent of Ron Yeats in 1961/62, but he was both adaptable and quick enough to switch to right-back to earn a Second Division title medal – two own-goals at Middlesbrough in the Reds' first defeat of the campaign provided a minor hiccup – before seeing out his career with Doncaster Rovers.

RICHARD WHITE	
BORN	Scunthorpe, Lincolnshire, 18 August 1931.
HONOURS	Second Division Championship 61/2.
OTHER CLUBS	Scunthorpe United 50/1-55/6 (133, 11); Doncaster Rovers 62/3-63/4 (82, 0).
DIED	Nottingham, 15 June 2002.

GAMES	216
GOALS	1

JOHNNY WHEELER

1956/57 → 1961/62

The twin peaks of Johnny Wheeler's career were both behind him when he arrived at Anfield as one of the first signings of new Liverpool boss Phil Taylor in September 1956.

Three years earlier the cultured right-half had played for Bolton Wanderers in the celebrated 'Matthews Final' at Wembley and in 1954 he had won his solitary England cap. But although Wheeler's prime had gone he still had plenty to offer an Anfield outfit locked in perennial struggle to escape from the Second Division, and on joining his home-town club he gave immediate value for money.

Wheeler, an adaptable performer who spent much of his first term with Liverpool as an inside-right playing behind his fellow forwards, was a graceful prompter, precise of pass, firm of tackle and never short of attacking ideas.

He was not a heavy scorer but sometimes surprised goalkeepers with snap-shots, one of his most memorable being a 20-yard drive past Harry Gregg in an FA Cup defeat by Manchester United in 1960.

Port Vale, though, had a more dramatic reason to remember his striking powers. With nine minutes remaining of a Second Division encounter at Anfield in November 1956 the score was 1-1. Enter Wheeler with a hat-trick in five minutes to transform the game.

On the debit side, there were times when quickness of thought was not matched by fleetness of foot. If possession was lost, Wheeler's recovery was not always rapid, which resulted in pressure on the defence, but more often his experience made him a joy to play alongside.

He spent only one season, 1958/59, as captain before the job passed to his cousin, Ronnie Moran, but Wheeler continued to exert a major influence, using his vast experience to nurse youngsters through their early matches.

In autumn 1959, aged 31, he was sidelined by injury and then suffered a spell of indifferent form. The end appeared to be nigh but he fought hack with some fine displays under new boss Bill Shankly, eventually giving way to youth in the form of Gordon Milne.

Johnny Wheeler, a kind and humorous character who went on to be trainer and assistant manager of Bury, won no medals at Anfield but could look back with satisfaction on a job impeccably well done.

JOHN EDWARD WHEELER		
BORN	Crosby, Liverpool, 26 July 1928.	
HONOURS	1 England cap (54).	GAMES **177**
OTHER CLUBS	Tranmere Rovers 48/9-50/1 (101, 9); Bolton Wanderers 50/1-55/6 (189, 18).	GOALS **23**

ALAN ARNELL

1953/54 → 1960/61

The scoring rate of Alan Arnell would be enough to have the majority of modern managers reaching feverishly for their cheque books. But the big, rangy centre-forward, who averaged a fraction short of a goal every two games for Liverpool during the middle and late 1950s, never established himself as a regular in the side.

Arnell – who was blooded by the Reds as an amateur, perhaps a sign of desperation in the quest for talent to lift the club back into the top flight – had all the attributes expected of a typical front-line hustler of his era.

He was strong, energetic and a menace in the air; his touch on the ball, while hardly of the delicate variety, was respectable enough; his distribution was adequate, and he toiled willingly.

During his most prolific campaigns, 1955/56 and 1956/57, he scored 23 times in 37 League outings yet failed to convince successive managers, Don Welsh and Phil Taylor, that Billy Liddell would be better employed on the wing than leading the line.

Some contemporary observers reckon Arnell was short of raw aggression and lacked the necessary drive to elbow aside even the challenge of fellow striker Louis Bimpson – who had a similarly unfulfilling Anfield career despite contributing plenty of goals – let alone those of the altogether more accomplished Dave Hickson and Roger Hunt at the end of the decade.

Nevertheless Alan Arnell enjoyed some triumphs as a Red, notably a courageous hat-trick after pulling a muscle early in the game at Huddersfield in 1956. He moved to Tranmere Rovers in February 1960, going on to maintain his strike-rate at Prenton Park and then at Halifax, before ending his playing days with non-League Runcorn.

ALAN JACK ARNELL

BORN   Chichester, Sussex, 25 November 1933.

OTHER CLUBS   Tranmere Rovers 60/1-62/3 (68, 33); Halifax Town 63/4 (14, 6).

GAMES	75
GOALS	35

FRED MORRIS

1958/59 → 1959/60

Fred Morris was a tall, dashing right-winger whose neck-or-nothing style was beloved of supporters; he was a clean striker of the ball who scored some rousing goals; and he was a joker, his face usually split in a wide grin.

In short, Morris was a soccer character. Unfortunately, despite several stirring displays – a two-goal show against Leyton Orient at Anfield in November 1959 comes to mind – he wasn't blessed with sufficient class to make the grade with Liverpool.

Morris was signed from Mansfield Town by Phil Taylor in March 1958 for £7,000. He was 28 at the time and perhaps had spent too long in the lower reaches of the League to make a successful transition.

After missing the first two games of the following season, he played in 40 without a break, netting a dozen times in the process, a creditable achievement. He was injured early in 1959/60 and had just reclaimed his place when Bill Shankly moved in at Anfield. Morris turned out in the next match, a 4-0 drubbing by Cardiff City, and was never selected again.

FREDERICK WILLIAM MORRIS
BORN   Oswestry, Shropshire, 15 June 1929.
OTHER CLUBS   Walsall 50/1-56/7 (210, 43); Mansfield Town 56/7-57/8 (57 17); Crewe Alexandra 60/1 (8, 1); Gillingham 60/1 (10, 1); Chester 61/2 (29, 3).
DIED   20 November 1998.

GAMES	48
GOALS	14

BOBBY CAMPBELL

1959/60 → 1960/61

The end of season 1959/60 came too soon for Bobby Campbell. The constructive wing-half was enjoying his most effective run in the Liverpool side and although the arrival of Tommy Leishman and Gordon Milne made his future challenging, to say the least, there were some grounds for optimism.

As the Reds completed their League programme with a 3-0 home victory over Sunderland, Campbell was in his element. His neat, creative skills were beginning to mesh impressively with fellow providers Jimmy Melia and Johnny Wheeler, and his tackling, never his strongest feature, was taking on a promising crispness.

But then, sadly, his impetus was shattered by the summer recess and it was never regained. He made only one more senior appearance for Liverpool before joining Portsmouth.

The major flaws in Campbell's game were a marked lack of pace and, because he was at his best going forward, a tendency to be lured out of position. This was never illustrated more aptly than against Cardiff City at Anfield in December 1959 when, offered the chance to create a favourable early impression on new boss Bill Shankly, he was given the run-around by the elusive Derek Tapscott.

Campbell went on to become a coach and manager with some success.

ROBERT CAMPBELL
BORN   Liverpool, 23 April 1937.
OTHER CLUBS   Portsmouth 61/2-65/6 (61, 2); Aldershot 66/7 (5, 0).
MANAGER   Fulham (76-80), Portsmouth (82-84), Chelsea (88-91).

GAMES	14
GOALS	1

JOHN MOLYNEUX

1955/56 → 1961/62

John Molyneux might have been the prototype for the popular image of a 1950s full-back. Tall and solidly constructed, he was far removed from the modern breed of overlapping defender, but when it came to doing his primary job of keeping out the opposition, there could be few complaints about his work during his seven years at Anfield.

Indeed, for six of those campaigns Molyneux was a first-team regular, performing with credit for three managers. Initially he served Don Welsh for nearly two seasons after arriving from Chester for £4,500, and then saw out the three-and-a-half year reign of Phil Taylor. But perhaps the greatest measure of his ability is that Bill Shankly was content for him to retain the right-back berth for 18 months as the decade closed.

Molyneux's primary attributes were his strength in the tackle and an instinct for danger which made goal-line clearances a much-appreciated speciality. His distribution was efficient and be formed a useful understanding with right-half Johnny Wheeler, but he could be exposed for lack of pace, a defect he tended to disguise by a cautious approach.

Fleet-footed wingmen such as Peter McParland of Aston Villa and Middlesbrough's Edwin Holliday sometimes posed problems, but on his day Molyneux could subdue the majority of Second Division speed merchants.

Getting forward was not one of his major concerns but he did allow himself the occasional flourish, one notable foray coming in an epic 4-4 draw at Villa Park in March 1960 when he struck one of his rare goals after combining, typically, with Wheeler.

John Molyneux, a dedicated all-round sportsman, ultimately lost his place when Dick White moved to right-back in the Shankly reshuffle of 1961/62. After that he returned to Chester for a second substantial spell.

JOHN ALLAN MOLYNEUX
BORN   Warrington, Lancashire, 3 February 1931.
OTHER CLUBS Chester 49/50-54/5 (178, 1) and 62/3-64/5 (67, 0).

GAMES   249
GOALS   3

JIMMY HARROWER

1957/58 → 1960/61

Jimmy Harrower was blessed with a treasure trove of natural ability; sadly, the Anfield career of the stocky Scottish inside-forward failed to do justice to his extravagant gifts.

When Phil Taylor persuaded Hibernian to part with the ball-playing under-23 international for £11,000 in January 1958, the Liverpool manager was optimistic that he had secured a man capable of scheming the Reds' return to the First Division.

There were few apparent defects to Harrower's game. His ball control was magnetic, his passing majestic; he possessed a savage, if sometimes wayward shot and he was strong with a low centre of gravity which made knocking him off the ball seem like removing a limpet from a rock. The one superficial flaw was a lack of pace, for which it was reasonably reckoned his other talents would compensate.

Several early displays confirmed his potential and one exhibition against Stoke in April 1958 had the Kop drooling as he stroked the ball around, giving full expression to his repertoire of delicate chips, lobs and dummies.

Unfortunately he could not attain consistency and often drifted through games making scant contribution, perhaps not benefiting from the presence of another play-maker, Jimmy Melia. The two frequently made pretty patterns together as they interchanged passes but frequently this joint artistry led nowhere in terms of team advantage.

An abrasive aspect to the Harrower game also surfaced. This sometimes provoked altercations, such as the series of petty clashes with Bristol City's Tom Casey which led to a booking in August 1959. More unwelcome was a certain cockiness which was entertaining when it took the form of saucy flicks and daring through-balls but unsavoury when it descended, on occasion, into petulance and the taunting of less skilful opponents.

As first Phil Taylor and then Bill Shankly explored every option in the push for promotion, Harrower was tried on the wing and as a deep-lying centre-forward, a role in which he shone briefly. Eventually Shankly opted to look elsewhere for inspiration and sold his fellow Scot to Newcastle for £15,000. An unfulfilling Anfield sojourn was at an end.

JAMES HARROWER

BORN   Alva, Clackmannanshire, 18 August 1935.
OTHER CLUBS   Hibernian 55/6-57/8 (36, 12); Newcastle United 60/1-61/2 (5, 0); Falkirk 61/2-62/3 (21, 3); St Johnstone 63/4-64/5 (42, 8); Albion Rovers 65/6 (22, 0).
DIED   Stirling, August 2006.

GAMES 105
GOALS 22

DAVE HICKSON

1959/60 → 1960/61

There have been some sensational Merseyside transfer tales down the years, involving the stellar likes of Alan Ball and Kevin Keegan, Ian Rush and Nick Barmby. But none has created a greater furore than the sale of Everton idol Dave Hickson to Liverpool in November 1959.

When Dave crossed Stanley Park, the neutral no-man's-land between the two neighbouring grounds, feelings ran so high that some Everton fans swore they would follow their hero and defect to the old enemy, while a contingent from the Kop pledged to make the opposite journey in protest at the £10,500 deal.

Phil Taylor's last signing before handing over the management reins to Bill Shankly, Hickson was a fiery, buccaneering centre-forward, utterly fearless and obsessed with scoring goals, whose distinctive blond thatch had stood out like a beacon in the Blues' attack during two successful spells.

His gladiatorial reputation had been forged by the raw-meat-and-razor-blades approach he had adopted ever since bursting on to the Everton scene in September 1951, and it was set in stone by his contribution to an FA Cup victory over Manchester United some 18 months later.

On an explosive Goodison afternoon with the whiff of cordite in the air, Hickson had endeared himself to the success-starved supporters (as they were at the time) by grabbing the winner after leaving the field for five stitches to be inserted in a gash above his eye. A few minutes later he reopened the wound with a header against an upright and his face was a bloody mask as he walked off at the end to a tumultuous ovation.

On his arrival at Liverpool, then, the stage was set for a bold entrance and Hickson obliged with a show that was pure theatre. He bagged both goals – one a glorious diving header – in a 2-1 win over Division Two pace-setters Aston Villa and exuded such swashbuckling charisma that the Anfield crowd cheered his every touch. Then, having transformed Liverpool's lacklustre season into one seething with possibilities, he consolidated with a run of dashing displays which yielded 21 strikes in 27 games.

While playing for Cheshire Army Cadets prior to his professional career, Big Dave had been coached by the legendary Dixie Dean, as his aerial work bore witness, but actually he boasted an accomplished all-round game, being particularly adept at subtle flicks to his sidemen.

One of his most lasting contributions to the Reds' cause was his part in the development of Roger Hunt, whom he relieved gladly of some of the scoring responsibility, and Roger always recalled him as one of the most effective partners he ever had.

Hickson continued to find the net freely in his second Anfield campaign, before the arrival of Ian St John rendered him surplus to requirements and he took his talents to fresh fields.

During his travels he was dubbed soccer's stormy petrel, a reference to assorted clashes with referees. Yet he was never perceived as malicious and his only major offence in a Liverpool shirt was a sending-off for retaliation – he was a constant victim of provocation – against Sheffield United, after which he was cleared of deliberate violent conduct. A quiet man off the pitch, Dave Hickson deserves to be remembered as a footballer, not a fighter.

DAVID HICKSON

BORN Salford, Lancashire, 30 October 1929.

OTHER CLUBS Everton 51/2-55/6 (139, 63) and 57/8-59/60 (86, 32); Aston Villa 55/6 (12, 1); Huddersfield Town 55/6-56/7 (54, 28); Cambridge City; Bury 61/2 (8, 0); Tranmere Rovers 62/3-63/4 (45, 21).

GAMES 67

GOALS 38

ALAN A'COURT

1952/53 → 1964/65

In full flight, left-winger Alan A'Court was a stirring sight. When he hared for the byline and crossed the ball at full stretch, he was one of the most difficult customers to confront Second Division full-backs in the late 1950s.

The blond Lancastrian wore a number-nine shirt for his Liverpool debut at Middlesbrough in February 1953 but his speed, directness and capacity to provide accurate centres marked him out as a natural wide-man.

Accordingly, with Billy Liddell usually occupying A'Court's favoured left flank, the youngster drifted in and out of the side during his first two seasons in serious contention for a place, getting a chance only when the Scottish international switched wings or was selected at centre-forward.

A'Court established himself during the Reds' first season following relegation to the Second Division and he was a linchpin in the struggle for promotion which was to last for eight often tortuous campaigns. Thereafter he remained a regular for half of Liverpool's initial term back among the elite in 1962/63 before giving way, temporarily, to Kevin Lewis.

His first-team ambitions were finally extinguished when the richly promising Peter Thompson was signed from Preston North End in August 1963. A'Court could be expected to scrap for a place with Lewis but, at such a late stage in his career, there could be no contest with the brilliant Thompson.

Though he was never a heavy scorer, A'Court packed a ferocious shot and had a blessed knack of finding the net when it mattered. For instance, Liverpool were on the threshold of promotion in March 1962 when they found themselves two down with ten minutes to go in the vital confrontation with fellow high-fliers Leyton Orient at Brisbane Road. In stepped the faithful A'Court with a brace of point-saving goals, neither as spectacular as his memorable strike against Chelsea in the FA Cup earlier that year, but of crucial significance.

By then, perhaps, despite the fact that he was an ever-present that momentous term, Alan was beginning to go past his peak and it was easy to forget that there had been a time when his left-flank fire, control and consistency had looked likely to win him a place in the game's higher echelons.

He played five times for England, including three appearances in the 1958 World Cup finals in Sweden against Brazil, Austria and the USSR, before becoming one of several players who lost out because of Bobby Charlton's short-term switch from inside-forward to the left wing. Bolton Wanderers' Doug Holden and Edwin Holliday of Middlesbrough suffered a similar fate.

But failure to become an international star should not detract from A'Court's achievements at Anfield before he left to see out his playing days with Tranmere, then coach at Norwich, Chester, Crewe, Stoke and in Zambia.

The teenager who caused a stir in his rugby-loving family by choosing soccer as his livelihood gave distinguished and loyal service to Liverpool. His deeds on the field spoke for themselves but also he was an inestimable asset to the club behind the scenes, keeping morale bubbling with his infectious humour and encouraging less experienced colleagues such as the rookie Ian Callaghan. Football would be incalculably richer for more men like Alan A'Court.

ALAN A'COURT

BORN	Rainhill, Lancashire, 30 September 1934.
HONOURS	Second Division Championship 61/2. 5 England caps (57-58).
OTHER CLUBS	Tranmere Rovers 64/5-65/6 (50, 11).

GAMES **382**

GOALS **63**

BERT SLATER

1959/60 → 1961/62

Bert Slater was fearless, agile and short. Unfortunately it was the last-mentioned characteristic which seemed to be constantly in the spotlight during his early days as Liverpool's number-one goalkeeper.

The modest, 5ft 8½ in Scot arrived at Anfield as part of the transaction which took his predecessor, Tommy Younger, to Falkirk in the summer of 1959, and he made a chequered start with his new club.

After performing heroics in a 3-2 reverse against Cardiff at Ninian Park on his debut, Slater blundered once against Bristol City and then twice against Hull. He was replaced by Doug Rudham and returned to the side only when the South African was injured.

Following several more alarming incidents, for which his lack of inches was usually blamed, Slater improved immeasurably and eventually hit brilliant form. Thus during the subsequent 1961/62 promotion campaign he was an ever-present, conceding only 27 goals in the first 29 games before surprisingly being axed – to the consternation of some team-mates – in favour of Jim Furnell.

Throughout that fine run he displayed exceptional handling on the ground and missed little in the air, benefiting enormously from an instant understanding with the dominant new centre-half Ron Yeats.

However, it was clear that there was no future for Slater at Anfield and he returned to Scotland to prove his class in Dundee's progress to the 1963 European Cup semi-finals.

In 1965 he headed south again to join Watford and two years later he defied Liverpool by keeping a clean sheet in an epic FA Cup draw at Vicarage Road. On retirement as a player in 1969, Slater became a coach with the Hornets, and when he left the game in 1975 he could look back on an accomplished and varied career.

ROBERT SLATER	
BORN	Musselburgh, Midlothian, 5 May 1936.
HONOURS	Second Division Championship 61/2.
OTHER CLUBS	Falkirk 53/4-58/9 (134, 0); Dundee 62/3-64/5 (70, 0); Watford 65/6-68/9 (134, 0).
DIED	Brechin, Angus, 21 July 2006.

GAMES	111
GOALS	0

TOMMY LEISHMAN

1959/60 → 1962/63

Long-striding, fierce-tackling Scot Tommy Leishman presented a menacing prospect when he arrived at Anfield in November 1959, just two weeks ahead of Bill Shankly. Gangly and gaunt, his dark features accentuated by a severe crew-cut, Tommy would have been a natural to play a trainee undertaker, if only he had been an actor! Instead he was destined for a relatively short, but generally effective tenure as Liverpool's left-half.

Leishman was signed from St Mirren, with whom he had won a Scottish Cup medal earlier that year, as a £9,000 replacement for Geoff Twentyman, whose role had not been filled satisfactorily since he had joined Ballymena United in the twilight of his career.

A part-timer with the Saints, Leishman benefited from Shankly's more rigorous training methods and soon he was turning heads on debut with an immensely promising display in a 2-0 victory against Charlton Athletic at Anfield.

He was quick off the mark for a big fellow, competitive in the air and admirably eager for the ball, though his distribution lacked the imagination and precision that were the hallmarks of his eventual successor, Willie Stevenson.

Nevertheless Leishman, a markedly left-sided performer who could be made to look awkward when forced towards the right, was a regular choice for two and a half seasons, including the 1961/62 promotion campaign in which his drive and enthusiasm were important assets.

He played 11 games on Liverpool's return to the top grade but it became evident that he lacked the class essential for a tilt at the Championship. Thus when Shankly turned to Stevenson, Tommy Leishman returned north of the border to perform creditably for Hibernian before becoming player-manager of leading Irish club Linfield.

THOMAS LEISHMAN
BORN   Stenhousemuir, Stirlingshire, 3 September 1937.
HONOURS   Second Division Championship 61/2.
OTHER CLUBS   St Mirren 57/8-59/60 (15, 1); Hibernian 62/3-64/5 (30, 1); Linfield, Northern Ireland, 65/6-67/8; Stranraer 67/8-69/70 (27, 4).
MANAGER   Linfield (65-68).

GAMES   119
GOALS   7

KEVIN LEWIS

1960/61 → 1962/63

The Anfield career of Kevin Lewis was a perplexing affair. Playing almost exclusively as a winger, he averaged better than a goal every two games and yet failed to find a niche as Bill Shankly built his great side of the mid-1960s.

The lanky flankman was recruited from Sheffield United in the summer of 1960 when Billy Liddell was on the verge of retirement and Ian Callaghan was adjudged too inexperienced.

Lewis began justifying his £13,000 fee immediately, netting on his debut at home to Leeds and going on to notch 19 goals in 32 games. Thus he became top scorer in his first term at Anfield, which was no mean feat with the likes of Roger Hunt and Dave Hickson in the side.

During the promotion campaign that followed, sharpshooter Lewis remained prolific. He scored in half his 20 games but was displaced by Callaghan and wasn't offered another run until midway through 1962/63 in Division One. Among the elite, he netted regularly and often spectacularly, only to be rewarded by Peter Thompson's arrival. Not surprisingly he departed, to Huddersfield Town, perhaps wondering what was needed to cement a Liverpool place.

A versatile performer – Lewis scored twice when standing in at centre-forward for the suspended Ian St John as the Reds clinched promotion against Southampton – he was quick, skilful and competent in the air, but at times he was brushed off the ball rather too easily, and he was inclined to be unpredictable.

Despite an outwardly casual manner, Lewis was nervous before games and maybe he wasn't temperamentally suited to the big time. He was lost to the British game when, still only 25, he emigrated to South Africa in 1965.

KEVIN LEWIS

BORN   Ellesmere Port, Cheshire, 19 September 1940.
HONOURS   Second Division Championship 61/2.
OTHER CLUBS   Sheffield United 57/8-59/60 (62, 23); Huddersfield Town 63/4-64/5 (45, 13); Port Elizabeth, South Africa.

GAMES	81
GOALS	44

JOHNNY MORRISSEY

1957/58 → 1960/61

Life was not easy for an aspiring young winger at Anfield as the 1950s drew towards a close. If he managed somehow to sidestep the great Billy Liddell and long-established Alan A'Court, there were still the likes of Ian Callaghan, Kevin Lewis and Fred Morris to contend with.

Even so, the denizens of the Kop reckoned they saw something special when little Johnny Morrissey broke through to the fringe of the team. He showed hardness unusual in a wingman, allied his pluck with cunning, carried a ferocious shot and was blessed with all-round natural talent. To confirm his place in their hearts, he hailed from the tough Scotland Road area of the city; in short, he was one of their own.

Limited chances during an unexpectedly brief Liverpool career allowed him to display his abilities to only intermittent effect but he was clearly a player of potential and it shocked supporters when he moved – to Everton, of all clubs – for £10,000 in August 1962.

There were stories of strife over the deal between the board and Bill Shankly, who was keen to keep Morrissey. Feelings among the fans ran higher still as he helped the Blues win the League Championship in his first season at Goodison Park before going on to give ten years' distinguished service to Harry Catterick's team.

	JOHN MORRISSEY		
BORN	Liverpool, 18 April 1940.	GAMES	37
OTHER CLUBS	Everton 62/3-71/2 (259, 43); Oldham Athletic 72/3 (6, 1).	GOALS	6

JIM FURNELL

1961/62 → 1963/64

Liverpool rescued Jim Furnell from the nether regions of professional football, where he had performed creditably but hitherto anonymously for Burnley's reserve teams for more than half a decade, and plunged him straight into the hunt for promotion in February 1962.

The popular Bert Slater had been controversially dropped and Furnell, who had been limited to two League outings with the Turf Moor club by the consistency of Adam Blacklaw, came in for the final 13 games of the campaign. He let no one down and the Reds duly made it to the First Division, where initially Bill Shankly kept faith with his £18,000 acquisition.

Though only rarely did he inspire the confidence of his defenders in the way his predecessor had, Furnell held on to his place in the top flight until he broke his finger 13 games into the season, an injury which effectively signalled the end of his Anfield career.

He was replaced by Tommy Lawrence, who proved to be an infinitely superior performer, and moved to Arsenal a year later. Furnell enjoyed a creditable mid-1960s spell with the Gunners before going on to do well with Rotherham United and, particularly, Plymouth Argyle, for whom he played until he was 39.

	JAMES FURNELL		
BORN	Clitheroe, Lancashire, 23 November 1937.		
HONOURS	Second Division Championship 61/2.	GAMES	28
OTHER CLUBS	Burnley 59/60-60/1 (2, 0); Arsenal 63/4-67/8 (141, 0); Rotherham United 68/9-69/70 (76, 0); Plymouth Argyle 70/1-75/6 (183, 0).	GOALS	0

JIMMY MELIA

1955/56 → 1963/64

Everything had gone Jimmy Melia's way in 1963, a year in which the creative inside-forward's subtle promptings had helped to lift Liverpool into a Championship-challenging position by late December.

The Merseysider was the ideas man of a side well on the way to becoming one of Britain's best and, though only just turned 26, already he had played nearly 300 times for the Reds. Recently his advance had been recognised with two England caps and, with such a blend of quality and experience, Melia seemed to be hovering on the very edge of greatness.

The soccer fates, however, are nothing if not unpredictable. A minor ankle injury sidelined the prematurely balding schemer shortly before Christmas and Bill Shankly was forced to make a radical change to his line-up. There was no obvious replacement for Melia so the manager improvised, moving Ian St John into a deep-lying position to take some of the midfield responsibility and introducing Alf Arrowsmith to partner Roger Hunt at the front. St John and Arrowsmith revelled in their new roles and although Melia made a brief and unconvincing reappearance when he regained fitness, his Anfield days were done.

Yet this rather abrupt exit should not obscure the earlier achievements of a player of enviable natural skills, who had celebrated his debut with a goal against Nottingham Forest in December 1955 and in the following seasons established himself in a side pushing perpetually for promotion.

The 1958/59 term, in which he netted 21 times, was a personally productive one, but his most impressive form was reserved for 1961/62 when, finally, the Reds left Division Two behind them.

At his best Jimmy Melia was one of the most constructive players Liverpool ever had, combining flair, industry and intelligence. He was the master of the penetrating through-pass and was adept at shielding the ball, though there were times when he retained possession too long and a delicate dribble might take him past the same opponent twice.

Such over-elaboration antagonised the Anfield fans, normally such an inspiration, and he was on the receiving end of some unreasonably barbed criticism. An occasional tendency to drift out of a match in which he had made a bright start also infuriated Kopites, who traditionally favoured players with a little more obvious fire about their games than Melia's more measured approach.

The abuse was particularly scathing when he missed a penalty five minutes from time against Brighton at Anfield – with the visitors a goal up – in October 1959. As ever, he demonstrated commendable resilience in the face of adversity and had the satisfaction of nodding the equaliser seconds ahead of the final whistle.

The same fortitude saw Melia survive the disappointment of a short, unsuccessful stint with Wolves before giving admirable service to Southampton, whom he helped to reach the First Division in 1966. There was to follow a wandering managerial career, perhaps the sweetest moment of which was the unceremonious ejection of Liverpool from the FA Cup by his Brighton side on the way to Wembley in 1983.

JAMES MELIA

BORN Liverpool, 1 November 1937.
HONOURS League Championship 63/4. Second Division Championship 61/2. 2 England caps (63).
OTHER CLUBS Wolverhampton Wanderers 63/4-64/5 (24, 4); Southampton 64/5-68/9 (139, 11); Aldershot 68/9-71/2 (135, 14); Crewe Alexandra 71/2 (4,0).
MANAGER Aldershot (69-72); Crewe Alexandra (72-74); Southport (75); Brighton and Hove Albion (83); Belenenses, Portugal, (83-85); Stockport County (86).

GAMES 287
GOALS 78

RONNIE MORAN

1952/53 → 1964/65

Ronnie Moran's inspired backroom work as Liverpool evolved into the dominant power in English football has tended to overshadow his playing career, a circumstance which does grave injustice to one of the Reds' sturdiest bulwarks throughout a testing period of their history and on to the dawn of the glory days.

A burly full-back with a penchant for dead-ball situations – his left foot was a devastating weapon from the penalty spot and at free-kicks – Moran ranks high among Anfield's most enthusiastic and effective defenders down the years. Indeed, some shrewd contemporary observers maintain that he should have won more representative honours than a brace of appearances for the Football League.

Ronnie's ample build might have suggested a lack of pace but he covered ground with deceptive speed and was rarely caught out of position. Robust in the tackle and combative in the air, he was a reassuring sight when his side came under pressure and his presence was never more appreciated than at Eastville in December 1959 when a rampant Bristol Rovers threatened to rout the Reds. The visiting defence wobbled visibly with the notable exception of Moran, who made three goal-line clearances and numerous last-yard tackles as Liverpool went on to win with two breakaway goals, a victory due largely to their indomitable left-back.

In his early days Moran concentrated so avidly on his defensive skills that he was rarely found in attack, but confidence came with maturity and he grew more adventurous. Ipswich bore the brunt of one telling excursion at Anfield in 1959 when he surged upfield, found Fred Morris on the wing and ran on to nod Morris' centre down for Roger Hunt to net.

Moran had made his League debut for an indifferent Liverpool outfit at Derby in November 1952, but failed to claim a regular place during the two-year struggle against relegation which ended unsuccessfully in the spring of 1954. His breakthrough came half-way through the first, acclimatising term in the lower grade when he ousted Frank Lock. Thereafter he missed only six League outings in the following five campaigns and enjoyed a spell as skipper at the end of the decade as his team strained unremittingly to escape from Division Two.

Then 16 months of injury problems removed Moran from the action and, with promotion finally beckoning, he seemed likely to miss out on the triumph after striving for so long to achieve it. Happily, he returned to fitness just in time to earn a richly deserved medal in 1961/62.

There was even better to come. In the Reds' second season back in the top flight they lifted the title and Moran capped his career by playing in 35 games on the way to the trophy. By then, though, he really was slowing down and in 1964/65 Chris Lawler came in at right-back, with Gerry Byrne switching to Moran's left-flank slot.

But one last bonus awaited the old campaigner before he turned his attention to coaching the club's youngsters. Byrne broke his collar-bone in the FA Cup Final against Leeds and Moran was called up to do battle in two European Cup semi-final encounters with mighty Internazionale of Milan, giving a creditable account of himself against the brilliant Brazilian, Jair. It was a fitting end to the playing days of one of the most dedicated one-club men who ever drew breath.

RONALD MORAN		
BORN	Liverpool, 28 February 1934.	
HONOURS	League Championship 63/4. Second Division Championship 61/2.	

GAMES	380
GOALS	16

GORDON MILNE

1960/61 → 1966/67

Gordon Milne was the first Shankly signing destined to play a role in Liverpool's triumphant march through the early and middle 1960s. He arrived with none of the fanfares which greeted the subsequent entrances of Ian St John and Ron Yeats, but in his own way he was as crucial a cog in the Anfield machine as his more famous team-mates.

A stocky and industrious right-half, Milne was never a player to grab a game by the scruff of its neck and dominate it. Instead, he was the fetcher and carrier of the side, rather like a middle man in a relay race; thus the job he did was indispensable to the team effort but he was rarely the centre of attention when it was time to hand out the plaudits.

Milne's approach was neat and unflashy, like the man himself. He was not a fearsome tackler, relying on anticipation to make interceptions before setting up attacks with admirably precise distribution, and he was adept at brisk one-two manoeuvres, a style which complemented the often more ambitious, probing methods of Willie Stevenson on his left.

Some believed that for a man who popped up so often around the opposition's penalty box Milne did not find the net regularly enough, but though his haul was admittedly on the meagre side, he had the knack of scoring vital goals. Match-winning efforts on the way to the 1965/66 title against fellow contenders Burnley, Leeds and Manchester United were typical.

Milne was bought from Preston in August 1960 and Bill Shankly could be unusually certain that he was getting value for his £16,000. He had known the Lancashire lad from the cradle and watched him grow up – having been a Deepdale colleague of Gordon's father, Jimmy, during his playing days – and judged that he was acquiring a 'hardy little boy who would fight for the Liverpool cause'.

In fact, Milne Junior made an indifferent start with his new club. After being preferred to the experienced Johnny Wheeler for an early eight-game run, he was ousted by the veteran, who was enjoying something of an Indian summer. But Gordon fought back with spirit, as Shanks knew he would. By the spring of 1961 he was firmly back in the reckoning and, growing in confidence all the time, was an ever-present in the Second Division title campaign that followed.

His performances had assumed a reassuring consistency and he won two Championship medals, but suffered the abiding disappointment of missing the 1965 FA Cup victory through an injury sustained in a 4-0 Good Friday defeat at Stamford Bridge. The only sad image of an otherwise glorious Wembley occasion for the Liverpool camp was of a forlorn and soggy Milne, seated on the bench in his tracksuit in the pouring rain as the team of which he was normally such an integral part enjoyed one of its finest hours.

In 1967 Milne was allowed to move up the coast to Blackpool although many supporters felt that, while his form had dipped, he had plenty to offer still. But Shankly had decided that his side, which was betraying slight hints of a relative slide, needed surgery and that, at 30, the dapper wing-half was needed no more. Milne, after a brief sojourn at Bloomfield Road, went on to an enterprising career in management.

GORDON MILNE	
BORN	Preston, Lancashire, 29 March 1937.
HONOURS	League Championship 63/4, 65/6. Second Division Championship 61/2. 14 England caps (63-64).
OTHER CLUBS	Preston North End 56/7-60/1 (81,3); Blackpool 67/8-69/70 (64, 4).
MANAGER	Wigan Athletic (70-72); Coventry City (72-81, executive manager until 82); Leicester City (82-86, general manager until 87); Besiktas, Turkey (87-95).

GAMES **279 (2)**
GOALS **19**

GERRY BYRNE

1957/58 → 1968/69

When Bill Shankly breezed into Anfield in December 1959, the career of full-back Gerry Byrne was going nowhere rather too quickly for comfort. After making only two first-team appearances in two seasons and performing but moderately for the reserves, the swarthy defender was on the transfer list and looked for all the world like a player who would loiter on the fringe of the big time for several years before drifting inevitably towards a lower grade of football.

The new boss, however, saw something that everyone else had evidently missed. He transformed Byrne from a Central League plodder into one of the most effective backs in the land – and although he couldn't have known it at the time, he was breathing life into the future of a man who, one rainy day in May 1965, was destined to become one of the true heroes of Liverpool soccer history

But even the most inspired manager needs a little help from fate and it came in the form of injuries to regular left-back Ronnie Moran. Byrne stepped in with a string of accomplished performances and then, when Moran returned to first-team duty, he continued his development by switching to right-back at the expense of Dick White.

Byrne was an ever-present in the 1961/62 promotion campaign and became an automatic choice throughout the heady triumphs of the mid-1960s, reclaiming his left-sided role when Chris Lawler replaced the ageing Moran.

Quiet and undemonstrative in both play and demeanour, Gerry brought a granite reliability to the Reds' defence. He wasn't over-endowed with pace but compensated by reading the game with cool assurance and with a tackle that was fearsome. Shankly was adamant that there wasn't a harder – or fairer – footballer in the game and, never a man prone to understatement, he described his protege's performance in the defeat of Belgian champions Anderlecht in late 1964 as 'the best full-back display Europe has ever seen.'

The match which clinched Byrne's place in Liverpool legend was the 1965 FA Cup Final against Leeds United in which he played for 117 minutes with a broken collar-bone, overcoming grinding pain and disguising his infirmity from Don Revie's men, who certainly would have taken advantage if they had recognised his plight.

Not only did he subdue the lively Johnny Giles, but also he laid on the Reds' first goal in extra time when he took a glorious pass from Willie Stevenson, reached the byline and swept over a cross for Roger Hunt to head home.

Having played a full part in taking two Championships as well as the FA Cup triumph, Byrne hurt a knee against Leicester City in August 1966 and was never quite the same dominant force again. When recurring knee trouble prompted premature retirement in 1969, leading to a spell as an Anfield coach, Shanks was again warm in his praise: 'When Gerry went, it took a big chunk out of Liverpool. Something special was missing.'

For a man who enjoyed so much success at club level, Byrne experienced little international joy. In the first of his two outings for England he endured a chasing from Scotland's Willie Henderson, and he lacked the outright class, perhaps, to mount a serious challenge to the immaculate Ray Wilson. Liverpool, though, knew his value – and it was immense.

	GERALD BYRNE		
BORN	Liverpool, 29 August 1938.	GAMES	332 (1)
HONOURS	League Championship 63/4, 65/6. Second Division Championship 61/2. FA Cup 64/5.	GOALS	4
	2 England caps (63-66).		

ROGER HUNT

1959/60 → 1969/70

It was the night they dubbed him 'Sir Roger'. More than 60,000 people had sallied forth in torrential rain, forsaking the comforts of hearth and home to bid farewell to one of Liverpool's favourite sons. Never mind that he had left the club more than two years earlier; he would have a place in their hearts forever. It was the testimonial match for one of the all-time great goal-scorers and no one wanted to miss the party.

Those locked out on that emotional evening in April 1972, when Anfield's capacity stood at 56,000, were left to listen to the roars from within and reflect on the supreme importance of Roger Hunt to the Reds throughout the fabulously successful 1960s, a decade in which his goals had been their staff of life.

Hunt's rise was little less than meteoric after scoring on his debut, as a 21-year-old with only amateur football and five Central League games behind him, against Scunthorpe United at Anfield in September 1959. Quickly he secured a regular place, netting 21 times in 36 games.

Then in 1961/62 his prolific partnership with Ian St John was born and Hunt struck 41 times in 41 outings, including five hat-tricks, to play a crucial role in turning the Reds' promotion dream into reality. Division One didn't know what was about to hit it.

The next six years brought an avalanche of goals – 149 in a mere 229 League games, to be precise – and it's no coincidence that Liverpool won the Championship in Roger's two most prosperous campaigns. In fact in 1965/66, the season of their second title triumph, the Reds didn't lose a First Division match in which he scored.

But there was more to Roger Hunt and his value to Liverpool than mere statistics. The explosive shot, the sudden and destructive pace, the strength which made him so hard to dispossess and his phenomenal work-rate were all well known. Less appreciated, perhaps, were his accomplished but unflashy ball control, neat distribution, refusal to hide when things were not going his way and an agile soccer brain which might have made him effective in a deep-lying role.

Goal-getting, though, was his golden gift and he employed it to the full. Never afraid to miss, Hunt scored spectacular goals and easy goals, those that he bludgeoned into the net, like the brutal volley that jolted Internazionale of Milan in the 1965 European Cup semi-final at Anfield, and those that he caressed past the 'keeper, such as the subtle touch that deceived Manchester United's Alex Stepney at Old Trafford in 1968.

His England record – 18 goals in 34 games, which included only two defeats – was outstanding, though he never received due credit for that, perhaps because he was one of those preferred, along with Geoff Hurst, to national hero Jimmy Greaves in the 1966 World Cup Final. That Hunt was maybe the least-lauded member of Alf Ramsey's team was the outrageous product of ignorance and bias, and it was scandalous that such a selfless player should be driven to end his England tenure voluntarily as a result of constant and often hysterical criticism.

Modest to a fault, even-tempered and unflinchingly honest, Roger was a referee's dream. The only moment of controversy came in March 1969, when he was substituted in an FA Cup defeat by Leicester and hurled his shirt into the dugout in frustration, a wholly untypical incident.

By then he had survived a post-World Cup dip in form to bounce back with a brief but bountiful liaison with Tony Hateley before his Liverpool days tailed off as Bill Shankly sought new faces to end a relatively lean period.

In December 1969 the 31-year-old Lancastrian moved to Bolton Wanderers, the club he had supported as a boy, to close a career which had seen him shatter the Reds' scoring record and bring unprecedented glory to the Anfield club.

With the exception of Bill Shankly himself, Hunt remains the most potent and enduring symbol of that wonderful 1960s combination. As one long-time supporter put it: 'They were all idols, every last man of them, but Roger was also the guy next door, an everyday sort of chap. Somehow he was playing not only for our team, but also for the folks in the ground who were kicking every ball with him. To me he was the heart of Liverpool FC, a magnificent footballer who fed people's dreams, yet without losing sight of reality. He symbolised all that was good about the club.'

So he did, and the fans loved him for it. A knighthood was the least they could offer . . .

ROGER HUNT

BORN Glazebury, Lancashire, 20 July 1938.
HONOURS League Championship 63/4, 65/6. Second Division Championship 61/2. FA Cup 64/5. 34 England caps (62-69).
OTHER CLUBS Bolton Wanderers 69/70-71/2 (76, 24).

| GAMES | 487 (5) |
| GOALS | 286 |

IAN ST JOHN

1961/62 → 1970/71

Ian St John was the spark that lit a flame destined to burn triumphantly for the next three decades and beyond. When quizzed by his board about the wisdom of paying Motherwell £37,500 for the Scottish international centre-forward, Bill Shankly described him as the man the Reds couldn't afford *not* to buy, the most urgently needed component of his brave new team. The manager's judgement, as usual, was impeccable.

From the night of St John's first appearance in a red shirt – a Liverpool Senior Cup Final against Everton at Goodison Park in August 1961 – it was clear that he and his new club were made for each other. He moved with a jaunty swagger, 5ft 7½in of concentrated aggression topped by a pugnacious crew-cut – and he scored a hat-trick. His rapport with the fans was instant and complete; a folk hero was born.

The opening matches of that Division Two title campaign showed that St John needed time to adjust but there was no doubting his quality. He was strong, cunning and courageous, devastating in the air for such a small man and adept at delicate flicks which did much to promote a fruitful scoring partnership with Roger Hunt. Ian notched 18 goals as the Reds went up, following that with 19 as a First Division new boy and 21 in 1963/64, on the way to the Championship.

That season saw a turning point which meant that 'The Saint' would never score as heavily again but would contribute even more significantly to the eternal Anfield trophy quest. When schemer Jimmy Melia was injured, Shankly withdrew St John into a deep-lying role in which he revealed his full potential for the first time. He became mastermind of the attack, feeding colleagues with possession and creating space for them to use it with his intelligent running. It didn't mean that the goals dried up entirely – he continued to contribute memorable strikes, such as the jack-knife header which won the FA Cup against Leeds United in 1965 – but simply that St John's vision, mobility and all-round skills were employed to bring a new dimension to Liverpool's game.

Hunt continued to be prime beneficiary of his former front-running comrade's talents, as he acknowledged after scoring against Standard Liege in the away leg of a European Cup Winners' Cup tie in December 1965. St John had sprinted half the length of the field, drawing defenders with him, before slipping the ball through for an unmarked Hunt to net.

By the dawn of the 1970s, with the Reds' first wave of Shankly-inspired honours behind them, St John was into his thirties and his fitness had declined but, used sparingly, he remained capable of transforming a game with his subtle touch and slick, close passing. Rumanians Dynamo Bucharest were the victims in December 1970 when he was taken off the bench to turn a shaky 1-0 lead into a comfortable 3-0 margin by laying on two late goals in the European Fairs Cup.

Throughout his playing days 'The Saint' was no stranger to controversy. Often he was criticised for flashes of bad temper, such as the clash with Preston North End's Tony Singleton in March 1962 which led to a joint dismissal, but fire was an integral part of his make-up and, crucially, there never appeared to he malice aforethought.

On retirement he tried coaching and then management but didn't excel as many people thought he might, though it might have been a different story had he not been pipped for the post of Leeds United boss by Brian Clough following the departure of Don Revie. As it was, he endured three years of travail on a shoestring at Portsmouth, where he felt he was betrayed by his employers.

Eventually he fashioned a new niche as a TV personality, but in years to come it should not be as Jimmy Greaves' amiable chat-show sparring partner that the Scot is primarily recalled.

In assessing his place in Liverpool's modern history, students of the Reds would do well to reflect on the answer to an earnest question posed on a placard outside a Merseyside church in the 1960s. Passers-by were asked: 'What would you do if the Lord came down?' Scrawled underneath was the gleeful response: 'Move St John to inside-left.'

How the author of that mischievous legend must have embraced the wisdom of the evangelically enthusiastic Shankly, when he grated solemnly: 'In the beginning was Ian St John.'

IAN ST JOHN	
BORN	Motherwell, Lanarkshire, 7 June 1938.
HONOURS	League Championship 63/4, 65/6. Second Division Championship 61/2. FA Cup 64/5. 21 Scotland caps (59-65).
OTHER CLUBS	Motherwell 57/8-60/1 (113, 79); Coventry City 71/2 (18, 3); Tranmere Rovers 72/3 (9, 1).
MANAGER	Motherwell (73-74); Portsmouth (74-77).

GAMES **420 (5)**

GOALS **118**

WILLIE STEVENSON

1962/63 → 1967/68

Frustration with life in the shadow of Jim Baxter drove Willie Stevenson from his native Scotland to the other side of the world, but he was to find his true niche much closer to home. The lanky left-half – as slim as Jim and with a similarly cultured style – had won League and Cup medals with Glasgow Rangers before being ousted by the arrival at Ibrox of the gifted but mercurial Baxter. Unwilling to languish in the reserves, Stevenson elected adventurously to sample soccer in Australia and it was while he was on loan Down Under that Bill Shankly stepped in.

The Reds had made a lacklustre start to their first campaign after regaining Division One status and the manager recognised that more class and creativity were needed. Accordingly he secured Willie for £20,000 in October 1962, outbidding Preston North End in the process, and then displayed admirable patience as his countryman took time to adjust to the demands of the English game.

Stevenson was skilful, that much was obvious, but the pace of First Division life was too hectic for him at first, and intolerant fans demanded the recall of Tommy Leishman. Shankly, as imperturbable as ever, kept faith with his new signing and was to reap rich rewards.

As Stevenson settled he began to exert a compelling influence. His biting tackle was the equal of Leishman's but the constructive side of his game was a class apart. A keenly intelligent tactician, he could change the emphasis of attack with a raking wing-to-wing pass or, more deadly still, drive a stiletto-thrust to the heart of the stoutest defence with the most crisp and piercing of through-balls.

He was seen at his best when winger Peter Thompson joined him on the left side of the Reds' 1963/64 Championship-winning team. Thompson was an ideal partner, adept at making the oblique runs which made the most of Willie's subtle ability to judge the weight and angle of a pass, and together they formed a crowd-pleasing duo.

The full Stevenson repertoire never received a better showcase than the FA Cup Final against Leeds United in 1965 when most observers made him man of the match. He revelled in the sweeping width of Wembley, with its bowling-green surface made lusher than ever by heavy rain, and did more than anyone to put Don Revie's dour side to the sword. Stevenson it was who strolled imperiously past two opponents and freed Gerry Byrne on the left for the full-back to lay on the first goal for Roger Hunt.

As the decade progressed, the one-time Ranger – a dressing-room joker who did much to boost team morale – continued to turn in immaculate performances, missing only nine games in four seasons and playing a valuable part in a second title triumph in 1965/66.

The campaign that followed was an anti-climax for Liverpool but Stevenson, as consistent as ever, did not seem in imminent danger of the axe. It materialised, however, in the shape of Emlyn Hughes and the 29-year-old schemer, finding himself out of the side with little prospect of a quick return, moved to Stoke City for £48,000 in December 1968.

Some fans were outraged, as they were over Gordon Milne's exit, at what they saw as premature dismissal of a loyal favourite, but Shankly was nothing if not decisive.

Stevenson, who missed out on an international career due to abnormally hot competition from the likes of Dave Mackay and Jim Baxter, thus left the club with plenty still to offer and spent six more years in the League. He will be remembered at Anfield as an entertainer in the classic mould, a thoroughbred who contributed royally to some of the Reds' most momentous triumphs.

WILLIAM STEVENSON		
BORN	Leith, Midlothian, 26 October 1939.	
HONOURS	League Championship 63/4, 65/6. FA Cup 64/5.	GAMES **240 (1)**
OTHER CLUBS	Glasgow Rangers 58/9-61/2 (73, 1); Stoke City 67/8-72/3 (94, 5); Tranmere Rovers 73/4 (20, 0).	GOALS **17**

ALF ARROWSMITH

1961/62 → 1967/68

Alf Arrowsmith was the shooting star who burst across the Anfield heavens to wreath himself in glory for four dazzling months before his brightness was abruptly and prematurely dimmed.

He rose sensationally to prominence in the second half of 1963/64 when the Reds' midfield general, Jimmy Melia, was injured. Ian St John moved back to assume the play-making role and the exuberant Alf came in to form a potent dual spearhead with Roger Hunt.

He signalled his intentions with a four-goal blitz on Derby County in the FA Cup and for the duration of the season the young man from Hollingworth, a Mancunian in all but name, could do little wrong, finishing with 15 League goals in 20 games and a Championship medal.

Appropriately two of his most significant strikes came against one of the Manchester clubs, United, in April 1964. By then Matt Busby's men had emerged as Liverpool's chief rivals for the League crown and a victory on Merseyside would have seen them move to within a point of Bill Shankly's pacesetters.

However, two Arrowsmith specials – a firm header and an adroit finish from ten yards – built decisively on the foundation of an earlier goal by Ian Callaghan to effectively settle the destination of the title on that tumultuous Anfield afternoon.

Boundlessly brave and imbued with refreshing innocence and verve, Arrowsmith ran at defences with unnerving pace and strength, often attempting the seemingly impossible with spectacular success. Several goals were thrashed home with savage power from acute angles, and a 12-yard back-heel which beat Chelsea at Stamford Bridge would have delighted Denis Law himself. Easier opportunities were sometimes spurned but a glittering future seemed to be in store.

It all went wrong that August in the Charity Shield clash with West Ham when Arrowsmith damaged a knee so badly that he was out of contention for the first half of 1964/65. Although he stayed at Anfield for another four years, he was dogged by injuries and never regained his impetus.

A popular, down-to-earth character, he went on to spells with Bury, who paid Liverpool £25,000 for his services in December 1968, and Rochdale.

ALFRED WILLIAM ARROWSMITH	
BORN	Hollingworth, near Manchester, 11 December 1942.
HONOURS	League Championship 63/4.
OTHER CLUBS	Bury 68/9-69/70 (48, 11); Rochdale 70/1-71/2 (47, 14).
DIED	May 2005.

GAMES	51 (4)
GOALS	24

GORDON WALLACE

1962/63 → 1966/67

Pocket-sized Scottish inside-left Gordon Wallace hogged the limelight in television's first *Match of the Day* when he scored twice, including an 87th-minute winner, against Arsenal at Anfield in August 1964. But that is undoubtedly a distinction he would trade for a small fraction of the glory predicted for him when he broke through to the fringe of the first team in 1962/63. Perhaps it was a typical piece of Shankly psychology when the perceptive Liverpool boss described Wallace as the nearest thing to Tom Finney since the war, but Bill was sincere in his regard for the abilities of a player whose career was cursed by what medical laymen might describe as brittle bones.

Wallace, also at home on the wing, was quick and skilful with a mesmeric body-swerve and on his debut at West Bromwich he tantalised England full-back Don Howe. When he deputised for appendix victim Ian St John and scored twice in the 1964 Charity Shield encounter with West Ham, it was the start of a six-goals-in-eight-days burst – including his brace on TV and two more against Reykjavik in the Reds' first European game – which might have established him at the top level. But then Wallace suffered a barren spell in his only extended run before a cruel succession of injuries ended his Anfield ambitions and he joined Crewe for £5,000 in October 1967.

GORDON HENRY WALLACE
BORN Lanark, 13 June 1944.
OTHER CLUBS Crewe Alexandra 67/8-71/2 (94, 20).

GAMES **21 (1)**
GOALS **6**

PHIL FERNS

1962/63 → 1964/65

No one can take away from Phil Ferns the achievement of winning a League Championship medal with Liverpool in 1963/64. He earned the honour by the sweat of his brow, making 18 appearances as Bill Shankly's squad was hit by injuries, but without remotely suggesting that he had the necessary class to forge a career in the First Division.

The hard-as-nails Merseysider stood in for Willie Stevenson at left-half, his most comfortable position, for a sequence of four games early in the campaign, returning later to deputise at full-back, first for Ronnie Moran and then for Gerry Byrne. His most memorable performance during this spell was at Old Trafford in November 1963, when he subdued Bobby Charlton as his side recorded a vital 1-0 victory.

Ferns, who was already 24 when he made his League debut at home to Manchester City in August 1962, was a rugged defender whose enthusiasm outstripped his ability. He was rather lacking in pace and ball skill but his versatility stood the Reds in good stead over three seasons. The emergence of younger players ended his usefulness at Anfield and he moved on, first to Bournemouth, for whom his son, Phil Jnr, was to play, and then to Mansfield.

PHILIP FERNS
BORN Liverpool, 14 November 1937.
HONOURS League Championship 63/4.
OTHER CLUBS Bournemouth 65/6 (46, 0); Mansfield Town 66/7-67/8 (56, 1).

GAMES **28**
GOALS **1**

ALLAN JONES

1959/60 → 1962/63

A Welsh schoolboy and youth international central defender, Jones was converted into a full-back at Anfield. He waited more than three years between his debut and a farewell run of four senior games, then joined Brentford for £6,000.

ALLAN POWELL JONES
BORN: Flint, 6 January 1940
OTHER CLUBS: Brentford 63/4-69/70 (248, 3).
DIED: 1993.

GAMES	5
GOALS	0

TOMMY LOWRY

1964/65

Right-back Lowry was the only one of the four youngsters whom Bill Shankly plucked from obscurity for the pre-Wembley trip to Wolverhampton in April 1965 who went on to flourish elsewhere. He set a club appearance record at Crewe.

THOMAS LOWRY
BORN: Liverpool, 26 August 1945.
OTHER CLUBS: Crewe Alexandra 66/7-77/8 (436, 2).

GAMES	1
GOALS	0

BOBBY THOMSON

1962/63 → 1963/64

A promising full-back who cost £7,000 from Partick Thistle in December 1962, Thomson was unable to emerge from the shadows cast by Messrs Byrne, Moran and Lawler. After his handful of starts, he was sold to Luton for £3,000 in August 1965.

ROBERT THOMSON
BORN: Menstrie, Clackmannanshire, 21 November 1939.
OTHER CLUBS: Partick Thistle 57/8-61/2;
Luton Town 65/9-66/7 (74, 0).

GAMES	7
GOALS	0

JOHN OGSTON

1966/67

A Scotland under-23 international goalkeeper, Ogston arrived from Aberdeen for £10,000 in September 1965 to provide cover and competition for Tommy Lawrence. However 'Tubby' could not oust 'The Flying Pig' and joined Doncaster.

JOHN KESSACK OGSTON
BORN: Aberdeen, 15 January 1939.
OTHER CLUBS: Aberdeen 58/9-65/6 (179, 0);
Doncaster Rovers 68/9-70/1 (70, 0).

GAMES	1
GOALS	0

BILLY MOLYNEUX

1964/65

An agile goalkeeper, who perhaps lacked the physical stature to dominate his area, Molyneux performed solidly enough on his one senior outing, being beaten only once at Wolves when deputising for Tommy Lawrence prior to the 1965 FA Cup Final.

WILLIAM STANLEY MOLYNEUX
BORN: Liverpool, 10 January 1944.
OTHER CLUBS: Oldham Athletic 68/9 (8, 0).

GAMES	1
GOALS	0

JOHN SEALEY

1964/65

Took on the Roger Hunt mantle at Molineux in April 1965, thus protecting the England man ahead of the FA Cup Final, and scored Liverpool's second goal in a 3-1 win. Later Sealey was transferred to Chester but didn't make a long-term mark.

ARTHUR JOHN SEALEY
BORN: Wallasey, Cheshire, 27 December 1945.
OTHER CLUBS: Chester 66/7-67/8 (4, 0).

GAMES	1
GOALS	1

ALAN HIGNETT

1964/65

One of four youngsters blooded by the Reds as they rested most of their first-team regulars in the run-up to the 1965 FA Cup Final, Hignett featured at right-half in a victory at Molineux. A subsequent move to Chester brought little joy.

ALAN JAMES HIGNETT
BORN: Liverpool, 1 November 1946.
OTHER CLUBS: Chester 66/7 (6, 0).

GAMES	1
GOALS	0

DAVID WILSON

1966/67

Viewed as one of the most talented young wingers in the land when signed from Preston for £20,000, the England under-23 star found his Anfield progress blocked by the consistent excellence of Ian Callaghan, and he returned to Deepdale unfulfilled.

DAVID CHARLES WILSON
BORN: Nelson, Lancashire, 24 December 1942.
OTHER CLUBS: Preston North End 60/1-66/7 (170, 31)
and 68/9-73/4 (111, 10); Bradford City on loan 71/2
(5, 0); Southport on loan 73/4 (2, 0).

GAMES	0 (1)
GOALS	0

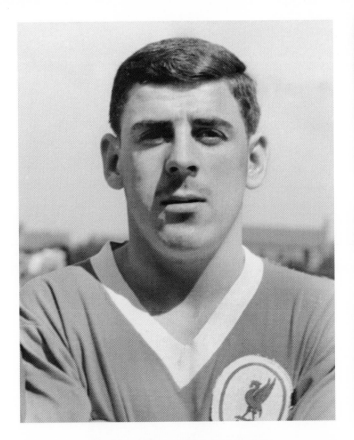

ALAN BANKS

1958/59 → 1960/61

The story of Alan Banks stands as an uplifting example to any young footballer who faces rejection by a leading club.

Having made an encouraging start with Liverpool, the stocky, dynamically direct marksman was released and left the League, but refused to give up on his hopes of a footballing future.

Instead he knuckled down with Cambridge City, knocked in more than a century of goals in the space of just two seasons, then returned to the League and became a folk hero in two massively productive stints with Exeter City.

As a 19-year-old Red, Banks netted on his senior debut, a 5-0 home victory over Brighton in September 1958, but then found himself queueing behind Alan Arnell and Louis Bimpson for a regular berth.

He remained on the sidelines until 1960/61, when Bill Shankly gave him a four-match run in the team and he responded with four goals, including a brace against Huddersfield.

However, Banks was replaced by Dave Hickson, who was returning from injury, and departed in the summer before rebuilding his career, playing a key role in transforming Exeter from Division Four strugglers to a promotion side in his first term. He went on to become the first man to score 100 goals for the Grecians, and remains one of the best-loved figures in the club's history.

PHIL CHISNALL

1964/65 → 1965/66

Phil Chisnall was a comprehensively talented young inside-forward with a unique claim to fame: he played under Sir Matt Busby, Bill Shankly and Sir Alf Ramsey, three of the most revered managers of all time.

After starting at Old Trafford, Chisnall seemed a certainty to seize a central role in the reconstruction of Manchester United following the Munich air disaster, displaying such lavish promise that Ramsey called him up for England under-23 duty and described him as 'probably the best passer of a ball in the country.'

However, he could not overcome ferocious competition for places in Manchester and accepted a fresh start with the newly-crowned champions, joining Liverpool for £25,000 in the spring of 1964.

Shanks believed he had stolen a march on Busby, his old friend and rival, but sadly Chisnall never met those colossal expectations during his three and a half years at Anfield.

He had his chances, being handed the number-nine shirt as a deputy for Ian St John at the beginning and end of 1964/65, but his partnership with Roger Hunt never prospered and he slipped inexorably out of contention.

In August 1967, a £12,000 deal took Chisnall to Southend, where he flourished; but three great football men were left to scratch their heads in perplexity over why he had not thrived at the top level.

ALAN BANKS		
BORN Liverpool, 5 October 1938.		
OTHER CLUBS Exeter City 63/4-65/6 (85, 43),		
Plymouth Argyle 66/7-67/8 (19, 5),	GAMES	8
Exeter City 67/8-72/3 (173, 58).	GOALS	6

JOSEPH PHILIP CHISNALL		
BORN Manchester, 27 October 1942.		
OTHER CLUBS Manchester United 61/2-63/4 (35, 8);		
Southend United 67/8-70/1 (142, 28);	GAMES	8 (1)
Stockport County 71/2 (30, 2).	GOALS	2

RON YEATS

1961/62 → 1970/71

'Take a walk around my centre-half, gentlemen.' The gleeful invitation came from master-of-banter Bill Shankly, introducing his mountainous new signing to assembled pressmen at Anfield in the summer of 1961. The colossus in question was a one-time slaughterman from an Aberdeen abattoir, name of Ron Yeats, and he had just arrived from Dundee United to become a cornerstone of the Liverpool legend.

Shankly's admiration for the 6ft 2in Scot dated back to his days in charge of Huddersfield Town, but the Yorkshire club didn't have the brass to prise Yeats from Tannadice. Thus, after failing in a bid for Jack Charlton of Leeds United, the Reds' boss parted willingly with the required £30,000 for a man he was confident would put the fear of God into the Sassenachs. Having already tempted the irrepressible Ian St John south of the border, he had the backbone of his first great side.

Yeats – inevitably nicknamed 'Rowdy' after Clint Eastwood's TV cowboy of that era – was made skipper within five months of his arrival and exercised monumental influence as the team galloped to promotion in his first season. Division Two centre-forwards seemed to be swallowed up by his all-pervading presence and even Sunderland's free-scoring Brian Clough, rampant against most opponents, was rendered ineffective.

Elevation to the top flight served only to emphasise Ron's talents. His aerial ability was awesome, his tackling thunderous and his distribution sensibly simple. Some said he was slow on the turn but, as Shankly revelled in pointing out, not many attackers got past him to find out.

He led the Reds to two Championships and through a succession of stirring European adventures but reserved some of his most rousing personal performances for the victorious 1965 FA Cup campaign. In fact, it all nearly went wrong at West Bromwich Albion in the third round when a mischievous whistler in the crowd gulled Yeats into picking up the ball in his own penalty area. Justice was done when Bobby Cram missed the resultant spot-kick.

In the fifth round at Bolton the Liverpool captain gave one of his bravest displays after pulling a muscle ten minutes into the match, yet going on to subdue the potent airborne menace of Wyn 'The Leap' Davies. Yeats garnered further glory by laying on Roger Hunt's winner in the quarter-final against Leicester and then comfortably snuffed out the threat of Leeds' potentially lethal Alan Peacock at Wembley

As the 1960s wore on the Yeats game, though still essentially rugged, acquired a little more polish and it was a rare adversary who could unsettle him. One who did was playing for Ajax on that infamous foggy Amsterdam night in December 1966 when the Reds were eclipsed 5-1, but Ron was neither the first nor the last defender to be given a chasing by Johan Cruyff.

By the end of the decade Yeats had turned 32 and was beginning to suffer back trouble, but when he yielded his place eventually to Larry Lloyd he still had the motivation to contribute a valuable stint at left-back.

Equal in stature to his footballing record were his off-the-field merits as skipper. Although he was quietly spoken, his imposing personality made him an impressive mouthpiece for colleagues in dealings with management, and he was a commendable influence on younger players.

Those admirable attributes remained in the club's service into the 21st century in his crucially important position of chief scout, but it is as an inspiring leader who never flagged that Ron Yeats will go down in Liverpool folklore. While Rowdy stood firm there was always hope. He was, in the words of his mentor Bill Shankly, a fantastic man.

RONALD YEATS	
BORN	Aberdeen, 15 November 1937.
HONOURS	League Championship 63/4, 65/6. Division Two Championship 61/2. FA Cup 64/5. 2 Scotland caps (65-66).
OTHER CLUBS	Dundee United 57/8-60/1 (95, 1); Tranmere Rovers 71/2-73/4 (97, 5).
MANAGER	Tranmere Rovers (72-75); Barrow (76).

GAMES	453 (1)
GOALS	16

TOMMY LAWRENCE

1962/63 → 1970/71

It's always a pity to waste a good nickname, especially one as colourful as 'The Flying Pig', coined affectionately and with no trace of an insult by the Kop to describe their solidly-built 1960s goalkeeper Tommy Lawrence.

But it was an alternative epithet, less vivid but more precise and with a little added subtlety, which most aptly summed up the vastly underrated Scottish international. Shrewd observers dubbed him 'the sweeper-keeper', a description which neatly captured his style and the way he fitted into the Liverpool system.

Lawrence operated behind a back four which pushed upfield whenever possible. When it was breached by a penetrating pass or an opponent's run from a deep position, it was imperative to have a last line of defence capable of reacting instantly to the danger.

This job called for anticipation, bravery and talent – qualities which Lawrence possessed in abundance. There wasn't another 'keeper of his era better acquainted with the bootlaces of First Division forwards; diving at feet was his speciality and when even the likes of Denis Law and Jimmy Greaves were through with only Tommy to beat, it was never a formality

The Reds were served royally by an intuitive understanding between their custodian and the mammoth centre-half Ron Yeats, who generally dominated the penalty area with his aerial strength. It was rare to see the two countrymen going for the same ball, and while Yeats was dealing with crosses, the unflappable 'keeper would be ready to protect his net with reliable handling and quite astonishing agility for a man of his bulk.

Although Lawrence was very much an under-praised stalwart throughout Liverpool's 1960s triumphs, Bill Shankly was well aware of his value. He knew there were matches which his team won, apparently convincingly, but in which the scorelines were wholly misleading, thanks in generous measure to the exploits of the undemonstrative Lawrence.

One such was a 4-1 home win against Blackpool in the victorious 1965/66 Championship campaign. Alan Ball was rampant and threatened to overturn the title aspirants as he sliced open their defence repeatedly with incisive service to front-runners Graham Oates and Ray Charnley. But the guardian of Liverpool's fortress was inspired, frustrating the Tangerines with a courageous and skilful display which enabled his side at first to survive, and then to take both points.

By then Lawrence was an experienced performer, having been first called to senior duty for the newly-promoted Reds some five years after his arrival at Anfield, pressed into action when Jim Furnell was injured in October 1962. He took the eye instantly, cementing his place with a run of impeccable form and earning an early cap for Scotland against the Republic of Ireland in June 1963.

The following season brought a Championship medal and Lawrence climaxed an accomplished first full term by repelling a George Eastham penalty in front of the Kop, a breathtaking save at a pivotal juncture of the 5-0 thrashing of Arsenal which clinched the title. At that point Liverpool were only a goal to the good, so strong nerves were demanded and Tommy was not found wanting.

Thereafter he built on this early success, earning a much-deserved reputation for consistency, and it was a double mystery that his international recall should have been delayed for six years and then been limited to a mere two games when it finally arrived.

Lawrence remained Liverpool's first-choice goalkeeper until February 1970, missing a mere five League games in eight seasons. Then, in company with Ian St John and Ron Yeats, he gave way to the challenge of youth, having kept his successor waiting for two and a half years.

The ultimate tribute to Tommy Lawrence is the identity of that young man who was forced to bide his time so patiently. It was a certain Ray Clemence.

THOMAS JOHNSTONE LAWRENCE	
BORN	Dailly, Ayrshire, 14 May 1940.
HONOURS	League Championship 63/4, 65/6. FA Cup 64/5. 3 Scotland caps (63-69).
OTHER CLUBS	Tranmere Rovers 71/2-73/4 (80, 0).

GAMES	390
GOALS	0

GEOFF STRONG

1964/65 → 1969/70

It is more than a tad ironic that Geoff Strong was perplexed by Arsenal manager Billy Wright's decision to switch him from his bounteously productive role as a free-scoring inside-forward to operate at wing-half.

The slim, wirily resilient Geordie was keen to occupy his favoured front-line slot, yet when he settled at Anfield he found himself, at one time or another, in virtually every outfield position and rarely had a shirt to call his own.

Strong had averaged more than a goal every two games during his Highbury spell and it seemed likely that Bill Shankly would use him as a striker alongside Roger Hunt in place of the seriously injured Alf Arrowsmith. But the £40,000 newcomer took time to adjust to the Reds' rigorous training regime following his arrival in November 1964, and by the time he was fully fit the side had a formidably stable look about it.

But neither player nor manager was dismayed. Shankly was adamant that he had bought Strong for his all-round talent, not for any specific task, and Geoff proceeded to become one of the most effective utility players the British game has known.

Indeed, as well as proving the most versatile man at the club, he showed also that he was one of the most accomplished. His midfield performances were notable for their skill and vision; at the back he was cool and resourceful; in attack he demonstrated an instinct for goals backed by a savage shot.

Strong's first major assignment on joining Liverpool was born out of heartbreak for Gordon Milne, when the right-half suffered an injury which put him out of the FA Cup Final against Leeds United.

In stepped the player who was to become Anfield's master-of-all-trades, to be handed the critical job of neutralising the threat of Don Revie's midfield general Bobby Collins. So well did he fare that Collins had but minor impact and Strong had time to test goalkeeper Gary Sprake with several stinging drives on his way to a winner's medal.

During the Championship campaign that followed, the ex-Gunner firmly established himself as the Reds' chameleon. At various times he stood in for Peter Thompson, Willie Stevenson, Chris Lawler, Gordon Milne and Roger Hunt; the only man whose position he did not cover was goalkeeper Tommy Lawrence, though if the green jersey had become vacant, it's a fair guess that Strong could have distinguished himself in it.

His finest hours that term came with two winning goals on the way to the final of the European Cup Winners' Cup, which Liverpool lost to Borussia Dortmund at Hampden Park. The first was a 25-yard thunderbolt off the underside of the crossbar against Juventus in the preliminary round; the second, scored despite a crippling knee injury, was a semi-final header past Celtic's Ronnie Simpson.

Such heroics didn't go unnoticed by the Kopites, who chanted Strong's name until he hobbled off the bench to take his bow when the title was clinched against Chelsea. It was a movingly emotional tribute to one of the game's most determined characters.

Over the next four years, as the manager began to experiment with his side, Geoff remained an integral part of the set-up. In his final two seasons on Merseyside his wanderings were largely halted, with an accomplished tenure at left-back. If he had a particular forte, however, it was perhaps as sweeper, a role denied him by the eminence of Tommy Smith.

But it was for the diversity of his gifts that he was most missed when, at the age of 33, he moved to Coventry City. Geoff Strong didn't leave one gap – he left ten.

GEOFFREY HUGH STRONG		
BORN	Newcastle, 19 September 1937.	
HONOURS	League Championship 65/6. FA Cup 64/5.	GAMES **194 (5)**
OTHER CLUBS	Arsenal 60/1-64/5 (125, 69); Coventry City 70/1-71/2 (33, 0).	GOALS **32**

PETER THOMPSON

1963/64 → 1971/72

When a sprightly, if rather distant Championship challenge withered in April 1963 – the Reds' first spring in the top flight for nine years – Bill Shankly made a momentous decision. He earmarked Peter Thompson as the one crucial ingredient missing from his title-winning recipe and signed the Preston winger, in the face of opposition from Juventus, Everton and Wolves, for a club record fee of £40,000.

A year later Shankly's mission was accomplished and the new man had played a thrilling part in the first of many triumphs before his Anfield days were done.

Peter Thompson was a soccer sorcerer, a pleaser of crowds and a teaser of full-backs; on his day he brought to the game a dancer's grace and the daring of a matador. True, when the Muse was not with him he was prone to over-elaboration and he could be the most frustrating man afield. But unlike certain other sumptuously gifted players, he offered no hint of the prima donna and, crucially, he was never afraid of hard graft.

Despite being right-footed, Thompson came into the side on the left flank where Alan A'Court and Kevin Lewis had both been judged deficient during the previous campaign. He made an eye-catching debut at Ewood Park, running at the Blackburn defenders, making them twist and turn in their efforts to stay with their elusive quarry and rendering an offside trap too perilous to contemplate.

As autumn turned to winter and the points piled up, Thompson and Ian Callaghan, whose more direct approach was in marked contrast to Peter's jinking and swaying, became the most formidable wing pairing in British club football.

The former Deepdale man's impact at Anfield could hardly have been greater, though there were those who said he should have scored more goals and that his final pass too often went astray. The fact was that his fierce shot could be a wayward weapon but his crosses, while not always matching the brilliance of his approach play, were as reliable as those of most contemporaries.

There was also a theory that Thompson should switch to the right to encourage him to reach the byline and cross with his favoured foot instead of being forced infield as he was on the left, but such a scheme took no account of the excellent Callaghan.

The nitpickers were predictably notable by their silence when Thompson capped his first, richly rewarding term as a Red with his most devastating display to date. He scored twice and turned the Arsenal defence inside out as Liverpool made certain of the title, drubbing the Gunners 5-0 in front of an ecstatic Kop.

Peter's progress continued as Shankly's men lifted the FA Cup in 1965. His personal highlight was waltzing past John Hollins and Marvin Hinton to grab the first goal in the semi-final against Chelsea with a fearsome left-foot drive between Peter Bonetti and his near post. Soon a second Championship medal followed but the nearest Thompson came to further Cup success was in 1971 when he joined the action from the substitutes' bench to breathe life into a hitherto dull final, which Arsenal won to clinch the League and FA Cup double.

By then he was plagued by knee trouble and in November 1973, after what seemed like ages on the treatment table, he moved to Bolton Wanderers for £18,000, a modest fee which reflected his fitness difficulties. Surprisingly in view of past injuries, he was able to put in four spirited years at Burnden Park before retiring, proving that his appetite for the game was as voracious as ever and that there was no substitute for sheer class.

One perennial gripe of Liverpool fans was Thompson's banishment for long periods to the international wilderness. After he had starred in Brazil in 1964, his appearances were cruelly curtailed by Alf Ramsey's decision to do without wingers, which cost him a part in the 1966 World Cup finals, though he did represent his country as late as 1970. But in the final analysis it is in a red shirt that Peter Thompson will be best remembered – as an entertainer, one of the most spellbinding of his time.

PETER THOMPSON		
BORN	Carlisle, Cumberland, 27 November 1942.	
HONOURS	League Championship 63/4, 65/6. FA Cup 64/5. 16 England caps (64-70).	**GAMES** 406 (8)
OTHER CLUBS	Preston North End 60/1-62/3 (121, 20); Bolton Wanderers 73/4-77/8 (117, 2).	**GOALS** 54

TONY HATELEY

1967/68 → 1968/69

When Tony Hateley opened his Liverpool scoring account with a rousing hat-trick against Newcastle United on the second Saturday of 1967/68, Anfield was the place to be. The stadium was bulging with nearly 52,000 people, the air was heady with the scent of triumphs to come and the 'H-Bombers' – Roger Hunt also scored twice in the 6-0 annihilation of the Magpies – had signalled their arrival as partners to be feared with a show of ruthless efficiency.

Bill Shankly, alarmed by a barren campaign after three seasons of glory, had paid Chelsea £96,000 for Hateley in the belief that the towering centre-forward would hit the target with sufficient regularity to arrest any slide before it gained momentum.

It was a euphoric start, despite being marred somewhat by a Hateley own-goal in an unexpected defeat at Highbury two days later, yet even allowing for the newcomer's exemplary overall strike-rate of a goal every two games, Shankly's expensive remedy was doomed to failure.

The problem was that Tony, a majestic header of the ball who needed constant aerial fodder to function, was utterly alien to Liverpool's style. That didn't bother Roger Hunt, who fed avidly off his knock-downs and enjoyed unaccustomed freedom as markers homed in on the big man, but the other players were used to a varied build-up along the ground. Understandably, after years of more subtle methods, they struggled to adjust to the tactic of repeatedly slinging high balls into the penalty area.

Thus, when that approach was non-productive, as often it was against top-class defenders who learned quickly, the Reds were left with few options because Hateley was too clumsy to employ a passing game. Lacking the control to hold the ball under pressure and the precision to lay it off accurately, he was the obstacle on which many of Liverpool's attacks broke down.

Despite these shortcomings, the big fellow had his moments. Twice he netted three times in League matches, and went one better in an FA Cup replay against Walsall to finish the season with 24 goals.

No one could accuse him of not doing his job, even if he failed to fit the team pattern, but it was no surprise when he was replaced, by young Alun Evans, early in the following campaign and joined Coventry City for £80,000. Through no fault of his own, an 'H-Bomber' had backfired.

	ANTHONY HATELEY		
BORN	Derby, 13 June 1941.	GAMES	56
OTHER CLUBS	Notts County 58/9-62/3 (131, 77) and 70/1-71/2 (57, 32); Aston Villa 63/4-66/7 (127, 68); Chelsea 66/7 (27, 6); Coventry City 68/9 (17, 4); Birmingham City 69/70-70/1 (28, 6); Oldham Athletic 73/4 (5, 1).	GOALS	28

BOBBY GRAHAM

1964/65 → 1971/72

When Bobby Graham struck a hat-trick as a 19-year-old debutant against Aston Villa at Anfield in September 1964, the skilful Scot seemed to have the perfect platform on which to build a long-term Liverpool career.

In retrospect his explosive start more closely resembled a curse. Though Bill Shankly was far too wise to be carried away on the strength of one performance, the expectations of the fans were elevated to the heavens, and the inexperienced Graham was not equal to them.

Although he scored in the next match, thereafter he suffered a dozen blank games and, often bedevilled by injuries, dropped out of serious contention for the next four seasons as other strikers held sway

But Bobby's chance came again – and this time he was ready. At the start of 1969/70, with Roger Hunt and Ian St John nearing the end of their illustrious Anfield days, Tony Hateley long gone and Alun Evans injured, a more mature Graham was pitched into a side in a state of extended flux.

Now he looked a different player to the boyish performer of half a decade earlier, adding new-found determination and confidence to his old virtues of pace and control.

That term the Scot was an ever-present, scoring 13 goals in a moderate campaign by the Reds' standards, and there were even whispers of an international call. But ten games into the following season the Graham bandwagon, now moving so smoothly, came to an abrupt halt when he broke his ankle against Chelsea at Anfield.

He didn't start another match for five months, by which time John Toshack was on the scene. When Kevin Keegan appeared in 1971/72 Graham was effectively crowded out and, bowing to the inevitable, he joined Coventry City for £70,000.

A short spell at Highfield Road and an even briefer loan period with Tranmere preceded a move to his native Motherwell, for whom he excelled for four years and earned plentiful praise. Even then he was not finished, spending another four seasons at Hamilton until retirement at the age of 36.

At Liverpool Bobby Graham was an unfortunate footballer, struck down at his peak. How well he deserved his belated recognition north of the border.

ROBERT GRAHAM

BORN	Motherwell, Lanarkshire, 22 November 1944.
OTHER CLUBS	Coventry City 71/2-72/3 (19, 3); Tranmere Rovers on loan 72/3 (10, 3); Motherwell 73/4-76/7 (132, 37); Hamilton Academical 77/8-80/1 (118, 42).

GAMES	124 (8)
GOALS	42

CHRIS LAWLER

1962/63 → 1975/76

Chris Lawler was hardly an eye-catching performer, seeming to saunter through games with all the apparent urgency of a man out walking his dog. There was no swagger, no tricks, no histrionics, but in time opponents came to realise – often ruefully, as they retrieved the ball from their net – that they ignored Liverpool's faithful right-back at their peril.

Not that his defensive capabilities weren't respected from the outset. It was obvious from early appearances deputising for centre-half Ron Yeats that the callow but composed Lawler had all the qualities of a future back-four stalwart.

No, what crept only gradually into the consciousness of opposing teams was an almost uncanny ability to ghost in behind his forwards and snatch goals when no threat seemed imminent. Presumably it was the result of instinctive anticipation, though sometimes it seemed like second sight.

The odd thing was that, unlike many defenders who pride themselves on hitting the target, Lawler was not a dead-ball specialist, never took penalties and did not possess a particularly powerful shot. Yet he can point to a career record of 61 goals, including ten in 1969/70 when he was the Reds' second-highest scorer, and 11 in European competitions, which saw some of his most famous efforts.

His most prolific continental campaign was that of the 1965/66 Cup Winners' Cup, in which he scored in three successive ties, starting with a deft header against Juventus before striking twice against Standard Liege and once against Honved.

Back in the First Division, Everton were twice the victims of the Lawler goal habit, both times at Anfield. In November 1970 Chris capped a stirring Liverpool comeback from a 2-0 deficit with a late winner and the following season scored with an overhead kick to complete a 4-0 rout.

Priceless though these attacking diversions were, Lawler never allowed them to distract him from his primary responsibilities at the back. In fact, he fulfilled those so well that he missed only one League game between October 1965 and November 1973, and that was when he was rested before the 1971 FA Cup Final.

He sprang to prominence for the first time in the 1963 semi-final, slotting into the middle of a reshuffled defence alongside Yeats, and then earned widespread praise when he stood in for the skipper in three Easter victories during the title run-in a year later.

In 1964/65, when the ageing Ronnie Moran stepped down and Gerry Byrne switched to the left flank, Lawler was handed the regular right-back berth. The slim, upright youngster took his chance with aplomb, underlining his progress by stifling the talents of speedy Leeds United winger Albert Johanneson at Wembley and claiming a Cup-winner's medal.

Calm, skilful and effective in the air, Lawler became a fixture and assisted in two Championship triumphs before a knee injury sustained at Loftus Road ended his proud record of consistency, effectively sidelining him for the rest of 1973/74.

Despite a handful of appearances the following term he was never the same again and, after a move to Manchester City was called off by Liverpool at the last minute, he joined Portsmouth, later returning to Anfield for a coaching stint.

Lawler's England outings were limited to four, though there might have been more had he possessed a little extra pace. Some would point to the considerable attributes of classy rivals such as Keith Newton and Paul Madeley, but Kopites would have none of that. For them the man they called 'The Silent Knight' – a reference to his quiet, modest nature – was simply the best right-back in the business.

CHRISTOPHER LAWLER
BORN Liverpool, 20 October 1943.
HONOURS UEFA Cup 72/3. League Championship 65/6, 72/3. FA Cup 64/5. 4 England caps (71).
OTHER CLUBS Portsmouth 75/6-76/7 (36, 1); Stockport County 77/8 (36, 3).

GAMES 549
GOALS 61

ALUN EVANS

1968/69 → 1971/72

If ever a young player seemed set for greatness it was perky, flaxen-haired Alun Evans in the autumn of 1968. Bill Shankly had just made him the first £100,000 teenager in British soccer and he had started his stint as Liverpool centre-forward with two richly promising displays crowned by three goals. But four years later, Anfield dream in tatters and potential unfulfilled, the golden boy had gone.

It might all have been so different. Evans started as a 17-year-old prodigy with Wolves and impressed mightily during his brief Molineux interlude. He gave one particularly precocious performance against Liverpool, having the temerity to rattle Ron Yeats and score a goal in the process. The Reds' boss was not a man to ignore such talent and when Evans became available Shankly made sure that Anfield was his destination.

He was procured as a long-term replacement for Tony Hateley and provided a stark contrast to his rather one-dimensional predecessor, bravery being the one quality they shared. Evans was quick and skilful, full of cute tricks and sudden changes of direction that threw defenders into disarray.

The mop-topped newcomer quickly unveiled his effervescent armoury, scoring after ten minutes of his debut at home to Leicester City and then netting two at Molineux in a 6-0 thrashing of his former employers.

Perhaps predictably, the young man's learning curve became more gradual and he managed only four more goals that season. The following campaign was one of total frustration, with injuries and a terrifying night-club incident – in which his face was badly scarred by broken glass – sidelining him for long periods, but he returned to something like top form in 1970/71.

Despite a cartilage operation, the result of playing on a bone-hard pitch in Bucharest, Evans scored ten League goals in 21 games and lit up Anfield with a brilliant hat-trick against Bayern Munich in the European Fairs Cup.

Fitness eluded him once more in 1971/72, a term which brought but one highlight, a breathtaking half-volleyed goal in a Cup Winners' Cup defeat by Bayern.

By then, though, Alun Evans was in the shadow of Messrs Keegan and Toshack and soon he took the road back to the Midlands, where a new start with Aston Villa was to add little joy to an unlucky, ultimately unsatisfying career.

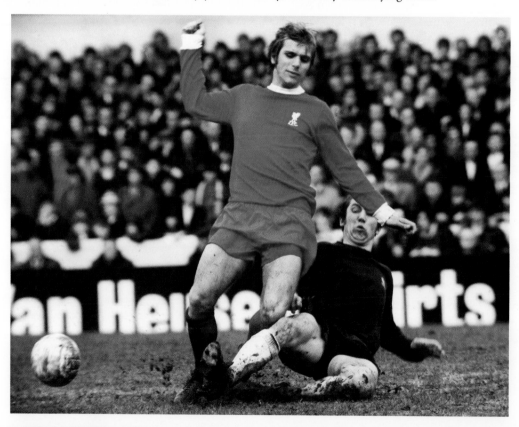

ALUN WILLIAM EVANS

BORN Stourport, Worcestershire, 30 September 1949.

OTHER CLUBS Wolverhampton Wanderers 67/8-68/9 (22, 4); Aston Villa 72/3-73/4 (60, 11); Walsall 75/6-77/8 (87, 7); Hellas FC, Melbourne, 78/9.

GAMES 105 (6)

GOALS 33

PHIL BOERSMA

1969/70 → 1975/76

Throughout his seven seasons on the fringe of the Liverpool team, Phil Boersma always seemed to be fighting a losing battle. A speedy utility forward with plenty of skill, occasionally he came agonisingly close to bridging the gap between Central League and First Division, but perpetually he failed to convince first Bill Shankly and then Bob Paisley that he was any more than a handy man to have about the squad.

Boersma first came into the reckoning on his 20th birthday in September 1969 when he was called on as a substitute for Alun Evans during a League Cup defeat at Manchester City. Several League outings followed, but at a time of team transition and strong opposition for forward places, the curly-haired youngster failed to establish himself.

There followed patchy progress over the next two campaigns, then in 1972/73 he seemed on the verge of a breakthrough, playing 31 times and scoring 13 goals in all competitions to claim League Championship and UEFA Cup medals.

He might have spoilt his encouraging work and precipitated a premature end to his Liverpool days when he walked out on Shankly on FA Cup Final day 1974. Boersma was outraged that after he had been used as a substitute in previous rounds, Chris Lawler was given the job at Wembley.

The manager understood his player's bitter disappointment and the differences were patched up, but he continued to find himself on the edge of the action.

Despite several settled runs, including one of 18 League matches in 1974/75, Boersma remained Anfield's 'nearly man' and, pushed yet lower in the pecking order by the emergence of David Fairclough, finally relinquished his hopes of a long-term future with the Reds in December 1975, when he joined Middlesbrough for £72,000.

Liverpool had lost a player of some verve, as anyone who saw his spirited dash into the box to make a late winner for Kevin Keegan against Southampton at Anfield in March 1973 would confirm. But Boersma's form was fitful and he wasn't helped by carping from over-critical fans, even if he was a split-second slower in reacting to opportunities than some of his international colleagues.

Subsequently he fared no better in the lower divisions and after injury forced early retirement he took up coaching and physiotherapy. Phil returned to the Reds in 1991 as the right-hand man of Graeme Souness, his second Anfield sojourn proving rather less memorable than his first.

PHILIP BOERSMA

BORN	Kirkby, Liverpool, 24 September 1949.
HONOURS	UEFA Cup 72/3. League Championship 72/3.
OTHER CLUBS	Wrexham on loan 69/70 (5, 0); Middlesbrough 75/6-76/7 (47, 3); Luton Town 77/8-78/9 (36, 8); Swansea City 78/9 (18, 1).

GAMES	99 (21)
GOALS	30

IAN ROSS

1966/67 → 1971/72

Any player who could subdue Franz Beckenbauer and Alan Ball and yet, unlike so many man-to-man markers, use the ball constructively when given the chance, would be guaranteed a first-team place at most clubs. Sadly for Ian Ross, it was not the case at Liverpool.

Ross, who eventually assumed the role of utility man vacated by Geoff Strong, made his debut as a substitute in January 1967. In the next two campaigns he stood in briefly for Smith, Byrne and Yeats at the back, impressing with his reliability and composure, before Bill Shankly began to employ his tenacious qualities to shackle specific opponents.

The blond Glaswegian did an effective job on Ball, then at his peak, when the Reds won 3-0 at Goodison in December 1969, but his finest achievement was the eclipse of 'Kaiser Franz' in a European Fairs Cup encounter with Bayern Munich in March 1971. He even found time to score Liverpool's only goal of the game as they reached the semi-final.

Ross enjoyed his longest unbroken run in 1971/72, wearing five different numbers during his spell of 20 games, before joining Aston Villa, for whom he performed with distinction alongside big centre-half Chris Nicholl. His success away from the furnace-hot competition of Anfield was well deserved.

IAN ROSS
BORN   Glasgow, 26 January 1947
OTHER CLUBS   Aston Villa 71/2-75/6 (175, 3); Notts County on loan 76/7 (4, 1); Northampton Town on loan 76/7 (2, 0); Peterborough United 76/7-78/9 (112, 1); Wolverhampton Wanderers 79/80-81/2 (0, 0); Hereford United 82/3 (15, 0).

GAMES 59 (9)
GOALS 4

DOUG LIVERMORE

1967/68 → 1970/71

Doug Livermore was a neat, workmanlike midfielder who simply didn't come up to the standard demanded at Anfield. He was handed the prompting role vacated by Ian St John when the Scot was axed after the Reds' shock FA Cup quarter-final exit at Watford in February 1970 and enjoyed a 13-match run to the end of the season as Bill Shankly set about reshaping his ageing team.

His displays revealed strength, honesty and some skill but he lacked pace and, most crucially, the inspiration for such an onerous task. After that sequence Livermore, who had made his debut as a substitute for Tony Hateley at Upton Park in April 1968, was never to start another League game for Liverpool and joined Norwich in November 1970 for £22,000.

Carrow Road saw the best years of his playing career as he helped the Canaries gain promotion to Division One in his first full campaign in East Anglia. Livermore, who later saw service with Bournemouth, Cardiff and Chester, went on to become a respected coach and worked with the Welsh national team. After a spell in charge at Tottenham, in 1994 he returned to his spiritual home of Anfield to assist his old team-mate, Roy Evans.

DOUGLAS ERNEST LIVERMORE
BORN   Prescot, Liverpool, 27 December 1947.
OTHER CLUBS   Norwich City 70/1-74/5 (114, 4); Bournemouth on loan 74/5 (10, 0); Cardiff City 75/6-77/8 (88, 5); Chester 77/8-78/9 (71, 6).
MANAGER   Tottenham Hotspur (92-93).

GAMES 14 (3)
GOALS 0

PETER WALL

1967/68 → 1969/70

Peter Wall was a cultured defender who once seemed likely to succeed Gerry Byrne as Liverpool's long-term left-back. He arrived from Wrexham in October 1966 as the junior partner in a £26,000 full-back package which included Stuart Mason. But while Mason was destined never to make a first-team appearance before returning to the Racecourse Ground, Wall made promising progress.

He made his debut at home to Burnley in March 1968, soon after Byrne had suffered the injury which was to end his career prematurely. Then, after makeshift stints by Tommy Smith and Ian Ross, Wall settled in for the remaining eight games of that season and the first 13 of the next.

The skilful Salopian revealed rare poise and a calm assurance under pressure which perhaps veered too close to being casual for Bill Shankly's peace of mind, and Geoff Strong was handed the number-three shirt for the duration of the campaign.

Wall, who maybe needed a shade more drive for a top-rank career, resurfaced for a nine-match spell half-way through 1969/70 but didn't become established and joined Crystal Palace for £35,000. At Selhurst Park he found his niche and served the Eagles admirably for eight years.

THOMAS PETER WALL		
BORN Westbury, Shropshire, 13 September 1944.		
OTHER CLUBS Shrewsbury Town 63/4-64/5 (18, 0);	GAMES	42
Wrexham 65/6-66/7 (22, 1); Crystal Palace 70/1-77/8		
(177, 3); Orient on loan 72/3 (10, 0).	GOALS	0

ROY EVANS

1969/70 → 1973/74

Roy Evans was an inspirational role model to the distressingly vast multitude of young professionals who discover that, contrary to initial expectations, they do not possess quite enough ability to make it as a player at the top level.

Crosby-born Evans was a skilful left-back who made his League debut against Sheffield Wednesday at Anfield in March 1970 as Geoff Strong's tenure was coming to an end and before Alec Lindsay became established. He was comfortable on the ball, passed well with his left foot and possessed boundless enthusiasm, but lacked the necessary pace to make the position his own.

Evans hung on as a reliable stand-by for four frustrating seasons but appeared to be destined for soccer oblivion until manager Bob Paisley stepped in with the offer of a job coaching the reserves. Still only 25, Roy must have been tempted to turn it down in favour of seeking a playing career elsewhere but perhaps felt, deep down, that Paisley was being realistic.

Accordingly, he accepted the opportunity and worked hard to make the most of it, leading his charges to the Central League championship at his first three attempts and going on to repeat his success regularly in the 1980s. Before long, Roy Evans was being mentioned as a possible Liverpool manager of the future . . .

ROY QUINTIN ECHLIN EVANS		
BORN Crosby, Merseyside, 4 October 1948.	GAMES	11
MANAGER Liverpool (94-98); Swindon Town (01).	GOALS	0

LARRY LLOYD

1969/70 → 1973/74

When strapping centre-half Larry Lloyd limped out of the Anfield action in early 1974, few observers could have guessed that the England international had played his last game for Liverpool. The thigh injury which had ended his interest in the encounter with Norwich City didn't seem serious and he was confidently expected to make a quick return.

It was never to be. The smaller but more skilful Phil Thompson was slotted in alongside Emlyn Hughes, bringing a continental style to the Reds' central defence, and the partnership prospered so fruitfully that Big Larry, an ever-present in the League Championship and UEFA Cup triumphs of the previous campaign, found himself discarded for good.

Bill Shankly bought the towering West Countryman, a dominant stopper in the Ron Yeats mould, from Bristol Rovers for £50,000 in April 1969. He saw him as the eventual successor to his vaunted colossus and so it proved. Lloyd made his entrance for a two-match spell when Yeats was injured early in 1969/70, but it was not until the last six games of the campaign, when Shankly was breaking up his beloved 1960s side, that the new man took his place on merit – and kept it until that fateful thigh strain changed the course of his career.

LLoyd assumed the burden of replacing a Liverpool legend with commendable confidence and, as his experience grew, he showed there was more to his game than the obvious asset of aerial power. Though lacking pace, he was capable of using the ball with precision, especially with his left foot, and he was exceptionally active in urging on his colleagues.

His huge physical presence in opposition penalty boxes brought Lloyd disappointingly few goals but he did make one vital strike, heading what was to prove the winner against Borussia Moenchengladbach in the 1972/73 UEFA Cup Final

Despite being out of the side already, Lloyd was devastated at missing the 1974 FA Cup Final and accepted a £225,000 move to Coventry three months later. He didn't settle there and Brian Clough got a bargain when he signed him for £60,000 in 1976. With Nottingham Forest, Lloyd played a leading role in League Championship and European Cup glories and, for one match, won back his England place. A rare resurrection was complete.

LAURENCE VALENTINE LLOYD

BORN	Bristol, 6 October 1948.
HONOURS	UEFA Cup 72/3. League Championship 72/3. 4 England caps (71-80).
OTHER CLUBS	Bristol Rovers 68/9 (43, 1); Coventry City 74/5-76/7 (50, 5); Nottingham Forest 76/7-80/1 (148, 6); Wigan Athletic 80/1-82/3 (52, 2).
MANAGER	Wigan Athletic (81-83); Notts County (83-84).

GAMES	218
GOALS	5

JOHN McLAUGHLIN

1969/70 → 1974/75

There was a time when Bill Shankly thought the slim, almost frail figure of schemer John McLaughlin would loom large in the 1970s as one of the foundations of his second successful side. Sadly Shanks' optimism proved groundless as McLaughlin's career withered and died in the harsh, hectic reality of First Division life.

His chance came during a period of transition for the Reds at the turn of the decade. The old order, so masterly in the 1960s, was now being swept away and places were there for the taking. McLaughlin was drafted in for the last match of 1969/70, a defeat at Stamford Bridge, and then was given 33 games in the following League campaign to establish himself.

He took the role of midfield creator and occasionally he looked the part, coolly employing his deft touch on the ball and ability to judge the weight of a pass to good advantage. But pace and stamina were lacking, frequently leaving John apparently out of his depth and struggling to have an effect on proceedings.

Having failed to make the most of his lengthy settled run, he faded away as new players came into contention for his place. Eventually, after a brief spell on loan at Portsmouth, a serious knee injury put him out of the game.

JOHN THOMAS McLAUGHLIN
BORN Liverpool, 25 February 1952.
OTHER CLUBS Portsmouth on loan 75/6 (5, 0).

GAMES **53 (2)**
GOALS **3**

JACK WHITHAM

1970/71 → 1971/72

Too much time on the treatment table robbed Jack Whitham of his chance to build a career at Anfield, and deprived Liverpool of a possible long-term successor to Roger Hunt. Whitham was a strong, all-action centre-forward who was signed from Sheffield Wednesday for £57 000 in April 1970, four months after Hunt's departure. At Hillsborough he had averaged only a little under a goal every two games but, alas, there was a catch. Jack had never started more than 18 games in a season thanks to a soul-destroying injury record; whenever he struck a patch of good form he was invariably sidelined before he could realise his potential.

He made his Reds debut as a stand-in for Bobby Graham in a goalless draw against Newcastle United at St James' Park early in 1970/71 but was offered only limited opportunities for the rest of that campaign. His first settled run came midway through the following season and he responded with five goals in eight games, including a powerfully-struck hat-trick in a 3-2 Anfield defeat of Derby.

This sequence ended, inevitably, with fitness problems. After a two-game absence he returned to score the only goal in a victory at Huddersfield in February 1972 before he was struck down again. Although Whitham was to remain at Anfield for another two years before joining Cardiff City, he was never to play another first-team game for Liverpool. His bad luck continued wherever he went and eventually he gave up football to run a pub.

JACK WHITHAM
BORN Burnley, Lancashire, 8 December 1946.
OTHER CLUBS Sheffield Wednesday 66/7-69/70 (63, 27); Cardiff City 73/4-74/5 (14, 3); Reading 75/6 (19, 3).

GAMES **16**
GOALS **7**

EMLYN HUGHES

1966/67 → 1978/79

A new adjective should have been invented for Emlyn Hughes; nothing in the dictionary captured adequately the essence of a man possessed by an almost demonic fervour for football in general and Liverpool in particular. Enthusiastic, energetic, ebullient – they've all been used and deserve to be discarded. Ask his old Anfield team-mates and they'll tell you that mere words could never do justice to the man who led them to some of their most memorable triumphs.

Emlyn's arrival in February 1967 marked the beginning of the end of an era. Bill Shankly was making his first, tentative moves towards dismantling his great 1960s side and the bubbly Barrow boy, who made a handful of appearances at left-back in place of the injured Gerry Byrne before permanently replacing left-half Willie Stevenson for 1967/68, was the first newcomer to claim a regular place.

Shanks' admiration of the rookie Hughes began one spring day in 1966 when he watched the 18-year-old – who was to become, in the lurid language of the Reds' boss, 'one of the major signings of all time' – make his debut for Blackpool. Bill was so impressed that he made a £25,000 offer straight after the game but had to wait ten months before securing his quarry for £65,000.

Having moved to Merseyside, Hughes wasted no time in making an impact. In his first game, at home to Stoke City, he dominated the Potters' play-maker George Eastham and four matches later he earned a famous nickname. From the day he felled Newcastle forward Albert Bennett with a rugby tackle – nothing malicious, more an example of youthful impetuosity – Hughes was branded 'Crazy Horse', a label that was his for keeps.

Not that such eccentric acts were needed to draw attention to such a promising player, for whom Leeds were soon willing to offer Peter Lorimer in part-exchange. Built like a dreadnought and with strength to match, the long-striding Hughes rampaged around the football grounds of England like a frisky rhino. If subtlety was lacking in his early approach, and if he did occasionally commit himself to rash tackles, his vast potential was always evident.

Left-sided but reliable with both feet, strong in the air and boisterously inspirational, Hughes became known for his dynamic surges into enemy territory. Southampton were on the receiving end at Anfield in April 1971 when he broke up an attack in front of his own goal, played the ball wide and steamed up the centre of the pitch. Arriving with uncheckable impetus on the edge of the Saints' box, he cracked a first-time shot into the net. Irresistible!

In 1973/74 Hughes replaced Tommy Smith as captain and moved into the centre of defence, forming a polished partnership with Phil Thompson. By this time his play had matured, his approach calmer and more reliant on anticipation than the buccaneering tactics of old. Though not as popular a skipper with team-mates as Smith or Yeats, Hughes was a motivator supreme, leading by example and unflagging in his zest. In five seasons in charge he held aloft the European Cup (twice), the UEFA Cup, the League Championship trophy (also twice) and the FA Cup.

At such moments his all-embracing grin – familiar to a wider audience following his emergence as a TV person – was an emblem of Anfield ascendancy although, always one to wear his heart on his sleeve, he could also radiate utter dejection more thoroughly than most. None who saw him drag himself up Wembley's 39 steps to accept an FA Cup loser's medal in 1977 will forget his despair.

Emlyn Hughes, who died tragically prematurely in 2004 after facing a drawn-out illness with characteristic fortitude, won more England caps as a Red than anyone else before him.

He was an emotional performer and a downright magnificent one who never knew when he was beaten. Thus, when he moved to Molyneux in August 1979, it was no surprise that he helped Wolves to League Cup glory. Somehow, though, that grin looked out of place above an old-gold shirt . . .

EMLYN WALTER HUGHES

BORN	Barrow, Lancashire, 28 August 1947.
HONOURS	European Cup 76/7, 77/8. UEFA Cup 72/3, 75/6. League Championship 72/3, 75/6, 76/7, 78/9. FA Cup 73/4. 62 England caps (69-80). FWA Footballer of the Year 77.
OTHER CLUBS	Blackpool 65/6-66/7 (28, 0); Wolverhampton Wanderers 79/80-80/1 (58, 2); Rotherham United 81/2-82/3 (56, 6); Hull City 82/3 (9, 0); Mansfield Town 83/4 (0, 0); Swansea City 83/4 (7,0).
MANAGER	Rotherham United (81-83).
DIED	Sheffield, 9 November 2004.

GAMES	665
GOALS	49

RAY CLEMENCE

1968/69 → 1980/81

Ray Clemence was possibly the most important factor in Liverpool's continued success throughout the 1970s. That assessment came from Bill Shankly, the man who paid Scunthorpe United £18,000 for the 19-year-old goalkeeper in June 1967 and then saw him rise to become one of the best – maybe, at his peak, the very best – in the world.

When Clemence arrived at Anfield, Shankly hinted that a first-team spot was there for the taking. But the canny Reds boss was either under-valuing the ability of 'keeper-in-residence Tommy Lawrence, which was not likely, or indulging in kidology to spur the new boy to greater efforts, which was. In the event Ray had to wait two and a half seasons to claim a place. By then, having tuned his talents to an irresistible pitch of readiness at the elbow of his helpful predecessor, he was itching to prove himself

His early games were played behind giant, aerially-dominant centre-halves – first Ron Yeats, then Larry Lloyd – and initially Clemence impressed with safe handling, sharp reflexes and a knack of getting down quickly to low shots. But as his confidence grew in subsequent seasons it was clear that he was a truly outstanding all-rounder; apart from a weakness in goal-kicking, on which he worked until it came up to scratch, there were no perceptible flaws.

Clemence combined a keen positional sense with shrewd anticipation, instinctively knowing when to leave his line and when to stay on it. This made for an unflashy technique but Shankly knew that acrobatics were a poor substitute for clean sheets and blessed the day he'd rescued Ray from Third Division obscurity.

Another immense Clemence virtue, so vital to the net-minder of a team such as Liverpool which spent long periods in their opponents' halves, was concentration, and he possessed it in abundance. He could spend lengthy chunks of a match marooned behind one of the world's most niggardly defences without getting a touch of the ball and it's a measure of his prowess that he could respond so magnificently when the need arose.

Indeed, but for the positive approach of this compulsive shouter and organiser, which demanded involvement and sometimes made him more sweeper than 'keeper, he might have spent his Anfield years as the loneliest man in English football!

Statistical proof of Clemence's excellence is plentiful. In his first full term, which ended with a brilliant display in the FA Cup Final defeat by Arsenal, he conceded only 22 goals in 41 games to help his defence equal the First Division record of 24 in a season. The achievement was destined to be eclipsed, however, as he let in a miserly 16 in 1978/79.

But it's saves rather than cold figures which live on in the memories of Reds fans, with penalty stops being particularly vivid. One in a goalless away leg against Dynamo Dresden on the way to winning the 1975/76 UEFA Cup, when he dived full-length to reach a firm, low shot, was a real heart-stopper.

Clemence, a dedicated trainer who relished scoring in five-a-sides and dubbed himself 'The White Pele', ended his 'Pool days on a surprising note in August 1981. Still at the peak of his powers, he announced the need for a new challenge and joined Spurs, for whom he went on to make more than 250 senior appearances. It's hard to see, though, what he hoped to find in the way of motivation at White Hart Lane that was missing at Anfield.

Running parallel to his club exploits was an illustrious international career throughout which he vied for the England jersey with Peter Shilton. The debate about who was the better will rage forever; suffice it to say that Kopites, like Clemence's new fans at White Hart lane, were a touch peeved with England manager Bobby Robson's final verdict.

RAYMOND NEAL CLEMENCE

BORN   Skegness, Lincolnshire, 5 August 1948.

HONOURS   European Cup 76/7, 77/8, 80/1. UEFA Cup 72/3, 75/6.
League Championship 72/3, 75/6, 76/7, 78/9, 79/80.
FA Cup 73/4. League Cup 80/1. 61 England caps (72-83).

OTHER CLUBS   Scunthorpe United 65/6-66/7 (48, 0); Tottenham Hotspur 81/2-87/8 (240, 0).

MANAGER   Barnet (94-96).

GAMES   **665**

GOALS   **0**

STEVE HEIGHWAY

1970/71 → 1980/81

When Steve Heighway burst irreverently on to a decidedly staid First Division scene in October 1970, it was like a fresh breeze sweeping through a musty bootroom. With Sir Alf Ramsey still in and wingers largely out – the likes of George Best and Eddie Gray were gilt-edged exceptions – the cobwebs were gathering thick and fast. The established order needed a kick up the backside and Heighway, an innocent abroad in the tough, serious world of professional football, delivered it in his own gloriously unorthodox style.

He arrived from non-League Skelmersdale to bring pace and width to the Liverpool attack. Heighway was a winger despite wearing the number-nine shirt, and rapidly it became clear that Bill Shankly had not burdened him with contemporary Division One protocol.

Instead of laying the ball off and running for a return pass in the accepted fashion, Steve had the audacity to take players on, and it confounded them. Knees high and elbows pumping, he ran at defenders and went past them – again and again.

Sometimes the Reds' raw flyer seemed to overstep himself and an opponent would be odds-on to rob him; but often Heighway, basin haircut bobbing and moustache bristling, would find an extra spurt of speed, stick out a toe and skip away with the ball. His raking stride made it hard for defenders to recover and his ability to cross accurately at full tilt gave a thrilling new dimension to the Liverpool front line.

Shankly had resisted the challenge of other top clubs to sign the athletic amateur but it was when Heighway was installed safely at Anfield that the manager pulled his master stroke. It would have been easy to dismiss the young Irishman's dashing approach as fine for the Cheshire County League but altogether too naive for the big time. Shanks, though, was too wise for that; having spotted something special he was not going to allow it to he coached into oblivion.

Heighway, who won his first Republic of Ireland cap the night after making his Liverpool debut, quickly turned heads with two-footed talents which enabled him to cut inside opponents or nip past them on the outside.

No one who saw him rescue an apparently lost cause in the Merseyside derby at Anfield in November 1970 had the slightest doubt about his pedigree. Everton were two up and coasting when Steve broke free to score from an acute angle; then he slipped past two defenders to make John Toshack's equaliser with a cross from the left wing. The Reds went on to win with a goal from Chris Lawler, but it was Heighway who had turned the tide.

He capped his first, exhilarating campaign, in which he had only rarely frustrated by over-elaboration, with a near-post shot which deceived Arsenal 'keeper Bob Wilson and gave Liverpool a short-lived lead in the FA Cup Final.

In the early years of his career 'Big Bamber' – a university graduate, as was Brian 'Little Bamber' Hall – seemed jaded at times but Shankly, that motivator supreme, was always able to supply the remedy and the arrival of another star, Kevin Keegan, removed much of the pressure.

By the mid-1970s Heighway, while less spectacular than in the past, had become a commendably consistent performer and spent much of his time in deep positions, prompting the Keegan-Toshack tandem. His touchline breaks, however, continued to be a potent attacking option and one such sortie set up the first goal for Terry McDermott in the 1977 European Cup Final.

At the end of the decade Heighway, in his thirties and faced with stiff competition for a place, crossed the Atlantic to end his playing days before returning to Anfield to coach youngsters, eventually to take charge of the club's opulent academy.

At the time it was felt that if he brought half as much flair to his new task as he had once displayed on the world's football fields, then Liverpool could look forward to a sparkling future. He retired in 2007, leaving an impressive legacy of young men rising excitingly through the ranks.

STEPHEN DEREK HEIGHWAY
BORN: Dublin, 25 November 1947.
HONOURS: European Cup 76/7, 77/8. UEFA Cup 72/3, 75/6. League Championship 72/3, 75/6, 76/7, 78/9. FA Cup 73/4. 34 Republic of Ireland caps (70-81).
OTHER CLUBS: Minnesota Kicks, USA, 81.

GAMES: 449 (24)
GOALS: 76

BRIAN HALL

1968/69 → 1975/76

Brian Hall was the man who made an art form out of being unobtrusive, but let none doubt the value to Liverpool of this perpetually busy and consistent footballer throughout the first half of the 1970s.

The diminutive Glaswegian claimed a regular place when Ian Callaghan suffered cartilage trouble in autumn 1970. Hall, whose previous League experience had been limited to substitute appearances, slotted neatly into the team on the right side of midfield, foraging energetically for the ball and passing it on with a minimum of fuss in time-honoured Reds tradition.

Bill Shankly was so pleased with the way the skilful, slightly round-shouldered deputy fitted into the team pattern that when Callaghan was fit again he returned in a central position, allowing Hall to continue in the wide role.

The newcomer kept his place for the rest of the season, making light of a slight deficiency in pace, and saw the Reds through to Wembley when he adroitly hooked home an Alun Evans cross to beat Everton in the FA Cup semi-final at Old Trafford. Arsenal won the final but the future beckoned promisingly.

The following term proved to be one of consolidation for Hall, despite several spells out of the side, as Shankly's task of replacing his first great team neared completion. Honours came in 1972/73 with triumph in the UEFA Cup and a Championship medal, though Brian was ousted for much of that campaign and the one that followed by the newly arrived Peter Cormack.

He fought back to play in the victorious FA Cup Final against Newcastle United in 1974 and then enjoyed his most active season in 1974/75, missing only seven League games. After that his first-team aspirations withered with the advent of Jimmy Case and he departed for Plymouth Arygyle, then Burnley.

On retirement as a player, Hall – a graduate who rejoiced in the nickname of 'Little Bamber', standing four inches shorter than 'Big Bamber' Heighway – became a teacher, then returned to Liverpool as a Football In The Community officer.

He will go down as an untiring worker who didn't have that vital turn of speed which might have lifted him to a higher plane. But in the final analysis there'll be no complaints from Anfield about the days in a red shirt of the loyal, dependable and, yes, talented Brian Hall.

BRIAN WILLIAM HALL	
BORN	Glasgow, 22 January 1946.
HONOURS	UEFA Cup 72/3. League Championship 72/3. FA Cup 73/4.
OTHER CLUBS	Plymouth Argyle 76/7-77/8 (51, 16); Burnley 77/8-79/80 (43, 3).

GAMES	198 (24)
GOALS	21

PETER CORMACK

1972/73 → 1975/76

Peter Cormack was one of the most naturally talented Reds of the mid-1970s; sometimes surprising, invariably subtle, he was a pleasure to watch about his business. Unlike so many midfielders, he was ready to risk losing possession to make a penetrating forward pass, often changing the pattern of play with a single touch.

Bill Shankly had been an admirer of the talented Scot since he was capped as a teenage winger with Hibernian but it was in the more central, constructive role Cormack adopted for Nottingham Forest that the Liverpool boss saw him making the greatest impact.

After paying £110,000 to prise him away from the City Ground in the summer of 1972, Shanks introduced Cormack to his Championship-chasing side at the expense of the more prosaic Brian Hall, and revelled in his success.

The new man quickly showed his mettle with incisive displays in which he employed his extensive repertoire of deft skills to full advantage and demonstrated that, for all his slight build, he was no shirker in the tackle.

Despite standing only 5ft 8in, he was also competitive in the air thanks to instinctive timing of the Ian St John variety, as Everton found out to their cost when he ghosted in at the near post to head the only goal of the October 1972 derby at Anfield.

Cormack found a particularly able collaborator in Kevin Keegan, the quick-witted pair often dazzling opponents with their lightning one-two exchanges, and soon after the all-Mersey clash Birmingham fell victim to their tricks in front of the Kop. The Cormack-Keegan tandem seemed to skate over the greasy, rain-soaked surface, inspiring a thrilling 4-3 win after being a goal down at the interval.

Despite his undeniable artistic attributes, however, there were times when the Cormack contribution could he peripheral, his abilities submerged in the hurly-burly of the game, and there were those who championed the more consistent merits of the worthy Hall.

But Shankly was convinced of Peter's values and he shared in League, FA Cup and UEFA Cup glory before a combination of cartilage trouble and the advance of other midfielders precipitated a November 1976 move to Bristol City. For three years he entertained fitfully at Ashton Gate before heading for Hibernian and home.

	PETER BARR CORMACK	
BORN	Edinburgh, 17 July 1946.	
HONOURS	UEFA Cup 72/3. League Championship 72/3, 75/6. FA Cup 73/4. 9 Scotland caps (66-71).	
OTHER CLUBS	Hibernian 62/3-69/70 (183, 76); Nottingham Forest 69/70-71/2 (74, 15); Bristol City 76/7-79/80 (67, 15); Hibernian 79/80-80/1 (20, 1); Partick Thistle 83/4 (1, 0).	
MANAGER	Partick Thistle (80-84); Anartosi, Cyprus; Botswana national coach.	

GAMES	169 (9)
GOALS	26

ALEC LINDSAY

1969/70 → 1976/77

Alec Lindsay was a man with a golden gift. Sadly, apart from three glorious seasons when arguably he was the best left-back in the land, he failed to make the most of it.

The talent in question was for passing, accurately and over long distances, with his left foot. To the casual observer that might not seem such a spectacular blessing but to anyone who has watched generations of defenders hoofing high balls hopefully in the general direction of their forwards, it was an asset to be cherished.

Lindsay cost Liverpool £67,000 when he arrived from his home-town club of Bury in March 1969 and, like so many newcomers to Anfield from the lower divisions, he went straight into the Central League 'finishing school'. He had been a wing-half with the Shakers and some respected judges were so impressed with his ball skills that they saw him developing along the lines of fellow Gigg Lane graduate Colin Bell.

After taking longer than many to settle with the Reds – Lindsay was not a 'natural' trainer – he made his debut and several more unremarkable appearances in midfield before switching to the left-back berth he was destined to grace so stylishly.

He created a favourable impression with two spells in 1970/71, making the position his own in the following campaign when he forged one of the most profitable Anfield partnerships of the 1970s. Much is heard of the Keegan-Toshack link but equally valuable, in a less obvious way, was Keegan's understanding with the resourceful blond defender.

Lindsay's long, raking passes to his front-men, often bent teasingly around helpless opponents, were made for Keegan, who was adept at bringing them under instant control before creating his own brand of mayhem. The full-back seemed to sense where his nippy target was going to run, playing the ball into space intelligently and with perfect weight, and the tactic had a major influence in the Reds' UEFA Cup and League Championship double of 1972/73.

Come the 1974 FA Cup Final against Newcastle and Lindsay was still in tremendous form. He was under-employed at the back, courtesy of the Magpies' feeble attacking efforts, but was prominent on the overlap as the Reds surged forward. It was from one such foray that he made the crispest strike of his life, driving a ferocious cross-shot past 'keeper Iam McFaul, only to have his joy cut short by an offside whistle.

Such a minor disappointment did nothing to sour an accomplished season and when Joe Mercer, England's caretaker manager, drafted him into the national side that summer the career of Alec Lindsay was at its zenith with, it seemed, only cloudless horizons ahead.

True, he had never been the quickest player and perhaps lacked the stamina for the midfield role which might have made more of his creative leanings; but he tackled well, read the game shrewdly and had found a productive niche.

Unfortunately, disillusionment was not far away. Linday's form faded badly in 1975 and he was replaced, first by Phil Neal and then by Joey Jones. For two years he strove in vain to regain his spot before taking that trusty left foot, briefly, to Stoke City and on to Oakland in Oregon. For all his undoubted success, the definitive epitaph on the playing days of Alec Lindsay must be that many men of inferior ability managed to achieve considerably more.

	ALEC LINDSAY		
BORN	Bury, Lancashire, 27 February 1948.		
HONOURS	UEFA Cup 72/3. League Championship 72/3. FA Cup 73/4. 4 England caps (74).	GAMES	246 (2)
OTHER CLUBS	Bury 64/5-68/9 (126, 14); Stoke City 77/8 (20, 3); Oakland, USA, 78.	GOALS	18

JOHN TOSHACK

1970/71 → 1977/78

John Toshack was the thinking man's version of that oft-maligned breed, the big, brave striker. While many of that ilk are strictly one-dimensional, ready to batter defences into submission or perish in the attempt, Toshack ultimately offered – after much hard work – a more varied range of attacking possibilities.

Of course, he had a distinct advantage over fellow members of the centre-forwards' union in that he was blessed for most of his Liverpool career with the presence of Kevin Keegan. The diverse talents of the towering Welshman and his nippy, opportunistic partner combined to give the Reds many of their finest hours.

Toshack, aged 21 and already an established international, was signed for £110,000 from Cardiff in November 1970 and lost little time in endearing himself to the Kop in the surest possible way – by dumping Everton on the seat of their pants. In one of the most rousing Merseyside derbies of modern times, Toshack helped to erase a two-goal deficit, climbing high above the Blues' Brian Labone to head the equaliser, before nodding down Alec Lindsay's cross for Chris Lawler to clinch an emotional victory.

Such exploits were clearly a recipe for deification by the fans, but John's immediate progress did not match his dynamic start. His last 18 games of the season, including the FA Cup Final defeat by Arsenal, failed to produce a goal and it was apparent that, though he was always a power in the air, other aspects of his game were in need of serious attention.

To his credit Toshack applied himself assiduously and, boosted by Keegan's breakthrough, gradually acquired more all-round skills, of which accurate distribution was the most notable. He used his newly-widened scope intelligently and often to devastating effect, laying on a steady stream of chances with subtle flicks to his effervescent accomplice and creating space by astute running off the ball.

But while this improvement enabled the Weshman to play an important role in winning six major trophies, his road to glory was rarely smooth. For most of his Anfield tenure he was dogged by a nagging thigh injury – only once did he exceed 30 League games in a campaign – and was engaged in perennial battle to defend his place. At various times he faced challenges from Bobby Graham, Alun Evans, Jack Whitham, Phil Boersma, Alan Waddle, Ray Kennedy, David Fairclough and David Johnson, seeing off all but the latter two. In fact, his shirt returned to him so often that eventually he called it Lassie!

Despite dropping Toshack sometimes, both Bill Shankly and Bob Paisley – who once agreed to sell him to Leicester only for the £160,000 deal to founder on a failed medical – liked him on duty for European encounters, in which he gave some of his finest performances.

One of the most unexpected came in the 1972/73 UEFA Cup Final first leg at home to Borussia Moenchengladbach, for which Tosh had been omitted. The match was abandoned because of heavy rain but Shankly had spotted that the Germans were vulnerable in the air. Accordingly the 6ft target man was recalled for the rescheduled game and laid on two goals for Keegan.

Toshack's most prolific term, though, was 1975/76, when he found the net 23 times, including three hat-tricks, on the way to a League title and UEFA Cup double. Thereafter fitness problems and hotter-than-ever competition for places preceded a move, as player-boss, to Swansea where phenomenal success put him on a management trail which was to take him all the way to Real Madrid. His stature as one of the greatest names in Welsh soccer history was confirmed.

JOHN BENJAMIN TOSHACK

BORN   Cardiff, 22 March 1949.

HONOURS   UEFA Cup 72/3, 75/6. League Championship 72/3, 75/6, 76/7. FA Cup 73/4. 40 Wales caps (69-80).

OTHER CLUBS   Cardiff City 65/6-70/1 (162, 75); Swansea City 77/8-83/4 (63, 24).

MANAGER   Swansea City (78-84); Sporting Lisbon, Portugal, (84-85); Real Sociedad, Spain, (85-89); Real Madrid, Spain, (89-90); Real Sociedad (91-94); Wales (94); Deportivo La Coruna, Spain, (95-97); Besiktas, Turkey, (97-99); Real Madrid (99); St Etienne, France, (00-01); Real Sociedad (01-02); Catania, Italy, (02-03); Murcia, Spain, (04); Wales (04-).

GAMES	237 (9)
GOALS	96

IAN CALLAGHAN

1959/60 → 1977/78

If ever one player embodied the multitude of qualities which built Liverpool into one of the world's greatest clubs then, undeniably, Ian Callaghan was that man. From the day he made his debut as a teenager against Bristol Rovers at Anfield in April 1960 – receiving an ovation from team-mates, opponents, the crowd, even the referee! – until his departure for Swansea nearly two decades later, he was, without ever being a star in the accepted sense, a shining example of everything a top footballer should be.

The Callaghan career divides neatly into two halves. He spent the 1960s as an orthodox right-winger, one of the best in the country, before converting into a chugging dynamo in central midfield, a role which was to win him a belated international recall at the age of 35.

He made his entrance as a diminutive professional of six weeks' standing with only four Central League games behind him. A man-size shirt hung loosely on his wiry frame but there was no suggestion of a little boy lost when he started to play. In that first match he revealed confidence, bags of natural ability and a precious instinct which told him when to hold the ball and when to release it.

A golden future awaited but Bill Shankly was wary of prematurely pitching his gifted rookie into the maelstrom of League football. A season and a half passed before he was awarded a regular berth and then he helped to win long-coveted promotion to the top flight.

Ian's game blossomed in the First Division. He formed a potent partnership with left-flank trickster Peter Thompson and the honours flowed. While Thompson was more devious, Callaghan was fast and direct, making it his business to reach the byline and feed Roger Hunt and Ian St John with a diet of crosses which did much to nourish the Reds' goal tally.

Though never a heavy scorer himself, Ian did contribute several memorable strikes. Particularly satisfying was an acute-angled side-foot from a well-rehearsed free-kick routine involving Hunt and Willie Stevenson that stunned Internazionale of Milan in the 1965 European Cup semi-final at Anfield, though more spectacular was a 30-yarder which sunk Everton in autumn 1963 as Shankly's men headed for their first Championship.

The watershed arrived in 1970/71. Liverpool were experiencing an indifferent patch but their reliable right-winger was playing as well as ever until a cartilage operation sidelined him for four months. In his absence newcomer Brian Hall prospered and there were fears that Callaghan's days in a red shirt were numbered. Such qualms were not shared by the manager, who doubted neither his man's resilience, nor his capacity to adapt, and simply handed him a new job in midfield.

Ian responded by missing only four games in the subsequent five seasons, during which he was awarded the MBE, became the club's first Footballer of the Year and played a major part in placing untold strain on the Anfield trophy cabinet.

His intelligence and enthusiasm, precise passing and limitless stamina were never seen to better effect and that return to the England side – he had been axed when Alf Ramsey abandoned wingers in 1966 – was a fitting reward. The cascade of tributes which followed genuinely puzzled the modest Cally, who felt his game had remained at the same consistent level throughout his years with the Reds.

When it was time to move on he could look back on an exemplary record. He had been the one common denominator in three fine teams, played more games than anyone in the club's history, never been cautioned by a referee and set a towering example of loyalty, dedication and skill. Ian Callaghan created a formidable standard; if others can meet it they will be great men indeed.

IAN ROBERT CALLAGHAN

BORN	Liverpool, 10 April 1942.
HONOURS	European Cup 76/7. UEFA Cup 72/3, 75/6.
	League Championship 63/4, 65/6, 72/3, 75/6, 76/7.
	Second Division Championship 61/2. FA Cup 64/5, 73/4.
	4 England caps (66-77). FWA Footballer of the Year 74.
OTHER CLUBS	Swansea City 78/9-79/80 (76,1); Cork Hibernian 80/1;
	Soudifjord, Norway, 80/1; Crewe Alexandra 81/2 (15, 0).

GAMES	851 (5)
GOALS	69

STEVE PEPLOW

1969/70

A pacy attacker who was given the chance to replace Roger Hunt as Bill Shankly was rebuilding his team, but who didn't seize it. Eventually Peplow did fashion a worthy career on Merseyside, but at Prenton Park instead of Anfield.

STEPHEN THOMAS PEPLOW
BORN: Liverpool, 8 January 1949.
OTHER CLUBS: Swindon Town 70/1-72/3 (40, 11); Nottingham Forest 73/4 (3, 0); Mansfield Town on loan 73/4 (4, 3); Tranmere Rovers 73/4-80/1 (248, 44).

GAMES	3
GOALS	0

DEREK BROWNBILL

1973/74

A product of local junior football, the blond attacker was plunged into the big time at Birmingham in September 1973. After being substituted by Brian Hall, he was never picked again and was sold to Port Vale for £6,000 in February 1975.

DEREK ANTHONY BROWNBILL
BORN: Liverpool, 4 February 1954.
OTHER CLUBS: Port Vale 74/5-77/8 (92, 13); Wigan Athletic 78/9-79/80 (48, 8).

GAMES	1
GOALS	0

CHRIS FAGAN

1970/71

A tall, slender defender whose sole senior outing for the Reds was as a stand-in for right-back Chris Lawler in a 2-2 draw at Manchester City in April 1971. Soon he crossed the Mersey to Tranmere, then switched to non-League Bangor City.

CHRISTOPHER JAMES FAGAN
BORN: Manchester, 5 June 1950.
OTHER CLUBS: Tranmere Rovers 71/2-74/5 (84, 2).

GAMES	1
GOALS	0

DAVE RYLANDS

1973/74

Rylands' only call to the Anfield banner was as a deputy for stopper Larry Lloyd in a surprising 2-2 FA Cup draw with Doncaster in January 1974. After joining Hereford he made only limited impact at Edgar Street and soon left the League.

DAVID ROBERT RYLANDS
BORN: Liverpool, 7 March 1953.
OTHER CLUBS: Hereford United 74/5-75/6 (22, 0); Newport County on loan 74/5 (3, 1); Hartlepool United on loan 75/6 (11, 0); Halifax Town 76/7 (5, 0).

GAMES	1
GOALS	0

STEVE ARNOLD

1970/71

A strong, versatile performer capable of filling both defensive and midfield roles, Arnold was a £10,000 recruit from Crewe in September 1970. However, he made little impact at Anfield and enjoyed his best spell in the Rochdale rearguard.

STEPHEN FRANK ARNOLD
BORN: Crewe, Cheshire, 5 January 1951.
OTHER CLUBS: Crewe Alexandra 68/9-70/1 (15, 0); Southport on loan 71/2 (16, 3); Torquay United on loan 72/3 (3, 1); Rochdale 73/4 (40, 1).

GAMES	1
GOALS	0

MAX THOMPSON

1973/74 → 1975/76

A hugely promising young defender who could not break through for Liverpool but who fetched a handsome £80,000 fee when he joined Blackpool in March 1978. Later he played under John Toshack at Swansea and helped to win the Welsh Cup in 1982.

MAXWELL STEWART THOMPSON
BORN: Liverpool, 31 December 1956.
OTHER CLUBS: Blackpool 77/8-80/1 (99, 6); Swansea City 81/2-82/3 (26, 2); Bournemouth 83/4 (9, 0); Port Vale on loan 83/4 (2, 0).

GAMES	1 (1)
GOALS	0

FRANK LANE

1972/73

When Bill Shankly needed an understudy for Ray Clemence, he paid Tranmere £15,000 for Lane, who marred an otherwise solid debut at Derby by carrying a cross from Alan Hinton over his goal-line. A capable custodian nonetheless.

FRANK LANE
BORN: Wallasey, Cheshire, 20 July 1948.
OTHER CLUBS: Tranmere Rovers 69/70-71/2 (76, 0); Notts County 75/6 (2, 0).

GAMES	2
GOALS	0

BRIAN KETTLE

1975/76 → 1976/77

An England youth international full-back who excelled for Liverpool's Central League side, then made his senior debut at Highbury in December 1975 at a time when the number-three position was unsettled. Later joined Wigan for £25,000.

BRIAN KETTLE
BORN: Prescot, Lancashire, 22 April 1956.
OTHER CLUBS: Houston, USA; Wigan Athletic 80/1 (14, 1).

GAMES	4
GOALS	0

TREVOR STORTON

1972/73 → 1973/74

When Bill Shankly traversed the Mersey to swoop on emerging Tranmere star Trevor Storton in the summer of 1972, the canny Anfield boss believed he was recruiting a key element of his next great side.

The sandy-haired six-footer, who had compiled more than a century of appearances for Rovers since breaking through at Prenton Park in the late 1960s, was adaptable enough to occupy practically any defensive or midfield role and his temperament seemed well suited to the top grade.

Duly, in his first September as a Red, Storton was blooded in a 2-1 win at Leeds, a crucial early blow in that title-winning campaign as it turned out. Standing in for Tommy Smith in the centre of defence, he performed efficiently enough to retain his place for a run of five successive matches until the iron man was available again.

There followed a handful of further opportunities, including two League Cup quarter-final outings against Spurs, but although Storton never disgraced himself it became evident that competition from the likes of Messrs Smith, Hughes and Thompson was a trifle too warm for him.

Thus in July 1974 he accepted an £18,000 move to Chester, for whom he went on to play nearly 500 games during a decade of sterling service. Later Storton managed former Football League club Bradford Park Avenue.

TREVOR GEORGE STORTON
BORN Keighley, Yorkshire, 26 November 1949.
OTHER CLUBS Tranmere Rovers 67/8-71/2 (118, 9); Chester 74/5-83/4 (396, 17).

	GAMES	11 (1)
	GOALS	0

ALAN WADDLE

1973/74 → 1976/77

The Liverpool career of gangling centre-forward Alan Waddle was a brief, unremarkable interlude enlivened by one moment of pure, unadulterated glory. It came after 68 goalless minutes of a Merseyside derby largely dominated by Everton at Goodison Park in December 1973.

Ian Callaghan broke free on the flank and put in a speculative cross which Waddle toe-poked at full stretch past stranded 'keeper David Lawson to win the match. It was the 6ft 3in striker's only goal in 22 appearances for the Reds – all made either deputising for John Toshack or as substitute – before he set off on a decade of travels which took him to six other League clubs.

Alan, a cousin of England winger Chris Waddle, never showed the necessary class to merit a prolonged stay at Anfield but at least he bowed out of the big time in an important match. He was called to the colours when Steve Heighway was injured in the 1977 European Cup semi-final second leg against FC Zurich at Anfield, but had little chance to impress and five months later was on his way to Leicester City for £45,000. His most productive spell came as a Toshack recruit at Swansea, whom he helped to rise from the Third Division to the First.

ALAN ROBERT WADDLE
BORN Wallsend, Northumberland, 9 June 1954.
OTHER CLUBS Halifax Town 71/2-72/3 (39, 4); Leicester City 77/8 (11, 1); Swansea City 78/9-80/1 (90, 34); Newport County 80/1-81/2 (27, 8); Mansfield Town 82/3 (14, 4); Hartlepool United 83/4 (12, 2); Peterborough United 83/4-84/5 (36, 12); Hartlepool United 84/5 (4, 0); Swansea City 84/5-85/6 (40,10).

	GAMES	16 (6)
	GOALS	1

KEVIN KEEGAN

1971/72 → 1976/77

Kevin Keegan is one of the pivotal figures in Liverpool history and despite a dozen years of unprecedented, Dalglish-inspired dominance, he remains the biggest star the Reds have ever had. That's not to say he was the greatest footballer – such a claim would be contentious, indeed – but for sheer charisma and public prominence there had been no one like him in the British game since the prime of George Best.

His initial impact after arriving from Scunthorpe for £35,000 in the spring of 1971 – 'robbery with violence' was how Bill Shankly later described the deal – was overwhelming. Keegan hit Anfield like a miniature tornado; he turned the hallowed training procedures upside down with an all-consuming urge to be first at everything, excelled on a pre-season tour of Scandinavia and, having been converted swiftly from deep-lying winger to striker, found himself in the team for the First Division opener against Nottingham Forest.

He scored after seven minutes, ran amok like a demented jack-in-the-box for the rest of the match and generally served notice that Shanks had finally found the elusive special additive needed to inspire his rebuilt side.

Keegan proved quickly that his grand entrance was no fluke with a series of galvanising performances which caught the imagination of media and fans alike. He was a darting, irrepressible imp of a player, scampering to all corners of his opponents' territory and not loth to forage for the ball in his own behalf.

Quick, brave and apparently inexhaustible, he possessed a sureness of touch with both feet which enabled him to trick defenders in tight spaces and, even at 5ft 8in, he carried a potent aerial threat. Keegan's most precious assets, though, were a nimble brain – a delicately drifted European Cup goal against St Etienne in 1977 was a vivid example of improvisation at speed – and almost fiendish determination, a quality greatly admired by Shanks and which did much to forge a deep bond between the two men.

Kevin, whose front-line understanding with John Toshack appeared to border on telepathy at times, was instrumental in many of the Reds' most stirring mid-1970s triumphs. Personal highlights included his two-goal show in the 1974 FA Cup Final against Newcastle and, three years later, that scintillating swansong when he ran Bertie Vogts and Borussia Moenchengladbach ragged as Liverpool won the European Cup for the first time.

Sadly, but perhaps inevitably, there was bitterness on Merseyside when Keegan announced his decision to take his talents to Europe. Having been honest enough to give a full season's notice of his intention, he endured, with commendable dignity, the cooling of the Kop's ardour and perfidious jibes about his so-called greed. It even became fashionable to question his stature in the game and there were constant, slighting references to a 'manufactured' footballer, one who had reached the top by application rather than natural talent.

How short were the memories of such mealy-mouthed critics, and how blindly they lashed out at a man who had given no more than half a dozen below-par performances in as many years at Anfield, had captained England and was to go on to become European Footballer of the Year in two consecutive seasons. Wherever he went thereafter, including Southampton and Newcastle (whom he was destined to transform as their manager in the 1990s before enduring a turbulent return more than a decade later), he gave princely value for money. A Pele or a Maradona he was not, but in his own way Kevin Keegan was one of the greats.

JOSEPH KEVIN KEEGAN

BORN: Armthorpe, Yorkshire, 14 February 1951.

HONOURS: European Cup 76/7. UEFA Cup 72/3, 75/6. League Championship 72/3, 75/6, 76/7. FA Cup 73/4. 63 England caps (72-82). FWA Footballer of the Year 76. PFA Player of the Year 82. European Footballer of the Year 78, 79.

OTHER CLUBS: Scunthorpe United 68/9-70/1 (124, 18); SV Hamburg 77/8-79/80; Southampton 80/1-81/2 (68, 37); Newcastle United 82/3-83/4 (78, 48).

MANAGER: Newcastle United (92-97), Fulham (chief operating officer 98-99), England (99-00), Manchester City (01-05), Newcastle United (08).

GAMES 323
GOALS 100

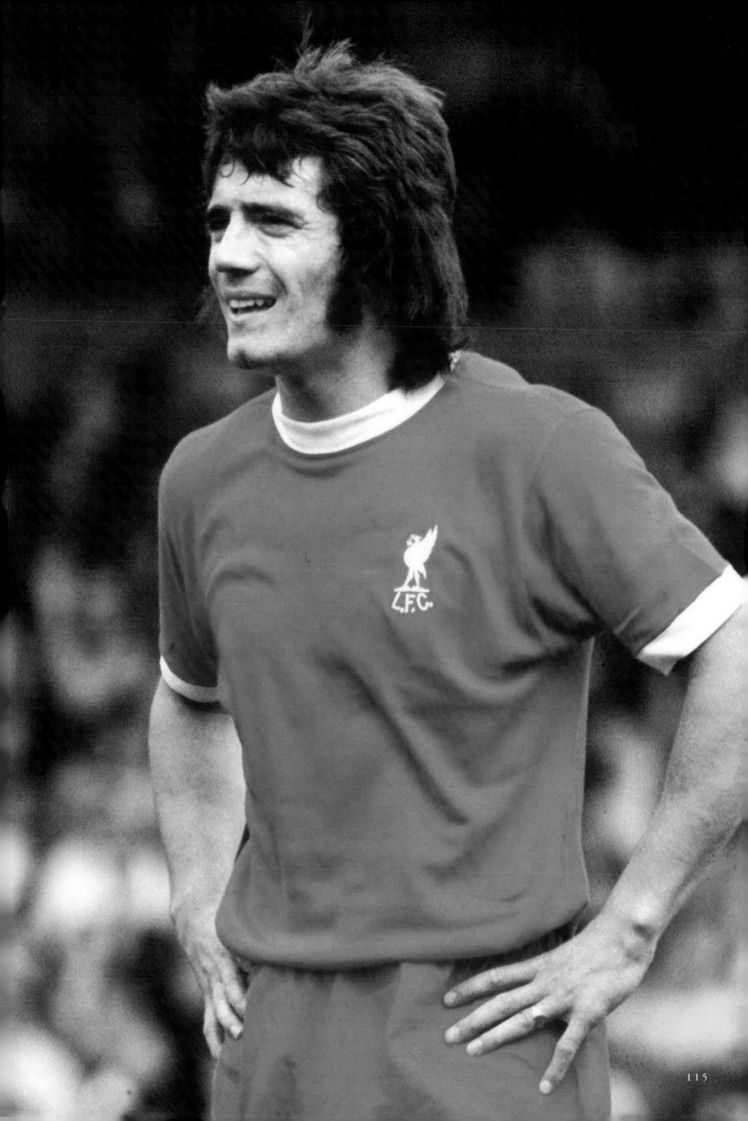

RAY KENNEDY

1974/75 → 1981/82

Ray Kennedy was a rare bird, a deceptively talented individual whose inimitable contribution to one of Liverpool's most imperious sides made a nonsense of any attempt to pigeon-hole him. Certainly, glib descriptions of a powerful midfielder, which he became at Anfield after years as a successful striker with Arsenal, failed dismally to do justice to his full, subtle range of distinctive abilities.

When Bill Shankly signed Kennedy for £180,000 in the summer of 1974 – his last act as the Reds' boss – he was rescuing a slightly overweight centre-forward, still eight days short of his 23rd birthday, who had seemingly lost his way after playing a crucial part in the Gunners' League and FA Cup double of 1970/71.

The newcomer found himself in at the dawn of the Paisley era and, despite an irritating injury which kept him out of the season's first four League games, impressed Bob enough to oust John Toshack from his front-running role. There followed a sequence of 24 games in which Kennedy managed ten goals, but then he lost his place as the Welshman was recalled in a bid to find a winning blend.

The turning point, however, was not far away. Towards the end of the campaign Paisley began experimenting with the former Highbury man in a deep-lying position behind the Keegan-Toshack spearhead, and liked what he saw. By November 1975 Kennedy was installed on the left of midfield where he was to help Liverpool lift ten major honours in six years of almost uninterrupted triumph.

His value to the team was incalculable, his footballing qualities legion, and if he didn't quite catch the eye like a Souness or a McDermott, Ray had much to offer the connoisseur. Still not the most athletic of figures, though more streamlined than on his arrival, he boasted a delicate touch for such a big man; he was adept at shielding the ball, a legacy of his days as a striker; and his distribution was intelligent, swift and decisive.

Like all top players who are short of pace, Kennedy read the game shrewdly and often he changed the emphasis of an attack with a sweeping crossfield pass, but perhaps his deadliest attribute was a knack of lurking unobtrusively on the left flank before making a late run into the box to finish off a move at the far post.

In the most important matches, habitually he spent the early minutes lying deeper than usual, doing a containing job before allowing his attacking flair to blossom as the game wore on, by which time unwary opponents had been cajoled into a false sense of security. This tendency was especially marked in European encounters, in which the England international contributed some of his most crucial strikes. An 83rd-minute away goal to upset Bayern Munich in the 1981 European Cup semi-final and a fierce second-half volley to turn the tide against Bruges when the Belgians were two up in the 1976 UEFA Cup Final are just a couple that remain sharp in the memory.

Ultimately squeezed out of the side by the youthful challenge of Ronnie Whelan in December 1982, Kennedy joined John Toshack's colony of former Reds at Swansea for only £20,000 less than his purchase price. A brief stint at Hartlepool preceded a spell as a publican and a coaching appointment at Sunderland, before it was revealed that he was suffering with Parkinson's disease, which he has battled for many years with characteristic courage.

Shanks, as usual, encapsulated the essence of a footballer better than most when he said of Ray: 'He played in no-man's land in a world of his own, but he gave the team balance. He had style and he reminded me of Matt Busby. Ray Kennedy was some player.'

RAYMOND KENNEDY

BORN Seaton Delaval, Northumberland, 28 July 1951.
HONOURS European Cup 76/7, 77/8, 80/1. UEFA Cup 75/6. League Championship 75/6, 76/7, 78/9, 79/80, 81/2. League Cup 80/1. 17 England caps (76-80).
OTHER CLUBS Arsenal 69/70-73/4 (158, 53); Swansea City 81/2-83/4 (42, 2); Hartlepool United 83/4 (23, 3).

| GAMES | 390 (3) |
| GOALS | 72 |

117

TOMMY SMITH

1962/63 → 1977/78

If the spirit of the Anfield Reds ever took on human form it would probably tackle like a two-legged ton of bricks, bark orders in broadest Scouse and answer to the name of Tommy Smith. Here was a man, born in the shadow of his beloved ground, who served Liverpool for 18 years and grew to be the very personification of his club. He will go down in folklore as one of the hardest men the game has known – and he was – but to write him off as a mere destroyer is a mistake. Oh yes, Tommy could play a bit, too.

He made his debut at home to Birmingham in May 1963 as a deputy for injured right-half Gordon Milne, but it was in an Anfield encounter with Anderlecht in November the next year that he made his first major impact. Wearing a number-ten shirt, he operated as an extra defender, confusing the Belgians as Liverpool won comfortably.

Instantly Smith became an integral part of Bill Shankly's first great side, initially combative in midfield before moving into central defence where he could more easily make light of a comparative lack of pace. 'Think of yourself as Ron Yeats' right leg,' Shanks told him, and he developed into a trusty buttress of Division One's most formidable rearguard.

Smith, a rumoured transfer target of Manchester United in his reserve days, was a confident, aggressive ball-winner whose distribution could rarely be faulted. His game, which always boasted more skill than he was given credit for, matured rapidly as he contributed vigorously to the 1965 Wembley victory over Leeds and the ensuing Championship campaign.

As the influence of better-known players waned with age, Smith's authority grew ever more marked and he was the obvious choice to succeed Yeats as captain in March 1970. Taking over a team in the throes of transformation, he was an inspiration, constantly driving his team-mates to greater efforts, not shrinking from the task even if off form personally, and standing up for their rights in off-the-field dealings.

Tommy relished the responsibility and in 1970/71 he delivered some of the finest performances of his life, being pipped only narrowly as Footballer of the Year by Frank McLintock and winning his sole England cap.

That season he led Liverpool to the FA Cup Final, which was lost to Arsenal, before going on to a then-unique double of the Championship and the UEFA Cup in 1972/73. His days as skipper were numbered, though, and he lost the job to Emlyn Hughes following a confrontation with Bill Shankly over being dropped in November 1973.

After nearly joining Stoke, Smith returned to the side at right-back in place of the sidelined Chris Lawler and helped to ensure a steady flow of trophies until, troubled by knee problems and with the team prospering in his absence, in early 1977 he announced that retirement was imminent.

How an injury to Phil Thompson changed all that! The old warhorse found himself back in central defensive harness to win a title medal, face Manchester United in the FA Cup Final and, most stirring of all, head the goal against Borussia Moenchengladbach in Rome that effectively won Liverpool their first European Cup. Fired anew with ambition, Smith stayed for another term and would have played in a second European Cup Final if he hadn't dropped a pick-axe on his foot.

After that the Reds offered him a one-year contract while John Toshack came up with a better deal at Swansea, which he accepted. Smith, who was to make a brief Anfield return as a coach, left in the knowledge that no one had ever fought more fiercely in the Liverpool cause. As one ex-opponent, himself no six-stone weakling, put it: 'There's a lot of very hard men – and then there's Tommy Smith!'

THOMAS SMITH

BORN Liverpool, 5 April 1945.
HONOURS European Cup 76/7. UEFA Cup 72/3, 75/6.
League Championship 65/6, 72/3, 75/6, 76/7. FA Cup 64/5, 73/4.
1 England cap (71).
OTHER CLUBS Swansea City 78/9 (36, 2).

GAMES 637 (2)
GOALS 48

PHIL NEAL

1974/75 → 1985/86

Phil Neal will take his place in soccer history as the man who combined two of the game's most priceless commodities, success and consistency, to a hitherto unknown degree. In the nine seasons between 1975/76 and 1983/84 it took Liverpool 538 games to win 16 major honours; Neal was absent from the starting line-up just four times. His haul of medals for the Reds is rivalled only by that of Alan Hansen, who missed more matches through injury and needed a little longer – without actually dragging his feet! – to assemble his collection.

A large slice of the credit for Neal's phenomenal record must go to Bob Paisley, who made the full-back his first signing when he handed Northampton Town a cheque for £66,000 in October 1974. It wasn't a case of plucking a teenage prodigy from the League's lower reaches as, despite the occasional flicker of interest from bigger clubs, Neal's six years of endeavour for the Cobblers had hardly secured him a national reputation. In Fourth Division circles, however, he was known for his consistency . . .

After arriving at Anfield it wasn't long before he was given a first-team chance, initially as deputy left-back for the injured Alec Lindsay in a goalless derby at Goodison Park, then came a short stint standing in for Tommy Smith on the right. Neal's calm, assured performances were enough to convince the manager of his ability and he became a fixture in the side. For 18 months he alternated between the two full-back roles before settling on the right, partnering first Joey Jones and then, more enduringly, Alan Kennedy as Liverpool continued to gratify English football's most gargantuan appetite for trophies.

Neal's attributes, though immeasurably valuable to his team's cause, were of the unspectacular variety. He was not a fearsome tackler, preferring to jockey an attacker into a corner before perhaps nudging the ball away or forcing a rash pass. An intelligent positional player, he was masterful at denying space to wingers who often had the edge on him for pace but who rarely gave him a chasing – Leeds' Eddie Gray was one man who did so occasionally – and he was strong enough in the air to be an emergency centre-half.

Excellent though Neal's defensive work was, the constructive side of his game was even more outstanding. His distribution was immaculate, whether playing the ball in neat triangles with his midfielders or finding the front-men with long, fluent passes down the inside-right channel, and he was adept at stealing forward to deliver crisp crosses.

The majority of his goals came from spot-kicks – his most famous sealed the 1977 European Cup Final victory over Borussia Moenchengladbach – but also there were several vital run-of-play strikes, the most notable being the prod which set Joe Fagan's side on the way to triumph in another European Cup Final, against Roma in 1984.

Dependable under pressure and an on-field talker who was constantly cajoling colleagues to greater efforts, Neal was well suited to succeed Graeme Souness as skipper for 1984/85 and he carried the responsibility impressively, although at 33 he was never going to be a long-term leader. Accordingly, half-way through the following term, reportedly mortified by the board's preference of Kenny Dalglish over himself as the next Anfield boss, he left to become player-manager of Bolton Wanderers.

Whatever the circumstances involving his exit, the playing achievements of Phil Neal, the most-capped England right-back of all time until his record was usurped by Manchester United's Gary Neville, will stand forever as a monument to dedication, fitness and not a little skill.

PHILIP GEORGE NEAL	
BORN	Irchester, Northamptonshire, 29 February 1951.
HONOURS	European Cup 76/7, 77/8, 80/1, 83/4. UEFA Cup 75/6.
	League Championship 75/6, 76/7, 78/9, 79/80, 81/2, 82/3, 83/4, 85/6.
	League Cup 80/1, 81/2, 82/3, 83/4. 50 England caps (76-83).
OTHER CLUBS	Northampton Town 68/9-74/5 (186, 29); Bolton Wanderers 85/6-88/9 (64, 3).
MANAGER	Bolton Wanderers (85-92); Coventry City (93-95); Cardiff City (96); Manchester City as caretaker (96).

GAMES 647 (2)
GOALS 60

JOEY JONES

1975/76 → 1977/78

Who ate the Frogs' legs, made the Swiss roll and topped the lot by munching Gladbach? Why, none other than Joey Jones, of course, that tattooed tiger of a left-back taken to the hearts of Kopites like few of their heroes before or since.

Jones, who grew up as a Liverpool fanatic and was as proud to wear the red of Anfield as that of his beloved Wales, enjoyed an affectionate rapport with the fans who loved his zealous approach, and they coined the colourful catchphrase for a banner to immortalise his spirited displays against the French, Swiss and West German champions on the way to lifting the 1977 European Cup.

He moved to Liverpool from Wrexham for £110,000 in July 1975, yet he was startled to discover that he wasn't to be granted the bedding-in period in the reserves which, in that era, Liverpool accorded to most recruits from the lower divisions. Instead he was pitchforked straight into senior action to replace the out-of-form Alec Lindsay, and he made an immediate impact with travelling Reds' supporters, thanks to a lung-bursting dash to clear off his goal-line on debut against Queen's Park Rangers at Loftus Road.

Soon Jones was delivering the clenched-fist salute that was to become his trademark, and his heart swelled with pride as whole terraces returned the gesture. For all that, though, his early displays indicated rather too many rough edges for immediate settlement in the top flight, so Phil Neal switched to left-back, Tommy Smith came in on the right and Joey was out.

That disappointment, however, was merely a prelude to his finest season; 1976/77 saw him claim a regular place in the side which took Europe's top prize, retained the Championship and narrowly lost the FA Cup Final to Manchester United.

Throughout that glorious campaign Jones played as though his life depended on it. Possessed with boundless enthusiasm, he was combative in the air and formidable in the tackle, though occasionally there was a tendency to commit himself to reckless challenges.

But there were more serious weaknesses; his distribution was often wayward and offered a sorry comparison to the silky skills of Lindsay, and his reading of the game was at times rudimentary. Thus it was no real surprise when Joey lost his place during the following term as Bob Paisley shuffled the Reds' defence to accommodate the increasingly impressive Alan Hansen.

In September 1978 Jones returned to Wrexham for a paltry £20,000 but he was not allowed to leave Anfield without a lovely spontaneous gesture from his personal fan club, the presentation of that famous 'Frogs' legs' banner. It was a keepsake which, he always maintained, meant even more to him than his European Cup medal.

Though that unforgettable night in Rome would remain the pinnacle of the Jones career, his days in the big time were not yet over. John Neal, his former boss at the Racecourse Ground, took him to Chelsea where he was doted on by the Shed as he had once been adored by the Kop, and Joey helped the Londoners win promotion to the First Division.

Next came a brief spell at Huddersfield, during which he overhauled Ivor Allchurch to become his country's most-capped player, an honour he retained for several years until his total of 72 was overtaken in turn by Peter Nicholas. Finally, and fittingly, Joey Jones put in a third stint with his first club, going on to serve the Red Dragons as a coach and to be tagged 'the unofficial Lord Mayor of Wrexham'. This time the doughty Welsh warrior was home for good.

JOSEPH PATRICK JONES

BORN Llandudno, Caernarvonshire, 4 March 1955.
HONOURS European Cup 76/7. League Championship 75/6, 76/7. 72 Wales caps (76-86).
OTHER CLUBS Wrexham 72/3-74/5 (98, 2) and 78/9-82/3 (146, 6); Chelsea 82/3-84/5 (78, 2); Huddersfield Town 85/6-86/7 (68, 3); Wrexham 87/8-91/2 (132, 11).

GAMES 100
GOALS 3

JIMMY CASE

1974/75 → 1980/81

It's a rare player who reaches his peak after leaving Liverpool but Jimmy Case was, after all, no ordinary performer. He bade farewell to the Reds at the age of 27, gave three and a half years' commendable but hardly remarkable service to Brighton, and then bloomed luxuriantly for Southampton in the play-maker's role denied to him at Anfield by the majesty of Graeme Souness.

Was he allowed to leave Merseyside too soon or was the change as good as a rest? The question will always hang over the Case career, but should not he allowed to detract from six seasons of stirring achievements under Bob Paisley

Jimmy, a £500 capture from non-League South Liverpool, made his debut at Anfield against Queen's Park Rangers in April 1975 in an attacking role wide on the right, but it was not until seven months later that his explosive talents earned a settled run in the team at the expense of midfielder Brian Hall.

He marked his new stature with a rousing hat-trick at home to Slask Wroclaw of Poland in the UEFA Cup and then, having also scored against Dynamo Dresden in the quarter-final, exerted a crucial influence on the home leg of the final against FC Bruges.

He had been omitted from the starting line-up in favour of David Fairclough but, with the Reds two down, was called on as substitute for John Toshack and immediately galvanised the side into three-goal retaliation. Rampaging ferociously down the right flank, Case unsettled the hitherto calm Belgian defence, creating several clear-cut chances and chipping in with the equaliser himself

Liverpool's vibrant, baby-faced rookie finished his first senior campaign with title and UEFA Cup medals and was clearly a prospect of prodigious potential. His value was twofold: in attack his pace, thrust and howitzer-style shooting offered a savage threat, while in deeper positions his lusty tackling, crisp distribution and general full-blooded vitality were a productive combination.

Yet despite such an impressive array of assets, Case's place in the side during the treble-hunting campaign which followed was not a formality. Until the spring of 1977, when he slotted in on the right of Terry McDermott, the two had fought a well-matched battle for the number-eight shirt. Come the run-in, Jimmy was on his mettle, playing an enterprising part in the League and European Cup triumphs and winning plaudits as the Reds' best player in the FA Cup Final against Manchester United. Though a Wembley loser, he had the consolation of scoring the game's finest goal, swivelling on the 18-yard line to beat Alex Stepney with a sweetly-struck half-volley.

Over the next three seasons his name was seldom missing from Liverpool's team-sheet and with Souness, McDermott and Ray Kennedy formed one of the world's most effective, and attractive, midfield units. But in 1980/81 Case was ousted by the industrious Sammy Lee and spent most of his time on the substitute's bench, clearly an unacceptable situation for a 27-year-old of his calibre.

With no likelihood of a swift recall, he was sold to Brighton for £350,000 and, in his second season with the Seagulls, had the huge satisfaction of returning to Anfield to score the goal which knocked his former team-mates out of the FA Cup. When, aged 30, he moved to the Dell for a token £25,000, Case's career looked to be petering out; half a decade and some 200 League matches later he was playing better than ever, maturity having revealed unsuspected depths of craft and insight. As his manager at the time, Chris Nicholl, put it: 'If the game is a language, then undoubtedly Jimmy is a professor.'

Even then he wasn't ready to retire, the Case history encompassing five more clubs until 1995, when a little matter of a suspected broken neck convinced him to step aside. A few days later Jimmy, his fears of serious injury laid to rest, put aside the temptation of a playing comeback but returned to the game for a demanding stint as boss of troubled Brighton.

	JAMES ROBERT CASE
BORN	Liverpool, 18 May 1954.
HONOURS	European Cup 76/7, 77/8, 80/1. UEFA Cup 75/6.
	League Championship 75/6, 76/7, 78/9, 79/80. League Cup: 80/1.
OTHER CLUBS	Brighton and Hove Albion 81/2-84/5 (127, 10); Southampton 84/5-90/1
	(215, 10); Bournemouth 91/2 (40, 1); Halifax Town 92/3 (21, 2);
	Wrexham 92/3 (4,0); Darlington 93/4 (1,0); Brighton 93/4-95/6 (32, 0).
MANAGER	Brighton (95-96).

GAMES	**244 (25)**
GOALS	46

TERRY McDERMOTT

1974/75 → 1982/83

There were suspicions during Terry McDermott's early days at Anfield that he was destined to be labelled as a £170,000 misfit; he became instead a creative inspiration in one of the Reds' most exhilarating combinations. At his irresistible best he was the free spirit in a beautifully balanced midfield quartet led by anchor man Graeme Souness, with Jimmy Case on the right flank and Ray Kennedy on the left. McDermott's roving commission gave full rein to a potent cocktail of vision and stamina which prised open many of the world's tightest defences.

It was not always thus. Bob Paisley signed the Liverpool-born schemer from Newcastle in November 1974 after he had impressed against his home-town club in that year's FA Cup Final. McDermott went straight into the side but failed to settle as the new manager experimented in an attempt to emulate the success of the Shankly era. When the trophies started rolling in, largely without Terry's assistance – Paisley's Reds won the Championship and UEFA Cup in 1975/76 – it seemed likely that he would be written off as a mistake, albeit an expensive one, and unloaded.

But Paisley kept faith with the wiry ex-Magpie and when, in the following campaign, Liverpool were pushing for a squad-sapping treble, McDermott began to blossom. After vying for a place with Case, whose stern tackling he could never remotely emulate, for most of the season, he became established in the spring and played a memorable part in a tumultuous run-in which saw the title and the European Cup end up at Anfield but the FA Cup slip away to Old Trafford.

McDermott was especially dangerous when running from deep positions and was adept at arriving late in the penalty area where his finishing, by turns powerful and subtle, could be deadly. His most valuable goal that term – and of his career, come to that – was the opener against Borussia Moenchengladbach in Rome where the Reds lifted Europe's top prize so gloriously. He ghosted, typically, down the inside-right channel to take a pass from Steve Heighway before curling the ball clinically past the German 'keeper. A month earlier there had been an even more mouth-watering piece of opportunism when Terry had spotted Everton's David Lawson off his line and chipped an exquisite goal in the FA Cup semi-final at Maine Road.

But the McDermott zenith was not reached until the arrival of Souness in 1978. The Scot's all-pervading influence on central midfield gave the newly-capped England international the liberty he needed to express his talents fully. A natural athlete, McDermott made runs to all corners of the pitch, often acting as a decoy and creating space for colleagues to exploit, and when he did gain possession his instinctive control and incisive passing ability usually made the most of it.

He remained in his pomp for three years – in 1980 he was the first man to win awards from the football writers and his fellow players in the same season – and two incidents against Spurs during this period emphasise his dual value, as team man and individual. In September 1978 at Anfield he started and finished a flowing end-to-end move that capped a 7-0 annihilation, and 18 months later at White Hart Lane he decided an FA Cup quarter-final with a spontaneous flighted shot from near the corner flag.

Despite winning title and League Cup medals in 1981/82, McDermott seemed to lose impetus and returned to Tyneside to help Kevin Keegan effect a Newcastle revival. That particular renaissance proved to be of the short-term variety. But when the two men were reunited at St James' Park a decade later, with Terry as assistant to manager Kevin, they transformed the Magpies into one of the most entertaining and dynamic sides of the 1990s.

TERENCE McDERMOTT

BORN   Kirkby, Liverpool, 8 December 1951.

HONOURS   European Cup 76/7, 77/8, 80/1. League Championship 76/7, 78/9, 79/80, 81/2. League Cup 80/1, 81/2. 25 England caps (77-82). FWA Footballer of the Year 80. PFA Footballer of the Year 80.

OTHER CLUBS   Bury 69/70-72/3 (90, 8); Newcastle United 72/3-74/5 (56, 6) and 82/3-83/4 (74, 12); Cork City 84/5; Apoel, Cyprus.

GAMES	317 (12)
GOALS	81

DAVID FAIRCLOUGH

1975/76 → 1982/83

The name of David Fairclough will forever occupy a cherished niche in Reds folklore, and deservedly so. That said, it is difficult to deny that he was at his most effective in a number-12 shirt, hardly a palatable circumstance for the young, ambitious striker to stomach. Fairclough loathed the much-touted 'Supersub' tag, feeling it implied an inability to create a major impact over 90 minutes, yet he was stuck with it for life.

He caused his first sensation when his goals in the spring of 1976 turned the title race with Queen's Park Rangers and Manchester United in Liverpool's favour. Coming on as a substitute, he clinched the points against Burnley, Everton and Stoke City at Anfield as well as netting in games which he actually started at Carrow Road and Maine Road.

The decisive strike in the Merseyside derby was especially momentous, arriving only two minutes from the end of a hitherto goalless encounter and involving a spellbinding dance past five or six opponents. As a stunned but delighted team-mate put it at the time: 'I don't think David himself knew what he was going to do, so the Everton lads couldn't have had a clue!'

Certainly, media and supporters were ecstatic; if this engaging newcomer could cause so much havoc at the tail-end of matches, they reasoned, what on earth could he do if he was there at the kick-off?

Fairclough, also known as the 'Bionic Carrot' in reference to his flaming hair and blistering pace, elevated his reputation to yet dizzier heights a year later when he notched what was arguably the most important goal in his club's history to that date. Near the end of the European Cup quarter-final at Anfield, St Etienne held the advantage of an away goal; the Reds had to score or perish and on came Fairclough for John Toshack.

Six minutes from time he received a pass on the left from Ray Kennedy, dribbled past three defenders and slipped the ball under the advancing 'keeper. He was practically canonised on Merseyside and Bob Paisley used him from the beginning of games with increasing frequency. However, over seven seasons in Liverpool's senior squad, only twice would his League starts reach double figures, with 26 in 1977/78 by far his highest.

Though that term was his most successful season overall – his European Cup Final appearance against Bruges was a personal highlight – it became disturbingly obvious that David was fractionally short of the all-round quality demanded at the top club level.

The England under-21 international did have an unorthodox knack of going past opponents, often stumbling with apparent clumsiness and getting rebounds from their legs, and continued to snatch the occasional important goal. But his overall form was patchy and over a full 90 minutes he tended to drift out of the action, seeming to lack both stamina and concentration.

As new players arrived at Anfield, Fairclough slipped out of contention, though he remained a paradox to the last: one minute displaying a gloriously unexpected touch, the next fluffing a simple pass. After leaving the Reds he failed to settle elsewhere and could be described as a player of whom the wider public, perhaps beguiled by heavily edited TV highlights, expected a little too much.

For all that, though, the very mention of St Etienne makes the eyes of every 1970s Kopite light up; David Fairclough made a lot of people deliriously happy and he will always be loved for it.

DAVID FAIRCLOUGH

BORN — Liverpool, 5 January 1957.
HONOURS — European Cup 77/8. UEFA Cup 75/6. League Championship 75/6, 76/7, 79/80.
OTHER CLUBS — Toronto Blizzard, Canada 82; Lucerne, Switzerland 83/4-84/5; Norwich City 84/5 (2, 0); Oldham Athletic 85/6 (17, 1); Beveren SK, Belgium, 86/7-88/9; Tranmere Rovers 89/90 (14, 1); Wigan Athletic 90/1 (7, 1).

GAMES 92 (62)
GOALS 55

DAVID JOHNSON

1976/77 → 1981/82

Reputations count for nothing at Anfield, as England centre-forward David Johnson discovered when he left Ipswich Town in August 1976 to become Liverpool's first £200,000 signing. During his initial two frustrating seasons with the Reds, neither international stature nor mammoth price tag was enough to guarantee him a regular place in the team. Not that Johnson, a chirpy, down-to-earth character, expected any favours; with characteristic grit he fought back to justify fully Bob Paisley's original faith, helping to assemble a prodigious collection of silverware and, for good measure, winning five further caps.

Merseyside-born Johnson checked in at Anfield, where he had once cheered his boyhood idols Roger Hunt and Ian St John, nine years after starting his career as an apprentice at Goodison Park. In fact, his delay in donning the red shirt would have been drastically reduced if either of Bill Shankly's bids to sign him in the early 1970s had paid off, but first Everton's Harry Catterick – who was adamant that no player of his would join the Blues' greatest rivals – and then Ipswich boss Bobby Robson rebuffed all overtures.

Having got their man at the third attempt, Liverpool pitched him straight into first-team action. There seemed no reason why Johnson would not be a hit; he was quick, skilful and unselfish, and his courageous approach, utterly refusing to be intimidated by the most physical of opponents, was guaranteed to endear him instantly to the Kop.

But the manager was blessed with a large and gifted squad and, in the course of his permutations, often David was the man to be left out. Not helped by a succession of niggling injuries, he managed only glimpses of his best form and, although he collected a title medal and figured in the FA Cup Final defeat by Manchester United, he missed out on European Cup glory

In 1977/78, with Keegan gone and Toshack soon to depart, it was hoped that a link with newcomer Kenny Dalglish would give the Johnson career renewed impetus, but frequently David Fairclough was chosen to play alongside the Scot and it was not until the spring that the ex-Ipswich striker began to look like his old self.

Then came bitter disappointment; with the European Cup campaign reaching a climax Johnson strained knee ligaments and was sidelined for the rest of the season. After beating FC Bruges in the final, sympathetic team-mates – who knew him as 'Doc' because his kit bag contained a remedy for most ailments – procured him a special medal from FIFA, but it was an unfulfilled, if typically determined David Johnson who prepared for 1978/79.

At last, however, his luck had changed. Given the luxury of two settled stints in harness, now he struck up a prosperous partnership with Dalglish which was to form the spearhead of one of the great Liverpool sides. After his lacklustre interlude, David was a revelation; his sharp control, work-rate and knack of taking up dangerous positions brought him 37 goals in 63 starts over two League campaigns and his comeback was fittingly crowned when he netted twice against Aston Villa at Anfield in May 1980 to seal a second successive Championship.

His scoring rate diminished in the following term and when a young fellow called Ian Rush came along, Johnson returned to his first club for £100,000. As the first man to score a derby winner for both Everton and Liverpool, he occupies a unique place in Merseyside folklore. But Anfield saw more of his prime than Goodison and it is as a Red, a title he wore with such pride, that Johnno will be best remembered.

DAVID EDWARD JOHNSON
BORN Liverpool, 23 October 1951.
HONOURS European Cup 80/1. League Championship 76/7, 78/9, 79/80, 81/2. 8 England caps (75-80).
OTHER CLUBS Everton 70/1-72/3 (50, 11); Ipswich Town 72/3-75/6 (137, 35); Everton 82/3-83/4 (40, 4); Barnsley on loan 83/4 (4, 1); Manchester City 83/4 (6, 1); Tulsa Roughnecks, USA, 84; Preston North End 84/5 (24, 3).

GAMES 177 (33)
GOALS 78

SAMMY LEE

1977/78 → 1985/86

Scouser Sammy Lee was the chunky bundle of energy whose skill and enthusiasm cut short the Reds career of Jimmy Case in its prime – only for his own Liverpool days to end in a similarly premature fashion.

Lee made his League debut as a substitute against Leicester City at Anfield in April 1978, scoring in a 3-2 victory, but was then stranded on the fringe of the side for the next two years. With such formidable opposition for a place – if Case seemed hard to dislodge it was hardly conceivable that he would oust Graeme Souness or Terry McDermott – his future seemed cloudy. Youngsters in that situation often fail to make the breakthrough, but Lee was made of stern stuff and in 1980/81 he displaced Case on the right side of midfield.

A buzzing support player and relentless marker, he endeared himself quickly to the fans with his never-say-die approach – on the Kop they reckoned the young Lee had the Liver Bird engraved on his heart – and he became a fixture in the team that won three successive Championships, two European Cups and four League Cups.

In some respects Sammy's play was reminiscent of Ian Callaghan's; he was a smooth passer, read the game well and had the ability to go past an opponent, though he lacked Cally's acceleration. His tackling, however, was fiercer than that of the great Anfield clubman and often he provided cover when full-back Phil Neal ventured forward. One of Lee's most valuable defensive contributions came against Roma in the 1984 European Cup Final as the Reds withstood periods of pressure before going on to win on penalties.

At the opposite end of the pitch his strike-rate was disappointing, especially as he possessed a potent shot – as demonstrated with a goal from a powerful free-kick on his England debut against Greece – and the fine touch to deliver the most tantalising of chips. But finding the net had never been his priority, and at the outset of 1984/85 Sammy Lee seemed set for many more seasons at the top; he was only 25, at the peak of his powers and an established international.

Sadly, it wasn't to be. Fitness problems and a loss of form conspired to shatter his confidence and, faced with the exuberant challenge of Craig Johnston, he faded out of contention. In August 1986 he left his beloved Merseyside for Queen's Park Rangers, but failed to settle and a year later headed for the sun with Osasuna of Spain. He performed creditably in the Spanish League, but in January 1990 he returned to England and signed for Southampton, where he linked up again with Jimmy Case.

After making little impact either at the Dell or Bolton's Burnden Park, the final port of call in his playing career, Sammy answered the summons from Graeme Souness to take over from Phil Thompson as Liverpool's reserve-team coach. Back where he had been happiest, the likeable Lee flourished in his new role, surviving the fall of Souness, then fitting seamlessly into the Roy Evans regime and taking on first-team duties.

Thereafter he became an integral part of Gerard Houllier's front-bench team and also earned rich praise for his invaluable work alongside successive England managers before becoming assistant to Sam Allardyce at Bolton. There followed a dispiriting six-month stint as boss of the Trotters until his sacking in August 2007, but his spiritual home remained at Anfield, and that's where he returned in 2008 as number-two to Rafael Benitez. Endlessly enthusiastic, hugely knowledgeable and popular with his starry charges, Sammy Lee was in his element as the Liverpool renaissance gathered pace.

	SAMUEL LEE	
BORN	Liverpool, 7 February 1959.	
HONOURS	European Cup 80/1, 83/4. League Championship 81/2, 82/3, 83/4, 85/6.	
	League Cup 80/1, 81/2, 82/3, 83/4. 14 England caps (82-84).	
OTHER CLUBS	Queen's Park Rangers 86/7 (30, 0); Osasuna, Spain, 87/8-88/9;	
	Southampton 89/90 (2, 0); Bolton Wanderers 90/1 (4, 0).	
MANAGER	Bolton Wanderers (07).	

GAMES	283 (7)
GOALS	19

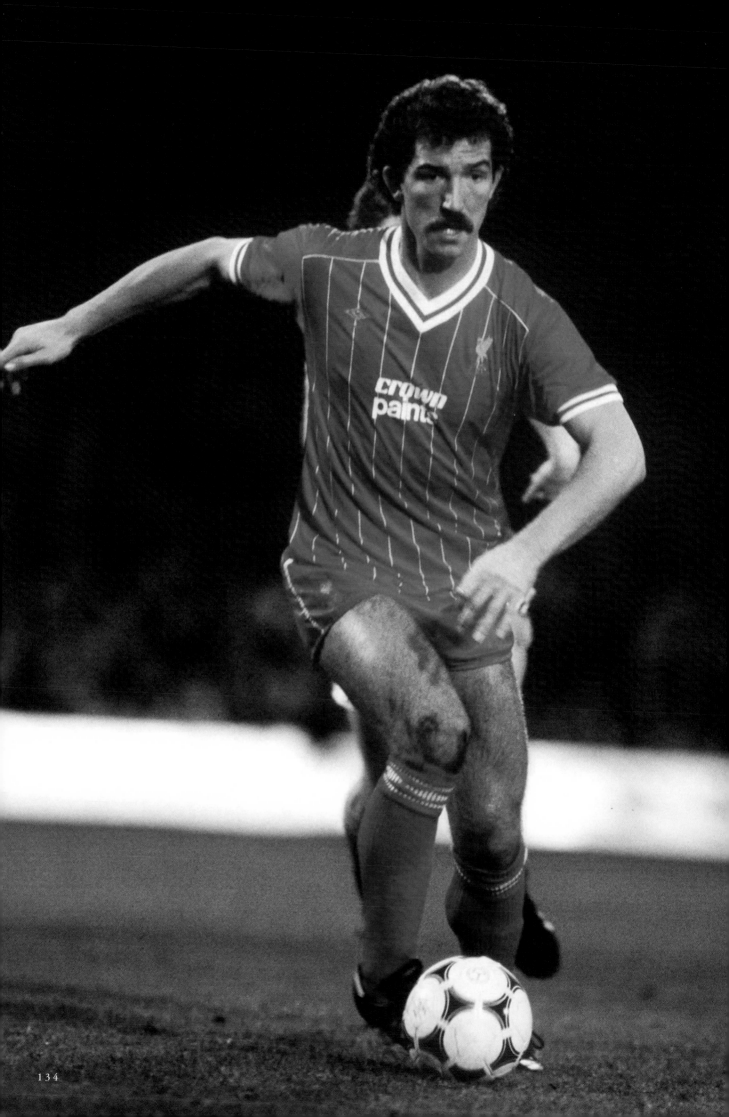

GRAEME SOUNESS

1977/78 → 1983/84

There can hardly have been a more all-pervading influence in the middle of a football field than that of Graeme Souness. In his pomp he was the emperor of Anfield, a dead-eyed dictator of all that came his way. He was one of the few British players of the 1980s to merit world-class status, but perhaps the greatest tribute to the lethal Souness combination of the devastatingly skilful and the crunchingly physical is that when he left for Italy in 1984 he was actually missed.

When the likes of Kevin Keegan and Ian Rush moved on, and even when Kenny Dalglish forsook the red shirt for the manager's tracksuit, Liverpool merely shuffled the pack, changed gear and carried on with the business of winning trophies. The Scottish international play-maker's departure, however, left a void which took a full season to fill.

Few would have predicted such an illustrious career for the 17-year-old rookie when, after signing for Spurs as an outstanding schoolboy he failed to settle in the south and left for Middlesbrough having spent only 26 minutes in the White Hart Lane first team. At Ayresome Park he began to realise his potential and looked every inch a star of the future just waiting for a wider stage.

That stage, of course, was Anfield and immediately after Bob Paisley signed him in January 1978 for £352,000 – then a record deal between Football League clubs – Souness began to hint at the riches to come. In his Reds debut at West Bromwich he scarcely misplaced a pass and settled quickly to become the hub of a midfield which already contained Terry McDermott, Jimmy Case and Ray Kennedy.

Souness' first taste of glory with his new club came four months after his arrival, when his incisive through-ball created the winner for Dalglish in the European Cup Final against FC Bruges. In the campaigns which followed, his dominance mushroomed as he orchestrated some of the most compelling football ever served up by a Liverpool side, spearing passes to all corners of the pitch and tackling with an implacable ferocity which at times bordered on the brutal.

Tottenham felt the Souness bite in March 1982 when he came on as substitute – he was returning after a back injury – with the Reds two goals down in a match dominated thus far by the strength of Graham Roberts and company. The abrasive number-12 soon made his mark, and the final score was 2-2.

Graeme supplemented his creative and ball-winning talents with occasional displays of potent finishing, none more emphatic than the thunderous volley which screamed past Paddy Roche into the Manchester United net at Anfield in February 1978, though his swivelling drive which beat Everton in the 1984 League Cup Final replay was even more significant.

Was Souness the complete player? Well, he lacked pace, though the side's pattern of play rendered the defect irrelevant, and for a man standing only an inch short of 6ft he was poor in the air. But such a trifle paled into nothingness compared with his overall contribution which, after a wretched team showing at home to Manchester City on Boxing Day 1981, increased still further when he replaced Phil Thompson as captain.

In his 29 months in charge Souness led Liverpool to three successive League titles, three League Cups and one European Cup, to become the most successful skipper in the club's history, forcibly demanding – and usually getting – the highest standards.

In June 1984 he made a £650,000 move to Sampdoria in Italy, where his brand of play was appreciated avidly, and he prospered there for two years before returning to Britain to have an even more significant effect on Glasgow Rangers than he had exerted on Liverpool.

'Suey' – a man held more in awe than affection by most fans – was once again stamping his authority on one of football's greatest institutions, though turbulent times awaited.

In due course, there would be a second coming at Anfield which would prove as traumatic as his first had been triumphant. More of that later; for now, it would he monstrously unjust if Graeme Souness' managerial tribulations were allowed to obscure his sheer majesty as a footballer.

	GRAEME JAMES SOUNESS
BORN	Edinburgh, 6 May 1953.
HONOURS	European Cup 77/8, 80/1, 83/4. League Championship 78/9, 79/80, 81/2, 82/3, 83/4.
	League Cup 80/1, 81/2, 82/3, 83/4. 54 Scotland caps (74-86).
OTHER CLUBS	Middlesbrough 72/3-77/8 (176, 22); Sampdoria, Italy, 84/5-85/6;
	Glasgow Rangers 86/7-89/90 (50, 3).
MANAGER	Glasgow Rangers (86-91); Liverpool (91-94); Galatasaray, Turkey, (95-96);
	Southampton (96-97); Torino, Italy, (97); Benfica, Portugal, (97-99);
	Blackburn Rovers (00-04); Newcastle United (04-06).

GAMES	357 (2)
GOALS	56

ALAN HANSEN

1977/78 → 1989/90

Alan Hansen is not a flamboyant man. If he were, if his football had exuded fire instead of ice, and he had greeted triumph with a swagger rather than his customary unassuming shrug, he would have received a more generous measure of the public acclaim which was his inalienable due as the outstanding British defender of the 1980s.

But no matter if his immaculate skills rarely earned the tabloid headlines. Hansen can be content that no one in the game, with the mysterious exception of successive Scottish team managers, undervalued his colossal contribution to 13 seasons of almost uninterrupted Anfield glory as he ploughed his elegant furrow at the heart of the Reds defence.

The £100,000 signing of the tall, spindly centre-back from Partick Thistle in May 1977 was arguably Bob Paisley's most canny excursion into the transfer market. In the subsequent campaign, a handful of appearances deputising for the injured Phil Thompson made it amply clear that the pale, dark-haired youngster was an inspired long-term investment, even if the characteristic calm that was later to be hailed as one of his supreme assets set off tremors of apprehension on the Kop.

Fans not familiar with the Hansen trademark of unflappability under pressure would gape as an apparently casual Alan would dribble his way out of the most perilous situation. Occasionally he would be caught in possession but, his confidence increasing as he replaced Emlyn Hughes as Thompson's regular partner in 1978/79, such errors grew so infrequent as to become collectors' items.

As a new decade dawned, Hansen matured into a well-nigh matchless performer, his cool approach so much a speciality that if he found touch it was construed as wild panic. An instinctive ability to read the game provided the platform for his more obvious skills and offset an apparent lack of pace, or was that merely an optical illusion due to the customary calm deliberation of his movement? Whatever, not many opponents showed him a clean pair of heels, although Gary Lineker managed it in the first half of the 1986 FA Cup Final.

Having won the ball, probably by an intelligent interception, invariably Hansen made the time and space to use it effectively, usually laying it off with the utmost precision. Rarely was a defender blessed with silkier distribution; for example, the chipped pass which tore open the Manchester United defence and enabled Steve McMahon to set up a John Aldridge goal at Old Trafford in November 1987 would have done credit to any play-maker. Alternatively he would embark on one of those imperious sallies deep into opposition territory, with all the magisterial dignity of a ship in full sail, offering his side an extra attacking dimension.

Of course, the more mundane tasks were not beyond Hansen. He was efficient both in the air and the tackle, though his economical, unobtrusive style meant that seldom did he seem stretched; certainly, it was unusual for him to land on his backside. An even temperament – Joe Jordan, in the 1979 FA Cup semi-final, was one of the few men to rattle him – made him an ideal choice to replace Phil Neal as captain in October 1985 and his leadership played a vital part in that season's League and FA Cup double.

Throughout an Anfield career which saw Hansen thrive in successive partnerships with Thompson, Mark Lawrenson, Gary Gillespie and Glenn Hysen and brought him 16 major honours, he often suffered knee trouble, but it was not until 1988/89 that he endured a lengthy lay-off.

After his retirement, aged 35 in 1990, there were persistent rumours linking him with the Liverpool managerial seat vacated so dramatically by his friend, Kenny Dalglish. But he had witnessed at first hand the personal sacrifices demanded by the job, and he opted instead for a quieter life as a BBC soccer pundit. As cool and decisive in the studio as once he had been on the field, Alan Hansen became more of a household name by talking amiably about the game than ever he did by playing it so majestically.

ALAN DAVID HANSEN	
BORN	Alloa, Clackmannanshire, 13 June 1955.
HONOURS	European Cup 77/8, 80/1, 83/4. League Championship 78/9, 79/80, 81/2, 82/3, 83/4, 85/6, 87/8, 89/90. FA Cup 85/6, 88/9. League Cup 80/1, 82/3, 83/4. 26 Scotland caps (79-87).
OTHER CLUBS	Partick Thistle 73/4-76/7 (86, 6).

GAMES 616 (4)
GOALS 13

RICHARD MONEY

1980/81

When Liverpool paid Fulham £300,000 for England 'B' and under-21 international Richard Money and promptly installed him in the reserves, it was no surprise to seasoned Anfield-watchers. It seemed inevitable that the Reds had signed up another promising youngster who would serve his time in the Central League before emerging a top-grade performer, as the likes of Ray Clemence, Larry Lloyd and Alan Hansen had done before him. Sadly for Money, the system was not infallible.

In his first term as a Red he made reasonable progress, twice deputising in the centre of defence – his favoured position – for Hansen and even managing, briefly, to oust Alan Kennedy at left-back. A classy operator who was strong in the air and comfortable on the ball, Money hinted at a big-match temperament with sound displays in the successful second legs of two semi-finals, away to Bayern Munich in the European Cup and at home to Manchester City in the League Cup.

But Hansen's resurgence in form and the arrival in August 1981 of Mark Lawrenson effectively closed the first-team door, and Money joined Luton for £100,000. He never fulfilled his early potential and eventually returned to his first club, Scunthorpe, before becoming a coach, then a manager. He took over Newcastle's youth academy in 2008.

RICHARD MONEY
BORN Lowestoft, Suffolk, 13 October 1955.
OTHER CLUBS Scunthorpe United 73/4-77/8 (173, 4); Fulham 77/8-79/80 (106, 3); Derby County on loan 81/2 (5, 0); Luton Town 81/2-82/3 (44, 1); Portsmouth 83/4-85/6 (17 0); Scunthorpe United 85/6-88/9 (100, 0).
MANAGER Scunthorpe United (93-94); AIK, Sweden, (03-04); Vasteras, Sweden, (04); Newcastle United Jets, Australia, (05-06); Walsall (06-08).

| GAMES | 15 (2) |
| GOALS | 0 |

HOWARD GAYLE

1980/81

According to the Kop, Howard Gayle was the quickest thing on two legs – and Bayern Munich would certainly not disagree. The West Germans fell victim to the young winger's blistering speed in the second leg of the 1981 European Cup semi-final when he was brought on as substitute for the injured Kenny Dalglish. The Reds, hunting an away goal to reach the final (eventually supplied by Ray Kennedy), sent on Gayle to run at the Bayern defenders and his pace had them floundering. Ultimately they were reduced to fouling him and when the enthusiastic rookie showed signs of retaliating he, in turn, was replaced by Jimmy Case.

It had been a performance of raw promise but the strongly-built Merseysider could not live up to it. Skilful and possessing a strong shot, Gayle excelled in the Central League where he spent four fruitful seasons, but perhaps he did not have the temperament for the big time. He was unfortunate also in that Liverpool at that time operated a four-man midfield which left little scope for a winger.

After various loan spells, Gayle joined Birmingham City for £75,000 in January 1983 and won England under-21 recognition during an often impressive First Division stay at St Andrews. Further travels brought limited success before he seemed to settle with Blackburn Rovers. Late in his career, he had achieved a degree of consistency at last.

HOWARD ANTHONY GAYLE
BORN Liverpool, 18 May 1958.
OTHER CLUBS Fulham on loan 79/80 (14, 0); Newcastle United on loan 82/3 (8, 2); Birmingham City 82/3-83/4 (46, 9); Sunderland 84/5-85/6 (48, 4); Dallas Sidekicks, USA, 86; Stoke City 86/7 (6, 2); Blackburn Rovers 87/8-91/2 (116, 29); Halifax Town 92/3 (5, 0).

| GAMES | 3 (2) |
| GOALS | 1 |

KEVIN SHEEDY

1980/81 → 1981/82

It didn't happen very often, but Liverpool let Everton escape with a rare gem when they sold Kevin Sheedy to the Blues for £100,000 in August 1982. True, the Reds were not exactly short of top-quality midfield creators with the likes of Graeme Souness and Terry McDermott on the payroll, but Bob Paisley's self-confessed uneasiness over the deal spoke volumes.

To be fair to Sheedy, he needed a move, understandably being fed up with life in the stars' shadows as he approached his 24th birthday, and he made the most of his opportunity by emerging as one of the prime movers in Everton's fabulous mid-1980s resurgence under Howard Kendall.

The Welsh-born Irishman, who commenced a decade-long international career soon after leaving Anfield, was a left-sided schemer who passed like a dream, the accuracy and vision of his dispatches providing perfect fodder for the likes of Goodison Park hit-men Graeme Sharp and Andy Gray. Sheedy was a spectacular finisher, too, reaching double figures in two title-winning campaigns and delivering the delicious chip which wrapped up European Cup Winners' Cup triumph in 1985.

Of course, Liverpool did not exactly flounder without Kevin Sheedy, but there must have been moments when successive Anfield bosses cast envious eyes at the artistic ex-Red prospering on the other side of Stanley Park.

KEVIN MARK SHEEDY
BORN Builth Wells, Brecon, 21 October 1959.
HONOURS 45 Republic of Ireland caps (83-93).
OTHER CLUBS Hereford United 75/6-77/8 (51, 4); Everton 82/3-91/2 (274, 67); Newcastle United 91/2-92/3 (37, 4); Blackpool 93/4 (26, 1).

| GAMES | 3 (2) |
| GOALS | 2 |

AVI COHEN

1979/80 → 1980/81

Avi Cohen was a back-four player of poise and class who had all the ability needed to enjoy protracted success with Liverpool but didn't stay long enough to do so. He stepped off the plane from Tel Aviv in May 1979 with a reputation as Israel's best all-round performer yet, at a cost of £200,000, he represented a sizeable gamble. Four months later in his first senior outing, replacing injured midfielder Ray Kennedy at Leeds, his peripheral showing proved he had plenty to learn about English football.

After six months of Reds-style training, Cohen reappeared at left-back as deputy for Alan Kennedy and managed to score at both ends against Aston Villa at Anfield in the game that clinched the Championship. The second goal, the one that beat the visiting 'keeper, sent the Kop into paroxysms of delight and seemingly signalled the birth of a new hero.

Cohen, as popular with team-mates as he was with the fans, complemented smooth distribution and shrewd anticipation with strength in the air and courage in the tackle, though his pace was unremarkable. In 1980/81 he enjoyed an early run which threatened to evict Kennedy from the side but then, perhaps yearning for sunshine, he returned to Tel Aviv. Six years later he braved another British winter to be reunited fleetingly with former Liverpool team-mate Graeme Souness at Glasgow Rangers.

COLIN IRWIN

1979/80 → 1980/81

Central defender Colin Irwin suffered two unhappy endings in a brief soccer career: hot competition brought his Liverpool days to a frustrating close and then, when he was making the most of a new start at Swansea, he was cruelly forced by injury into early retirement.

Irwin had been an Anfield professional for nearly five years before making his debut in August 1979 at home to West Bromwich Albion. He gave a tidy display alongside Phil Thompson and that season enjoyed 14 appearances, deputising in turn for Alan Hansen and left-back Alan Kennedy.

It was a valuable grounding for his big chance in 1980/81, when knocks to Hansen and Thompson gave him an unbroken run of 17 League matches, with bonuses of a Wembley trip for the drawn League Cup Final against West Ham and a place in the away clash with Bayern Munich which put the Reds in the European Cup Final.

Strong but never quite commanding, Irwin did a steady job once again without revealing the class to suggest a first-team future, and when John Toshack's £340,000 offer to take him to Vetch Field coincided with the arrival of Mark Lawrenson, he was allowed to leave. He captained the Swans to sixth position in the First Division before bowing out, a sad casualty of soccer misfortune.

ABRAHAM COHEN		
BORN: Tel Aviv, Israel, 14 November 1956.		
HONOURS: 51 Israel caps (76-88).	GAMES	20 (3)
OTHER CLUBS: Macabbi Tel Aviv (twice); Glasgow Rangers 87/8 (7, 0).	GOALS	1

COLIN THOMAS IRWIN		
BORN: Liverpool, 9 February 1957	GAMES	40 (4)
OTHER CLUBS: Swansea City 81/2-83/4 (48, 0).	GOALS	3

KENNY DALGLISH

1977/78 → 1989/90

There were Stanley Matthews and Tom Finney, Bobby Charlton and Jimmy Greaves, Denis Law and George Best; to list the absolute cream of British forwards in the half-century which followed the Second World War is not an arduous task. But now sufficient time has elapsed to stand back from the playing career of Kenny Dalglish, and his achievements can be seen in true perspective, it is fitting that the name of the Scottish master be added to that exalted company.

His exploits for Celtic alone would fill a book but it was the sublime gifts he displayed for Liverpool that lifted him on to the very highest plane. Dalglish was one of those rare performers who brought true beauty to sport, his football at once exhilarating and aesthetic; some of his goals were acts of supreme artistic creation and those who saw him at his peak were privileged indeed.

He arrived at Anfield from Parkhead in August 1977 for £440,000, then a record fee between British clubs, and inherited the number-seven shirt from Kevin Keegan. After a quiet start against Manchester United in the Charity Shield, he marked his League debut with a goal at Middlesbrough and soon it became apparent that the Reds had made an inspired investment. Dalglish's first Anfield term yielded 30 strikes in 59 matches but that represented only the most obvious aspect of his value; such was his prodigious natural ability that he gave a new dimension to the team.

Endowed with magnetic control and a deadly instinct for releasing the ball with nigh-perfect precision and timing, he brought the best out of team-mates, often creating for them precious extra seconds in which to capitalise on his skills. The Dalglish genius – yes, he was that good – was most eye-catching in crowded penalty areas. Wriggling like some muscular eel, he would feint one way, turn another and squeeze a vicious shot or exquisitely weighted pass through the narrowest of gaps.

He was never a sprinter of Lineker-type velocity; Dalglish's primary speed was of thought, one telling example being the way in which he turned what would have been a defect in a lesser player – his lack of heading prowess – to his advantage. When faced with hulking defenders he would not waste time on ineffectual aerial challenges, instead looking to where the ball might drop, often as not arriving in exactly the right spot with almost uncanny anticipation.

Crucially, too, Dalglish had a tough streak. Solidly built with a low centre of gravity, he tackled with his whole body-weight and was strong enough to take most of the knocks which inevitably came his way, as his appearance record – he was ever-present in five of his first six League campaigns – reveals eloquently.

But rich and varied though Dalglish's all-round talents were, it was his goals, so often the product of sheer virtuosity, that evoked the most wonder and created countless immortal memories: the subtle, Greaves-like dink to end the deadlock against FC Bruges in the 1978 European Cup Final; the delicate chip and curling, top-corner drive past poor Paul Cooper of Ipswich in two late-1970s League encounters; the 1981 League Cup Final winner, a delicious volley on the turn against West Ham; and the Stamford Bridge strike which secured the 1985/86 Championship, when Kenny took a Jim Beglin pass on his chest and, with characteristic calm, clipped the ball imperiously past Tony Godden. Golden moments all, though any Liverpool fan could recall another dozen equally thrilling and timeless examples of Dalglish magic.

In 1985 Kenny, the only Scot to win 100 caps, took over as the Reds' boss and by decade's end, before his enigmatic departure from Anfield, his managerial achievements were rivalling his playing triumphs. However, they could never outshine the on-the-field glory of the man who could justly be called the greatest footballer in Liverpool's history.

KENNETH MATHIESON DALGLISH

BORN Dalmarnock, Glasgow, 4 March 1951.
HONOURS European Cup 77/8, 80/1, 83/4. League Championship 78/9, 79/80, 81/2, 82/3, 83/4, 85/6. FA Cup 85/6. League Cup 80/1, 81/2, 82/3, 83/4. 102 Scotland caps (71-87). FWA Footballer of the Year 79, 83. PFA Footballer of the Year 83.
OTHER CLUBS Celtic 68/9-76/7 (204, 112).
MANAGER Liverpool (85-91); Blackburn Rovers (91-95); Newcastle United (97-98).

GAMES **493 (17)**
GOALS **170**

ALAN KENNEDY

1978/79 → 1985/86

Alan Kennedy was the buccaneering Wearsider who solved Liverpool's nagging left-back problem at the end of the 1970s and went on to earn Anfield immortality by scoring the goals which won two European Cups – even if one of them, as he emphasises still with typical modesty, was in a penalty shoot-out.

Bob Paisley turned to Kennedy, one of the few Newcastle players to impress against the Reds in the 1974 FA Cup Final, in August 1978 after deciding to replace the worthy but unpolished Joey Jones. The fee of £330,000 was considered a massive outlay for a full-back but, at 26, Alan was in his prime and there was every reason to believe that his game would benefit from playing alongside top-class performers.

Unlike a number of other expensive Liverpool investments, the newcomer became an instant first-team regular, catching the eye with a scorching turn of speed which compensated amply for a sporadic tendency to commit himself to challenges in forward positions. He could be beaten on the half-way line but recover to win the ball before his opponent, believing Kennedy to be trailing safely in his wake, could reach the Reds' penalty area.

His adventurous streak, characterised by surging left-flank runs which often took him past defenders and occasionally culminated in stinging strikes on goal, was combined with an uncompromising tackle and indefatigable enthusiasm. It all amounted to an appealing package which endeared him to Kopites, who affectionately dubbed him 'Barney Rubble' after the cartoon buddy of Fred Flintstone.

At first Kennedy was slightly disconcerted by the need to adapt to the Liverpool method of building attacks from the back. At St James' Park he had been accustomed to slinging long balls forward for Malcolm Macdonald and John Tudor; now he was expected to play it short to Ray Kennedy, Terry McDermott or Kenny Dalglish. His distribution, initially a little erratic, improved with experience and eventually he became especially adept at one-two combinations with Dalglish.

Overall, the former Magpie clearly vindicated Paisley's decision to buy him, playing a spirited part in the Championship triumphs of his first two campaigns, and when his character was put to the test in 1980/81 it was not found wanting. He had struck an inconsistent patch of form and the manager experimented with both Richard Money and Avi Cohen in the number-three shirt, but Kennedy, though troubled by injuries, fought back to regain his place in time for the European Cup Final against Real Madrid, a game that was to bring the most memorable moment of his Reds career.

With nine minutes left and the score tied at 0-0, Alan received a throw-in from Ray Kennedy on the left and moved into the Spaniards' half. Unmolested by a defence which presumably expected a cross, the enterprising left-back cut in to arrow the ball over the 'keeper's shoulder for the winner.

As if inspired by that supreme moment, Alan took on new stature. He came under pressure on the arrival of Mark Lawrenson but once again he re-established himself to take three more (consecutive) title medals, being ever-present in 1982/83 and 1983/84. Then came his decisive penalty in the 1984 European Cup sudden-death defeat of Roma and a belated England call-up – he had dropped out with injury when picked nine years earlier.

When finally ousted by Jim Beglin in the autumn of 1985, Alan Kennedy joined Sunderland, his home-town club, for £100,000. He could walk out of Anfield with his head held high, secure in the knowledge of a job well done.

ALAN PHILIP KENNEDY

BORN   Sunderland, County Durham, 31 August 1954.

HONOURS   European Cup 80/1, 83/4. League Championship 78/9, 79/80, 81/2, 82/3, 83/4.
League Cup 80/1, 81/2, 82/3, 83/4. 2 England caps (84).

OTHER CLUBS   Newcastle United 72/3-77/8 (158, 9); Sunderland 85/6-86/7 (54, 2);
Hartlepool United 87/8 (5, 0); Beerschot, Belgium, 87/8; Wigan Athletic 87/8 (22, 0);
Wrexham 89/90-90/1 (16, 0).

GAMES   **355 (2)**

GOALS   21

PHIL THOMPSON

1971/72 → 1982/83

The wiry, almost scrawny frame of Phil Thompson was a source of much amusement to Bill Shankly. But the Reds' wisecracking boss knew an outstanding player when he saw one and his quips about 'the matchstick man with sparrow's legs' masked a profound respect and admiration for the former Kopite who lived for Liverpool. To be honest, Thompson's spindly appearance hardly tied in with the popular image of a top footballer but, as most forwards of his era would testify, there wasn't a more awkward central defender to be found in the First Division, and precious few with more skill.

Originally a midfielder, Thompson made his debut as a substitute at Old Trafford in April 1972 and went on to squeeze in just enough appearances in assorted positions to qualify for a Championship medal in the following season. He impressed with precise passing and improbably fierce tackling but often was found wanting for pace, and it became clear that his prospects in his chosen role were strictly limited. Shankly, however, had spotted a rich vein of potential and when centre-half Larry Lloyd was injured in February 1974 it was to Thompson that the manager turned to partner Emlyn Hughes in the middle of his back four.

The enthusiastic Scouser was a natural in his new role. Though not as aerially dominant as his predecessor, he was an exquisite reader of the game who brought a new dimension to the Reds' defence. Whereas in the days of Yeats and Lloyd, towering headers were often the preferred option for clearances, Thompson was more likely to play his way out of trouble in European style, retaining possession and setting up attacks with his neat distribution.

One of the first to experience his cool, ruthless efficiency was Newcastle United's garrulous centre-forward Malcolm Macdonald, who had trumpeted imprudently to the world how he was going to bring Liverpool to their knees at Wembley in 1974. In the event it was Macdonald who partook of humble pie as Thompson blotted him out of what proved to be the most one-sided FA Cup Final for years.

The Hughes-Thompson combination grew steadily in authority, remaining at the heart of the Reds' rearguard as the trophies piled up throughout the second half of the 1970s. Ultimately, it was broken in 1978/79 when Emlyn relinquished his place to Alan Hansen and the captaincy went to Phil, who proved an inspiring and highly vocal motivator.

The new pairing prospered with the Scot's sophisticated, often adventurous style dovetailing comfortably with his skipper's more simple but equally effective approach. When Liverpool were pouring forward en masse it was invariably Thompson who held his position at the back, ready to deal with breakaway threats, and few British defenders were more accomplished in one-on-one encounters.

Liverpool's success did not abate during his spell in charge and he led his side to two League titles and 1981 European Cup victory over Real Madrid, making up for missing the 1977 final through injury, before Graeme Souness took over in 1981/82. Thompson, who had a short stint as England skipper during a distinguished international career, went on to win two more Championship medals and retained his Reds place until injuries and the excellence of Mark Lawrenson accelerated his demise.

After 18 months with Sheffield United he returned to Anfield as a coach, and there were those who reckoned one of Liverpool's most loyal sons was a realistic candidate to manage the club at some future stage. Unfortunately for Phil, sitting boss Graeme Souness had other ideas, dismissing his former team-mate in 1992. However, six years on, the story took another fascinating twist when Thompson made another comeback as number-two to Gerard Houllier.

	PHILIP BERNARD THOMPSON
BORN	Liverpool, 21 January 1954.
HONOURS	European Cup 77/8, 80/1. UEFA Cup 75/6.
	League Championship 72/3, 75/6, 76/7, 78/9, 79/80, 81/2,
	82/3. FA Cup 73/4. League Cup 80/1, 81/2.
	42 England caps (76-82).
OTHER CLUBS	Sheffield United 84/5-85/6 (37, 0).
MANAGER	Liverpool (caretaker, 01-02).

GAMES **470 (7)**
GOALS 13

CRAIG JOHNSTON

1981/82 → 1987/88

Craig Johnston was an Anfield enigma from first to last. He arrived in a whirlwind of raw energy and ebullience, threatening to turn the place upside down in the manner of Kevin Keegan. It didn't happen, but he stayed to win nine major honours in seven seasons – despite rarely being assured of a first-team place – and to make his name as possibly the most untypical Liverpool player of modern times. Finally, forever his own man, he effectively tore up his contract and walked out on the Reds to start a new life in Australia.

Bob Paisley paid Middlesbrough £575,000 for the South African-born attacking midfielder in the summer of 1981 and Johnston started the new season as a substitute with high expectations. But it was not until the middle of March, with Liverpool just embarking on a surge that was to take them from an unaccustomed mid-table position to the title, that the effervescent newcomer ousted Terry McDermott.

Raiding gleefully down the right, those long, curly, dark locks flying in his wake, Johnston offered a fitful flair which was distinctly at odds with the Anfield tradition for consistency. His searing pace and exhilarating skill were a delight to behold, but often nothing would come of them. There was an all-too-frequent resemblance to a headless chicken as he disappeared into a blind alley or wasted a faultless dribble by capping it with a wayward cross.

Over the successful 1982/83 and 1983/84 campaigns, Johnston, whose work-rate bore witness to his supreme fitness, was more often in the team than out of it, but both Paisley and his successor, Joe Fagan, were wary of his headstrong element. Paisley, while a confirmed admirer of the overall Johnston package, summed up the managerial dilemma aptly: 'Putting Craig alongside ten men who were pacing themselves through a busy period was like throwing a firework into a box of safety matches.'

As the Reds endured a disappointing season in 1984/85, Johnston found himself on the fringe of the action, but Kenny Dalglish's appointment as manager the following term changed his luck and he became a regular in the side which won the League and FA Cup double.

Dalglish harnessed the midfielder's verve and persistence to the team effort and he became less unpredictable, more productive; one minute he would be winning the ball in his own half, the next scoring a vital goal such as the one which put Liverpool on top against Everton at Wembley.

Though Johnston's name wasn't always on the teamsheet, a campaign of consolidation followed, and by 1987/88 he was at his peak. But Anfield security was not to be his; ironically, soon after Craig's progress had been recognised by selection for an England squad, Dalglish bought Ray Houghton and the former Middlesbrough man returned to the periphery.

In May 1988 he announced there was more to life than kicking a bag of wind and returned to Australia, where he had lived before moving to England, for domestic reasons. Johnston became a full-time photographer and thus the English sporting scene bade farewell to one of its more individual talents.

Later he resurfaced as a boot designer and a passionate campaigner for redistribution of wealth in the world game. For a man who admitted candidly that he had fallen out of love with football, Craig Johnston retained plenty of trenchant views on the subject.

CRAIG PETER JOHNSTON
BORN   Johannesburg, South Africa, 25 June 1960.
HONOURS   European Cup 83/4. League Championship 81/2, 82/3, 83/4, 85/6, 87/8.
FA Cup 85/6. League Cup 82/3, 83/4.
OTHER CLUBS   Middlesbrough 77/8-80/1 (64, 16).

GAMES **227 (37)**
GOALS 39

MARK LAWRENSON

· ·

1981/82 → 1987/88

There was a time in the mid-1980s when Mark Lawrenson looked the equal of any central defender in the world. He had the lot: speed, power, ball control, anticipation, passing ability, strength in the air. There was no discernible defect, and together with the impeccable Alan Hansen he formed what was arguably the finest middle-of-the-back-four combination in British football history

Bob Paisley broke the Reds' transfer record when he signed Lawrenson from Brighton for £900,000 in August 1981, beating off stiff opposition from Manchester United and Arsenal. Undeniably the Lancashire-born Eire international – an Irish father qualified him to play for the Republic – was a top-class addition to the Liverpool squad, but with Hansen and Phil Thompson in consistently excellent form there were those who reckoned he was an ultra-expensive luxury. Paisley reasoned, however, that such pedigree performers seldom became available and were not to be missed when they did. The manager's wisdom was borne out emphatically in the seasons that followed.

In his initial term at Anfield, Lawrenson demonstrated his versatility, flitting around the teamsheet like some latter-day Paul Madeley, the former Leeds United utility man. First came a stint replacing Alan Kennedy at left-back before relief duty took him to both midfield and centre-back. The opening months of 1982/83 told a similar story before a serious injury to Thompson allowed the ex-Seagull to cement the link with Hansen, which was not seriously disturbed for more than three years.

For most of that time the Reds revelled in a dominance of the First Division then-unequalled since the all-conquering exploits of Arsenal half a century earlier. With Lawrenson's influence becoming ever more majestic, they completed a hat-trick of titles in his first three campaigns, monopolised the League Cup and in 1984 defeated Roma to lift the European Cup for the fourth time, a performance in which the tall defender's multiple talents were showcased to brilliant effect.

Throughout much of the second half of a tense struggle between two well-matched sides, Joe Fagan's men were pinned back as the Italians strove to end the 1-1 deadlock, but Mark, a natural ball-winner through timing rather than ferocity, was immaculate in both his tackling and his reading of the game. If Graziani or Falcao seemed on the point of breaking through, invariably a long Lawrenson leg would snake out to frustrate them, and but for the inspired work of the Reds' number four the penalty shoot-out which landed the trophy might well not have been reached.

The first hint of a split in the partnership with Hansen appeared when Lawrenson took a knock during a 6-0 thrashing of Oxford United at Anfield in March 1986. Gary Gillespie stepped in and the Republic of Ireland star might have missed the Wembley win over Everton which clinched the League and FA Cup double had his immensely capable deputy not fallen ill.

But the blow which was to lead to the premature end of a glittering career fell a year later in the home encounter with Wimbledon, when he sustained a serious Achilles tendon injury. Despite several short-lived comebacks, Lawrenson had lost too much pace and elasticity to continue, and he was forced to retire at the age of 31. It was a poignant departure for such a smooth, experienced and shrewdly economical performer, who might have been expected to play on for another half-decade.

It was difficult to accept that no more would that gangling yet curiously graceful figure, sleeves pushed up and head rolling as he ran, patrol the Reds' back line. Club, and country, had been deprived of a true thoroughbred.

Thereafter he turned to management, then broadcasting, linking up eventually with old mate Hansen, bringing commendable clarity, objectivity and humour to the BBC mix.

MARK THOMAS LAWRENSON
BORN Preston, Lancashire, 2 June 1957.
HONOURS European Cup 83/4. League Championship 81/2, 82/3, 83/4, 85/6, 87/8.
FA Cup 85/6. League Cup 81/2, 82/3, 83/4.
38 Republic of Ireland caps (77-87).
OTHER CLUBS Preston North End 74/5-76/7 (73, 2); Brighton and Hove Albion
77/8-80/1 (152, 5).
MANAGER Oxford United (88); Peterborough United (89-90).

GAMES 338 (9)
GOALS 17

DAVID HODGSON

1982/83 → 1983/84

Rangy front-runner David Hodgson, a £450,000 acquisition from Middlesbrough in the summer of 1982, started his Reds career with a flourish only to fizzle out in sad anti-climax within two seasons.

Playing alongside Ian Rush and Kenny Dalglish, the robust England under-21 international notched four goals in his first six games. His most impressive display came at home to Nottingham Forest in September when his willingness to chase apparently lost causes brought him two goals in a 4-3 victory.

Hodgson's greatest asset was his pace and he could be particularly dangerous cutting in from the flanks. But once in a threatening position often he was betrayed by a lack of finesse and the opening would be wasted.

At times he was guilty of failing to do the basic things well, and faced with competition as a wide attacker from the more skilful Craig Johnston – with the intimidating presence of Rush and Dalglish closing off other avenues of advancement – he was, perhaps, destined inevitably for a short Anfield tenure.

In Hodgson's opening campaign, manager Bob Paisley gave his fellow north-easterner plenty of chances to impress. In truth, he didn't disgrace himself during an unbroken midwinter spell of 15 matches and his title medal was well earned.

But in 1983/84, with Joe Fagan now in charge and Michael Robinson on the scene, his opportunities were fewer, partly due to injuries, and he accepted a £125,000 move to Sunderland. There followed spells with several other clubs but Hodgson still gave little sign of fulfilling the promise which had first prompted Paisley to take him from Ayresome Park.

DAVID JAMES HODGSON	
BORN	Gateshead, County Durham, 6 August 1960.
HONOURS	League Championship 82/3.
OTHER CLUBS	Middlesbrough 78/9-81/2 (125, 16); Sunderland 84/5-85/6 (40, 5); Norwich City 86/7 (6, 1); Middlesbrough on loan 86/7 (2, 0); Jerez, Spain, 87/8; Sheffield Wednesday 88/9 (11, 1); Metz, France; Swansea City 91/2 (3, 0).
MANAGER	Darlington (95, 96-00 and 03-06).

GAMES	33 (16)
GOALS	10

MICHAEL ROBINSON

1983/84 → 1984/85

Four years after a rash gamble by Malcolm Allison had threatened to blight Michael Robinson's career, Liverpool offered the honest, uncomplicated, head-down-and-run striker a second chance at the top level.

Big Mal had astounded the football world by paying £756,000 to take the then-unknown youngster from Preston to Manchester City during one of the wildest spending sprees in the game's history. Understandable failure at Maine Road had been followed by a steady spell with Brighton when Joe Fagan ventured £200,000 to make him a Red in August 1983.

Robinson was pitched straight into first-team action, forming a joint spearhead with Ian Rush as Kenny Dalglish withdrew to a deeper position, and when he went eight games without a goal the tongues of the I-told-you-so brigade were wagging avidly.

But then a European Cup brace at home to BK Odense of Denmark and a cracking League hat-trick at Upton Park three games later restored his credibility, and despite losing his place as the manager tried various permutations, the burly Republic of Ireland international remained in the reckoning for most of the campaign.

Though capable of the occasional artistic touch, Robinson was not blessed with a wide range of delicate skills and, with commendable common sense, played to his strengths. He liked to run on to the ball rather than have it played to his feet and was often at his best when foraging on the flanks.

His wholehearted efforts were deservedly rewarded with title and European Cup medals – he took the field as substitute for Dalglish in the 1984 final against Roma – but it was no surprise when, half-way through his second season at Anfield, Robinson was allowed to join Queen's Park Rangers for £100,000.

Certainly he had proved a short-term investment but, this time around in the big league, it would be an exceedingly exacting critic who called him a flop.

A personable and enterprising individual, Michael Robinson went on to become a hugely successful broadcaster in Spain.

MICHAEL JOHN ROBINSON

BORN   Leicester, 12 July 1958.
HONOURS   European Cup 83/4. League Championship 83/4. 23 Republic of Ireland caps (80-86).
OTHER CLUBS   Preston North End 75/6-78/9 (48, 15); Manchester City 79/80 (30, 8); Brighton and Hove Albion 80/1-82/3 (113, 37); Queen's Park Rangers 84/5-86/7 (48, 6); Osasuna, Spain, 87/8.

GAMES	46 (6)
GOALS	13

BRUCE GROBBELAAR

1981/82 → 1993/94

Bouquets and brickbats rained on the head of Bruce Grobbelaar with equal intensity after that most eccentric of soccer entertainers succeeded Ray Clemence as Liverpool goalkeeper in 1981/82. Many shrewd observers claimed that, during his lengthy Anfield reign, he was the most accomplished custodian in the land and maintained that his habitual brilliance more than outweighed his well-publicised errors; others reckoned that his slapstick antics and catalogue of clangers prevented the Reds from lifting an even greater share of honours.

Another strand to the debate went that, whatever his technical merits, football needed the Zimbabwe international for the sheer fun he brought to a game beset with problems, a poignantly ironic reflection in view of his subsequent embroilment in bribing and match-fixing allegations, both of which he denied.

Whatever the truth at the heart of that tawdry scandal, from a purely sporting viewpoint the third theory would have received the shortest of shrift from Liverpool's pragmatic management. Surely, the key to Grobbelaar's worth lay in the fact that three bosses of England's most successful club were content with Bruce's unorthodox efforts in his prime. Had Bob Paisley, Joe Fagan and Kenny Dalglish in turn not been convinced that they had the best 'keeper available, he would have been ruthlessly replaced.

Grobbelaar arrived at Anfield in March 1981 as a £250,000 signing from Vancouver Whitecaps, and had little time to settle before being plunged into regular first-team action. He might have benefited from a couple of seasons as understudy to his illustrious predecessor, as Clemence himself had once learned from Tommy Lawrence, but with the England man moving to White Hart Lane that summer there was no such chance.

Reds supporters realised they were getting an unknown quantity but they were hardly prepared for the culture shock which the newcomer represented. They loved the stunning saves, a product of a natural athlete's startlingly sharp reflexes, and were impressed by the way he sought to dominate his penalty area. They were not so sure, on the other hand, about the occasional flailing attempt to gather a cross which had passed way over his head or the disturbing tendency to leave his penalty area to snuff out an attack not far from the half-way line!

The acid test, however, was whether Liverpool won as many trophies with Grobbelaar as they did in the pre-Bruce days. And certainly they did. He was an ever-present in the five seasons between 1981/82 and 1985/86, during which the team lifted four League Championships and five major cups. Better still, the triumphs were spiced with humour, an irresistible combination to the Scouse legions.

When Grobbelaar was confronted with a penalty shoot-out at the end of the 1984 European Cup Final against Roma, he eased the tension with his famous leg-wobbling act and, crucially, he had the last laugh by finishing on the winning side. If he was pelted with coins on an away ground, as 'keepers are apt to be, he might pocket them to get the crowd on his side, and he was always ready with a spontaneous reaction to fans' banter.

After plentiful alarms and excursions in his early Anfield years, Bruce appeared more consistent in the mid-1980s, and after winning his place back from Mike Hooper after a bout of meningitis in 1988/89, he struck an inspired vein of form as the side went unbeaten for 22 games. Perversely. the odd howler crept back in during 1989/90 and the doubts resurfaced. Nevertheless, the old soldier battled on, increasingly error-prone and frequently irascible, but in the side more often than out of it until spring 1994, when he was unseated finally by David James.

Given a free transfer that summer, Grobbelaar joined Southampton and continued to hold his own in the top flight, even, for a time, after being assailed with those damning claims of dishonesty. For the record, he was found guilty of taking bribes, while the fixing charge was never proved.

But whatever uncertainties might persist about Grobbelaar, no one should doubt that he took his trade seriously. As one former team-mate remarked: 'Inside that clown is a dedicated perfectionist.' On his day that perfection was sometimes achieved; on others . . . well, at least it was never dull.

BRUCE DAVID GROBBELAAR

BORN	Durban, South Africa, 6 October 1957.
HONOURS	European Cup 83/4. League Championship 81/2, 82/3, 83/4, 85/6, 87/8, 89/90.
	FA Cup 85/6, 88/9, 91/2. League Cup 81/2, 82/3, 83/4.
	20 Zimbabwe caps.
OTHER CLUBS	Vancouver Whitecaps, Canada; Crewe Alexandra on loan 79/80 (24, 1);
	Stoke City on loan 92/3 (4, 0); Southampton 94/5-95/6 (32, 0);
	Plymouth Argyle 96/7 (36, 0); Oldham Athletic 97/8 (4, 0);
	Bury 98/9 (1, 0); Lincoln City 98/9 (2, 0).

GAMES	620
GOALS	0

JAN MOLBY

1984/85 → 1994/95

Few top-flight managers could put their hands on their hearts and say they did not covet the ability of Jan Molby. Yet the Danish international midfielder, a rare and at times irresistible combination of dainty skills and bear-like strength, became a shadowy figure on the fringe of the Anfield action long before reaching the veteran stage and being freed to become player-boss of Swansea City in February 1996.

Joe Fagan took him to Anfield as a £200,000 recruit from Ajax of Amsterdam in August 1984 and pitched him straight into the team. The initial impression was of a sluggish, rather corpulent individual who lacked the speed to make the most of his natural gifts. Molby played on for the first half of the campaign before being replaced by Kevin MacDonald, and a brief end-of-term reappearance as sweeper was not enough to prevent many critics from writing him off.

Never a man to be swayed by the media, Kenny Dalglish was of a different opinion. The new Liverpool manager installed a slightly slimmer Molby in his side for 1985/86, and his faith was quickly repaid. The Dane, having had time to adjust to the frenetic demands of the British game, exuded authority as the Reds' creative fulcrum, supplying Ian Rush in particular with a nourishing diet of exquisitely weighted through-balls.

Like Souness before him, Molby laced his constructive merits with formidable power, and his dead-ball expertise – he scored nine of his 19 goals that season from the penalty spot – was indispensable. His finest hour came in the FA Cup Final at Wembley, in which Liverpool were distinctly second-best to Everton until the hefty schemer began to exert his influence. First he put Rush through to level the scores at one-apiece and then opened up the match with a succession of flowing crossfield passes, which led ultimately to two more goals.

Molby's Anfield future was apparently assured. Not only was he a success on the pitch, he also became a personal favourite with the fans, who delighted in his Danish-Scouse accent and general willingness to embrace the Merseyside way of life. The way ahead, however, was paved with problems.

After playing well enough for a slightly below-par 'Pool during the following season, he broke his foot in training and missed most of the vintage 1987/88 campaign. Molby was back for 1988/89, deputising in defence for Alan Hansen, but soccer was forced to take a back seat as he was sentenced to three months in prison for a driving offence.

To his credit, Jan survived the trauma with dignity, returning to fight for his place. But, though arguably still the most artistic play-maker in the land, as he showed repeatedly during 1991/92 by contributing upliftingly to Liverpool's FA Cup triumph, the affable Dane seemed to have lost the impetus of earlier days.

Part of the reason was his eternal battle with his weight; if he could have controlled that ample girth as ably as he mastered a football then, surely, Molby must have attained true greatness. But also he suffered appallingly with injuries, which plagued him mercilessly throughout the first half of the 1990s. In addition, there were times when the team's pattern of play, with so many attacking ideas stemming from more fleet-footed colleagues, simply did not suit his measured approach.

For all that, there is no escaping the truth that the sumptuous talents of Jan Molby remained frustratingly peripheral at a time when they should have been reaping their richest bounty. By any reckoning, that amounts to a dreadful waste.

JAN MOLBY	
BORN	Kolding, Denmark, 4 July 1963.
HONOURS	League Championship 85/6, 89/90. FA Cup 85/6, 91/2. 33 Denmark caps (82-90).
OTHER CLUBS	Ajax, Amsterdam; Barnsley on loan 95/6 (5,0); Norwich City on loan 95/6 (2, 0); Swansea City 95/6-97/8 (42, 8).
MANAGER	Swansea City (96-97); Kidderminster Harriers (99-02 and 03-04); Hull City (02).

GAMES 253 (30)
GOALS 58

STEVE NICOL

1982/83 → 1994/95

No player is indispensable at Liverpool. Neither the departure of Ian Rush nor the retirement of Kenny Dalglish left a vacuum which was not filled swiftly and successfully; that is the Anfield way. But, throughout most of the 1980s and the early 1990s, if there was one performer who might have been missed more than any other, one for whom the manager might have longed most wistfully, especially in the depths of an injury crisis, that man was Steve Nicol.

The versatile Scottish international, Footballer of the Year in 1989, acquitted himself with distinction in every back-four and midfield position, and epitomised all that was best about the modern Reds.

Boundlessly enthusiastic and determined, Nicol boasted a rich range of soccer assets: his touch on the ball – despite his need for size-14 boots – was sure and often subtle, his passing was accurate and imaginative, his tackle was firm. He was rarely found to lack power in the air or pace in a sprint, he possessed boundless stamina, and his classy finishing put many a striker to shame.

Nicol was imported to Anfield as £300,000 worth of raw teenage talent from Ayr United in October 1981. Then principally a right-back, immediately he found himself in the shadow of the consistent Phil Neal and was consigned to the reserves to complete his soccer education. If there were ever any doubts about Nicol's potential they were quickly stilled in an early Central League encounter in which he picked up the ball in his own penalty box and beat five opponents as he ran the length of the field to score the winner.

His initial outings deputising for Neal, on the infrequent occasions that the England stalwart was injured, boded well for the future. Despite his inexperience, Nicol revelled in the responsibility, revealing an eagerness for the ball and the initiative to use it constructively; clearly it could not be long before he claimed a first-team place.

The breakthrough arrived in October 1983 when Craig Johnston was injured and Steve slotted into midfield. His 19 League appearances were enough to earn a title medal and he went on to play his part in that term's European Cup Final, joining the action as substitute against Roma and volunteering to take Liverpool's first penalty in the deadlock-breaking shoot-out. He missed, but still he went home with a winner's medal.

The following campaign saw him cement his place, mainly at the expense of Sammy Lee, before he reverted to right-back when Neal left the club early in the League and FA Cup double campaign of 1985/86. Back in his original role, Nicol was magnificent, but any chance of settling there was destroyed by groin problems which kept him out of action for two thirds of the ensuing season.

A return to full fitness saw him reach yet greater heights of form and over the next three years he gave full rein to his adaptability. A competent spell at centre-back in the absence of Alan Hansen revealed a new aspect of his talent, though the right side of midfield was perhaps his most effective niche. From that position he had the scope to be a potent attacking force and contributed some memorable goals, notably a crisp hat-trick – including a sublime chip over the advancing 'keeper – at Newcastle in September 1987, and the sweetest of lobs against Southampton in the FA Cup in February 1990.

The sight of Steve, spiky red hair dripping with sweat and huge feet dancing over the ball, became an inspiring and reassuring one for Reds fans during a period of fabulous success and on into leaner times.

Injuries and the advancing years reduced his effectiveness slightly during his final days at Anfield, but often his experience proved priceless as the team underwent a time of transition. When he was freed to join Notts County in January 1995, Liverpool were not short of high-quality replacements; but those promising young men would have needed rare mettle, indeed, to equal the durability and achievements of Steve Nicol.

STEPHEN NICOL	
BORN	Irvine, Ayrshire, 11 December 1961.
HONOURS	European Cup 83/4. League Championship 83/4, 85/6, 87/8, 89/90.
	FA Cup 85/6, 88/9, 91/2. 27 Scotland caps (84-91). FWA Footballer of the Year 89.
OTHER CLUBS	Ayr United 79/80-81/2 (70, 7); Notts County 94/5-95/6 (32, 2);
	Sheffield Wednesday 95/6-97/8 (49, 0); West Bromwich Albion on loan 97/8 (9, 0).
MANAGER	New England Revolution, USA (02-).

GAMES 441 (17)
GOALS 45

PAUL WALSH

1984/85 → 1987/88

When England striker Paul Walsh left Luton for Liverpool in the close season of 1984, Reds fans drooled and rival supporters quaked. The prospect of a partnership between the waspish Walsh, then the most promising front-runner in the country, and the mighty Ian Rush seemed a breathtaking one for Kopites dreaming of ever more extravagant triumphs.

Walsh, who shortly before his £700,000 move had been voted Young Player of the Year by his fellow professionals, was exquisitely equipped for the Anfield challenge. Quick, lithe and abundantly skilful, he was that increasingly rare phenomenon, a central attacker who ran at defenders and took the ball past them. In confined spaces he could turn to deadly effect, like some pencil-slim Sassenach version of Dalglish, and he possessed a rasping shot to cap his exciting approach work.

Expectations were sky-high, and Walsh's early performances hinted at riches to come, despite a slight inclination to over-elaborate and an occasional tendency to drift on the edge of the action. After marking his home debut against West Ham with a goal on 15 seconds, the eel-like newcomer was working hard to establish an understanding with Rush when injury ruled him out for two months and that was to set the sorry pattern for the rest of his Liverpool days. Whenever he managed to put together a run of matches, usually Walsh would impress and the pundits would predict the long awaited breakthrough; then he would be sidelined again and his impetus would be lost.

Despite such frustrations, 1984/85 saw Paul maintain his average career strike-rate of roughly one goal every three starts and in the following term, again after missing a clutch of matches, he ran into splendid early-winter form. Two goals at home to his former Luton team-mates began an almost unbroken, 16-game sequence in which he netted ten times, and in the November encounter

with West Bromwich Albion Walsh was again at his irresistible best, setting up three and scoring one as the Kop roared its approval. There was another brilliant performance, crowned by two goals, against Watford at Vicarage Road in January 1986 before an Anfield injury a month later against Manchester United kept him out of the run-in to the League and FA Cup double.

There were similar tribulations in 1986/87, after which the advent of Peter Beardsley, John Aldridge and John Barnes relegated him to the role of perpetual substitute. Accordingly, in February 1988 Walsh opted for a much-needed clean slate and accepted a £500,000 move to White Hart Lane. Roughly a third of his time at Anfield had been spent recovering from a cartilage injury, a hernia, torn ankle ligaments and a broken wrist, and certainly he deserved better fortune with Spurs. However, consistent first-team action continued to elude one of the top flight's most tantalising talents.

PAUL ANTHONY WALSH

BORN	Plumstead, London, 1 October 1962.
HONOURS	League Championship 85/6. 3 England caps (83-84).
OTHER CLUBS	Charlton Athletic 79/80-81/2 (87, 24); Luton Town 82/3-83/4 (80, 24); Tottenham Hotspur 87/8-91/2 (128, 19); Queen's Park Rangers on loan 91/2 (2, 0); Portsmouth 92/3-93/4 (73, 14); Manchester City 93/4-95/6 (53, 16); Portsmouth 95/6 (21, 5).

GAMES **86 (19)**
GOALS 35

JOHN WARK

1983/84 → 1987/88

John Wark never quite lived up to his billing at Anfield, partly through injury but also, perhaps, because his game lacked the all-round qualities needed to flourish with Liverpool.

He was signed from Ipswich Town in March 1984, three months before the much-dreaded departure of fellow Scottish midfielder Graeme Souness to Sampdoria of Italy. At Portman Road Wark had been a kingpin of Bobby Robson's refreshing side, scoring heavily with powerful shots and ferocious headers, and such was his reputation that Reds boss Joe Fagan was widely considered to have completed a sizeable coup in capturing the thrustful Glaswegian for £450,000.

Initial impressions were excellent as Wark slotted smoothly into the side, replacing Craig Johnston for the title run-in. He scored on his debut in a 2-0 win at Watford, and though there were not enough games left for him to win a medal in that campaign it seemed only a matter of time before his barrel chest would be covered in gongs.

In the event, immediate life after Souness proved non-productive for Liverpool as they failed to lift an honour in 1984/85, but Wark acquitted himself with

gusto, even exceeding his Ipswich strike-rate with 18 League goals – highlighted by a hat-trick at West Bromwich and including only two penalties – in 40 games and contributing five more on the way to the ill-fated European Cup Final against Juventus at the Heysel Stadium.

Kenny Dalglish replaced Fagan for 1985/86 and, often deprived of John's services by niggling knocks, prospered without his countryman. The swarthy, moustachioed international's cup of woe finally ran over in March when he broke his leg, missing out not only on the League and FA Cup double but also Scotland's World Cup trip to Mexico. The following term presented the challenge of breaking back into the team but, though the Reds won no trophies, Wark was called up for only a handful of senior outings.

A magnificent striker of the ball who was at his most dangerous arriving late in the penalty area behind the front-runners, John had little outstanding to offer if his goals dried up. Admittedly he was strong in the air and firm in the tackle but his distribution lacked precision at times and he could match neither the vision of Molby nor the flair of Johnston.

In January 1988 he rejoined Ipswich for £100,000 and gave doughty and memorably lengthy service during two more stints at Portman Road, at first in his former role and later in defence, soldiering on gamely and effectively into his late thirties.

Looking back, John Wark could count himself unlucky that his best Anfield term coincided with one of the Reds' rare barren seasons.

	JOHN WARK		
BORN	Glasgow, 4 August 1957.		
HONOURS	29 Scotland caps (79-84). PFA Footballer of the Year 81.		
OTHER CLUBS	Ipswich Town 74/5-83/4 (296, 94) and 87/8-89/90 (89, 23); Middlesbrough 90/1 (32, 2); Ipswich Town 91/2-96/7 (154, 18).	GAMES	**93 (12)**
		GOALS	**42**

KEVIN MacDONALD

1984/85 → 1988/89

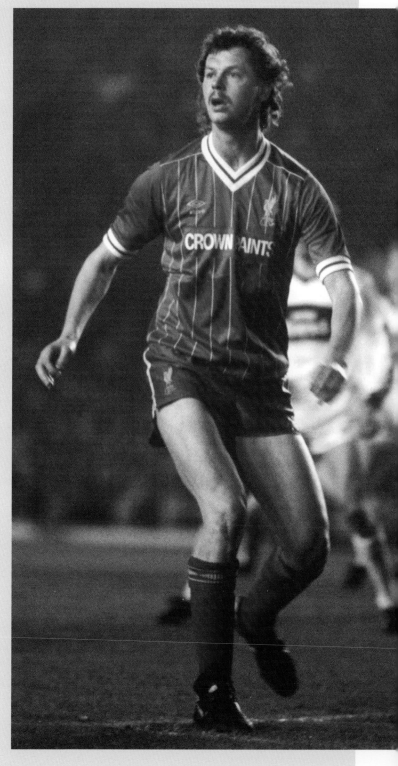

There were times during Kevin MacDonald's first 18 months at Anfield when his form emitted echoes – admittedly faint, but encouraging nevertheless – of that departed king of play-makers, Graeme Souness. Joe Fagan paid £400,000 for the promising midfielder, who had caught the eye as an inspiring skipper of Leicester City, in November 1984 after the Reds' early-season progress had fallen short of expectations.

The newcomer was introduced quickly into a side suffering noticeably from the absence of Souness and, though short of pace, he impressed immediately with his assured distribution and wiry strength. One display in an FA Cup quarter-final at Barnsley in March 1985, when his imaginative approach work played an influential part in a 4-0 victory, was particularly accomplished and MacDonald seemed poised for success.

Somehow, though, the lanky Scot never quite became established and in 1985/86, with the likes of Jan Molby and Steve McMahon in direct competition, he slid out of the reckoning until injuries to team-mates precipitated a comeback during the run-in to the League and FA Cup double. He seized his opportunity and gave a series of enterprising performances, including an assertive contribution against Everton at Wembley.

That might have been the platform for greater achievements but all hopes of consolidation were smashed when he broke his leg at Southampton in September 1986, an accident which effectively ended his Anfield career.

After two operations MacDonald fought back to fitness with commendable determination, but the combination of a strong squad and further injury trouble denied him a Liverpool future. After spells on loan with former club Leicester and – ironically – Souness' Glasgow Rangers, he joined Coventry City on a free transfer in the summer of 1989.

KEVIN DUNCAN MacDONALD

BORN   Inverness, 22 December 1960.
HONOURS   League Championship 85/86. FA Cup 85/6.
OTHER CLUBS Leicester City 80/1-84/5 (138, 8); Leicester City on loan 87/8 (3, 0); Glasgow Rangers on loan
            88/9 (3, 0); Coventry City 89/90-90/1 (31, 0); Cardiff City on loan 90/1 (8, 0);
            Walsall 91/2-92/3 (53, 6).

GAMES   44 (14)
GOALS   3

JIM BEGLIN

1984/85 → 1987/88

All was right with Jim Beglin's world as he ran out for the League Cup quarter-final against Everton in January 1987. The 23-year-old Eire international, who had played a telling part in the League and FA Cup double of the previous campaign, was apparently on the threshold of a long career as the Reds' left-back.

He was firmly established and there seemed little likelihood of a more accomplished rival emerging to fill what often had proved a problem position at Anfield. But by the end of that fateful Goodison encounter, Beglin's leg had been shattered in a tackle with Gary Stevens – and with it his Liverpool ambitions.

Beglin, who cost a small fee on his arrival from Shamrock Rovers in May 1983, made his Reds debut 18 months later in midfield but was not tried in his favoured role until he deputised for Alan Kennedy at the end of 1984/85, a stint which culminated in the European Cup Final at the Heysel Stadium. Kennedy started 1985/86 back in favour but soon Beglin ousted him for good and, apart from one four-match spell, the Irishman held sway for the rest of a triumphant term.

His talents typified those demanded of a modern Liverpool defender: he had close control, used the ball with precision and intelligence – it was his interception and pass to Jan Molby which initiated Ian Rush's equaliser against Everton in the 1986 FA Cup Final – and read the game shrewdly. In addition Beglin was fast, competitive in the air and effective in attack. If he had a weakness it was when an opponent cut inside him, but he was working on that when injury struck.

While his leg was mending, Beglin suffered the frustration of watching a succession of youngsters – Gary Ablett, Steve Staunton, David Burrows – impress in his job and when he regained fitness the old confidence was missing. In June 1989 he took a free transfer to Leeds, only for ligament problems and arthritis to force premature retirement. Happily, Jim found a new niche in broadcasting.

	JAMES MARTIN BEGLIN
BORN	Waterford, Republic of Ireland, 29 July 1963.
HONOURS	League Championship 85/6. FA Cup 85/6. 15 Republic of Ireland caps (84-86).
OTHER CLUBS	Shamrock Rovers, Republic of Ireland; Leeds United 89/90 (19, 0);
	Plymouth Argyle on loan 89/90 (5, 0); Blackburn Rovers on loan 90/1 (6,0).

GAMES 91
GOALS 3

STEVE McMAHON

1985/86 → 1991/92

Steve McMahon was a winner, plain and simple. The fact was etched in every flicker of expression, every gesture, every line of his combative frame as he patrolled the Reds' midfield like some hunter who knew that his prey was at his mercy and that it was only a matter of time before he claimed it. Like Graeme Souness before him, he exuded ruthlessness, and again like the formidable Scot, he had the footballing qualities to fulfil his ambitions.

Liverpool-born McMahon took an unorthodox road to Anfield, joining Everton from school and serving as a Goodison Park ball-boy before becoming one of the most promising Blues of the early 1980s. But he was not happy on Merseyside; after rejecting Howard Kendall's offer of a new contract, also he spurned the chance to join the Reds, electing instead to make a new start with Aston Villa in May 1983.

McMahon failed to settle in the Midlands, and when Kenny Dalglish offered £350,000 to take him home two years later, the deal was completed swiftly. It was the first signing by Liverpool's new boss, but few were to prove wiser.

Not that the blond play-maker immediately revealed the form which was to make him one of the club's most influential performers by the end of the decade. His abrasive ball-winning qualities, precise distribution and dynamic shooting – ironically his first goal for Liverpool was the winner at Goodison in September 1985 – were already in evidence, but the creative heights which transformed him into the hub of the side still lay ahead.

In that first season as a Red he won a Championship medal, but vied for a place with Kevin MacDonald and missed the FA Cup Final victory against Everton. The following campaign, which brought no trophy, saw a maturing of his talents, and the through-pass which freed Ian Rush to score the opener in the League Cup Final clash with Arsenal was a foretaste of delights to come.

But it was not until 1987/88, and the arrival of John Barnes and Peter Beardsley, that McMahon began to realise his full potential. He was the perfect provider for the gifted newcomers and, as his confidence grew, so did his authority in the centre of midfield. Fierce tackling remained a basic part of his game, but now he revealed creativity and vision at which he had previously only hinted; his passing, both long and short, grew in control and penetration, and he carried the ball with both purpose and grace.

Though never a prolific scorer, McMahon continued to contribute a significant quota of spectacular goals, possessing the enviable ability to hit his shots hard and low. a nightmarish combination for goalkeepers. Oxford United were on the receiving end of one particularly fearsome strike at the Manor Ground on Boxing Day 1987, and Manchester United's Chris Turner, rooted to his line as he was passed by a 25-yard piledriver at Anfield three months later, will also vouch for the velocity of McMahon's missiles. Power, however, did not provide his only means of finding the net, as he demonstrated with a cheeky chip in the 9-0 demolition of Crystal Palace in the autumn of 1989.

As the 1990s dawned, Steve had broken into the England squad and had most of a five-year contract with the Reds to run. He was at his peak and still playing as though his life depended on it, but he never flourished under the leadership of new boss Graeme Souness, despite a spell as captain when Ronnie Whelan was injured.

As his form declined, he appeared to become tetchy on the field and, with the side struggling for direction, he was sold to Manchester City for £900,000 in December 1991. It was an anti-climactic exit for such an influential individual, who made little impact at Maine Road but went on to show promise as an abrasive (what else?) player-boss at Swindon.

Though never quite matching the omnipotence of Souness as a performer, Steve McMahon was close enough for the comparison to be made. And praise doesn't come much higher than that.

STEPHEN McMAHON	
BORN	Liverpool, 20 August 1961.
HONOURS	League Championship 85/6, 87/8, 89/90. FA Cup 88/9. 17 England caps (88-90).
OTHER CLUBS	Everton 80/1-82/3 (100, 11); Aston Villa 83/4-85/6 (75, 7); Manchester City 91/2-94/5 (87, 1); Swindon Town 94/5-97/8 (42, 0).
MANAGER	Swindon Town (94-99); Blackpool (00-04); Perth Glory, Australia (05).

GAMES **268 (2)**
GOALS **49**

GARY ABLETT

1986/87 → 1991/92

Gary Ablett did little wrong over six seasons in and out of the Liverpool team, picking up two Championship medals and one FA Cup winner's gong along the way. Yet, somehow, there was always a nagging suspicion that he was not destined to secure a regular long-term niche – and so it proved.

If the versatile defender ever harboured doubts about the paramount need for patience as he fought for that berth, a dramatic rise in the temperature of competition for places during 1989/90 must have removed them unceremoniously. Thereafter, it seemed, unless he was prepared to play the role of perpetual stopgap, it was a question of whether he moved on sooner or later.

Ablett, the first Liverpudlian since Sammy Lee to appear in more than a handful of matches for the Reds, had made steady progress since making his League debut at Charlton in December 1986. Deputising in both full-back slots and in the middle of the back four, he had distinguished himself with a succession of sound, composed performances.

Gaunt of build and spidery of movement, he was not the paciest of operators but he timed his tackles well, was solid in the air and boasted a neat line in unfussy distribution. His temperament was impeccable and, after missing only the first three League games of 1988/89, he might have been excused for feeling that he was established.

But then the arrival of Glenn Hysen, together with the rapid strides made by Steve Staunton and David Burrows, relegated Ablett in the pecking order and his opportunities in the new campaign were limited. Yet a measure of his standing was that when Middlesbrough offered £700,000 for him, Kenny Dalglish answered in the negative, just as Joe Fagan had four years earlier when Ablett had attracted a six-figure offer from Derby County.

Liverpool's refusal to part must have given him confidence, and the England under-21 international continued to make the most of limited chances. Certainly he impressed when standing in at centre-back, arguably his best position, in the League Cup defeat at Highbury in 1989, but when Hysen and Alan Hansen returned he was sidelined again.

Gary deserved better than to be a permanent reserve and, after looking uncomfortable during the early months of the new Souness regime, he joined Everton for £750,000 in January 1992.

In 2006 there began a new chapter in the Liverpool-Ablett relationship when he returned to Anfield to coach the reserves, whom he led to their national championship in 2008. A year, however, he left to manage Stockport.

	GARY IAN ABLETT
BORN	Liverpool, 19 November 1965.
HONOURS	League Championship 87/8, 89/90. FA Cup 88/9.
OTHER CLUBS	Derby County on loan 84/5 (6, 0); Hull City on loan (86/7 (5, 0); Everton 91/2-95/6 (128, 5); Sheffield United on loan 95/6 (12, 0); Birmingham City 96/7-98/9 (104, 1); Wycombe Wanderers on loan 99/00 (4, 0); Blackpool 99/00 (10, 1).
MANAGER	Stockport County (09-).

GAMES	137 (9)
GOALS	1

NIGEL SPACKMAN

1986/87 → 1988/89

During the two eventful years they spent in each other's company, Nigel Spackman and Liverpool were undeniably good for each other.

Kenny Dalglish parted with £400,000 to sign the tall, strong Chelsea stalwart in February 1987 when the Reds' midfield department was sorely depleted by injuries. Spackman's early performances demonstrated that while he might lack the creative skills to unlock a stubborn defence singlehandedly, there was no one more adept at doing the simple thing well.

He had the underrated ability to play short passes quickly and with precision, and became a reliable foil for the more extravagant talents around him.

This was particularly evident in 1987/88 when the former Bournemouth man, who spent much of the season deputising for the injured Ronnie Whelan, was joined in the team by John Barnes and Peter Beardsley.

Spackman played in more than half the matches as the Reds cruised exhilaratingly to the title, time and again proving the need for a workhorse among the artists.

His stout attributes were never more sharply defined than in the much-lauded 5-0 demolition of Nottingham Forest at Anfield in April 1988 when, unselfish to a fault, he laid on two of the goals for colleagues when he might have found the net himself. That was especially admirable as Nigel was never to score in his 63 appearances for the club.

He went on to play in the FA Cup Final against Wimbledon, but in the subsequent season a fitter squad increased the manager's options and even the versatile Spackman, who helped out occasionally in defence, found it hard to win a place.

In February 1989, his job done, he left for Queen's Park Rangers (on his way to Ibrox employment by Graeme Souness, as it transpired), taking with him a Championship medal and a wealth of glorious memories. Liverpool had received two years' doughty service and now they picked up a £100,000 profit. Splendid business for all concerned.

NIGEL JAMES SPACKMAN

BORN	Romsey, Hampshire, 2 December 1960.
HONOURS	League Championship 87/8.
OTHER CLUBS	Bournemouth 80/1-82/3 (119, 10); Chelsea 83/4-86/7 (141, 12); Queen's Park Rangers 88/9-89/90 (29, 1); Glasgow Rangers 89/90-92/3 (100, 1); Chelsea 92/3-95/6 (67, 0); Sheffield United 96/7 (23,0).
MANAGER	Sheffield United (97-98); Barnsley (01); Millwall (06).

GAMES **50 (13)**

GOALS **0**

JOHN ALDRIDGE

1986/87 → 1989/90

It was like a worthy but run-of-the-mill county cricketer taking over from prince of batsmen Viv Richards, or a rookie rider climbing into the saddle of master jockey Lester Piggott; when John Aldridge replaced Ian Rush as Liverpool centre-forward public expectations were not especially high.

But Scouser John had the perfect response. He scored so freely that Rush was not missed and when the prodigal hero did return after a frustrating year in the Italian sun he found that reclaiming the role of the Reds' goalscorer-in-chief was no formality. Indeed, a hefty slice of the Welshman's first campaign back at Anfield was spent on the bench as he languished in the shadow of his so-called stand-in.

Aldridge had achieved his lifetime ambition of joining Liverpool in January 1987 when, with Rush's departure in the offing, Kenny Dalglish signed him from Oxford United for £700,000. His Manor Ground strike-rate of around 1.5 goals every two games might have made him one of the most feared strikers in the land yet, strangely, there was widespread reticence in recognising his achievements.

True, he had never played for a glamorous club and his style was efficient rather than flashy, but that record, which included 18 months of First Division experience, surely would have made it surprising if he had failed at Anfield. How perverse, then, that in many quarters his success was greeted with downright amazement.

In his first half-term as a Red, Aldridge started only two League matches but, significantly, scored in both, although it wasn't until 1987/88 that the headlines started coming his way. Even when he netted in the opening nine League matches – admittedly six of his strikes were from the penalty spot – he was accorded but a fraction of the acclaim deservedly bestowed on John Barnes.

As the season wore on, however, it dawned gradually on the media that perhaps the unobtrusive front-runner who rounded off so many flowing moves with the minimum of fuss should be given a share of the credit. After all, his finishing was clinical and he was better in the air than Rush; his selfless running created countless openings for Messrs Barnes and Beardsley, and if Aldridge could match neither the ball skills of his team-mates nor the pace of his predecessor he made up for it with the positional sense of a born opportunist.

Add to that his inbuilt passion for Liverpool – never more evident than in his utter devastation on missing his first penalty for the club in the 1988 FA Cup Final against Wimbledon – and his all-round value becomes apparent.

Despite the triumphs of his first full term at Anfield, in which he scored 26 times on the way to a title medal, it was widely predicted that he would shuffle quietly out of the limelight when Ian Rush returned for 1988/89.

Once again Aldridge confounded the pundits. Rush spent most of the League opener against Charlton in the Selhurst Park dugout before replacing not Aldridge but Beardsley; John, meanwhile, was weighing in with a little matter of a hat-trick! That performance set the tone for a campaign in which Aldo outscored an often unfit Rush and capped his Reds career by sweeping home the opening goal against Everton in the 1989 FA Cup Final with icy assurance.

Come 1989/90 it was clear that Dalglish must make a choice between the two men and, not surprisingly, he chose the one for whom he had paid more than £2 million. Aldridge, though, had one more moment of glory before joining Real Sociedad for £1 million. Just days before his September move, 'Pool were five up at home to Crystal Palace when they won a penalty and the Kop called for the Republic of Ireland international. The boss betrayed evidence of a heart by sending him on, and duly he signed off with a goal; the man whom the critics had continually expected to fail had succeeded to the last.

Even then, Aldo's Merseyside exploits were not finished. After two years of prospering in Spain, he signed for Tranmere as a 32-year-old in 1991, going on to become player-boss and to register well in excess of a century of League strikes over the next seven campaigns. Wherever he played, at whatever level, John Aldridge scored freely. It is tempting to wonder just what he might have achieved had he been allowed to remain at Anfield in 1989.

JOHN WILLIAM ALDRIDGE
BORN Liverpool, 18 September 1958.
HONOURS League Championship 87/8. FA Cup 88/9. 69 Republic of Ireland caps (86-96).
OTHER CLUBS Newport County 79/80-83/4 (170, 69); Oxford United 83/4-86/7 (114, 72); Real Sociedad, Spain, 89/90-90/1 (63, 33); Tranmere Rovers 91/2-97/8 (242, 138).
MANAGER Tranmere Rovers (96-01).

GAMES 89 (15)
GOALS 63

JOHN BARNES

1987/88 → 1996/97

As the veteran John Barnes applied himself industriously to a comparatively unspectacular midfield anchor role during the Reds' mid-1990s renaissance, it was inevitable that he was outshone by the generation of new stars shining incandescently around him. But it should never be forgotten that, not so long before, he was hailed as one of the most brilliant entertainers to grace British football since the war.

More than that, he achieved something which eluded every Anfield player before him: he became, for a while, the national symbol of the game at its most attractive. In the same way that George Best's name was once a byword for soccer excellence, even among people who didn't follow sport, so in the late 1980s was that of the Jamaican-born England forward.

As an all-round performer he did not equal Dalglish at his peak, and for sheer pop-idol appeal, he did not match Keegan. But in terms of presence and charisma John left the Scotsman standing, and for all Kevin's admirable qualities, he lacked the magical skills with which the former Watford winger was so plenteously endowed. Thus, it was John Barnes, more than anyone else, who finally bestowed upon Liverpool the glitter and panache which had been the traditional preserve of Spurs and Manchester United.

Yet for all the plaudits heaped on his close-cropped head, Barnes was seen as something of a gamble when he headed north for £900,000 in the summer of 1987. His extravagant talents were acknowledged, but at Vicarage Road these had been tempered with inconsistency and there were fears that he was not the Anfield type. Any misgivings, however, withered as Barnes produced a string of scintillating early performances which dazzled even the sceptics.

To say he gave the Reds a new dimension is a gross understatement. A big, powerful man blessed with a sublime first touch, he was lethal when he received the ball in a deep left-flank position and ran at defences. He had the guile to gull those who stood in his way, the strength to ride tackles and a deceptive pace which took him loping away from his stricken prey.

One moment Barnes would be hemmed in by several opponents, two feints later he would be yards away, jockeying for a shooting chance. And unlike many wingers, he could capitalise on his own approach work, scoring goals from almost any angle or distance. Indeed, so stunning was his marksmanship that some critics reckoned he was best employed as a central striker.

John's reward for his inspired efforts during that first Anfield campaign was a title medal and Footballer of the Year awards from fellow professionals and soccer writers alike. Understandably, much was expected of him in the 1988 European Championships but he disappointed, as he did often in the international arena, looking more like the wayward performer who had alternately thrilled and frustrated in his Watford days. Perhaps he needed his regular top-class colleagues to bring the best out of him, for on his return to club duty he was as deadly as ever, apart from the occasional game when he seemed to drift.

Despite his catalogue of gifts, however, Barnes experienced a relatively fallow career interlude, which coincided loosely with the Souness reign. Injuries laid him low and he put on weight, looking sluggish and ill at ease when he did play. Happily, he shed pounds and regained vitality in 1994, confounding the popular belief that he was finished, and he became a subtly cohesive link-man, passing so beautifully that he was known to go through an entire game without losing possession.

Yes, there were times when he was overrun by heel-snapping speedsters, and some reckoned he was too cautious, not delivering enough 'killer' balls. There was no denying, either, that the 'miracle man' of yesteryear had gone forever. But in his place was a canny general, offering his precocious young lieutenants much-needed guidance, sometimes with a firmness surprising in one so placid, and it was clear that he had plenty to offer still.

However, after he was dropped for the second leg of the Cup Winners' Cup semi-final against Paris St-Germain in April 1997, it became apparent that he was no longer wanted and come August, by then aged 33, he was freed to pursue a brief Indian summer at Newcastle.

It is to be hoped that those fans who had noisily demanded his exit have since restored him, in their minds, to the place of honour merited by his exceptional service. Truly, John Barnes was one of Liverpool's finest.

JOHN CHARLES BRYAN BARNES

BORN Kingston, Jamaica, 7 November 1963.

HONOURS League Championship 87/8, 89/90. FA Cup 88/9. League Cup 94/5. 79 England caps (83-95). FWA Footballer of the Year 88, 90. PFA Footballer of the Year 88.

OTHER CLUBS Watford 81/2-86/7 (233, 65); Newcastle United 97/8-98/9 (27, 6); Charlton Athletic 98/9 (12, 0).

MANAGER Celtic (chief coach, 99-00), Jamaica (08-09); Tranmere Rovers (09).

GAMES **402 (4)**

GOALS **107**

170

PETER BEARDSLEY

1987/88 → 1990/91

Shoulders hunched and mouth habitually agape, Peter Beardsley hardly cut an heroic figure on the field. Until, that was, the ball arrived at his feet. Then, suddenly, the multi-talented Geordie looked what he was – a daring, elusive firecracker of a player, lurking with intent on the very verge of world class.

For four seasons, presumed at the time to be his peak, he plied his trade to coruscating effect for Liverpool; then, having entered his 31st year and with his confidence evidently in decline, he was allowed to slip away. Wisdom comes easily after the event, but how ill-judged Graeme Souness' decision to sell him was to appear after Beardsley put in another half-decade and more of sheer magnificence for Everton and Newcastle, finding time to resurrect his England career along the way.

Beardsley's early days at Anfield were not easy. When he moved from Newcastle for £1.9 million in the summer of 1987, he carried the burdensome tag of Britain's most expensive footballer. As if that were not enough of a challenge, his arrival coincided with that of John Barnes, a circumstance which both helped and hindered his efforts to make an instant impact. The England winger's sensational form deflected much of the media attention from Beardsley, giving him much-needed extra time to bed in, but also it set a dauntingly high standard, especially as Barnes' transfer fee had been less than half his own.

For several months, while by no means a flop, the stocky, deep-lying marksman failed to rivet the eye and by the turn of the year he had contributed only four goals. The Reds, however, remained unbeaten in the League and Kenny Dalglish pronounced himself well satisfied with Peter's progress.

As 1988 dawned, the manager's faith was shown to be cannily placed, his record signing turning in a sparkling New Year's Day performance against Coventry. The former Magpie, whose route to St James' Park had taken in a frustrating one-match sojourn at Old Trafford, scored twice and had the Kop purring with pleasure at his all-round skills as he began to fulfil his immense potential.

That day, and for the rest of the campaign, Beardsley was irresistible, whether employing his speed and ball control to skip past defenders as he ran from deep positions, or slicing deadly, perfectly angled passes through a crowded penalty area. With his self-belief at last sky-high, he revealed the full repertoire of tricks which had endeared him to Tyneside and, at Anfield later that month, Arsenal fell victim to a typical piece of Beardsley cheek. Nutmegging an astonished Michael Thomas, he moved forward to chip the ball over towering 'keeper John Lukic to put the match beyond the Gunners' reach.

Quick-witted and a natural improviser, Peter confirmed his stature over subsequent seasons, though he would have risen to yet greater heights in a red shirt if his finishing had been more consistent. Often he would appear on the edge of the box, jink past a couple of defenders and then spoil his work with a weak attempt on goal. The Beardsley boot could dispatch a devastating shot, be it blistering drive or tantalising curler but, in those days at least, reliable it was not.

Unlike some gifted individuals, Beardsley could never be faulted for his work-rate, even if he did seem to run out of steam now and then. Also there were days when he was unable to get into the swing of the action, which resulted in periodic controversial omissions from an increasingly out-of-sorts side – by Anfield standards, that is – as the Dalglish era approached its stunning end. Those absences and occasional form-losses offered proof positive of Beardsley's enormous influence: when the England striker was sidelined or below-par, the Reds' overall performance suffered significantly, their attacking options drastically reduced without his normally incisive input.

For Liverpool fans who bemoan, to this day, what they lost after Peter's £1 million sale to Everton in August 1991, there is one telling consolation – at least they enjoyed four years of Beardsley brilliance. At Manchester his sole appearance ended in substitution; how United must have rued the decision to let him go after just one hour of first-team football.

PETER ANDREW BEARDSLEY

BORN   Newcastle, 18 January 1961.
HONOURS   League Championship 87/8, 89/90. FA Cup 88/9. 59 England caps (86-96).
OTHER CLUBS   Carlisle United 79/80-81/2 (104, 22); Vancouver Whitecaps 82; Manchester United 82/3 (0, 0, Peter's one appearance was in a League Cup tie); Vancouver Whitecaps 83; Newcastle United 83/4-86/7 (147, 61); Everton 91/2-92/3 (81, 25); Newcastle United 93/4-96/7 (129, 47); Bolton Wanderers 97/8 (17, 2); Manchester City on loan 97/8 (6, 0); Fulham 97/8-98/9 (21, 4); Hartlepool United 98/9 (22, 2).

GAMES   **158 (15)**
GOALS   59

RAY HOUGHTON

1987/88 → 1991/92

Kenny Dalglish's ceaseless quest for perfection took Ray Houghton to Anfield in the autumn of 1987. Even at that early stage of the season, the Reds were apparently cantering away with the Championship and playing some of the most exhilarating football the First Division had seen in years. Surely the manager could not ask for more? But, of course, he could!

Craig Johnston was doing a splendid job as a right-sided attacking midfielder, but Dalglish believed that Houghton would be an improvement. So, after a protracted cloak-and-dagger transfer saga, he paid £825,000 for the stocky Glaswegian.

Houghton, who had been dumped by West Ham after one appearance and then rebuilt his career with Fulham and Oxford United, played his first match for Liverpool at home to Norwich and made an instant impact, the game finishing goalless through no fault of the newcomer. The Kop warmed to Ray as he created a series of chances with his busy runs and accurate crosses, and as the weeks went by it became clear that Dalglish had made yet another astute purchase.

The Eire international – he qualified for the Republic by virtue of an Irish father – was a tireless forager who relishing picking up the ball inside his own half and dribbling it deep into opposition territory. On reaching his destination, he was less prone than Johnston to squander possession, and often he startled goalkeepers with snap shots from outside the penalty area.

Houghton was in the habit, also, of popping up for vital close-range strikes, as he did twice with FA Cup goals in early 1988, a header which beat Everton at Goodison Park and a magnificently adroit mid-air side-footed volley against Manchester City at Maine Road.

With Houghton providing a thrustful threat on the right and John Barnes casting his magic spell on the left, the Reds were superbly balanced. They were ideally equipped to rip open the most clam-like of defences, and in that glorious 1987/88 campaign, they did so frequently,

Houghton capped the impressive start to his Liverpool career with some enterprising performances for his adopted country, linking smoothly with clubmates John Aldridge and Ronnie Whelan in the 1988 European Championships.

His dash and skill on the wider stage prompted the interest of assorted Italian clubs and huge sums were mentioned, but Dalglish understandably refused to part with his new-found gem. Houghton confirmed his stature with exemplary form in the following term, being an ever-present in the team which failed narrowly to take the title and giving an outstanding display in the FA Cup Final win over Everton.

Injuries caused him to miss much of 1989/90, but he bounced back for the hectic climax to that title-winning season and was the Reds' most consistent performer during the two turbulent campaigns which followed. Accordingly, his £825,000 departure to Aston Villa in July 1992 provoked considerable consternation among Kopites, who were mystified by Graeme Souness' sale of a player who had so much still to offer at club and international level.

Their qualms were amplified by Houghton's emergence as a key figure in the Villa side which pushed Manchester United most of the way in the 1992/93 Championship race, then assumed positively gargantuan proportions when he struck the sensational goal which beat Italy in the Republic of Ireland's opening game at the 1994 World Cup Finals.

RAYMOND JAMES HOUGHTON

BORN	Glasgow; 9 January 1962.
HONOURS	League Championship 87/8, 89/90. FA Cup 88/9, 91/2. 73 Republic of Ireland caps (86-97).
OTHER CLUBS	West Ham United 81/2 (1, 0); Fulham 82/3-85/6 (129, 16); Oxford United 85/6-87/8 (83, 10); Aston Villa 92/3-94/5 (95, 6); Crystal Palace 94/5-96/7 (72, 7); Reading 97/8-98/9 (43, 1).

GAMES	193 (7)
GOALS	37

RONNIE WHELAN
1980/81 → 1993/94

At best inspirational, at worst remarkably consistent, Ronnie Whelan was at the heart of almost every Liverpool triumph of the 1980s. The Eire international's deceptively simple, almost matter-of-fact midfield method exerted a powerfully pervasive influence which increased with the passing years.

When the sandy-haired Dubliner breezed into Bob Paisley's side in 1981, he made an exciting impact with spectacular goals and an infectious, ambitious style of play which, though exhilarating when Whelan was on song, sometimes resulted in the ball being lost unnecessarily. Maturity taught him to do the simple thing, and to do it well, with the result that he could be counted on to perform reliably in any company, on any occasion.

When Ronnie – whose father, Ron Snr, also wore the Republic's green shirt – left Home Farm in October 1979, his destination might have been Old Trafford rather than Anfield. He had spent three summer holidays with Manchester United as a schoolboy but was allowed to slip through their recruitment net.

The Red Devils' loss was to be Liverpool's gain and, some 18 months after crossing the Irish Sea, he marked his League debut, against Stoke City in front of the Kop, with a goal. It was October 1981, however, before he outstripped his countryman Kevin Sheedy, who was later to build a successful career with Everton, in the race to replace Ray Kennedy on the left side of the Reds' midfield.

In his first campaign as a regular, Whelan could do little wrong. As well as picking up a title medal, he scored twice in the League Cup victory over Spurs at Wembley and received a Young Player of the Year award. To cap it all, no less a judge than Joe Mercer compared him to that great Northern Irish inside-forward of several decades earlier, Peter Doherty.

Whelan maintained his progress during the following season, contributing another League Cup Final winner, this time against Manchester United, but suffered a setback in 1983/84 when a hand injury kept him out of the side until November. On his return he seemed to have lost impetus and there were fears that he was drifting out of long-term contention, but the exit of Graeme Souness changed all that.

In the absence of the former skipper, Ronnie tightened up his game and accepted new responsibility to become a better all-round player than ever before. His distribution became more efficient, his tackling attained a keenly abrasive edge, and there was a new purpose about everything he did. As a bonus, the new Whelan retained his habit of scoring sensational goals, none more breathtaking than the first-time 25-yard curler past Gary Bailey which took the 1985 FA Cup semi-final against Manchester United into extra time.

As his medal collection burgeoned, so did his versatility. At various times he occupied all the midfield positions and filled in effectively at left-back when Jim Beglin broke his leg in early 1987. Then, in the subsequent season when costly newcomers were grabbing all the headlines, Whelan enjoyed his best term to date. Moving into a central role to create extra space for John Barnes on the left, he was a revelation, his quickfire passing and selfless running off the ball winning new and much-deserved acclaim. His enthusiasm and level-headed approach were rewarded with the captaincy when Alan Hansen was sidelined for most of 1988/89 and he led the Reds to FA Cup triumph over Everton at Wembley.

Come 1990, Whelan was vastly experienced though not yet 30 and he was expected to play a pivotal role as Liverpool sought to extend their dominance of English football into a new decade. Sadly, his outings over ensuing seasons were to be curtailed cruelly by injuries, and, surprisingly, when he was fit he was not always selected by Souness.

In September 1994, he was freed to join Southend United and ten months later was promoted to player-boss. After an encouraging start, there followed difficult times and an acrimonious exit from Roots Hall, then Whelan went on to test his managerial mettle in Greece and Cyprus.

RONALD ANDREW WHELAN

BORN   Dublin, 25 September 1961.

HONOURS   European Cup 83/4. League Championship 81/2, 82/3, 83/4, 85/6, 87/8, 89/90. FA Cup 85/6, 88/9. League Cup 81/2, 82/3, 83/4. 53 Republic of Ireland caps (81-95).

OTHER CLUBS   Home Farm, Republic of Ireland; Southend United 94/5-95/6 (34, 1).

MANAGER   Southend United (95-97); Panionios, Greece; Olympiakos Nicosia, Cyprus.

GAMES **467 (18)**

GOALS **73**

GARY GILLESPIE

· ·

1983/84 → 1990/91

The shrewd acquisition of centre-back Gary Gillespie in July 1983 typified the meticulous planning which helped Liverpool retain their position of supremacy in English football for so long. When new manager Joe Fagan paid Coventry £325,000 to make Gillespie his first signing, it was hardly credible that the classy Scot was going to see first-team service in the foreseeable future. Fagan was blessed already with the masterly combination of Alan Hansen and Mark Lawrenson, and despite five years experience as a First Division defender, the tall, angular newcomer seemed destined to serve an Anfield 'apprenticeship' in the reserves.

Sure enough, a whole season passed in which the former midfielder and occasional full-back made but a solitary senior appearance, at home to Walsall in the League Cup semi-final first leg. But 1984/85 brought intermittent opportunities and Gillespie made the most of them. He revealed a commanding aerial presence in both penalty areas, cultured and precise distribution, and a penchant for loping forward like some runaway giraffe to play slick one-two passing combinations.

His campaign culminated with a promising European Cup Final display against Juventus, despite conceding the penalty which cost Liverpool the match, after coming on for the injured Lawrenson just 90 seconds into the action. By then, of course, all footballing considerations had been rendered irrelevant by earlier events on that tragic Heysel night.

Gillespie was to get no further chance until January 1986, when he put together an impressive run, highlighted uncharacteristically by an Anfield hat-trick against Birmingham, and finally he became established in the team. With Lawrenson sidelined once again, the former Sky Blue dovetailed seamlessly with Hansen and played enough matches to earn a title medal. Even when Mark was fit again, Gary retained his place and looked set to face Everton in the FA Cup Final, but he was laid low by a virus and missed what would have been his first Wembley date.

Over the next two terms he played some of the best football of his career, showing ever more skill and composure as his confidence grew. He was rewarded by international caps but this encouraging progress was interrupted by injuries which put him out of contention for most of 1988/89 and 1989/90. With Glenn Hysen added to the squad, suddenly Gillespie's prospects were not so bright, though he returned in the spring of 1990 to help clinch the Championship. However, he did not figure in Graeme Souness' plans and joined Celtic for £925,000 in August 1991.

		GAMES	199 (8)
		GOALS	6

GARY THOMPSON GILLESPIE

BORN   Bonnybridge, Stirlingshire, 5 July 1960.
HONOURS   League Championship 85/6, 87/8, 89/90. 13 Scotland caps (87-90).
OTHER CLUBS   Falkirk 77/8 (22, 0); Coventry City 78/9-82/3 (172, 6); Celtic 91/2-93/4 (69, 3); Coventry City 94/5 (3, 0).

BARRY VENISON

1986/87 → 1991/92

Barry Venison deserves top marks for initiative. In the summer of 1986 the England under-21 international full-back felt his career was going nowhere with Sunderland, who had narrowly escaped relegation to the Third Division. It had been a second successive disappointing campaign for Venison, who in 1985 had become the youngest captain in a Wembley final when the Wearsiders had tasted League Cup defeat and dropped out of the top flight. So he wrote to Liverpool to ask if he was wanted at Anfield; the result was a £250,000 transfer and a place in the first team at the start of the new term.

He settled in with a series of composed displays, usually at right-back but occasionally switching flanks, and missed only a handful of League games. Determined and positive in his approach, Venison tackled efficiently, he was always on the alert for opportunities to link with his attack, and often he crossed the ball effectively, though sometimes his overall distribution was scrappy.

He started 1987/88 as the first choice right-back, but then injuries to Achilles tendon and calf were followed by an appendix operation and his season was in tatters. As new defenders such as Gary Ablett, Steve Staunton and David Burrows came into the reckoning, it looked as though Venison might be pushed to regain his role.

The next campaign, in which he started only 14 First Division matches but won an FA Cup medal, proved indeterminate, but in 1989/90 he enjoyed his most settled run for three years. His use of the ball, as exemplified by the pass which cut through the Chelsea rearguard to set up a goal for Peter Beardsley at Stamford Bridge in December 1989, was improving and he was beginning to look like a long-term proposition.

However, further injuries and stern competition for places precipitated a £250,000 transfer to Newcastle United in July 1992 and it proved the making of him. Given extra responsibility with Kevin Keegan's Magpies, the forthright north-easterner excelled in both central defence and midfield, and earned a full England call-up in the latter role.

Later Venison played briefly under Graeme Souness in Turkey before taking his considerable nous and experience to Southampton, only for a back problem to end his career prematurely. By then his flaxen locks and flamboyant dress had become familiar to viewers of Sky TV, for whom he had worked as a summariser, and he went on to become a successful broadcaster.

BARRY VENISON

BORN   Consett, County Durham, 16 August 1964.
HONOURS   League Championship 87/8, 89/90. FA Cup 88/9. 2 England caps (94).
OTHER CLUBS Sunderland 81/2-85/6 (173, 2); Newcastle United 92/3-94/5 (109, 1);
           Galatasaray, Turkey, 95/6; Southampton 95/6-96/7 (24, 0).

GAMES 137 (18)
GOALS 2

STEVE STAUNTON

1988/89 → 1990/91 & 1998/99 → 2000/01

When Steve Staunton was freed to join Aston Villa in December 2000 most Liverpool fans nodded in approval; the Irishman was enduringly popular but there was general recognition that his best days were gone. What stark contrast to the outrage among Kopites when Staunton had been dispatched to Villa Park nearly a decade earlier in a transaction denounced scathingly as arguably the club's most ill-conceived sale since the war.

As the 1990s began, the callow £20,000 recruit from Dundalk had just broken through and it was clear that he possessed the talent, temperament and versatility to become an Anfield cornerstone. Only a year later new manager Graeme Souness struck that perplexing £1.1 million deal – and, sure enough, the 22-year-old developed into one of the Premiership's finest left-backs. Meanwhile, Liverpool struggled depressingly for quality in what often was a problem position.

True, there were mitigating circumstances, although none that impressed the livid critics. Liverpool, like other top clubs, were hamstrung by the restriction on non-English players that then pertained, and for this purpose Staunton was classed as a 'foreigner'. Secondly, in Souness' judgement David Burrows was a promising left-back and, in fairness,

some people agreed. In addition, though Staunton had already picked up League and FA Cup honours as a Red, his confidence had been buffeted by cruel barracking by a small but noisy section of so-called supporters, who used him as a scapegoat for the team's indifferent form. On top of all that, the Anfield coffers were not exactly bulging in 1991 and, measly though the fee seems in retrospect, it was not negligible at the time.

Exactly what had Liverpool lost with Steve's departure? A defensively sound, tireless overlapper capable of truly destructive distribution – his speciality was the wickedly curling, low-trajectory cross – who could play also in midfield, central defence or even up front; indeed, he helped himself to a League Cup hat-trick as a substitute for Ian Rush at Wigan in September 1989.

Ironically, he would have been ideally suited to Roy Evans' fluid 3-5-2 formation in the mid-1990s and the Anfield boss made two failed attempts to re-sign him. However, Staunton remained in the Midlands until July 1998, when finally he was freed to rejoin the Reds, always his first love.

Surprisingly enough, he made a disappointing start to his second Liverpool sojourn, performing shakily at left-back, but went on to regain a measure of his former assurance when switched to central defence.

Soon, though, a formidable posse of new recruits arrived, and Staunton slipped so far out of contention that he declared jokingly that Gerard Houllier had forgotten he had loaned him to Crystal Palace. Accordingly he headed south to thrive once more, replacing Roy Keane as Eire skipper during the 2002 World Cup Finals and completing his century of caps. Steve Staunton's career had been one of shining accomplishment; what a shame that its prime was not spent at Anfield.

	STEPHEN STAUNTON	
BORN	Drogheda, Republic of Ireland, 19 January 1969.	
HONOURS	League Championship 89/90. FA Cup 88/9. 102 Republic of Ireland caps (88-02).	
OTHER CLUBS	Dundalk, Republic of Ireland, 85/6 (3, 0); Bradford City on loan 87/8 (8, 0); Aston Villa 91/2-97/8 (208, 16) and 00/01-02/03 (73, 0); Crystal Palace on loan 00/01 (6, 0); Coventry City 03/04-04/05 (70, 4); Walsall 05/06 (7, 0).	
MANAGER	Republic of Ireland (06-07), Darlington (09-).	

GAMES **125 (22)**
GOALS **6**

DAVID BURROWS

1988/89 → 1993/94

When Kenny Dalglish prised rookie defender David Burrows away from West Bromwich Albion for £500,000 in October 1988, dashing the hopes of a posse of rivals in the process, the word sped down the soccer grapevine that the Liverpool boss had pulled off a sizeable coup.

The fiercely enthusiastic Midlander, already an England under-21 international despite having fewer than 50 League appearances under his belt, was viewed widely as one of the finest prospects outside the top flight.

Indeed, there was a certain something about 'Bugsy' which was reminiscent of another all-action youngster who, more than 20 years earlier, had also moved to Anfield for a hefty fee.

In his unbridled sense of adventure, his almost frenzied commitment and his downright hatred of being beaten, Burrows evoked memories of no less a competitor than Emlyn Hughes. Sadly, though the former Throstle gave the Reds five years of doughty service encompassing nearly 200 senior outings, he was never even to approach the standard set by his eminent predecessor.

Having arrived with Liverpool in the throes of an injury crisis, Burrows found himself in immediate first-team action. Pressed into service at both left-back and the left side of midfield, he revealed bullish strength and enough skill to suggest that hard work could turn him into an accomplished player, despite a disturbing inclination to commit himself to horribly rash tackles.

His long stride made him an effective overlapper and his galloping gait was becoming a familiar sight when returning regulars and the emergence of fellow hopeful Steve Staunton edged him out.

Burrows fought back to play a full part in the title triumph of 1989/90 and was not often absent from the side for the next three seasons, impressing particularly as a midfield marker and proving a gutsy stand-in at centre-half.

However, he remained headstrong, his tactical acumen seemed rudimentary and, overall, his game did not progress as expected. Accordingly, it was no surprise when he was dispatched to West Ham as a makeweight in the deal that took Julian Dicks to Anfield.

Thereafter, while enjoying a solid enough career, he never settled anywhere for long and those extravagant early expectations were never met. Certainly, as the veteran campaigner threw himself into Sheffield Wednesday's battle to avoid relegation to the Second Division in the spring of 2003, the Anfield glory days of David Burrows seemed a long, long time ago.

DAVID BURROWS

BORN	Dudley, Worcestershire, 25 October 1968.
HONOURS	League Championship 89/90. FA Cup 91/2.
OTHER CLUBS	West Bromwich Albion 85/6-88/9 (46, 1); West Ham United 93/4-94/5 (29, 1); Everton 94/5 (19, 0); Coventry City 94/5- 99/00 (111, 0); Birmingham City 00/01-01/02 (25, 0); Sheffield Wednesday 01/02-02/03 (21, 0).

GAMES **181 (12)**
GOALS **3**

IAN RUSH

1980/81 → 1986/87 & 1988/89 → 1995/96

Every now and then, no more than once or twice in a generation, there arises in top-flight football an individual with a certain predatory instinct; no matter how exciting or beautiful the talents of more artistic performers may be, this man's special gift – the knack of scoring goals in large numbers and at regular intervals – is the most valuable asset in the game. In modern times, certainly since the golden days of Jimmy Greaves and Denis Law, no British player has demonstrated a more ruthless aptitude for long-term net-finding than Ian Rush. The Welshman's record is all the more remarkable because so many of his goals have come in high-profile matches with trophies at stake, a testimony to temperament as well as supreme skill.

Yet there was a time, shortly after his £300,000 move to Liverpool from Chester in April 1980, when Rush looked destined to flop. In his early days at Anfield he could hardly manage to get on the Central League scoresheet, and there had even been talk of a swift exit. Then came a chance in the 1981 League Cup Final replay against West Ham and, suddenly, confidence seemed to surge through the rookie striker's lean frame. Streaking down the left flank, at last revealing a glimpse of the searing pace that was to make him feared throughout the football world, the raw Flintshire lad gave a broad hint that the Reds' investment had not been a rash one.

But it was not until the following campaign that the real Ian Rush stood up. Then the goals came with a vengeance; they started with a trickle, increased to a steady flow, and over the next five seasons swelled to a veritable torrent. Between 1981/82 and 1986/87 Rush hit the target nearly 200 times, averaging around two strikes every three games. Ironically, he was particularly pitiless towards Everton, whom he had supported as a boy, his most savage execution taking place at Goodison Park in 1982 when he scored four.

Rush's most obvious asset was the speed which carried him beyond defenders, but it was by no means his only weapon. He was a clean, powerful striker of the ball and had the finely honed positional sense of all the best poachers; his first touch was usually sure and he was willing to forage for possession, though for a six-footer he was surprisingly weak in the air.

So integral was Rush to the Liverpool set-up that when it was revealed he was on his way to Juventus for £3.2 million – the deal was announced a year before he left in June 1987 – there was consternation on the Kop. In the event he was hardly missed, thanks to the Aldridge, Barnes and Beardsley triumvirate, and many observers thought the Reds were foolish to part with £2.8 million to get him back.

Certainly, after a year of frustration and illness, the old Rush fire needed patient rekindling and there were moments when it seemed the spark had gone. But by then he was no longer merely a spearhead; instead he was leading the line, often receiving the ball with his back to goal, which demanded different skills. Naturally it took time to adapt, but two opportunist strikes which beat Everton in the 1989 FA Cup Final signalled that his rehabilitation was complete.

Thereafter, Rush proved a more accomplished all-rounder than ever before. His former pace never quite returned, his scoring-rate was not as formidable, but his own more-than-respectable tallies were augmented by the countless assists he contributed to team-mates and by a capacity for work which seemed to grow as he got older.

But most telling of all was the way Ian Rush reacted to a challenge. When dropped by Graeme Souness he came back with all guns blazing to earn the captaincy, only to face an even more daunting double threat from Messrs Fowler and Collymore in 1995. With two such virile young bloods hunting his job, most thirtysomethings might have shuffled off to find a more comfortable berth. But not Rushie: he just battled harder, and first Fowler, then Collymore, was omitted to accommodate the old fella.

Eventually a cartilage injury cost him his place, but still Rush showed no signs of stepping meekly aside, continuing to give his all until accepting a free transfer to Leeds United in May 1996. True grit from a true great.

IAN JAMES RUSH

BORN	St Asaph, Flintshire, 20 October 1961.
HONOURS	European Cup 83/4. League Championship 81/2, 82/3, 83/4, 85/6, 89/90.
	FA Cup 85/6, 88/9, 91/2. League Cup 80/1, 81/2, 82/3, 83/4, 94/5.
	73 Wales caps (80-96). FWA Footballer of the Year 84.
	PFA Footballer of the Year 84.
OTHER CLUBS	Chester 78/9-79/80 (34, 14); Juventus 87/8 (29, 7);
	Leeds United 96/7 (36, 3); Newcastle United 97/8 (10, 0);
	Sheffield United on loan 97/8 (4, 0); Wrexham 98/9 (17, 0).

GAMES **625 (30)**

GOALS **340**

RONNY ROSENTHAL

1989/90 → 1993/94

When Ronny Rosenthal was pitched into the title race in the spring of 1990 it was like a fistful of *Alka Seltzers* hitting a bucket of water. Not that Liverpool were ailing – they were firmly in pole position – but they were in need of a tonic after the trauma of FA Cup semi-final defeat by Crystal Palace. Cue Ronny, an instant one-man pick-me-up.

Kenny Dalglish had signed the Israeli international striker on loan from Standard Liege just minutes ahead of the transfer deadline, eventually closing a £1 million deal the following summer after Rosenthal had proved his worth in stirring fashion.

After impressing as a substitute against Southampton at Anfield, he was a sensation in his first full appearance, destroying Charlton at Selhurst Park with a scintillating hat-trick. It wasn't just the goals but the manner of them which captivated travelling Kopites; there was one with his left foot, one with his right and a diving header.

Through pace, verve and crisp finishing, he produced further crucial strikes that term and, though he might not have been the easiest man to play alongside – he was always full of running but not always in the right direction – Reds fans salivated at the thought of more defence-shredding cavalry charges to come.

However, it transpired that while he could lift crowds and colleagues alike, Rosenthal was at his most effective when rising from the bench, unpredictability being his chief virtue, and he remained on the fringe of the side for four years.

In January 1994, as one of his last acts as Liverpool boss, Graeme Souness sold the Israeli to Tottenham for £250,000. Rosenthal left Anfield declaring that he had never been given a fair chance, understandable from his standpoint but not a view shared by most observers.

At White Hart Lane, he found himself in a similar supporting role at first, until in 1995/96 he enjoyed his longest unbroken run of senior appearances since arriving in English football, playing a typically energetic part in Spurs' latest attempt at renaissance. Subsequently Rosenthal moved to Watford, where he completed his career.

RONNY ROSENTHAL

BORN   Haifa, Israel, 11 October 1963.

HONOURS   55 Israel caps (84-97).

OTHER CLUBS   Macabbi Haifa, Israel; FC Bruges, Belgium; Standard Liege, Belgium; Tottenham Hotspur 93/4-96/7 (87, 4); Watford 97/8-98/9 (33, 8).

GAMES   41 (56)

GOALS   22

GLENN HYSEN

1989/90 → 1991/92

During the first of his three campaigns at Anfield, Glenn Hysen cut an imposing figure. Tall, muscular and handsome, he radiated authority and charisma – and that was before he ran on to the pitch. When Sweden's centre-half and captain actually began to play, the impression of power, almost majesty, tended to be reinforced. He was courageous, skilful and audaciously calm, accustomed to aerial dominance and resourceful enough to counter most ground-level thrusts. Accordingly, in stately tandem with Alan Hansen, he helped Liverpool lift the title in 1989/90.

But then, like a footballing enactment of *The King's New Clothes*, the hitherto regal Hysen was, quite simply, found out and his weaknesses exploited. That icy assurance appeared to evaporate, revealing a frequently disturbing clumsiness in its place; his lack of pace was laid bare; he appeared casual, at times to the point of complacency, and he was caught in possession with alarming frequency.

With his previous club, Fiorentina of Italy, Hysen had been the well-protected linchpin of a packed defence. Thus, surrounded by colleagues and threatened by comparatively fewer forwards, his physical presence and arrogant skill were enough to command most situations. But in the more frenetic, attack-minded English game, he found himself increasingly isolated and vulnerable as his flaws were rumbled.

Hysen had arrived on Merseyside in the summer of 1989 – thus jilting Manchester United, who had expected to sign him – and early indications were that Kenny Dalglish had acquired an accomplished and imperious leader for his £650,000. Hearteningly, too, the Nordic newcomer was willing to scrap, as he proved in two bone-shaking confrontations with United's Mark Hughes. The combative Welshman put Hysen's resolve and ability to the most searching of tests and they were not found wanting.

Come 1991, though, that distinguished iron-grey head was looking ever more forlorn. Hysen did not relish the new Souness regime, and did not last long under it. He was stripped of the captaincy, dropped, then freed in January 1992 to complete a poignant fall from grace.

GLENN INGVAR HYSEN

BORN   Gothenburg, Sweden, 30 October 1959.
HONOURS League Championship 89/90. 68 Sweden caps (81-90).
OTHER CLUBS Warta, Sweden; IFK Gothenburg, Sweden (twice); PSV Eindhoven, Holland; Fiorentina, Italy; GAIS Gothenburg, Sweden.

GAMES	91 (2)
GOALS	3

DAVID SPEEDIE

1990/91

David Speedie crackled into Anfield as a Championship shock-trooper, introducing himself in characteristically explosive fashion, only to fizzle out in dismal anti-climax and leave largely unmourned. Though there were few public hints of the Liverpool manager's desperation at the time, Kenny Dalglish was already under enormous personal pressure when he paid Coventry £700,000 for the aggressive, cocky little Scot in February 1991. The Reds were losing ground in the title race and the beleaguered boss thought, presumably, that the battle-scarred 30-year-old attacker might prove a short-term inspiration, that perhaps he could do for Liverpool what Andy Gray had once done for Everton.

At first it seemed that Dalglish had pulled a rabbit out of the hat, even if Speedie had more in common with a ferret. On his debut his volley secured a share of the spoils at Old Trafford, then he netted twice in three minutes – a deft header and an adroit side-foot – to furnish victory in the Merseyside derby at Anfield. It was an astonishing start against the Reds' two fiercest rivals but, thereafter, it was all downhill. Dalglish departed and the Championship slipped away, while Speedie floundered, particularly when deployed in midfield, where he worked hard but his technique was found to be wanting. He was an able harasser of opponents, and some might have been intimidated by his volcanic temperament, but he could not dovetail with the side's traditional passing game and it was no surprise when Graeme Souness sold him to Blackburn for £500,000 that August. Thus a prospective title talisman had become a gamble that failed, albeit a fascinating one.

DAVID ROBERT SPEEDIE		
BORN Glenrothes, Fife, 20 February 1960.		
HONOURS 10 Scotland caps (85-89).		
OTHER CLUBS Barnsley 78/9-79/80 (23, 0); Darlington 80/1-81/2		
(88, 21); Chelsea 82/3-86/7 (162, 47); Coventry City 87/8-90/1		
(122, 31); Blackburn Rovers 91/2 (36, 23);		
Southampton 92/3 (11, 0); Birmingham City on loan		
92/3 (10, 2); West Bromwich Albion on loan 92/3	GAMES	9 (5)
(7, 2); West Ham United on loan 92/3 (11, 4);		
Leicester City 93/4 (37, 12).	GOALS	6

JIMMY CARTER

1990/91 → 1991/92

Prodigiously pacy but plain and predictable, £800,000 winger Jimmy Carter was a relative unknown when he arrived at Anfield from Millwall in January 1991 and, sad to say, seemed hardly less anonymous when he departed some nine months and four senior starts later.

In retrospect it is easy to question Kenny Dalglish's judgement of the right-sided flankman, who had helped the Lions lift the Second Division crown in 1987/88, yet in the year before he became a Red, Carter had attracted substantial bids from Rangers, Arsenal and Coventry City.

Perhaps it was all a matter of confidence. Despite early encouragement from the Kop, the Londoner seemed tentative, as if terrified of failure. Somehow, too, despite those winged heels, there was a lack of urgency about his play and also the suspicion that he became disheartened rather too quickly when the ball didn't run his way. Harking back to happier days at the Den, Carter had displayed a delightful change of pace, neat footwork and reliable crossing ability. For Liverpool it appeared, at times, that his legs moved too fast for his footballing brain, while his control was barely adequate and his distribution erratic.

There had been suggestions that he was to be groomed as the long-term successor to John Barnes, who had been linked with a possible move abroad, but the very thought seemed increasingly preposterous. Soon it became apparent that Carter had no future at Anfield and Liverpool were relieved, perhaps, when Arsenal demonstrated their continued belief in the player by paying £500,000 for him in October 1991. However, he fared little better at Highbury before returning to the second flight.

JAMES WILLIAM CHARLES CARTER		
BORN Hammersmith, London, 9 November 1965.		
OTHER CLUBS Millwall 86/7-90/1 (110, 10);		
Arsenal 91/2-94/5 (25, 2); Oxford United on loan		
93/4 (5, 0) and 94/5 (4, 0); Portsmouth 95/6-97/8	GAMES	4 (4)
(72, 5); Millwall 98/9 (16, 0).	GOALS	0

MIKE HOOPER

1986/87 → 1992/93

As the man who kept both Bruce Grobbelaar and David James out of the Liverpool team on merit for substantial spells, Mike Hooper was clearly not short of goalkeeping quality. Unfortunately for the red-haired six-footer, natural talent alone is never enough at the top level, especially in such an exposed, high-pressure position. As indispensable as the knack of stopping shots or catching crosses is a generous supply of confidence, a commodity of which Hooper appeared to be parlously short.

Unquestionably he had plenty of opportunities to cement a regular place following his £50,000 arrival from Wrexham in October 1985. There were several competent stints deputising for Grobbelaar, followed by four months in 1988/89 when the personable Bristolian seemed on the verge of becoming the Reds' regular 'keeper.

While Grobbelaar fought to overcome meningitis, Hooper enjoyed a sequence of 24 consecutive games in which he won praise for his safe handling and quick reactions, and turned in several outstanding displays. Even when Grobbelaar was fit, Kenny Dalglish persisted with Hooper, and an end to the long reign of the flamboyant Zimbabwe international was suddenly conceivable. But the presence of the still-eager veteran brought added tension, and after some uncertain showings, Hooper was dropped.

Still the door remained ajar, though, with Graeme Souness preferring him to Grobbelaar and newcomer James for two months in mid-1992/93. However, Anfield was going through a harrowing interlude then, and as poor results produced inevitable criticism, Hooper was unseated again.

Certainly his £550,000 move to Newcastle United in September 1993 was in his best interests but, sadly, Hooper was unable to make the most of it.

MICHAEL DUDLEY HOOPER
BORN Bristol, 10 February 1964.
OTHER CLUBS Bristol City 84/5 (1, 0); Wrexham 84/5-85/6 (34, 0); Leicester City on loan 90/1 (14, 0); Newcastle United 93/4-94/5 (25, 0).

GAMES 69 (2)
GOALS 0

NICKY TANNER

1989/90 → 1992/93

Nicky Tanner was a moderately talented but exceptionally dedicated stopper who deserves credit for exceeding most expectations when Liverpool were hit by an appalling sequence of injuries during 1991/92. However, at a club accustomed to central defenders of the highest calibre, the tall, blond Bristolian didn't seem likely to retain his place when the crisis was past.

A £30,000 acquisition in the summer of 1988 from Bristol Rovers, for whom most of his outings had been at full-back or in midfield, Tanner made little initial impact at Anfield. Though competent in the air, competitive in the tackle and blessed with deceptive pace, his ball work and reading of the game left something to be desired. In short, he didn't look like a Liverpool player.

But when Mark Wright was sidelined in August 1991, obvious deputies were thin on the ground and Tanner had the chance of an extended run in the side. He responded nobly, playing the best football of his life by keeping it simple and eradicating risk.

Two examples that come to mind are his efficient part in the away UEFA Cup win over Swarovski Tirol and his shackling of Gary Lineker at White Hart Lane. Duly his progress was rewarded by a new three-and-a-half-year contract in January 1992.

Though doubts persisted in many quarters, Tanner seemed to have arrived, but the reversal of fortune was short-lived. He lost his place through injury and, when fit again, looked ordinary in the extreme. Thereafter he slipped down the pecking order before being forced into premature retirement by a back problem.

NICHOLAS TANNER
BORN Bristol, 24 May 1965.
OTHER CLUBS Bristol Rovers 85/6-87/8 (107, 3); Norwich City on loan 89/90 (6, 0); Swindon Town on loan 90/1 (7, 0).

GAMES 51 (8)
GOALS 1

KEVIN KEWLEY

1977/78

Attacking midfielder Kewley was a product of local junior football who turned professional in 1972. His sole senior outing was as a substitute for Terry McDermott in the home win over Middlesbrough in January 1978, a month before he left.

JOHN KEVIN KEWLEY

BORN Liverpool, 2 March 1955.

GAMES	0 (1)
GOALS	0

MARK SEAGRAVES

1985/86

The peak of the big central defender's Reds career was playing in the first leg of a League Cup semi-final against QPR. Later he excelled for Bolton, helping them to become Division One runners-up in 1992/93 and beat Liverpool in the FA Cup.

MARK SEAGRAVES

BORN Bootle, Lancashire, 22 October 1966.
OTHER CLUBS Norwich City on loan 86/7 (3, 0); Manchester City 87/8-89/90 (42, 0); Bolton Wanderers 90/1-94/5 (157, 7); Swindon Town 95/6-97/8 (60, 0).

GAMES	2
GOALS	0

STEVE OGRIZOVIC

1977/78 → 1980/81

After understudying Ray Clemence and Bruce Grobbelaar at Anfield, Ogrizovic became one of the most durable and respected goalkeepers in the land with Coventry, whose appearance record he holds. He played Premiership football into his forties.

STEVEN OGRIZOVIC

BORN Mansfield, Nottinghamshire, 12 September 1957.
OTHER CLUBS Chesterfield 77/8 (16, 0); Shrewsbury Town 82/3-83/4 (84, 0); Coventry City 84/5-99/00 (507, 1).

GAMES	5
GOALS	0

ALAN IRVINE

1986/87 → 1987/88

A tall, rangy striker who started with Hibernian, became established with Falkirk, then joined Liverpool for £75,000 in November 1986. He made little impact, though, and soon he re-crossed the border, with the Reds making a £25,000 profit.

ALAN JAMES IRVINE

BORN Broxburn, West Lothian, 20 November 1962.
OTHER CLUBS Falkirk 82/3-86/7 (116, 18); Dundee United 87/8 (7, 0); Shrewsbury Town 87/8-88/9 (37, 6).

GAMES	0 (4)
GOALS	0

COLIN RUSSELL

1980/81

A diminutive marksman whose prolific exploits for Liverpool reserves earned him a £15,000 move to Huddersfield in September 1982. That term his 16 goals helped to secure promotion from Division Three, then he became a soccer wanderer.

COLIN RUSSELL

BORN Liverpool, 21 January 1961.
OTHER CLUBS Huddersfield Town 82/3-83/4 (66, 23); Stoke City on loan 83/4 (11, 2); Bournemouth 84/5-85/6 (68, 14); Doncaster Rovers 86/7-87/8 (43, 5); Scarborough 87/8 (13, 2); Wigan Athletic 88/9 (8, 3).

GAMES	0 (1)
GOALS	0

BRIAN MOONEY

1986/87

A ball-playing midfielder who failed to break through at Anfield, but who became such a crowd favourite at Deepdale that Preston fans protested vociferously when he was sold to Sunderland for £225,000. Sadly he was not a hit at Roker Park.

BRIAN JOHN MOONEY
BORN Dublin, 2 February 1966.
OTHER CLUBS Home Farm, Republic of Ireland; Wrexham on loan 85/6 (9, 2); Preston North End 87/8-90/1 (128, 20); Sunderland 90/1-92/3 (27, 1); Burnley on loan 92/3 (6, 0).

GAMES	0 (1)
GOALS	0

PHIL CHARNOCK

1992/93

During his fleeting Anfield sojourn Charnock, an industrious, sweet-passing, left-sided midfielder, reminded some observers of Ray Kennedy. Later he shone for Crewe, including a stint as an emergency left-back, though injury hampered his progress.

PHILIP ANTHONY CHARNOCK
BORN Southport, Lancashire, 14 February 1975.
OTHER CLUBS Blackpool on loan 95/6 (4, 0), Crewe Alexandra 96/7-01/02 (157, 8); Port Vale 02/03 (18, 1); Bury 03/04 (3, 0); Linfield, Northern Ireland, 03/04.

GAMES	1 (1)
GOALS	0

JOHN DURNIN

1986/87 → 1988/89

A tough, versatile performer who didn't make the senior grade as a forward with the Reds, but fetched a £225,000 fee on joining Oxford in 1989. Durnin went on to give sterling midfield service elsewhere, and could play in defence at need.

JOHN PAUL DURNIN
BORN Bootle, Lancashire, 18 August 1965.
OTHER CLUBS West Bromwich Albion on loan 88/9 (5, 2); Oxford United 88/9-92/3 (161, 44); Portsmouth 93/4-99/00 (118, 31); Blackpool on loan 99/00 (5, 1); Carlisle United 99/00 (22, 2); Kidderminster Harriers 00/01 (31, 9); Port Vale 01/02-02/03 (47, 2).

GAMES	1 (1)
GOALS	0

BARRY JONES

1991/92

A utility defender who tasted his sole moment in the limelight when he rose from the bench to replace the injured David Burrows during a 1-0 UEFA Cup defeat to Kuusysi Lahti in Finland. Later Jones became a stalwart in the lower divisions.

BARRY JONES
BORN Prescot, Lancashire, 30 June 1970.
OTHER CLUBS Wrexham 92/3-97/8 (195, 5); York City 97/8-00/01 (134, 5).

GAMES	0 (1)
GOALS	0

ALEX WATSON

1987/88 → 1988/89

Big Alex, the brother of Everton and England stopper Dave Watson, made a bright start to his senior Reds career at full-back before accepting a £150,000 switch to Bournemouth in 1991 and maturing into a doughty central defender.

ALEXANDER FRANCIS WATSON
BORN Liverpool, 5 April 1968.
OTHER CLUBS Derby County on loan 90/1 (5, 0); Bournemouth 90/1-94/5 (151, 5); Gillingham on loan 95/6 (10, 1); Torquay United 95/6-00/01 (202, 8); Exeter City 01/02-02/03 (46, 1).

GAMES	6 (3)
GOALS	0

LEE JONES

1994/95 → 1996/97

It was hoped that the £300,000 recruit might follow in the prolific bootsteps of another pacy Welshman, Ian Rush, but it wasn't to be. Instead Jones joined Tranmere for £100,000, then became the first man to sign for Wrexham on four occasions.

PHILIP LEE JONES
BORN Wrexham, North Wales, 29 May 1973.
OTHER CLUBS Wrexham 90/1-91/2 (39, 10); Crewe Alexandra on loan 93/4 (8, 1); Wrexham on loan 95/6 (20, 9), Wrexham on loan 96/7 (6, 0); Tranmere Rovers 96/7-99/00 (86, 16); Barnsley 00/01-01/02 (40, 5); Wrexham 01/02-03/04 (49, 14).

GAMES	0 (4)
GOALS	0

MIKE MARSH

1988/89 → 1993/94

Anyone who watched Mike Marsh in training during his two best seasons at Liverpool will he mystified by the comprehensively capable midfielder's failure to secure a long-term Anfield future. A superb passer and a game trier who never backed away from a challenge, the enthusiastic Scouser frequently dominated sessions at Melwood, his all-round skills standing out even among so many exalted colleagues.

Yet during 1991/92 and 1992/93, when he was rarely absent from Graeme Souness' line-ups, Marsh transferred that outstanding form to matches only in fitful bursts. It wasn't that he let the side down, simply that he didn't live up to his vast potential, becoming frustratingly peripheral at times.

Of course, there were exceptions, notably one scintillating display against Crystal Palace at Anfield in November 1992. That night Marsh was irresistible as he scored one goal – a fulminating 30-yard drive after an exquisite feint past an opponent – and set up two more with an immaculate through-ball to Ronny Rosenthal and a precise cross for Don Hutchison.

He was versatile, too, excelling in a spell as Rob Jones' deputy at right-back, defending stoutly and joining in attacks with commendable enterprise, such as when he headed a neat equaliser in the passionate home encounter with Auxerre during the 1991/92 UEFA Cup campaign.

However, Marsh never quite made himself indispensable and when he was needed to help facilitate the purchase of Julian Dicks from West Ham in September 1993, he was dispatched to Upton Park, valued at £1 million.

He didn't settle in London, nor in Coventry, nor with Souness in Turkey, but then, under the tutelage of former Liverpool hero Ronnie Whelan, he became an instant favourite at Southend. Still it seemed, with all due respects to Roots Hall, that Marsh's place was in the Premiership, but the matter became poignantly academic in 1997 when a knee injury ended his League career when it might have been approaching its peak.

Ironically he regained fitness, but could not return to the League because of an insurance pay-out. Thus after leading Jan Molby's Kidderminster Harriers out of the Vauxhall Conference, he took his talents to Southport, then Boston United, then Accrington Stanley. And remarkably, after everything, in 2002/03 Mike Marsh remained as resiliently competitive as he had been in his prime.

MICHAEL ANDREW MARSH

BORN   Kirkby, Liverpool, 21 July 1969.
OTHER CLUBS   West Ham United 93/4-94/5 (49, 1); Coventry City 94/5 (15, 2); Galatasaray, Turkey, 95/6 (3, 0); Southend United 95/6-97/8 (83, 11).

GAMES   **70 (31)**
GOALS   **6**

DEAN SAUNDERS

1991/92 → 1992/93

Dean Saunders was a footballer of numerous admirable qualities, a vivacious entertainer and expert marksman with ample ability to have flourished at the top level. However, buying him for Liverpool, and then not playing to his strengths, was a glaring mistake.

Graeme Souness beat Everton to the Saunders signature in July 1991, paying Derby County £2.9 million for a striker who had been excitingly successful in a struggling team. Just imagine, went the argument, what he could achieve alongside better players at Anfield.

Sadly, that theory neglected to take into account the two clubs' contrasting styles. During his Baseball Ground days, invariably Derby had been under pressure and many of his goals had come from latching on to clearances punted into vast areas of empty space. In such situations the dashing Deano was undeniably deadly, his eager industry, searing pace and frequently clinical finish being exactly what was needed.

But Liverpool played a patient passing game, which demanded a surer first touch than the Welsh international possessed and a positional sense which he never seemed to acquire. All too often, beautifully measured moves would break down with the ball squirting tantalisingly out of his reach.

Oddly enough, though, once in possession he could run with the ball under control, sometimes taking on opponents to devastating effect. Indeed, it should be stressed that, despite his limitations, Saunders was not an unmitigated flop. Far from it.

The crowd warmed to his engaging enthusiasm and non-stop effort, while that characteristic tip-tap gait was positively Keeganesque. His overall strike-rate was some distance in front of respectable, too, even if it was massaged by a disproportionately prolific 1991/92 UEFA Cup campaign which, incidentally, featured several goals of the highest quality.

At his lowest ebb, during one especially arid scoring drought, Saunders – whose father, Roy, was a Reds wing-half in the 1950s – found himself under intense media pressure, and earned admiration for facing it so manfully. In October 1992, Souness tacitly owned up to his error by selling the troubled striker to Aston Villa for £2.3 million.

In his first season at Villa Park, Saunders demonstrated his enduring ability by helping to engage Manchester United in a meaningful race for the League title. Come 1995 he resumed his wanderings, eventually returning to the Premiership and playing until within a few months of his 37th birthday. There followed a coaching career, and in 2008 he took charge of Wrexham's bid to regain Football League status.

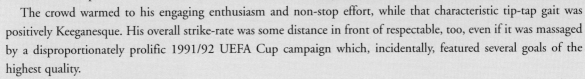

DEAN NICHOLAS SAUNDERS

BORN	Swansea, Glamorgan, 21 June 1964.
HONOURS	FA Cup 91/2. 75 Wales caps (86-01).
OTHER CLUBS	Swansea City 83/4-84/5 (49, 12); Cardiff City on loan 84/5 (4,0); Brighton and Hove Albion 85/6-86/7 (72, 21); Oxford United 86/7-88/9 (59, 22); Derby County 88/9-90/1 (106, 42); Aston Villa 92/3-94/5 (112, 37); Galatasaray, Turkey, 95/6 (27, 15); Nottingham Forest 96/7-97/8 (43, 6); Sheffield United 97/8-98/9 (43, 17); Benfica, Portugal, 98/9 (17, 5); Bradford City 99/00-00/01 (44, 3).

GAMES	61
GOALS	25

TORBEN PIECHNIK

1992/93 → 1993/94

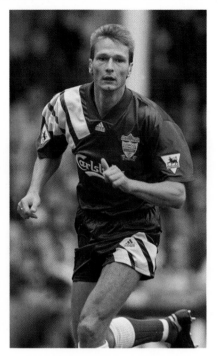

Even by the wretched overall standard of Graeme Souness' transfer record as manager of the Reds, the unfortunate Torben Piechnik appears as a mammoth blot. The 29-year-old central defender was signed from his home-town club, BK Copenhagen, in the wake of his finest hour, helping Denmark to amaze the soccer world by lifting the European Championship in the summer of 1992. The £500,000 move was completed that September, and a few days later Piechnik was experiencing the first of too many embarrassing afternoons in a Liverpool shirt.

It cannot have done much for the Anfield boss's peace of mind that the newcomer's tormentor-in-chief was the recently-sold Dean Saunders, but that day at Villa Park it was the Welshman's pace and nimbleness that exposed the Danish debutant most cruelly. While allowances could fairly be made for understandable first-match nerves, the omens were ominous.

As autumn turned to winter, the Piechnik purchase became ever more perplexing. At a time when, because of European competition rules, Liverpool were expected to seek young English talent, Souness had invested in an ageing, dithering Dane who was adequate in the air but ponderous on the turn, an unreliable passer and not the best at positioning. In short, he looked hopelessly out of his depth. Piechnik was dropped soon after suffering another chasing by Saunders in January and never regained a regular place. He was freed to return to Denmark during the 1994 close season.

TORBEN PIECHNIK
BORN   Copenhagen, Denmark, 21 May 1963.
HONOURS   15 Denmark caps (91-96).
OTHER CLUBS   BK Copenhagen; Aarhus, both Denmark.

GAMES   **23 (1)**
GOALS   0

ISTVAN KOZMA

1991/92 → 1992/93

It would be easy to pillory Graeme Souness over his purchase of Istvan Kozma, the little-known play-maker who cost £300,000 from Dunfermline Athletic in January 1992, only to be freed just 20 months and three senior starts later. Of course, the manager was not blameless in the matter of the Hungarian's dismal failure, but he could be excused, perhaps, for being captivated by delicious ball skills that positively shamed the technique of most Britons.

Like some throwback to the 'Magnificent Magyars' of the 1950s, Kozma could mesmerise an opponent, charm a crowd, by his total command over a football. The trouble was, he appeared utterly unable to apply that rare mastery in the hectic arena of the English game. In many a reserve encounter, he would bemuse a defender with outrageous, two-footed trickery, but then, instead of delivering a telling pass, Kozma would pause, as though admiring his own work. In that instant, almost invariably, he would be robbed and left to shuffle ineffectually on the fringe of the action until his next moment of unproductive inspiration.

Sadly, as the months passed he showed few signs of adapting to his new circumstances and his passion for the job seemed questionable. Clearly no English club, and certainly not Liverpool, could afford such a luxury and it is significant that by August 1993 lstvan had not played enough first-team games to qualify for a new work permit. Accordingly Souness, who had been impressed by the Kozma quality during meetings between Dunfermline and Glasgow Rangers, allowed the disenchanted schemer to return to his native land.

ISTVAN KOZMA
BORN   Paszto, Hungary, 3 December 1964.
HONOURS   40 Hungary caps (86-95).
OTHER CLUBS   Ujpest Dozsa, Hungary (twice); Dunfermline Athletic 89/90-91/2 (90, 8); Apoel, Cyprus; Videoton, Hungary.

GAMES   **3 (7)**
GOALS   0

NIGEL CLOUGH

1993/94 → 1995/96

He might have been made for Liverpool: a clean-cut, intelligent young man blessed with sumptuous natural ability, dedicated to the work ethic and with ambition to burn. His combination of vision and dexterity, flair and courage, marked him out as a thoroughbred, the type who has flourished at Anfield since Bill Shankly readjusted the club's horizons. And that is why Nigel Clough qualifies as the saddest, most distressing example of Graeme Souness' transfer market travail. Signed from his father Brian's Nottingham Forest for £2.275 million in June 1993, Nigel began brilliantly, playing up front alongside Ian Rush and scoring twice on his debut against Sheffield Wednesday. Comparisons with Kenny Dalglish were invidious yet understandable, the newcomer's smoothness of touch and quickness of thought evoking echoes of the great man. But disillusion was not far away.

A lean spell of results presaged the rise of Robbie Fowler and Clough was omitted, then employed in midfield. The team toiled, his confidence evaporated and suddenly his one major fault, his lack of pace, appeared to outweigh his catalogue of merits. Apart from a two-goal contribution to the rousing 3-3 draw with Manchester United in January 1994, Clough was rarely to bestride centre stage with real certainty again. For two more years he strove manfully but vainly to gain a place, but seemed ill at ease, spawning theories that his subtle gifts were increasingly unsuited to the speed of the modern game. That thought gained poignant momentum when neither a £1 million move to Manchester City in early 1996, nor a subsequent loan spell with Forest, produced a reversal of fortune, and he entered management with non-League Burton Albion.

DON HUTCHISON

1991/92 → 1993/94

Liverpool fought a long, frequently tiresome battle to induce Don Hutchison to realise his extravagant potential. Disappointingly for the club, self-destructively for the player, it was a conflict doomed to end in frustration and defeat as a sorry catalogue of unsavoury off-the-field incidents scuppered his Anfield career. The lean, leggy midfielder cost some £300,000 from Hartlepool United in November 1990, an apparently shrewd investment for the future. At the time he was touted as having talent to equal that of another, more famous north-easterner; unfortunately he shared certain other of Paul Gascoigne's characteristics, too.

After two years of honing his skills in the Central League, Hutchison won a regular senior berth in 1992/93, and became one of the most eye-catching members of Graeme Souness' transitional side. A perceptive passer blessed with impeccable ball control and a stern tackle, he was an expert finisher also, and became noted for audacious runs ahead of his forwards which yielded ten goals that term. Such form should have guaranteed Hutchison a key long-term role with New Liverpool, but the indiscretions continued until even the patient Roy Evans, who had replaced Souness, could tolerate no more.

Accordingly, the troubled midfielder was sold to West Ham for £1.5 million in August 1994 and, used frequently as a striker, made a major contribution to the Hammers' late escape from relegation. However, Hutchison did not settle in east London, but went on to captain Everton and shine with Sunderland, achieving sufficient consistency to make a deserved international breakthrough with Scotland. Ultimately his longevity in the game was immensely commendable.

NIGEL HOWARD CLOUGH
BORN Sunderland, County Durham, 19 March 1966.
HONOURS 14 England caps (89-93).
OTHER CLUBS Nottingham Forest 84/5-92/3 (311, 101); Manchester City 95/6-96/7 (38, 4);
Nottingham Forest on loan 96/7 (13, 1);
Sheffield Wednesday on loan 97/8 (1, 0).
MANAGER Derby County (09-).

GAMES	**34 (10)**
GOALS	9

DONALD HUTCHISON
BORN Gateshead, County Durham, 9 May 1971.
HONOURS 26 Scotland caps (99-03).
OTHER CLUBS Hartlepool United 89/90-90/1 (24, 2); West Ham United 94/5-95/6 (35, 11); Sheffield United 95/6-97/8 (78, 5); Everton 97/8-99/00 (75, 10); Sunderland 00/01-01/02 (34, 8); West Ham United 01/02-04/05 (63, 5); Millwall 05/06 (11, 2); Coventry City 05/06-06/07 (38, 4); Luton Town 07/08 (21, 0).

GAMES	**44 (16)**
GOALS	10

MARK WALTERS

1991/92 → 1994/95

It was easy to see why Liverpool bought Mark Walters. When Graeme Souness paid Glasgow Rangers £1.25 million to be reunited with his former star in August 1991, he was acquiring an international winger in his prime, an enthralling entertainer and a match-winner, ostensibly the man to fill the void which seemed likely to be created by the oft-mooted departure of John Barnes.

However, it didn't work out quite like that. Walters never played for England again, he thrilled only sporadically and made crucial contributions to only a handful of games. Oh yes, and John Barnes stayed.

The relative failure of the gentle Brummie on Merseyside was perplexing, not least because there was no denying his abundance of natural talent. On song he could be an enchanting swashbuckler, all bewitching step-overs, outrageous backheels and venomous snap-shots, and it should be stressed that he did have his moments as a Red.

The most memorable of these climaxed what was probably the most joyous Anfield night during the Souness stewardship, when Liverpool came from behind to beat Auxerre in a 1990/91 UEFA Cup tie, Walters sliding home the winner with cool expertise while the Kop went wild. Other highlights included his two-goal home demolition of Blackburn Rovers in December 1992, and his mesmeric gulling of four Spurs defenders before laying on a goal for Robbie Fowler in an FA Cup quarter-final in March 1995.

Sadly, such telling interventions were the exception rather than the rule. Too often, particularly when the team was struggling, Walters' influence was negligible and the fans let him know, in stringent terms, exactly what they thought about it. He was slammed for not going past defenders, for inaccurate crossing, for dallying ineffectually on the ball, for not scoring enough goals and, most damning of all, for not showing sufficient fire and determination.

Increasingly Mark, whose middle name happened to be Everton, became a scapegoat, at times almost an aunt-sally figure, and his confidence drained away until he was little more than a cipher. As Roy Evans' exciting new side took shape it became clear that the flankman's future lay away from Anfield and in January 1996 he joined Southampton on a free transfer. Mark Walters might have meant so much to Liverpool, but in the end he meant so little.

MARK EVERTON WALTERS	
BORN	Birmingham, 2 June 1964.
HONOURS	1 England cap (91).
OTHER CLUBS	Aston Villa 81/2-87/8 (181, 39); Glasgow Rangers 87/8-90/1 (106, 32); Stoke City on loan 93/4 (9, 2); Wolverhampton Wanderers on loan 94/5 (11, 3); Southampton 95/6 (5, 0); Swindon Town 96/7-99/00 (112, 25); Bristol Rovers 99/00-01/02 (82, 13).

GAMES	82 (42)
GOALS	19

STIG BJORNEBYE

1992/93 → 1998/99

Across from the left foot of Stig Inge Bjornebye could be a thing of rare, almost aesthetic beauty. It seemed to float from the Norwegian's boot before curving inexorably away from the goalkeeper, arcing tantalisingly beyond the reach of desperately back-pedalling defenders to fall perfectly for an oncoming attacker to smack it netwards.

Never was this scenario realised more sweetly than on one tumultuous evening at Anfield in January 1994 when Bjornebye's sublime delivery enabled Neil Ruddock to complete Liverpool's comeback from a three-goal deficit against Manchester United. Such precision was exactly what Graeme Souness paid Rosenborg £600,000 to acquire in December 1992, though it must be said that Bjornebye was to suffer bouts of morale-sapping inconsistency between periods of admirable competence.

He had impressed with a fine display against England in the summer before the transfer and when David Burrows suffered a

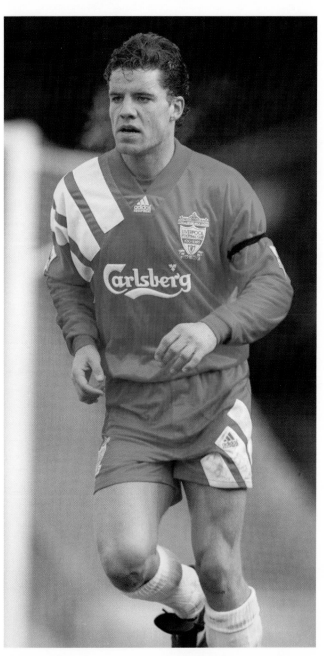

serious injury, the Reds boss felt the sturdy defender – a seasoned campaigner with five years of international experience at the tender age of 23 – was ideal for the English game.

However, Bjornebye took time to adjust to the pace of the Premier League and, during intermittent appearances over the next season and a half, was subjected to sometimes senseless criticism from fans frustrated by their side's general travail. But 1994/95 brought a change of fortune, at least initially, as Bjornebye secured a regular place as the left wing-back.

Strong, well balanced and composed, he tackled firmly and showed neat ball control, although that was prone to slip under severe pressure. His passing, irreproachable at times, was prone to infuriating lapses of accuracy, as were the crosses which became his speciality.

Nevertheless, Bjornebye was a respected member of the team that beat Bolton to lift the League Cup, his one Wembley disappointment coming when he shot against the post instead of ending his scoring duck for Liverpool. That minor regret was placed in perspective a few days later when he broke his leg in a freak accident against Southampton, his studs sticking in the grass as he strained to reach the ball.

On recovery. he found himself in a daunting queue for a first-team place, but with Rob Jones and Steve Harkness unavailable for the start of 1996/97, he capitalised by earning a regular berth. That term Bjornebye was a revelation, oozing quiet confidence at the back and attacking with more consistent potency than ever before.

Seemingly marginalised by the return of Steve Staunton for 1998/99, Bjornebye rallied resiliently to make 31 generally effective senior appearances before a combination of injury and an influx of new players ended his Anfield stay.

He was far from finished, though, and in June 2000 he joined Blackburn for £300,000, linking once more with Graeme Souness, the man who had first spotted his rich potential.

STIG INGE BJORNEBYE		
BORN	Elverum, Norway, 11 December 1969.	
HONOURS	League Cup 94/5. 76 Norway caps (89-00).	
OTHER CLUBS	Strommen, Kongsvinger, Rosenborg, all Norway; Blackburn Rovers 00/01-01/02 (56, 1).	

GAMES	175 (9)
GOALS	4

JULIAN DICKS

1993/94

Expensive signings tend to provoke avid and enjoyable anticipation among fans of the buying club, yet when Graeme Souness paid West Ham the equivalent of £2.5 million for Julian Dicks in September 1993, there was no shortage of Anfield regulars who cringed in disbelief.

Not that anyone doubted the footballing credentials of the Hammers' left-back; his skill, power and commitment were all undeniable. Rather it was his appalling disciplinary record – eight sendings-off and 20 yellow cards in his career to that date – and his general image of crude machismo that filled them with dismay.

The gist of their attitude was 'Have Liverpool really come to this?', a feel-bad factor exacerbated by the departure of the popular Mike Marsh and David Burrows as part of the deal. Souness, though, was content with his capture, confident that he could moderate Dicks' wilder excesses, and he predicted that the 25-year-old England 'B' international would go on to win full caps.

To be fair, though continuing to exude an aura of provocative bravado, the pugnacious Bristolian made a promising and peaceful start. Though his positional play gave cause for concern, his passing was assured, his tackling aggressive but usually fair, and he packed a savage left-foot shot. However, knee problems disrupted his training, which he had not appeared to relish anyway, and a subsequent fall-out over his fitness level with new boss Roy Evans led to the defender's £1 million return to Upton Park in October 1994.

Had he joined a successful Liverpool side, rather than a transitional one, Julian Dicks just might have met Souness' expectations. As it was, he is remembered at Anfield as a piece of very bad business.

JULIAN ANDREW DICKS
BORN Bristol, 8 August 1968.
OTHER CLUBS Birmingham City 85/6-87/8 (89, 1); West Ham United 87/8-93/4 (159, 29) and 94/5-98/9 (103, 21).

	GAMES	28
	GOALS	3

PAUL STEWART

1992/93 → 1993/94

Opinion was divided when Liverpool paid Spurs £2.3 million for England midfielder Paul Stewart in the summer of 1992. On the face of it, the burly but skilful Mancunian appeared to be a magnificent acquisition, just the player to replace the ball-winning bite so markedly missed since the departure of Steve McMahon. In addition, the former striker was expected to add to the Reds' goal power, probably operating just behind the front-men and making late runs into the box.

However, amid the immediate euphoria of pipping rival clubs for the Stewart signature, there were those who warned that he was a costly flop waiting to happen. After all, he had endured dire periods at Tottenham before his conversion to the central role in which he had earned England caps and had yet to prove himself a long-term prospect at the top level.

In the event, the doubters were proved sadly but overwhelmingly correct. Throughout most of his troubled, injury-plagued Anfield sojourn, Stewart looked sluggish and unimaginative, never mastering the Liverpool concept of pass-and-move, failing even to be an effective tackler. Following the sale of Dean Saunders, he was moved forward briefly to partner Ian Rush but that did not work and his lack of fulfilment became apparent in his petulant on-the-field demeanour.

He never returned to the senior side after 1993 and his value plummeted during two and a half years divided between treatment table, the Reds' reserves and loan stints elsewhere. A free transfer to Sunderland in 1996 must have been a relief to all concerned.

PAUL ANDREW STEWART
BORN Manchester, 7 October 1964.
HONOURS 3 England caps (91-92).
OTHER CLUBS Blackpool 81/2-86/7 (201, 56); Manchester City 86/7-87/8 (51, 26); Tottenham Hotspur 88/9-91/2 (131, 28); Crystal Palace on loan 93/4 (18, 3); Wolverhampton Wanderers on loan 94/5 (8, 2); Burnley on loan 94/5 (6, 0); Sunderland 95/6-96/7 (35, 5); Stoke City 97/8 (22, 3).

	GAMES	38 (4)
	GOALS	3

STEVE HARKNESS

1991/92 → 1998/99

Steve Harkness had no rivals for the title of Liverpool's unluckiest player of 1995/96. After several frustrating seasons on the fringe of the side, the combative Cumbrian had confounded his critics by winning a regular berth, proving a revelation at wing-back on the left flank of Roy Evans' enterprising 3-5-2 formation. Having been given his chance through Stig Inge Bjornebye's broken leg, Harkness performed so splendidly in defence, attack and all points between that he made it impossible for his manager to drop him, even when the Norwegian regained fitness.

Clearly, only suspension or serious injury was going to unseat him – and he was destined to suffer both before the term was out. After being ever-present until January, including an able emergency stint at centre-half, Harkness was banned for collecting six bookings. The resultant reshuffle, which saw Rob Jones switch from right to left, proved so successful that Steve was out in the cold once more. Admittedly, it could be said that his sentence was self-inflicted but his misdemeanours owed far more to enthusiasm than malice and it was difficult not to feel sorry for him.

But even greater mortification was in store. An injury crisis resulted in a springtime recall which ended in agony, both physical and mental, when his leg was shattered by an uncharacteristically wild tackle from Coventry's John Salako. Ever resilient, Harkness

returned in early 1997, bypassing no less than Ruddock, Babb and Matteo to play in central defence. His progress continued as he unseated Bjornebye on the left of the rearguard during 1997/98, but while his passing and overlapping were periodically impressive, they were not as consistent as his doughty work at the back and his chances of a long-term berth receded.

Harkness, a former England youth team skipper, was signed from his home-town club, Carlisle, for £75,000 in July 1989 and made his Reds debut some two years later. Playing as an orthodox left-back, he did well enough but wasn't quite ready for the top flight and was contemplating the possibility of a move when Bjornebye's mishap gave him a lifeline in April 1995. Thereafter Steve played like a man burning to prove a point and, though his high-octane aggression was channelled sensibly, brick walls with Harkness-shaped holes sprang irresistibly to mind.

Something a little more sophisticated was required by new boss Gerard Houllier and in March 1999 Steve's former mentor, Graeme Souness, paid £750,000 to take him to Benfica. Soon the pair were reunited yet again at Blackburn, then injury continued to dog the footsteps of the serially unfortunate Harkness during a stint with Sheffield Wednesday.

STEVEN HARKNESS
BORN Carlisle, Cumberland, 27 August 1971.
OTHER CLUBS Carlisle United 88/9 (13, 0); Huddersfield Town on loan 93/4 (5, 0); Southend United on loan 94/5 (6, 0);
Benfica, Portugal, 98/9 (9, 0); Blackburn Rovers 99/00-00/01 (17, 0); Sheffield Wednesday 00/01-01/02 (30, 1).

GAMES **119 (18)**
GOALS **6**

MICHAEL THOMAS

1991/92 → 1997/98

After a beguilingly bright beginning, it took several seasons of debilitating, injury-induced frustration before Graeme Souness' judgement in paying Arsenal £1.5 million for Michael Thomas in December 1991 was borne out. But when vindication finally came, in the winter and spring of 1995/96, it was so handsome that the former England midfielder came close to winning an international recall.

Of course, the name of Thomas was already burned indelibly into the consciousness of Kopites, thanks to his barely credible, last-gasp Anfield strike which won the 1988/89 title for the Gunners, but all was forgiven as Michael emerged as one of Liverpool's FA Cup heroes of 1992.

A precision-tooled quarter-final winner against Aston Villa was followed by a rasping 15-yard volley to open the Wembley scoring against Sunderland; the Londoner had completed the transition from bane to paragon and seemed set for a key role in Liverpool's future.

Then came sickening anti-climax. Fitness problems, mainly a snapped Achilles tendon, sidelined the newcomer for some two and a half campaigns and, with a wave of fabulous young players emerging, he missed out on the start of the renaissance inspired by new boss Roy Evans.

The torment ended with a worthy first-team run at the end of 1994/95 but it was not until the fitness gremlins transferred themselves to Jamie Redknapp in the following November that the real Michael Thomas had the opportunity to stand up.

He seized it avidly, displaying all his former box-to-box athleticism, allied to smooth distribution, assured control and the type of stern tackling which enabled him to fill in as a full-back or central defender at need.

Though surrounded by extravagant talents, he contributed a succession of outstanding performances, often at his most impressive in a holding position which allowed John Barnes the freedom to attack. As a result, towards the end of the season he was offered a new contract which be duly signed, but only after protracted speculation that he wanted to play abroad, and reported feelings of insecurity regarding his Anfield prospects.

Any such misgivings could only have heightened when he was dropped for the returning Redknapp after Liverpool's first defeat in 20 games, but they were not to linger into the subsequent campaign.

During 1996/97 a more contented Thomas' well-grooved consistency proved a telling factor in the Reds' renewed drive for honours. He was ever-present until a suspension in January and the team never functioned more smoothly than when he was beavering unobtrusively at its hub.

That often-underrated value was highlighted with vivid clarity in the FA Cup debacle against Chelsea, which saw a two-goal lead transformed into an astonishing 4-2 deficit. Had the reliable former Gunner been on duty, it is inconceivable that midfield possession would have been squandered with such wanton frequency as it was on that sorry Sunday afternoon.

However, such is the uncertainty of football that Thomas was unable to win back a regular place after his ban and, though he started 1997/98 in favour, the presence of Messrs Ince, Redknapp, Carragher, Murphy and Thompson prompted a loan spell at Middlesbrough in the New Year.

That summer he was freed to renew his association with Souness at Benfica, but the Thomas career marked time at the Stadium of Light and he finished his playing days with Wimbledon.

MICHAEL LAURISTON THOMAS

BORN   Lambeth, London, 24 August 1967.
HONOURS   FA Cup 91/2. 2 England caps (88-89).
OTHER CLUBS   Arsenal 86/7-91/2 (163, 24); Portsmouth on loan 86/7 (3, 0); Middlesbrough on loan 97/8 (10, 0); Benfica, Portugal, 98/9-99/00; Wimbledon 00/01 (8, 0).

GAMES   **128 (35)**
GOALS   **12**

MARK WRIGHT

· ·

1991/92 → 1997/98

Consider the sorry plight of Mark Wright in the late summer of 1994. A former England centre-half in his 32nd year and niggled by injuries, he had spent three seasons at Liverpool during which he had not lived up to expectations. Now his aspirations and, no doubt, his pride had been dented massively by the expensive arrival of John Scales and Phil Babb, two of the League's most accomplished defenders. Already at Anfield were the fearsome Neil Ruddock and the talented youngster Dominic Matteo. As if that wasn't enough, the one-time World Cup star had just clashed publicly with Reds boss Roy Evans, who had criticised his attitude and axed him from the senior squad. Job prospects? Forget them.

Yet, from that seemingly bottomless pit of professional and personal anguish, Wright emerged with a fresh outlook to play the finest football of his life. Indeed, in both 1995/96 and 1996/97 he was the pick of Liverpool's impressive posse of stoppers, a majestically assured performer whose class, strength and new-found maturity played an integral part in his club's spirited quest for honours and won him a richly-deserved international recall.

The sandy-haired six-footer was an international of seven years' standing when Graeme Souness signed him for £2.2 million from newly-relegated Derby County in July 1991. Anfield appeared the perfect platform for such a stylish individual approaching his prime, and when he skippered the side to FA Cup glory in his first campaign it was easy to assume that undiluted success would follow

But something was not right. Even allowing for an Achilles problem that would not quite clear up, Wright did not exude true authority. Yes, there was a certain arrogance about him but – and this annoyed many fans – his form simply did not justify it. He was splendid in the air but his slowness on the turn made him horribly vulnerable when faced with nippy opponents, who would draw him out of position, then leave him for dead. And, though smoothly comfortable on the ball, he strolled so languidly at times that possession would be squandered dangerously.

This situation simmered frustratingly through 1992/93 and 1993/94 before coming to a head when the dissatisfied Evans dispensed his home truths to such devastating effect. Now Wright was faced with a stark choice: leave Liverpool on such a low note that it might prove difficult to resurrect his career, or stay and fight against overwhelming odds in a bid to make the most of his undeniable quality.

After what must have been some painful self-examination, Wright opted courageously for the latter course and he worked ferociously, only for injuries to make an already steep mountain all but unclimbable. There were few opportunities in 1994/95 but the ex-captain continued to buckle down and, gradually, the pendulum swung. With Scales sidelined at the start of the following term, Wright found himself in the team – and how he made the most of it.

Looking fit and alert, the old cockiness replaced by a more measured confidence, he was a goliath alongside Babb and Ruddock in the Reds' back-three formation and earned repeated man-of-the-match accolades. As aerially dominant as ever, now he was using his experience to read the game more astutely than ever before; tackles were timed to perfection, sloppiness was eradicated, passes were sensible or probing by turn, but never foolhardy. Indeed, it might have been an optical illusion, but such was Wright's aura of control that he even seemed to run faster than in the dark, ponderous days of previous campaigns.

As age and injuries were catching up with him during 1997/98, if he paused to consider what he might have achieved on Merseyside given a different approach from the beginning, he might have shuddered. But at least he could be proud of his response when granted a late shot at revealing his true worth. For that majestic resurrection in the twilight of his playing days, which ended with retirement in the autumn of 1998, Mark Wright deserved eternal credit.

MARK WRIGHT

BORN Dorchester, Oxfordshire, 1 August 1963.
HONOURS FA Cup 91/2. 45 England caps (84-96).
OTHER CLUBS Oxford United 81/2 (10, 0); Southampton 81/2-87/8 (170, 7); Derby County 87/8-90/1 (144, 10).
MANAGER Oxford United (01); Chester City (02-04, 06-07, 08-09); Peterborough United (05-06).

GAMES **206 (4)**
GOALS **8**

ROB JONES

1991/92 → 1997/98

In the late 1990s, when accolades were being showered like so much confetti on a vibrant new wave of multi-talented Reds, it was all too easy to treat Rob Jones a tad uncharitably, like some less-favoured sibling in a family of prodigies. But to do so was unfair, and quite monstrously so.

It should never be forgotten that after bursting abruptly on to the Anfield stage as a 19-year-old virtually unknown outside the homely confines of Gresty Road, Crewe, then ascending to international heights within a few fantastic months, Jones was held back from even greater achievement only by a veritable catalogue of maladies, the most damaging of which was to bring a sickeningly premature end to his football career.

In such harrowing circumstances, it was hardly surprising that his form hit something of a plateau. It didn't mean that he was no longer one of the finest young full-backs to emerge since the war, merely that he was human after all, that only rarely could he perform at optimum fitness, and that his script was not penned by the same author as Roy of the Rovers'.

The grandson of stalwart post-war Liverpool utility man Bill Jones, Rob was discovered by Graeme Souness when the Reds boss was weighing up the merits of another player. A deal was struck in October 1991, with Crewe receiving £300,000 down, £150,000 after the right-back had played 20 senior games, and a further £50,000 if he won five England caps. Though clearly Jones was an outstanding prospect, the Cheshire club could hardly have expected to pocket the full amount as soon as they did.

Just two days after the deal was completed, the slim, pale rookie was thrown in at the deepest of ends, facing high-riding Manchester United at Old Trafford and astonishing seasoned observers with his poise and aplomb amid the non-stop frenzy which characterises clashes between the north-west rivals. Jones was skilful, tough and could run like the wind, and, not surprisingly with the team going through a lean period in the League, became a first-team regular on the spot.

By February he was a full international, in May he helped Liverpool beat Sunderland to win the FA Cup and Alexandra must surely have received the balance of the fee that summer but for Jones' affliction with shin splints, an agonising condition which left him barely able to walk after games. As it was he missed a substantial slice of 1992/93 and, while doing enough to demonstrate that his phenomenal potential was unimpaired, laboured a little to regain his early impetus, though still the Crewe coffers were swollen by their final instalment in 1994.

Thereafter, despite difficulties with knee and back and a worrying susceptibility to viruses, Jones began to acquire the top-flight experience he still lacked. Though he was no longer quite as prominent in a side in which the overall standard was steadily increasing, his maturity and pace, his acute positional sense in defensive situations and the impeccable timing of his tackles all continued to impress. Going forward he could take part delightfully in Liverpool's short-passing triangles, though his self-belief appeared to waver as he reached opponents' penalty areas. Indeed his crossing and shooting cried out for attention – he remained goalless after more than 200 senior outings for the Reds – especially as Roy Evans' 3-5-2 system saw him overlapping more frequently than before.

Season 1995/96 brought competition in the shape of newcomer Jason McAteer, who emerged as a startlingly effective right-sided wing-back. As a result the thoroughly right-footed Rob was switched to the left flank, where he performed competently enough if with rather reduced impact, leaving an inescapable feeling that he had been marginalised.

An even more distressing development was in store. The Jones back had been causing ever-worsening pain for a year and, only three days after facing Manchester United in the FA Cup Final, he was told to rest for six months or risk becoming a cripple.

On his return to the squad, with McAteer and Bjornebye ensconced as wing-backs, Jones found himself out of the team, then suffered further niggling injuries. Once more he bounced back, unseating the Irishman at the outset of 1997/98, only to be sidelined again with a pulled hamstring. He recovered, then McAteer broke a leg and the Welsh-born Englishman was restored to senior duty, only to be afflicted by a hernia in the spring of 1998.

He didn't know it, but poor Jones would never play another senior game. After enduring yet another injury-ravaged term, he was freed to join West Ham on a non-contract basis in summer 1999, but his body could take no more and he was forced to retire while still in his twenties. For all his enormous talent and abundant grit, Rob Jones was finally undone by that most destructive of all adversaries – rotten luck.

ROBERT MARC JONES	
BORN	Wrexham, North Wales, 5 November 1971.
HONOURS	FA Cup 91/2; League Cup 94/5. 8 England caps (92-95).
OTHER CLUBS	Crewe Alexandra 87/8-91/2 (75, 2).

GAMES	241 (2)
GOALS	0

STEVE McMANAMAN

1990/91 → 1998/99

The venomous resentment generated among many erstwhile fans by Steve McManaman's tediously trailed departure from Anfield to join Real Madrid in the spring of 1999 offered a woefully inappropriate farewell to one of the most enchanting home-grown entertainers British football has produced in modern times.

True, scandalised Kopites had been in a state of extended agitation over their favourite's future ever since the Reds had reportedly accepted a £12.6 million offer from Barcelona in 1997/98; now they could scarcely credit that Steve, having run down his contract, was decamping to the Bernabeu on a 'Bosman', and that their club was losing a world-class star without banking a bean.

But such transactions, despise them or not, are a fact of modern sporting life, and the understandably passionate emotions surrounding the McManaman deal should not be allowed to obscure due recognition of the mild-mannered Merseysider's magical, if mercurial, talent.

Admittedly, even after he had helped Real to become champions of Europe in two of his first three seasons in Spain, McManaman's contribution could be frustratingly fitful. But at his scintillating best he made matches dance to his tune, showing why terms like joy and beauty could be applied still to a game plagued by greed and fear and tawdriness. Even better, by doing so he achieved the well-nigh impossible: to all but the blind, the bigoted and the most chronically biased, Steve McManaman transcended allegiance. Okay, perhaps that last assertion is going a bit far, but let's put it this way – he ought to have transcended allegiance.

What made him special was his mesmeric knack of dribbling a football past opponent after opponent, not through awesome acceleration in the manner of, say, Andrei Kanchelskis, but through a heavenly alliance of touch and balance, wit and resilience and, most precious of all, sheer instinct. He loped towards intended victims gently, like some inoffensive lone pedestrian almost begging to be mugged; he carried the ball so close to their feet that robbery with violence seemed inevitable; then came an apparently effortless shuffle and they were tackling empty air while the floppy-haired England flankman skipped lightly towards his next challenge. Like Stanley Matthews in another age, McManaman employed a deceptively simple method of showing the ball to defenders, then snatching it away. But, thanks to his immaculate timing, even though they knew what was coming, more often than not they were helpless to prevent it.

When Liverpool were flying, McManaman was one of half a dozen potential match-winners, but often it was when the Reds' rhythm was missing a beat that his value could be felt most keenly. He had his faults, but one of them was not a proclivity for disappearing when the going got tough. In all but a very few games – the 1996 FA Cup Final comes to mind – he created chances sooner or later, thus providing appreciable insurance against a poor team display.

Those defects? Well, given the number of menacing positions his sorcery placed him in, he did not score enough goals. Oh, he could finish with cool élan, notably the brace which capped his wonderful display in the 1995 League Cup Final victory over Bolton and the sublime curler at the end of a typically beguiling weave late on against Celtic at Parkhead in September 1997. But, season in and season out, quantity was lacking.

Other criticisms were that he surrendered possession too frequently with misplaced or underhit passes, that his skittish dribbles could interrupt the Reds' smooth flow, and that too many of Liverpool's attacks were channelled through him, so that if opponents did manage to stifle him then the team was at a loss.

Such misgivings were all part of the compelling McManaman story, which had begun with his arrival on the top-flight scene as a clearly gifted but distinctly frail-looking 18-year-old in 1990/91. Despite his telling contribution to the FA Cup triumph against Sunderland in 1992, in ideal circumstances he might have been blooded more gradually than the club's prevailing injury situation permitted. As it was he suffered fitness problems of his own and did not progress as rapidly as expected over the next two campaigns. For all his fabulous skill, fears began to surface that he lacked direction, even that he appeared a tad too casual at times.

Come 1994/95, that all changed. Whether the words boot and backside might have been applied in conjunction at this stage is not known, but now McManaman was beginning to dominate games, especially when given a roving commission which made him hideously tricky to mark. In many of the matches that term, and frequently throughout the rest of the decade, his input was colossal, not only for his goals and assists, but for the attention he commanded among opposing defenders and the space thus liberated for marauding colleagues.

What made his rise all the more meaningful to local supporters – and rendered that controversial 'adios' all the more painful – was that he was the first Liverpudlian lad since Sammy Lee to become a long-term regular after working his way through the junior ranks. Meanwhile, to the rest of the nation Steve McManaman was, purely and simply, a rare pleasure to watch.

	STEVEN McMANAMAN	
BORN	Bootle, Lancashire, 11 February 1972.	
HONOURS	FA Cup 91/2; League Cup 94/5. 37 England caps (94-01).	
OTHER CLUBS	Real Madrid 99/00-02/03 (92, 8); Manchester City 03/04-04/05 (35, 0).	

GAMES	348 (16)
GOALS	65

NEIL RUDDOCK

1993/94 → 1997/98

Neil Ruddock was a giant who never attained his full footballing stature. He had it within him to be as dominating and talismanic a figure as, say, Ron Yeats in the 1960s, but despite spells of excellence – such as the 1994/95 season, when he was capped by England – the mountainous Londoner continued to fall short of the consistently inspirational standard set by Bill Shankly's skipper.

At his best Ruddock was an awesome central defender, his implacable, rock-like presence, uplifting spirit and strident assertiveness combining with often underestimated natural ability to produce an abrasively dynamic focal point around which any team would unite.

But that was not always the Ruddock on view. Occasionally his concentration seemed to desert him and his defects, mostly related to lack of pace, were thrown into sharp relief. Then he could be a lumbering, lunging figure, slow at closing down opponents, worryingly vulnerable on the turn and prone to concede free-kicks in dangerous positions through rash challenges, though he should be congratulated for reining in the volatile temper which marred his early development.

Most Spurs fans would have been only too happy to bear with Ruddock's infrequent lapses when his £2.5 million move to Liverpool was agreed in July 1993. Having returned for a second stint with the north Londoners only a season earlier, he had played the finest football of his career and had assumed cult-hero status at White Hart Lane.

Kopites greeted him fervently. He was the warrior king they craved, perhaps a new heartbeat for their talented if slightly tentative team, but for some time he did not live up to such vivid billing. Though mighty in the air and comfortable enough against big men whom he could match physically, Ruddock was made to look clumsy by nippier strikers, and too often he would go for the same ball as his partner, Mark Wright. Maybe a mite complacent following his move to Merseyside, he put on weight, too, and it took a word in his ear from former mentor Terry Venables, among others, to help re-establish his priorities.

Indeed, had 'Razor' not sharpened up his act, surely he would have slipped prematurely out of the Liverpool reckoning in 1994/95. Top centre-backs John Scales and Phil Babb were recruited and the rumour machine had it that Neil would be shipped out, probably to Glasgow Rangers. But the slimmed-down Ruddock would have none of it.

He started the term in such imperious form that manager Roy Evans could not countenance dropping, let alone selling him, and Ruddock settled seamlessly into a back-three system alongside the speedy newcomers, who offered ideal cover if he was caught flat-footed. Displaying immense composure on the ball – in fact, there were times when he was a little too laid-back – he also revealed impressive accuracy in his long-distance distribution. In particular his trademark delivery, swept majestically from the left-back slot to the inside-right channel, offered telling and much-needed variety to Liverpool's short-passing game.

International recognition, deputy stints as Reds skipper and a League Cup winner's medal completed a memorable season. Thus the platform for consolidation as an Anfield cornerstone was in place but Ruddock's progress during 1995/96, a term complicated by personal problems, was not wholly smooth. He played passably well but without making himself indispensable and had to endure spells in the reserves after returning from suspension. His first-team security was lessened by the phenomenal renaissance of Mark Wright and he was omitted from the 1996 FA Cup Final line-up.

The next campaign brought more chequered fortune, with Ruddock's opportunities being limited by the advance of Matteo and the arrival of Kvarme. Come 1997/98, however, he made the line-up for opening day, looking lean and hungry, only to suffer injury, after which he drifted tamely out of contention. He had descended, in his own words, 'from hero to zero' and Liverpool fans who had believed in Neil Ruddock as a potential touchstone for long-term glory felt sorely disillusioned. The following July, when he joined West Ham for £100,000 plus possible increments depending on appearances, the sense of missed opportunity was overwhelming.

NEIL RUDDOCK
BORN   Wandsworth, London, 9 May 1968.
HONOURS   League Cup 94/5. 1 England cap (94).
OTHER CLUBS   Tottenham Hotspur 86/7-87/8 (9, 0); Millwall 88/9 (2, 1); Southampton 88/9-91/2 (107, 9);
Tottenham Hotspur 92/3 (38, 3); Queen's Park Rangers on loan 97/8 (7, 0);
West Ham United 98/9-99/00 (42, 2); Crystal Palace 00/01 (20, 2); Swindon Town 01/02 (15, 1).

GAMES   146 (6)
GOALS   12

JAMIE REDKNAPP

1991/92 → 2001/02

Jamie Redknapp . . . ah, what might have been. For the better part of a decade, the universally popular, opulently talented midfielder seemed just a stride away from blossoming into the play-maker for whom Kopites yearned, the inspirational general whose creative promptings would lead Liverpool out of the Championship wilderness.

But it never came to pass. Instead Redknapp's Anfield career was blighted by a savage succession of injuries, the worst of which prevented him from kicking one ball in earnest as the Reds claimed their momentous treble in 2001. Then, a year later when he was still only 29 and should have been in his prime, he was given a free transfer, slipping away to make a fresh start with Spurs, for whom he had played as a schoolboy.

Yet only a few years earlier, it could be held that if Redknapp had been dreamed up for a work of fiction, he would have been dismissed as too good to be true. The sumptuously sleek skills, the self-assurance untainted by arrogance, the personable character and matinee-idol looks: put them all together and they beggared credibility.

But Harry's boy was for real, looking every inch a thoroughbred after making his League entrance as a 16-year-old for Bournemouth, then managed by Redknapp senior. Certainly Kenny Dalglish thought so, backing his judgement to the tune of £350,000 to make the novice schemer his last major Anfield signing in January 1991.

Soon, with his natural gifts enhanced by above-average physique and maturity for his years, Jamie made an instant impression on new Reds boss Graeme Souness, who gave him his senior debut in the taxing atmosphere of a UEFA Cup clash with Auxerre in Burgundy a mere nine months after his departure from Dean Court.

The following season he enjoyed a lengthy settled run in the side and thereafter he claimed a regular place, his game spiced deliciously with wit, guile and imagination, yet underpinned also with the more mundane, but equally important, attributes of stamina, strength and determination. Indeed, the Redknapp style was buttressed so firmly by steel that certain pundits' earlier suspicions that he might lack a touch of 'devil' were banished emphatically.

Of course, it was his control, breadth of vision and precision of distribution, both long and short, which offered particular delight, even if his repertoire of passes was not quite comprehensive. Maddeningly, he would miss the occasional inviting opportunity to deliver a killing short through-ball around the edge of the box, the type at which Souness had been a master.

No matter, Redknapp lacked little else. Beautifully balanced, he could feint past opponents on the run, was adept at supplying all manner of crosses and was versatile enough for England manager Glenn Hoddle to experiment with him as a sweeper. But for sheer crowd-pleasing spectacle, pride of place went to his long-distance shooting, of which there was no more sensational example than the fulminating 30-yarder away to Spartak Vladikavkaz in September 1995.

Though some observers maintained that it remained rare for him to turn a game that was not going Liverpool's way already, he was in the midst of his finest spell to date when he pulled a hamstring on international duty in November 1995. His confidence appeared to be battered by the setback and for the next year or so, still troubled by nagging injuries, his development became unexpectedly static.

Later, on returning from a broken leg suffered while playing for England against South Africa in summer 1997, his eagerness to make up for lost time was almost tangible and he excelled periodically alongside new midfield partner Paul Ince. But no sooner was Redknapp back on track than recurring knee trouble jolted his momentum early in 1998.

Now his top priority was to overcome that infuriating stop-go syndrome, and in the first half of 1999/2000 he seemed to have succeeded. Elevated to the role of club skipper, he embarked on a crucial phase of his career in vigorously influential form, only to be struck down yet again in midwinter. A brief springtime return raised hopes of long-term recovery, but then came that agonising absence throughout the treble-winning campaign, rendered all the more poignant when Robbie Fowler and Sami Hyypia pushed him forward to accept the FA Cup. It was a moving gesture, a warm tribute to the vast personal esteem in which he was held and to the steely resolution he had shown in the face of serial adversity. Yet, understandably, he seemed a tad embarrassed; somehow, with the likes of Gerrard, McAllister and company flourishing so admirably, already Jamie seemed part of the past.

So it was to prove, as he managed only a handful of outings in 2001/02 before being released by the club he had come to love. All who wished Jamie Redknapp well, and there was an army of such folk on Merseyside, were hoping that some day he would know the joy of lifting a trophy when not wearing a suit. But it wasn't to be, and he limped away from stints with Spurs and Southampton to take his genial presence to the TV studios, where he set about carving a successful niche.

JAMIE FRANK REDKNAPP

BORN   Barton-on-Sea, Hampshire, 25 June 1973.
HONOURS   League Cup 94/5. 17 England caps (95-99).
OTHER CLUBS   Bournemouth 89/90-90/1 (13, 0); Tottenham Hotspur 02/03-04/05 (48, 4); Southampton 04/05 (16, 0).

GAMES   **270 (38)**
GOALS   **42**

PHIL BABB

1994/95 → 1998/99

In the space of one breathless year, Phil Babb went from being a promising but little-known youngster with Coventry to winning lavish acclaim in the World Cup finals and becoming, for a time, the most expensive defender in British football history. Perhaps understandably after such a demanding journey, the leggy, exceptionally pacy Londoner, who was once freed by Millwall, struggled to justify the inevitable hype created by a combination of his international profile and the £3.75 million fee Liverpool paid for him in September 1994.

In the immediate wake of his USA '94 exertions, Babb made a tentative start in a red shirt and before long his game was being placed under an uncharitable media microscope. Some criticised him for an inconsistent first touch and for rushing his creative passing, which led to mistakes; others drew attention to his questionable positional sense and felt he dwelt on the ball with apparent casualness when danger threatened. Against that, his phenomenal speed could get him out of most scrapes as well as offering superb cover to colleagues, his tackling technique was slickly effective, he was a smotheringly tight man-marker and usually he was capable in the air.

Arguably his luck ran out from the day he was asked to play on the left of the Reds' rearguard of three, rather than as a centre-back in a 4-4-2 formation, the role in which he had risen to prominence and which left him less isolated and exposed than on the flank.

Whatever, Roy Evans was quick to deny speculation that Babb might make a rapid exit from Anfield and, despite formidable competition for his place and too many edgy displays for comfort, he missed few games over nearly two campaigns before he was injured in the spring of 1996. On his return to fitness the 25-year-old faced a stern challenge to become re-established. To his credit, he met it head on and was rewarded with an FA Cup Final place at the expense of Neil Ruddock.

Over the next two terms, during which he was plagued incessantly by injury, there was a gradual upturn in his form – especially after the reversion to 4-4-2 in 1997/98 – although still it came as no surprise when a string of solid performances was followed by a distinctly uneasy one.

Sadly, in 1998/99 Babb's consistency dipped again and after a succession of dithering displays he became a scapegoat to fans dissatisfied by the team's progress. Predictably his confidence suffered further, clangers proliferated and eventually he was discarded.

There followed a disappointing loan stint with Tranmere before he rebuilt his career with Sporting Lisbon, helping to lift Portugal's League and Cup double in 2001/02.

PHILIP ANDREW BABB	
BORN	Lambeth, London, 30 November 1970.
HONOURS	League Cup 94/5. 35 Republic of Ireland caps (94-02).
OTHER CLUBS	Bradford City 90/1-91/2 (80, 14); Coventry City 92/3-94/5 (77, 3); Tranmere Rovers on loan 99/00 (4, 0); Sporting Lisbon, Portugal, 00/01-01/02; Sunderland 02/03-03/04 (48, 0).

GAMES	164 (6)
GOALS	1

JOHN SCALES

1994/95 → 1996/97

When he signed John Scales from Wimbledon in September 1994, Roy Evans reckoned his £3.5 million recruit had been the steadiest defender in the League for some time. Not many observers were arguing with the Liverpool manager then and, two seasons of immaculate service down the road, still fewer were taking issue.

Yet early in 1996/97 a combination of nagging injuries, consequent loss of form and the forthcoming arrival of Bjorn Tore Kvarme saw Scales join Spurs in an unexpected £2.5 million deal. Until then the athletic Yorkshireman had been an unflappable, speedy and almost metronomically reliable component of the Reds' back-three formation, whether operating at its heart or on its right side.

His economical style – tackling cleanly, covering intelligently and eschewing risks by playing percentage passes rather than succumbing to over-ambition – had meshed smoothly with a variety of partners. Indeed, the more swashbuckling Neil Ruddock, the gifted but sedate Mark Wright and the less experienced Phil Babb and Steve Harkness had all benefited immeasurably from the consummate Scales professionalism.

John, who won his first England cap in the summer of 1995, attained his eminence only after paying his dues in full. Rejected by Leeds as a teenager, he underwent footballing rehabilitation with Bristol Rovers, then continued his development with Wimbledon, for whom he appeared as a Wembley substitute to help foil Liverpool's League and FA Cup double aspirations in 1988.

For six more seasons Scales flourished as a steely but untypically restrained member of the Crazy Gang and his stature was underlined by a moving, near-tearful farewell from Sam Hammam. The Dons' owner mourned the loss of a gladiator and comrade-in-arms, honouring his exemplary attitude to the game, particularly his coolness under fire, and accurately predicting his international future.

Thereafter Scales settled quickly into the Reds' more sophisticated system, his solidity and common sense offering reassuring security to an extravagantly entertaining side. Some believe he should have attacked more, but his safety-first approach worked admirably and he looked set for a lengthy Anfield sojourn.

Then came that surprising transfer, which delighted Spurs supporters at the time, though they were rather less content after the poor fellow had suffered four seasons of misery with serial injuries.

JOHN ROBERT SCALES

BORN: Harrogate, Yorkshire, 4 July 1966.

HONOURS: League Cup 94/5. 3 England caps (95).

OTHER CLUBS: Bristol Rovers 85/6-86/7 (72, 2); Wimbledon 87/8-94/5 (240, 11); Tottenham Hotspur 96/7-99/00 (33, 0); Ipswich Town 00/01 (2, 0).

GAMES 93 (1)

GOALS 4

ROBBIE FOWLER

1993/94 → 2001/02 & 2005/06 → 2006/07

Once upon a time Robbie Fowler was the most complete British striker of his generation; he was practically deified by Liverpool's hardcore fans and he professed an undying devotion to the club for which he had burned so brightly during comparatively lean years. Yet at the age of 26, with the Reds reaching for the sky once more, he was sold to one of their principal rivals. Those are the bald facts, but they do not tell anything like the whole story.

The truth was that, despite emphasising his undying quality with some of the most brilliant and significant goals in the Anfielders' modern history, Fowler had trodden an ominously turbulent path since recovering from a potentially career-threatening knee injury in February 1998.

Thereafter, with further fitness problems contributing to a decline in strike-rate, there was a succession of unsavoury, self-destructive incidents; instead of radiating the confidence and wellbeing of an ultra-gifted athlete in his prime, too often Robbie's performances and demeanour signalled that he was at odds with himself and the world, and his exit became sadly inevitable.

As the enormity of his £11 million switch to Leeds in November 2001 sunk in, it was poignant to recall the sensational impact of the teenage Fowler when he emerged in autumn 1993. A League Cup goal on debut against Fulham was followed by five in the return leg, before Robbie began his first settled senior sequence. Though obviously uncut, he was clearly a jewel and finished his first campaign with 18 goals, the majority plundered with his favoured left foot.

The Toxteth-born imp weighed in with another 31 strikes in his second season and 36 in his third. So many of that 1995/96 vintage were breathtaking in both conception and execution – the exquisite chip on the run that left Peter Schmeichel helpless at Old Trafford, the smooth swivel past Steve Staunton followed by a pinpoint 25-yard scorcher against Aston Villa at Anfield – and there was still time for a few tap-ins along the way. Robbie of the Reds continued to give a fair impression of Roy of the Rovers as the credits continued to pile up in 1996/97, another 31 of them, and Liverpool missed their main man sorely when suspension removed him from their abortive title run-in.

But the next term brought that fateful, knee-shattering collision with Everton 'keeper Thomas Myhre, and although there was hardly a drought when he reappeared in 1998/99 – 18 successes in 31 starts would be the envy of most hitmen – he no longer carried himself like the audacious young hero who had beaten even his illustrious mentor, Ian Rush, to the 100-goal mark.

Though there was always a mischievously engaging aspect to the Fowler persona – as illustrated by his unveiling of a T-shirt in support of striking Merseyside dockers – there was also a darker side. Now this surfaced in a boorish insult to Chelsea's Graeme Le Saux and a tasteless simulation of cocaine-sniffing after netting against Everton, both of which brought misconduct bans before injury sidelined him again.

Perhaps he felt undermined by endless comparisons with Michael Owen, but that seemed less of an issue when he was created vice-captain for 1999/2000, apparently rejuvenated and plundering an early wonder-goal against Arsenal. A delighted Gerard Houllier referred to 'another Bergkamp in the making', but then prolonged absence with ankle trouble and the arrival of Emile Heskey sparked non-stop speculation about Fowler's future.

The 2000/01 campaign brought new responsibility as Robbie deputised for Jamie Redknapp as skipper, but initially the old certainty was missing and he railed against the striker-rotation policy espoused by Houllier, who urged him to work harder. But bids from Chelsea and Aston Villa were rejected and in the spring it was as though Fowler was born again, lighting up the Millennium Stadium with a fabulous volley against Birmingham in the League Cup Final. Soon he was lifting the FA Cup, too, then he rose from the bench to contribute an unforgettable goal to the UEFA Cup Final triumph over Alaves and netted adroitly against Charlton as the Reds ensured their Champions League berth.

All the old fluency and ebullience were back, he was linking beautifully with Owen and supporters dared to hope for a happy ending, but their optimism was dissipated the following August when a training ground spat with Phil Thompson saw Fowler suspended until he issued a public apology.

He did so, and duly returned, but it couldn't last. Thus with Houllier's patience exhausted, the club afraid of losing a major asset for nothing at the end of his contract, and the player desperate for regular football, Liverpool and one of its most beloved sons adjusted to a painful parting of the ways.

But there was to be an unexpected postscript. In January 2006, following an injury-marred sojourn with Manchester City, a more mature and wholesomely accessible Fowler rejoined Liverpool on a free transfer. Clearly Rafael Benitez was not acting out of sentiment, and there was a genuine belief on the Kop that Robbie could prove a priceless catalyst in the Reds' burgeoning revival, maybe not as the team's chief marksman but as a talismanic figure still capable of lethal contributions. It was a second coming redolent with joyous possibility, but there was to be no fairytale finale. The old sharpness was gone and, after a season and a half of negligible impact, Robbie Fowler left Liverpool for the second and last time, joining Cardiff on a free transfer.

ROBERT BERNARD FOWLER

BORN Liverpool, 9 April 1975.
HONOURS UEFA Cup 00/01. FA Cup 00/01. League Cup 94/5, 00/01. 26 England caps (96-02).
OTHER CLUBS Leeds United 01/02-02/03 (30, 14); Manchester City 02/03-05/06 (80, 20); Cardiff City 07/08 (13, 4); Blackburn Rovers 08/09 (3, 0); North Queensland Fury, Australia, 09-.

GAMES 309 (60)
GOALS 183

STAN COLLYMORE

1995/96 → 1996/97

After a brief but blissful honeymoon, the marriage between Stan Collymore and Liverpool was threatened by an ugly, embarrassingly public tiff. Even at that early stage it seemed the differences might be irreconcilable, but a heart-to-heart talk and a little give and take on both sides soon had the partners kissing and making up. Alas, the cosy concord was not to last. Thereafter the relationship was intermittently fulfilling but strained by periodic turbulence, and friends of the handsome couple were not surprised when it culminated in sudden divorce.

Yet the initial consummation had been joyful, indeed. It took place on a sunny afternoon at Anfield in August 1995, just 60 playing minutes into the Reds career of the multi-talented striker for whom Roy Evans had obliterated the British transfer record by paying Nottingham Forest £8.5 million a few weeks earlier.

Collymore was heavily marked as he received the ball with his back to goal some 25 yards out; he turned sinuously, held off one challenger and feinted past another before calmly dispatching the most delicious of top-corner curlers with his unfavoured left foot. He was the match-winner, he ran to the crowd, he was received with rapture. Happy ever after? Not a bit of it.

The next outing brought injury, then Collymore suffered illness and there followed a run of anonymous performances, leavened by only one more goal, another 'miracle' strike at home to Blackburn. Now, for the most part, the tall Midlander was looking like some moody stranger with a grudge against the world. An undercurrent of impatience began to emanate from the stands and he was dropped.

Collymore's predicament was that he was used to being the focal point of Forest's counter-attacking game, with the whole team playing to his main strength, which was dashing thrillingly at and past defenders. Liverpool espoused a more intricate, patient build-up, involving long passing sequences which, at this stage, were alien to him.

A sensitive fellow who had encountered a number of personality clashes during his progress through six clubs in the previous six years, he became so disillusioned with the Anfield experience that he talked of quitting, which was bad enough. What made it many times worse, however, was that he chose to bare his soul in a magazine, his morose reflections being seized upon and magnified by the rest of the media. As the debate raged about who was to blame, player or club, Glenn Moore of *The Independent* likened Roy Evans to a man who had discovered his bold new Ikea sofa did not match his pretty-pattern Laura Ashley fittings, an eloquently telling summation. Suddenly, unthinkably, a split was not out of the question.

But Collymore, clearly chastened by a 'headmaster's study' session with his manager, apologised for his indiscretion and then regained his first-team place following injury to Ian Rush. Now, slowly but inexorably, he began to settle. He adapted his approach to suit Liverpool and, to a certain extent, the Reds bent to accommodate their costly acquisition.

At last there was a spring in the Collymore step and he began to integrate into the team method; an understanding with Robbie Fowler started to flower, the side flourished and Stan was scoring goals again. Hitherto disgruntled fans began to sing his praises as they revelled in his pace, power and control, his exciting excursions to either flank and the high-quality crosses he supplied to his predatory partner. Collymore's off-the-ball work improved, too, especially his defending from the front, yet all this was achieved without sacrificing his glorious capacity for the unexpected which could turn a game on its head.

During 1996/97, however, there were spells when the ex-Forest star remained peripheral, listless, even disenchanted, and he was ousted occasionally by Patrik Berger. But he scored prolifically as the Reds strove for the title, upped his all-round involvement and won an England recall in the spring. It seemed the general trend was positive and that, having survived some debilitatingly stormy interludes, Stan Collymore just might be staying at Anfield after all. But then, two days after season's end, nuptial vows were exchanged with Aston Villa, a £7 million settlement was arranged and another honeymoon began . . .

STANLEY VICTOR COLLYMORE

BORN   Cannock, Staffordshire, 22 January 1971.

HONOURS   3 England caps (95-97).

OTHER CLUBS   Crystal Palace 90/1-92/3 (20, 1); Southend United 92/3 (30, 15); Nottingham Forest 93/4-94/5 (65, 41); Aston Villa 97/8-99/00 (45, 7); Fulham on loan 99/00 (6, 0); Leicester City 99/00-00/01 (11, 5); Bradford City 00/01 (7, 2); Real Oviedo, Spain, 00/01.

GAMES   71 (10)

GOALS   35

JASON McATEER

1995/96 → 1998/99

The leaving of Liverpool can have hurt few players more profoundly than Jason McAteer. All his life, the bright-eyed, self-confident Scouser had been desperate to enlist at Anfield and when a £4.5 million deal took him there from Bolton in September 1995, he was ecstatic. But some three and a half years later, an unfulfilled McAteer was on his way out of his spiritual home, his cherished ambition of winning medals with the Reds now just a broken dream.

The unscheduled exit must have been all the more harrowing because he had arrived the hard way. After his mother had refused to let him follow his boxing uncles, Pat and Les McAteer, into the ring, he had majored on soccer and clawed his way up through non-League ranks with Merseyside-based Marine. Eventually he made the grade with the Trotters, starring as they reached the League Cup Final of 1995 – in which they lost to Liverpool, ironically – and earned promotion to the top flight.

If Jason's own expectations had been colossal after turning down Arsenal and reigning champions Blackburn to achieve his heart's desire, then certainly they were matched by those of his new fans, who rejoiced at the recruitment of the grittily dynamic Republic of Ireland international. In fairness, too, it should be stressed that for a long time, after manager Roy Evans made up his mind how to employ him, the eager newcomer did not disappoint.

Though he had thrived in central midfield at Bolton, terrorising opponents with his driving runs and employing his box-to-box energy to compelling effect, he slotted into the Anfield jigsaw as a right wing-back, initially because of injury to Rob Jones. However, it wasn't long before his zest and verve in that key position won him preference. His defensive work was generally competent, if occasionally naive, but it was his attractively direct attacking contribution that captured the imagination

The McAteer speciality was his mastery of the accurate cross. Jason offered remarkable consistency and variety, whether on the run or stationary, under pressure or in acres of space. He could float them, drive them or whip them in with a wicked bend, such as the glorious delivery which laid on an equaliser for Stan Collymore as the classic Anfield encounter with Newcastle in March 1996 boiled towards its frenzied finish.

But despite having made an emphatic mark, McAteer suffered extended travail in 1997/98, during which he was dropped at the outset in favour of Jones, then sustained a broken leg in February. To his credit he reacted to both setbacks with characteristic fighting spirit, working hard and regaining his place on merit each time.

However, the arrival of Vegard Heggem for 1998/99 eased him to the margins, and although he might have relished an extended opportunity in his old Bolton role of central midfield, that was always unlikely with Paul Ince and Jamie Redknapp in possession. Thus Jason McAteer, perhaps with a tear in his eye, accepted a £4 million switch to Blackburn in January 1999.

JASON WYNN McATEER		
BORN	Birkenhead, Cheshire, 18 June 1971.	
HONOURS	52 Republic of Ireland caps (94-04).	
OTHER CLUBS	Bolton Wanderers 92/3-94/5 (110, 8); Blackburn Rovers 98/9-01/02 (72, 4); Sunderland 01/02-03/04 (53, 5); Tranmere Rovers 04/05-06/07 (81, 4).	GAMES **119 (20)** GOALS **6**

DOMINIC MATTEO

1993/94 → 1999/2000

Being lumbered with the ludicrous label of 'the new Alan Hansen' didn't do him a lot of favours, but it wasn't often that Dominic Matteo put a foot wrong for Liverpool, and he could consider himself mightily unfortunate that Gerard Houllier did not mark him out for a long-term future with the Reds.

Vivid testimony to the versatile six-footer's all-round quality was furnished only a few months after his £4.25 million move to Leeds United in August 2000. Though he had played for England at youth, under-21 and 'B' level during his Anfield years, and been called into full international squads, he had never been awarded a cap. So Craig Brown pounced.

Knowing that Matteo had been born north of the border – actually he has an English mother, Scottish father and Italian grandparents – the Scotland manager offered him a place in his side. Dominic accepted and soon received an extra boost from Sven-Goran Eriksson, who described him as 'the outstanding left-sided midfielder in the country' and mooted the possibility of attempting to persuade him to switch allegiance back to England!

What made this an even more encouraging judgement was that although Matteo had garnered some early midfield experience at Anfield, and Leeds boss David O'Leary had been quick to deploy him in an advanced left-flank role, he had spent the bulk of his career to date as a stylish centre-half or left-back.

Tellingly, this was not the first time Matteo had been in brisk demand. Back in 1996, Roy Evans received no less than 30 inquiries about the leggily coltish 22-year-old, but had refused to part.

As it happened, Matteo had passed the '96 close-season soul-searching over why he had not emulated his chum, Robbie Fowler, in claiming a regular spot. Accordingly, he emerged from the break burning with renewed enthusiasm to prove himself, and virtue had its own reward when injuries to Ruddock and Scales offered an immediate back-three opportunity.

Matteo had never looked out of his depth during his sporadic first-team outings to date; but now, having added muscle to a previously spindly physique, and with a distinctly more ruthless approach, he was a revelation. Whether operating in the middle or on the left, he exuded calm authority, tackling and heading in approved stopper fashion and displaying enviable pace and athleticism for such a tall fellow. He read the game intelligently, was immensely comfortable on the ball and could use it with crisp perception. Crucially, too, he could surge forward in possession, not indiscriminately but at telling junctures, as Chelsea discovered at Anfield that September. After intercepting confidently, he ran practically from box to box before choosing the optimum moment to release Patrik Berger for a lovely goal.

Thereafter, without quite managing to make himself indispensable, Matteo became steadily more impressive, excelling especially as a firm but creative left-back in a 4-4-2 formation, notably in 1999/2000. How perplexing that it should be his final season as a Red.

DOMINIC MATTEO

BORN   Dumfries, Scotland, 28 April 1974.

HONOURS   6 Scotland caps (00-02).

OTHER CLUBS   Sunderland on loan 94/5 (1, 0); Leeds United 00/01-03/04 (115, 2); Blackburn Rovers 04/05-05/06 (34, 0); Stoke City 06/07-07/08 (23, 1).

GAMES	137 (18)
GOALS	2

DAVID JAMES

1992/93 → 1998/99

A catalogue of calamitous blunders in the spring of 1997 reduced David James from his widely perceived status as England's finest young 'keeper to a sad, almost abject figure, utterly bereft of confidence and an accident waiting to happen on the Liverpool goal-line. Throughout this period of public purgatory, James remained a magnificent shot-stopper but his ineptitude at dealing with crosses became a millstone to a title-chasing side, begging the question: why had the Reds no experienced reserve to spare the 6ft 5in international such prolonged embarrassment?

To his credit, he soldiered on with dignity, interspersing some spellbinding saves with the demoralising misjudgements, and when manager Roy Evans recruited Brad Friedel in December 1997, in a belated attempt to provide meaningful competition, James responded in commendable manner. Indeed, he produced his finest form for more than a year and kept the American on the sidelines for several months before being forced aside, a distressing pattern that was to be repeated in 1998/99.

Such crises were not the first James had faced since his £1.3 million transfer from Watford in July 1992. On arrival he was pressed straight into senior action in Graeme Souness' struggling team and was found to be out of his depth. He proved particularly vulnerable in the air, losing his place first to Bruce Grobbelaar, then to Mike Hooper, before earning a late-season recall. Though immensely promising, James languished in the Zimbabwean's intimidating shadow during 1993/94 and he came close to joining Southampton, remaining at Anfield only after a swap deal involving Tim Flowers fell through.

The turning point for James, who took over once more when Grobbelaar was injured in the February, came the following summer when Bruce left the club. With the spectre of yet another return by his ultra-competitive predecessor no longer haunting him, the younger man began to flourish, exuding presence and charisma that had previously lurked behind a somewhat brooding public demeanour.

He was an ever-present during 1994/95, making several fine saves during the League Cup Final victory over Bolton, and his game continued to progress apace in the subsequent term. James seemed to fill the goal, barring the way like some huge and muscular spider, whether arching his back to make stupendously agile stops or plucking shots from the air with deceptively casual ease. He improved in one-on-one situations and the speed of his reflexes when adjusting his direction to deal with deflections could be phenomenal.

Still, though, there persisted doubts about his aerial prowess. Though more reliable than in earlier campaigns, he continued to lose his way a little too often for comfort during 1995/96. Unfortunately for Liverpool, there was one vivid example in the FA Cup Final against Manchester United, when his disastrous dash and weak punch led to Eric Cantona's winning goal, thus marring an otherwise faultless display. It should be said that there was solid evidence of David's progress, too, with his fellow professionals naming him as the season's best goalkeeper in the Premiership, though with the likes of Peter Schmeichel and David Seaman on the scene, this layman was not alone in finding the players' verdict a tad perplexing.

And so to 1996/97 which, to be fair, James began in splendid style, maintaining generally excellent form until the turn of the year. There were signs of the jitters in the League Cup upset at Middlesbrough in January but it was not until March that alarm bells began to ring. Errors in the seven-goal thriller against Newcastle set the tone, before mistakes at Nottingham Forest, at home to Coventry, away to Paris St-Germain, then most excruciatingly of all in the crucial Anfield clash with Manchester United, piled up in painful procession. His ability to catch high crosses under challenge appeared to have vanished, taking his self-belief along with it, a mystifying and debilitating situation as the campaign approached its climax.

Ironically, he was called up for his full England debut during this traumatic interlude and though Glenn Hoddle left him out of his next squad, Roy Evans retained faith in the troubled custodian, hoping to reap the benefit in the seasons ahead. Unfortunately, his inconsistency continued unabated, yet James remained a huge natural talent and a self-critical perfectionist who strove diligently to get back on track.

It came as no surprise when Gerard Houllier decided that enough was enough in the summer of 1999, bringing in Sander Westerveld, allowing James to join Aston Villa for £1.8 million. At his new club, and later at West Ham, Manchester City and Portsmouth, he continued to demonstrate vast strength of character in putting his Anfield tribulations behind him, returning to prime form and earning more international caps.

DAVID BENJAMIN JAMES

BORN Welwyn Garden City, Hertfordshire, 1 August 1970.
HONOURS League Cup 94/5. 48 England caps (97-).
OTHER CLUBS Watford 90/1-91/2 (89, 0); Aston Villa 99/00-00/01 (67, 0); West Ham United 01/02-03/04 (91, 0); Manchester City 03/04-05/06 (43, 0); Portsmouth 06/07- (109, 0).

GAMES 277 (1)
GOALS 0

PATRIK BERGER

1996/97 → 2002/03

Patrik Berger was a captivating, if inconsistent Anfield hero, a swashbuckling Pied Piper who seduced the eye as he swayed and darted behind enemy lines, all athletic grace topped off by the threat of imminent explosion. But maddeningly for the Liverpool fans who came to love him, he lost impetus after a high-octane start and, by the spring of 1998, appeared ready to leave. Then, granted a reprieve as the managerial reins passed from Roy Evans to Gerard Houllier, he regained prime form, only to be cut down by a savage succession of injuries which ultimately sabotaged his Reds career.

The tall, slim Czech arrived on Merseyside in the summer of 1996 at a cost of £3.25 million from Borussia Dortmund, having just helped his former employers to lift the Bundesliga title and his country to reach the final of Euro '96, albeit without quite fulfilling his boundless potential as an entertainer during the tournament. However, it wasn't long before his new supporters were enraptured by the Berger repertoire.

Patrik announced himself as a major Premiership force at Filbert Street in September, appearing after the interval as a substitute for the troubled Stan Collymore. Almost instantly he transformed a hitherto drab stalemate with a joyous infusion of attacking bravado, running at and past Leicester defenders seemingly at will and contributing two brilliant goals to a 3-0 victory. Lest anyone feared that the newcomer's performance was a fluke, he repeated the dose in the next game against Chelsea, then made it five goals in two and a half outings with a strike against MyPa-47 of Finland.

Kopites rejoiced and wondered: had they found their talisman, an Anfield answer to Old Trafford's Eric Cantona, a player capable of changing the balance of power on the English soccer scene? After all, the Czech was endowed with sumptuous skills, endearing enthusiasm – clearly he wasn't the type to sulk when things went wrong – and thrilling flair. Messiah material, surely.

In fact, it was not to be that simple. Despite his early impact as a marksman, Berger was essentially a left-sided play-maker rather than a specialist front-runner. He was in his element deployed just behind the main striker, frequently a crowded area given Liverpool's plethora of attackers, and vacancies were hard to find. Thus, after a short run of senior starts in which his influence was understandably fitful as he adjusted to the English game, manager Evans used the man from Prague more sparingly, often from the bench.

His vision, passing and crossing remained exquisite at times and there was always the hint of the unexpected. The crowd adored him, Alice-band and all, but he tired of life on the periphery and, understandably enough, with the likes of Benfica and Roma displaying interest, he expressed eagerness for a fresh start. With the climax of the 1997/98 season approaching, the Reds refused to release him, but it seemed inevitable that a diverting, if enigmatic, Anfield sojourn was about to end.

That all changed in the summer with the advent of Gerard Houllier, and Berger started the new season on the left side of midfield, having ousted Oyvind Leonhardsen. Working tirelessly to marry his offensive instincts to defensive responsibilities, he re-emerged as a major force, a little less of a cavalier but still an embodiment of Liverpool's traditional verve and, crucially, a more effective all-rounder than ever before.

Over two campaigns, 1998/99 and 1999/2000, Berger made 75 senior starts for Liverpool and supplied 18 goals, plenty of them unforgettable. For instance, there was a fulminating 30-yarder to cap a dazzling personal display against Kosice in Poland in September 1998, a sublimely curled free-kick to engender fleeting hope in a reverse at White Hart Lane three months later, a tracer-bullet drive at home to Leeds in February 2000 and, best of all, an unstoppable 25-yarder at Old Trafford the following month.

But heartache was in store. A torn cruciate ligament in autumn 2000 sidelined Berger for seven months of that treble-winning term, and although he returned in time to make a telling springtime contribution – including the beautifully flighted pass to set up Michael Owen's FA Cup winner against Arsenal – never again would he exert a consistent influence.

Further knee problems ruined Patrik's next two seasons and he was given a free transfer in the summer of 2003.

PATRIK BERGER

BORN Prague, Czechoslovakia, 10 November 1973.

HONOURS UEFA Cup 00/01. FA Cup 00/01. 2 Czechoslovakia caps; 44 Czech Republic caps (94-01).

OTHER CLUBS Slavia Prague, Czech Republic, 91/2-94/5 (89, 24); Borussia Dortmund, Germany, 95/6 (25, 4); Portsmouth 03/04-04/05 (52, 8); Aston Villa 05/06-07/08 (29, 2); Stoke City on loan 06/07 (7, 0); Sparta Prague, Czech Republic, 08/09- (11, 5).

GAMES	136 (60)
GOALS	35

PAUL INCE

1997/98 → 1998/99

Paul Ince did not have a bad first campaign as a Liverpool Red, injecting extra bite and dynamism into a midfield unit not always renowned for those qualities. But did he consistently exert the same towering, passionate influence as in his Old Trafford pomp? Were there games which he seized and shaped to his will, simply refusing to countenance defeat? Any realistic answer must be in the negative, and after a turbulent second season in which his declining effectiveness was mirrored by tetchiness and arrogance, allegedly off the pitch as well as on it, new boss Gerard Houllier surprised no one by ushering the self-styled 'Guv'nor' to the Anfield door.

When Internazionale's England star appeared on the market in the summer of 1997, the newspapers linked his name with most of the Premiership's leading clubs, though there was a peculiar hiatus when it seemed nobody was that interested. Certainly Manchester United didn't want him back and as other feasible employers began to rule themselves out, there was a suggestion that he might remain in Italy despite all the hullaballoo. However, lurking in the background were Liverpool, for whom he seemed ideally suited.

For a long time the Merseysiders had craved a warrior at the team's heart, a man who would lead by rousing personal example, who could sort out the physical side but also play some football. A second Graeme Souness would have been perfect, but in the absence of such an improbable being, Paul Ince was eminently acceptable.

A fee of £4.2 million was agreed with Inter, then followed excruciatingly protracted negotiations over personal terms until, finally, a wisp of white smoke appeared over Anfield and Roy Evans announced that the Reds had a new captain.

Despite his wide experience in the English top flight with the Uniteds of West Ham and Manchester, it was reasonable to suppose that Ince would need some sort of re-acclimatisation period following his two-year sojourn in Milan. After all, although he believed he was both a more complete player and a more mature character in the wake of his San Siro service, the pace in *Serie A* was not as frenetic as the Premiership's.

It was not surprising, therefore, that as he strove to make an early impression, he received a string of bookings which resulted in suspension by November. His footballing input, meanwhile, was worthy enough but a tad pallid in comparison with the expectations of Kopites who recalled, all too vividly, the United swashbuckler of seasons past. He was hard, undeniably improving the side's competitiveness, yet he seemed uncharacteristically tentative about pressing forward, perhaps reasonably given the wealth of attacking talent on parade.

However, come the turn of the year, with Liverpool clearly off the pace in the Championship race, Ince appeared to shrug off any inhibitions and threw himself into the fray as of yore. No doubt encouraged by a growing understanding with Jamie Redknapp – the Reds were unbeaten in the 15 League games the two England men started in harness – he became a more dominant figure, especially in the attacking half.

One welcome upshot was a spell of three crucial springtime goals, a close-range equaliser in a pulsating Anfield clash with Everton, a thundering header in the 2-1 home victory over Bolton and a balletic overhead kick from six yards in the stirring 3-3 encounter with Tottenham at White Hart Lane.

As he appeared steadily to gather momentum ahead of England's summer assault on World Cup glory in France, the snarl was back on the face of the tiger – wonderful news, indeed, for the Anfield camp. Still only 30 as 1998/99 got under way, he should have had plenty left to give, but as an unsatisfactory term progressed it became clear that all was not well in the world of Paul Ince.

His form was patchy, perhaps partly due to niggling injuries; there was a series of petulant, pointless rucks with opponents and referees; and stories circulated about troubles behind the scenes with the new managerial regime. Gerard Houllier confronted the problem squarely and dealt with it decisively, selling his skipper to Middlesbrough for £1 million in August 1999.

Sadly Ince's exit was not a gracious one. He might have left the fans with memories of his uproariously greeted late equaliser against Manchester United at Anfield in May. Instead he chose to depart with a fusillade of abuse at Houllier and his assistant, Phil Thompson. The taste it left was decidedly sour.

	PAUL EMERSON CARLYLE INCE		
BORN	Ilford, Essex, 21 October 1967.		
HONOURS	53 England caps (92-00).		
OTHER CLUBS	West Ham United 86/7-89/90 (72, 7); Manchester United 89/90-94/5 (206, 25); Internazionale of Milan, Italy, 95/6-96/7 (54, 9);		
	Middlesbrough 99/00-01/02 (93, 7); Wolverhampton Wanderers 02/03-06/07 (115, 10); Swindon Town 06/07 (3, 0);		GAMES 81
	Macclesfield Town 06/07 (1, 0).		GOALS 17
MANAGER	Macclesfield Town (06-07); Milton Keynes Dons (07-08, 09-); Blackburn Rovers (08).		

OYVIND LEONHARDSEN

1997/98 → 1998/99

Oyvind Leonhardsen appeared to be exactly what Liverpool needed. A buzzing fetcher and carrier in the Ray Houghton mould, he combined pace and directness with immense technical skill and formidable physical presence. At Wimbledon he had proved himself in the Premiership fire as a driving midfielder whose range of operations stretched from ahead of his side's front-men to his own goal-line and the Norwegian's half-century of international caps served to underline his genuine quality. Yet he made scant impact on Merseyside under Roy Evans, who had bought him, then was discarded early in the managerial reign of Gerard Houllier.

Certainly Leonhardsen endured a disappointing first season at Anfield following his arrival from Selhurst Park in the summer of 1997. He got off to a luckless start, missing the first two months of the campaign with a hamstring injury, but when he enjoyed a sparky debut in a 2-0 League Cup victory at West Bromwich in October, it seemed only a matter of a little bedding-in time before the Reds started reaping a royal benefit from their £4.5 million investment.

It never happened. Though Leonhardsen was as eager and energetic as expected, his contribution to match after match was largely anonymous. That is not to say much of his work wasn't valuable, but it was mainly unobtrusive, such as covering for defensive colleagues when they ventured forward, and he received precious little credit from the fans.

So why was such an experienced performer, who had excelled so comprehensively with the Dons, under-achieving on the grander stage with Liverpool? The simple answer appears to be that he spent most of his time playing out of position. As a right-footer on the left flank his options were limited and he became numbingly predictable, always being forced to cut inside where, invariably, he would be crowded out.

Of course, his preferred right-sided position was occupied by the wandering Steve McManaman, while Jamie Redknapp and Paul Ince tied up the middle, so it could be argued that manager Roy Evans had little choice. For Leonhardsen, this must have been supremely frustrating.

At the outset of 1998/99 his problems deepened as the left-side berth was allotted to Patrik Berger; thus the man who helped Rosenborg lift three successive domestic titles and who excelled for his country in the 1994 World Cup finals found his career in a state of suspended animation.

It was a bewildering turn of events for a player of such considerable pedigree and the inevitable outcome was a transfer, to Tottenham Hotspur for £3 million in August 1999. Perplexingly the ultra-professional Leonhardsen did not thrive at White Hart Lane, either, and he sought unavailingly to revive his fortunes with Aston Villa.

OYVIND LEONHARDSEN

BORN	Kristiansund, Norway, 17 August 1970.
HONOURS	86 Norway caps (90-03).
OTHER CLUBS	Molde, Norway, 89-91 (64, 9); Rosenborg, Norway, 92-94 (63, 20); Wimbledon 94/5-96/7 (76, 13); Tottenham Hotspur 99/00-01/02 (23, 3); Aston Villa 02/03 (19, 3); Lyn Oslo, Norway, 04-05 (37, 2); Stromgodset, Norway, 06-07 (41, 7).

GAMES	42 (7)
GOALS	7

KARLHEINZ RIEDLE

1997/98 → 1999/2000

It is more of a compliment to Michael Owen than a condemnation of Karlheinz Riedle that the star German marksman, who had been everywhere and done everything, languished in the shadow of the English *wunderkind* for much of 1997/98.

When Liverpool announced their £1.8 million purchase of Riedle from Borussia Dortmund in July 1997, a tremor of apprehension intruded on the annual summer celebration of Manchester United supporters, and on the followers of others clubs with genuine title aspirations.

Clearly the Reds were not messing about: they had signed a man whose goals had just secured the European Cup, who had helped to win the World Cup in 1990, who had played and prospered in Italy's ultra-demanding *Serie A*. True, he was nearly 32 and past his absolute pomp but it was easy to imagine this tall, dark stranger having the same sort of impact as did Jurgen Klinsmann during his first coming at White Hart Lane.

As it turned out, the phenomenal Owen advance combined with the presence of Robbie Fowler confined Riedle to the sidelines far more frequently than expected, but that is not to denigrate the German's exceptional class or his impeccable influence on his colleagues as a professional athlete of the highest order.

To run through the Riedle roster of attributes is to describe the well-nigh perfect centre-forward. He was superb in the air and possessed of beautiful all-round technique; his play was an amalgam of delicacy and power, intelligence and sophistication. His awareness of the overall attacking picture, abhorrence of wasting possession and commendable unselfishness made him the ideal team man, while his flashes of individual brilliance offered a thrilling bonus.

Of these, none was more compelling than his first Premiership goal at Elland Road in August, which he secured with a ravishing

20-yard chip after gulling a Leeds defender. For a moment, it was as though Kenny Dalglish, no less, had reappeared in a red shirt.

However, the presence of the two young Englishmen and a succession of debilitating injuries limited his senior starts to less than a dozen after October and as the season ended there was an unavoidable feeling that Liverpool had not garnered a full harvest of the Riedle bounty.

Karlheinz reacted positively, proving he was not a wholly spent force by starting the new term brightly with three goals in six outings before receding to the bench, but in 1999/2000 he was overtaken finally by the passing of time, as well as the arrival of new strikers Titi Camara and Erik Meijer. Having entered his 35th year, that September Riedle joined Fulham for £250,000, leaving behind him at Anfield an abundance of respect and affection which was entirely appropriate.

KARLHEINZ RIEDLE		
BORN	Simmerberg-Weiler, Germany, 16 September 1965.	
HONOURS	42 Germany caps (88-94).	
OTHER CLUBS	Blau-Weiss Berlin, Germany, 86/7 (34, 10); Werder Bremen, Germany, 87/8-89/90 (86, 38); Lazio, Italy, 90/1-92/3 (84, 30); Borussia Dortmund, Germany, 93/4-96/7 (87, 24); Fulham 99/00-00/01 (35, 6).	GAMES **42 (34)** GOALS 15

BJORN TORE KVARME

1996/97 → 1998/99

The rickety form of Bjorn Tore Kvarme during his first full Premiership campaign was rendered all the more mortifying by memories of his unflappable excellence in the months immediately following his arrival at Anfield in January 1997 in the wake of John Scales' departure to Tottenham.

Indeed, after looking faintly bemused by the pace of proceedings during the first ten minutes of his debut at home to Aston Villa, the blond Norwegian international stopper went on to be voted the man of that particular match. Thereafter, he performed so efficiently on the right of Liverpool's back three that, by May, it appeared that Roy Evans had pulled off a major coup, especially as new European transfer regulations meant that no fee had changed hands.

Furthermore, Kvarme was fiercely committed to the cause, having been so keen to join the Reds that he had left Rosenborg as the Trondheimers were preparing for a European Cup quarter-final against Juventus.

There was nothing complicated about the Kvarme method: when his team had the ball he defended sensibly; when Liverpool were in possession he slotted easily into their smooth passing game. Quick, strong and exceptionally calm, he tackled forcefully, displayed power and timing in the air, and took up intelligent covering positions. Add to that an assured touch, tidy distribution and

the versatility to double as a full-back, and the picture seemed satisfyingly complete. Yes, there had been a few isolated moments of aberration, but they had been deemed permissible for a foreigner settling in.

However, the new season brought sharp disillusionment. It wasn't that Kvarme became a duffer overnight, but mistakes became unacceptably frequent. At Everton in October, he dithered over a clearance, allowing Danny Cadamarteri to run on and score; at home to Manchester United in December, Andy Cole dispensed similar treatment. As winter wore on Bjorn's displays became increasingly ragged until his reputation was finally shredded by Darren Huckerby during the January FA Cup knockout at home to Coventry.

After that, he was dropped for the first time since joining the Reds, but not the last. Recalled when colleagues were injured in February, Kvarme appeared devoid of confidence and soon he was axed again. It represented a demoralising turnaround for an experienced performer, who had looked more comfortable in his back-three slot than in the middle of a back four, to which Roy Evans had switched in the autumn.

Hopes that he might recover lost ground in 1998/99 proved illusory and the disappointed 27-year-old was sold to St Etienne for £1 million during the following summer. At Least Liverpool had turned a profit on the deal, but that was scant consolation.

BJORN TORE KVARME

BORN	Trondheim, Norway, 17 June 1972.
HONOURS	1 Norway cap (97).
OTHER CLUBS	Rosenborg, Norway, 91-96 (88, 2); St Etienne, France, 99/00-00/01 (53, 0); Real Sociedad, Spain, 01/02-03/04 (84, 0); Bastia, France, 04/05 (10, 0); Rosenborg 05-08 (27, 0).

GAMES	48 (6)
GOALS	0

MARK KENNEDY

1994/95 → 1997/98

'It seems I'm good enough to play for Ireland, but not good enough for Liverpool.' Thus spoke a frustrated Mark Kennedy during 1997/98, his final season at Anfield, and his assessment, which might or might not have been intended ironically, was spot on.

After arriving on Merseyside as British football's most expensive teenager in March 1995, the confident Dubliner had set about justifying his £2 million fee in refreshingly sparky manner. Just 19 days after his move from Millwall, the left-sided raider, still overwhelmed at joining the club he had worshipped as a boy, was called on as a substitute at home to Leeds. He tormented the visitors' defence with the pace, strength and unpredictability of his dashing runs and only the crossbar prevented a sensational 30-yard debut goal.

Kennedy, a former centre-forward, consolidated with several more cameo gems on the left flank before season's end and the feeling was that, before long, the Reds' hefty investment would be considered a steal. True, he was naive in his work off the ball, which was only to be expected in one so young, but he was willing, fearless and gifted, an irresistible combination.

But Kennedy's meteoric rise was destined for a summary halt. Injury disrupted his preparation for the 1995/96 campaign in which so much was expected of him and thereafter his form proved so indifferent that he was unable to advance beyond the fringe of Roy Evans' side, where he remained until his £1.75 million transfer to Wimbledon in March 1998.

BRAD FRIEDEL

1997/98 → 1999/2000

Though Brad Friedel emerged as one of the Premiership's most reliable goalkeepers in the early years of the 21st century, it would be harsh to blame Gerard Houllier for allowing the USA international to slip away from Anfield on a free transfer in December 2000.

After all, there was no deafening chorus of disapproval when Friedel was dispatched to Blackburn Rovers, having failed to carve a niche for himself at Anfield following his £1 million signing from Columbus Crew.

That deal had been completed three years earlier, following a tortuous three-month saga during which Liverpool had laboured mightily to secure a work permit for the muscular 6ft 3in custodian.

The most immediate effect of the 26-year-old's arrival was to provoke a dramatic improvement in the hitherto erratic form of incumbent 'keeper David James, thus consigning Friedel to the sidelines until the Englishman faltered again.

Eventually the newcomer was called up in February, making a solid start despite playing behind a distressingly leaky rearguard – one brilliant block on Ryan Giggs at Old Trafford remains vivid in this writer's memory – and retaining his place until season's end.

But soon he was ousted once more by James, then Sander Westerveld was acquired and Friedel, who had neither flopped nor consistently shone during his intermittent sojourn as the Reds' number-one, was snapped up for nothing by the canny Graeme Souness.

As it turned out, and as noted in the previous edition of this book well in advance of his departure for Ewood Park, the big American just might have been worth Liverpool's wait . . .

MARK KENNEDY
BORN Dublin, 15 May 1976.
HONOURS 34 Republic of Ireland caps (95-02).
OTHER CLUBS Millwall 92/3-94/5 (43, 9); Queen's Park Rangers on loan 97/8 (8, 2); Wimbledon 97/8-98/9 (21, 0); Manchester City 99/00-00/01 (66, 8); Wolverhampton Wanderers 01/02-05/06 (167, 12); Crystal Palace 06/07-07/08 (46, 1); Cardiff City 08/09- (36, 0).

GAMES	5 (16)
GOALS	0

BRADLEY HOWARD FRIEDEL
BORN Lakewood, United States of America, 18 May 1971.
HONOURS 82 United States caps (92-05).
OTHER CLUBS Brondby, Denmark; Galatasaray, Turkey; Columbus Crew, United States, 96-97 (38, 0); Blackburn Rovers 00/01-07/08 (288, 0); Aston Villa 08/09- (38, 0).

GAMES	30 (1)
GOALS	0

JAMIE CARRAGHER

1996/97 →

Jamie Carragher is Liverpool's Tommy Smith for the new millennium, the Reds' most consistently mighty back-line performer throughout the first titanic half-decade of the Benitez reign. A cult-hero with hard-core Kopites long before recognition of his immense merit filtered through to the national consciousness, Carragher was for several seasons the most reliable pure defender in the land as well as being deceptively skilful. Ludicrously, it was 2006 before his star finally attained its rightful zenith and when few would have argued if the persuasive lobby to make him Footballer of the Year had succeeded.

A boyhood Evertonian he might have been, but he grew into an uplifting emblem of modern Liverpool's pride and dignity, a bluff, honest yeoman with a huge fighting heart – and unlike his fellow Scouser Steven Gerrard, he can state categorically that he has never even contemplated the possibility of leaving Anfield while still in his pomp.

There are no flashy flourishes or extravant gestures about the Carragher game; he merely gets on with his job, holding his position shrewdly, making tackles and heading clearances as if his life depended on them. Never was this illustrated more vividly than during his epic contribution to the 2005 European Cup miracle in the Ataturk Stadium.

With the score at 3-3 towards the end of normal time Jamie made heroic saving challenges on Kaka and Shevchenko, who had the goal virtually at their mercy. Then, still in pain despite treatment for cramp during the extra period, he continued to hurl himself at Milan's raiders, defiant to the last as the siege intensified. As Johan Cruyff put it eloquently, he looked like a marathon runner whose legs had turned to jelly, but who somehow always found more energy in the last ditch.

Once the overwhelming emotion of that climactic night had sunk in, it was appropriate to reflect on the rise of Jamie's star since the closing months of the Houllier era, when his case had been a perplexing one. By common consent at that time the Premiership could boast few, if any, more capable defensive full-backs than the tall, athletic Carragher. He tackled with ferocious dynamism; his supplies of courage, resolution and resilience were clearly boundless; and he could concentrate forever.

But going forward, an increasingly crucial facet of a flank defender's responsibilities, he exerted minimal impact. In promising situations he appeared hidebound by caution, presumably by instruction rather than personal inclination, and this was the crux of the matter for an increasingly vociferous faction of supporters embittered by what they perceived as their team's excessively unadventurous approach. What galled them sorely was that earlier in his career he had demonstrated amply that he was a multi-talented, all-purpose footballer, having performed classily in midfield and at centre-half as well as at full-back.

A key member of the Reds' 1996 FA Youth Cup-winning combination, he experienced a steady introduction to the big time as a substitute for right-back Rob Jones in the League Cup defeat at Middlesbrough in January 1997. Not for one moment did the 18-year-old look out of place, doing the simple things well in time-honoured Liverpool tradition. His full debut, filling in for midfielder John Barnes ten days later at home to Aston Villa, was considerably more eventful. In the first minute Jamie was booked for a foul but he appeared utterly unfazed, turning in a confident performance which he capped with the first goal towards a comfortable 3-0 victory. In 1997/98 his progress continued as he became an integral part of the England under-21 side, for which he was to make a record 27 appearances, and enjoyed some 20 senior club outings spread between defence and midfield. During the following term he claimed a regular berth, beginning in central defence and making a favourable individual impression in what was a shaky edifice overall. It was in that position that he earned full international recognition in the spring, while his prowess as a midfield anchorman was showcased by a single-mindedly gritty display in the sad defeat by Celta Vigo in Spain.

Come 2000/01, the right-footer settled successfully at left-back, proving a redoubtable bulwark in the treble-winning combination, keeping his place ahead of Christian Ziege. Indeed, such was his composure under ferocious pressure that his manager was heard to sigh for a team of 11 Carraghers, opining that the steely Scouser would be willing to turn out even with a broken leg.

Certainly he proved capable of shackling world-class performers, the likes of David Beckham and Barcelona's Luis Enrique, and at that point there was little criticism by fans of his game. But thereafter Markus Babbel's distressing illness necessitated a switch to right-back and by 2002/03, with League and European disappointments biting deep, his contribution came under increasing scrutiny. Though Carragher was still revered for his value in the rearguard trenches, the failure to make the most of his all-round quality was questioned by those who felt it would be a crying shame if his full potential were to remain unexplored.

Then came Rafa Benitez, more expansive than his predecessor. He posted Jamie in central defence, where he dovetailed brilliantly with Sami Hyypia, proving reassuringly rocklike but also encouraged to be constructive when the opportunity arose. After returning from a broken leg suffered at Blackburn in September 2003, the boy from Bootle just got better and better, riding out his extremely rare patches of poor form with characteristic grit.

Still only 31 in the spring of 2009, Jamie Carragher possessed all the credentials to remain a colossal Anfield influence for the foreseeable future, perhaps even beyond his playing days. Strong minded, passionate and articulate enough to take issue with anyone – even Rafael Benitez when necessary – he might just be a Liverpool manager in waiting. The words 'Fergie' and 'perch' come to mind.

JAMES LEE DUNCAN CARRAGHER
BORN   Bootle, Merseyside, 28 January 1978.
HONOURS   European Cup 04/05. UEFA Cup 00/01. FA Cup 00/01, 05/06. League Cup 00/01, 02/03. 34 England caps (99-07).

GAMES	556 (21)
GOALS	4

DANNY MURPHY

1997/98 → 2003/04

He was dumpy and unglamorous, and from time to time he was pilloried mercilessly by a venomously strident faction of the Anfield faithful. Yet to many connoisseurs of Liverpool's traditional game – passing and movement spiced with imagination and flair – Danny Murphy was the Reds' most consistently creative performer during 2002/03, a core player wholly undeserving of the bile heaped at his door. However, after one more season, and despite a glowing appraisal by new boss Rafael Benitez, he was gone.

At least Murphy, who fought back from a potentially terminal career blip not long after his recruitment from Crewe in July 1997, was appreciated by those who mattered most. Gerard Houllier, after admitting that 'not many people notice him', paid warm tribute to his schemer's vision and tactical awareness, while Phil Thompson declared that Murphy was as important to Liverpool as David Beckham was to Manchester United.

A goal-scoring, sweet-passing play-maker as clever as he was industrious, Murphy proved influential both in harness with Steven Gerrard or when England's young leviathan was missing. Though clearly suited best to the central midfield berth denied him by more stellar colleagues, he proved capable of sparkling from either flank, usually the left.

Eager for constant involvement and pugnaciously aggressive, Murphy was adept at breaking up opponents' moves, then launching quickfire attacks to which he was splendidly equipped to apply the finishing touch. His inventiveness and capacity for the unexpected was exemplified at Ewood Park in August 2002 when he backheeled to Abel Xavier, sprang into space to accept the return and netted with a controlled clip from the edge of the box. But the Murphy goals which remain most vivid in the collective memory of Anfielders are those which secured three rapturously acclaimed triumphs at Old Trafford in the space of four seasons.

In December 2000 his exquisitely arced free-kick delivered the Reds' first win at the enclave of the old enemy for more than a decade. Then, 13 months later, he was fed majestically by Gerrard before lobbing with infinite delicacy over the stranded Fabien Barthez, a major factor in United losing their League crown. Finally there was a penalty in April 2004. Yet how typical that the second of those Murphy masterpieces was crafted only three days after he had been jeered off at Anfield following a tame draw with Southampton.

What volumes it speaks for Danny's character that, despite the brickbats, he never appeared short of confidence. Certainly self-belief was not lacking when he was called from the bench for his Premiership debut, against Wimbledon at Selhurst Park in August 1997, and within five minutes Liverpool were awarded a penalty. With regular spot-kicker Robbie Fowler absent, the sassy newcomer piped up to volunteer his services, and although the job went to Michael Owen, the incident offered a telling illustration of the Murphy persona.

Later that term Danny, who had cost £1.5 million plus an appearances-based top-up, demonstrated his versatility as a stand-in front-man, excelling in isolation at Old Trafford after the dismissal of Owen. But soon his progress slowed unexpectedly; now he gave the impression that he was coasting, perhaps seduced by a taste of stardom, and there followed a painful heart-to-heart with new manager Houllier, which resulted in a disillusioned Murphy being loaned back to Crewe in February 1999.

To his credit he reacted positively, first playing a key role in the Alex's successful scrap to avoid relegation to the Second Division, then slaving like a demon to regain his place in the Liverpool squad. At that juncture a poor pre-season must have sounded his Anfield death knell but, having learned a hard lesson, he regained lost ground in 1999/2000.

Next came a significant contribution to the treble-winning campaign – 47 appearances, albeit 19 of them as a substitute, and ten goals – before deservedly he attained a regular slot in 2001/02, when his renaissance was rewarded by a first England cap.

Murphy's new stature was reflected by his call-up to Sven-Goran Eriksson's World Cup finals party as a replacement for the sidelined Gerrard, only for a broken foot to force his own mortifying withdrawal. Undaunted, he recovered to show exceptional form in 2002/03, shining even during Liverpool's horrible mid-season slump and clipping an audacious winner at Goodison, yet there persisted an unreasonable minority to whom he remained a scapegoat.

Though it was grotesquely unfair, Murphy's back appeared broad enough to cope, and still his Anfield prospects seemed healthy. But then a less consistent 2003/04 and an offer of £2.5 million from Charlton Athletic presaged a reluctant exit, virtually on the eve of the next campaign.

DANIEL BENJAMIN MURPHY
BORN Chester, Cheshire, 18 March 1977.
HONOURS UEFA Cup 00/01. FA Cup 00/01. League Cup 02/03. 9 England caps (01-).
OTHER CLUBS Crewe Alexandra 93/4-96/7 (134, 27) and on loan 98/9 (16, 1); Charlton Athletic 04/05-05/06 (56, 7); Tottenham Hotspur 05/06-07/08 (22, 1); Fulham 07/08- (71, 10).

GAMES **178 (71)**
GOALS 44

23.0

MICHAEL OWEN

1996/97 → 2003/04

When Michael Owen chose to abandon the Reds for Real Madrid in August 2004, he provoked bitter resentment from thousands of disillusioned Kopites who could barely believe that the 24-year-old national hero was turning his back on Anfield, seemingly because he doubted Liverpool's ability to tilt for the game's top prizes.

As he had only a year left on his contract, they believed he had effectively forced the club to sell for a comparatively paltry £8 million before his market value plummeted to zero. True, on a strict business level he owed Liverpool nothing after so many seasons of scintillating service. After all, any worker has the right to take his talent where he pleases and, as Steve McManaman had demonstrated in 1999, such transactions are commonplace, no matter how heart-rending for the fans. Yet a widespread notion on Merseyside was that there should be more to football than such a cool bottom line.

The rancour resurfaced 12 months later when, with Real keen to offload Owen but demanding a £16 million fee, Michael stated his preference for Anfield, but then joined Newcastle United instead of standing his ground.

For all who loved Liverpool it was a sorry situation, but it should never be allowed to obscure the essential sporting truth that Michael Owen remained a once-in-a-generation goal-scoring genius, an incandescent performer whose phenomenal achievements in his teens and early twenties for both club and country beggared belief.

Consider: he was Liverpool's leading scorer in each of his seven full seasons at Anfield, averaging better than a goal every two games; he was the youngest England player of the 20th century; in 1998 he lit up the World Cup Finals with a fantastic strike against Argentina after entering the tournament with only three hours of international experience behind him; three years later he became the first British-based European Footballer of the Year since George Best in 1968.

As if all that were not enough, he is blessed with an impeccable temperament which enables him to cope stoically with periodic media pannings, and the enviable facility of invariably bouncing back from rare lean spells with spectacular goal rushes.

Not for half a lifetime, since the emergence of Jimmy Greaves, has a rookie marksman erupted on to the English scene with such compelling force, and while Owen's eminent predecessor was a predator of a vastly different type, in terms of sheer impact the comparison is valid.

Of course, the impish Londoner was an incomparable opportunist in confined areas rather than a maker and taker of chances like the blindingly pacy Owen, who is at his most lethal when racing into space. But both caught the imagination of a public who were ready to believe that, for them, nothing was impossible; both were quicksilver in thought and deed, able to transform any match with a split-second of dazzling brilliance; both were brimming with exuberant vitality, incapable of being overawed.

A boyhood prodigy, Owen was snapped up by Liverpool, shattered virtually every junior scoring record and was given his senior debut at 17 during the closing stages of a crucial Premiership encounter with Wimbledon at Selhurst Park in May 1997. Within minutes he had stroked a lovely goal with a veteran's aplomb and came close to forcing the draw which would have extended the title race.

Unveiled to a national audience that evening were his deft technique, startling change of pace and astonishing strength for one so slightly built, while aficionados were gasping, too, over his uncanny knack of taking up dangerous positions. Unsurprisingly Owen started the new season in the first team, and soon it was unthinkable that he should be anywhere else.

Duly a first full campaign of unrelenting excellence was climaxed by his World Cup derring-do, and after returning from France '98, he did little to correct the impression that nothing was beyond him. Certainly that was the feeling when he plundered a wondrous hat-trick for his country in the 5-1 humbling of Germany in Munich in September 2001, while the brace of opportunistic strikes which turned around the FA Cup Final against Arsenal six months earlier encapsulated the Owen magic in microcosm. After labouring for 80 minutes with barely a sniff at goal, Michael pounced on a Markus Babbel knockdown to equalise with an acrobatic volley, then he hared past two defenders before clipping a clinical winner with his weaker left foot.

That day, Michael Owen was the difference between victory and defeat, and frequently that was the case over subsequent campaigns. There were plenty who believed that Liverpool relied on him too heavily, that the expectations on his still-youthful shoulders were unfairly vast. They contended that too often he was expected to slave selflessly while being offered inadequate service, and that such a relentlessly demanding role exacted a daunting price in injuries. Indeed, some feared he might become frustrated, and seek fulfilment elsewhere, and so it proved.

Owen's character appeared open and appealingly clean-cut, but there was steel there, too, a rampant hunger for success and a certainty of ambition which dictated that, sooner or later, he must play for a team tilting regularly at League titles and Champions League glory. Ironically, had he remained at Anfield, he would have been an integral part of the European Cup dream in 2005. The future? While he was toiling grimly for struggling Newcastle, a handful of supporters still yearned for an emotional return to Liverpool. However, many more were unwilling to let bygones be bygones, a hardline attitude which his next transfer set in stone.

MICHAEL JAMES OWEN

BORN	Chester, Cheshire, 14 December 1979.
HONOURS	UEFA Cup 00/01. FA Cup 00/01. League Cup 02/03. 89 England caps (98-). European Footballer of the Year 01.
OTHER CLUBS	Real Madrid 04/05 (35, 13); Newcastle United 05/06-08/09 (71, 26); Manchester United 09/10-.

GAMES **267 (30)**
GOALS **158**

VEGARD HEGGEM

1998/99 → 2000/01

If a few more defenders attacked with the zest, vitality and invention of Vegard Heggem, then football would be an infinitely more entertaining game. The nimble Norwegian right-back arrived at Anfield in July 1998, brimming with brio and so eager to sample life in the Premiership that he passed up the certainty of a Champions League campaign with Rosenborg, who pocketed £3.5 million as Roy Evans and Gerard Houllier completed the first signing of their joint managerial reign.

Immediately Liverpool fans were beguiled by his buccaneering approach. They relished the bright-eyed 22-year-old's undisguised swagger as he danced past opponents in the manner of a conventional winger, all intricate skills and sudden sidesteps, his sure-footed balance matched by his power, pace and resilience.

That first autumn and winter he shredded a succession of rearguards by bursting into space shrewdly vacated by his forwards, notably at home to Coventry and Newcastle, and unforgettably at Middlesbrough, where he flitted beyond three defenders before netting with an adroitly stabbed cross-shot.

True, sometimes there was a price to pay if Heggem became stranded upfield, or failed to keep tabs on the man he was marking, such as when Coventry's Noel Whelan escaped to score at Highfield Road in January 1999. There were occasions, too, when his distribution seemed careless, or even cavalier, but overall he was a tonic, a player with a bit to learn but a seeming certainty to become an Anfield fixture.

Alas, it was not to be, as Heggem suffered serial hamstring problems. After a handful of outings in 2000/01, and despite harrowing attempts at recovery, he never played for Liverpool again.

VEGARD HEGGEM
BORN Trondheim, Norway, 13 July 1975.
HONOURS 21 Norway caps (98-00).
OTHER CLUBS Rosenborg, Norway, 95-98 (57, 5).

GAMES 46 (19)
GOALS 3

RIGOBERT SONG

1998/99 → 2000/01

It was impossible to miss Rigobert Song on a football field. It wasn't merely the wildly flailing dreadlocks which riveted the eye, but the flamboyantly frenetic style, as the lithe, muscular Cameroon international patrolled his defensive patch like some exuberant Doberman with a meal on its mind.

When Song was recruited from Italian *Serie A* side Salernitana for £2.8 million in January 1999, he carried with him a reputation both eminent and lurid. On the positive side, he had accumulated half a century of caps by the age of 23 and appeared in two World Cups. Less commendably, he had been sent off in both tournaments, and though Gerard Houllier had rated Rigobert highly ever since watching him excel for his first club, Metz, the Song sojourn at Anfield was destined to be brief.

He was given opportunities both in his favoured slot of centre-half and at right-back, and there were aspects of his game which appealed instantly to the home crowd, with whom he struck up a good-natured rapport. He was fast and powerful, an explosive attacker of the ball on the ground and in the air, and he was endlessly persistent.

But there was no disguising Rigobert's rashness. Many of his challenges were impetuous, and he conceded unnecessary free-kicks; his marking was only fitfully disciplined and sometimes he appeared confused and disorganised. Thus, with defensive stability a Houllier priority, it came as no surprise in November 2000 when West Ham's £2.5 million offer was cordially accepted.

Song went on to flourish overseas, becoming the Cameroon's most capped player, with more than a century of appearances.

BAHANAG RIGOBERT SONG
BORN Ncanglicock, Cameroon, 1 July 1976.
HONOURS 124 Cameroon caps (93-).
OTHER CLUBS Metz, France, 94/5-97/8 (123, 3); Salernitana, Italy, 98/9 (4, 1); West Ham United 00/01-01/02 (24, 0); Cologne, Germany, on loan 01/02 (16, 0); Lens, France, 02/03-03/04 (63, 3); Galatasaray, Turkey, 04/05-07/08 (108, 4); Trabzonspor, Turkey, 08/09- (20, 0).

GAMES 30 (8)
GOALS 0

DAVID THOMPSON

1996/97 → 1999/2000

David Thompson was a spiky little Scouser who operated anywhere across the midfield and the fans hailed him as one of their own. Unquestionably he was endowed with every shred of ability and desire required to become a long-term Liverpool favourite, yet somehow he lost his way at Anfield and departed to prosper elsewhere.

The Thompson possibilities were illustrated compellingly with a goal at home to Crystal Palace in April 1998, one which might have been fashioned by any of the club's great play-making combinations of the past few decades. David seized possession in centre-pitch, sprayed the ball wide to Steve McManaman on the right, then sprinted into the Londoners' box to slide home the return pass from six yards. Beautifully simple, devastatingly effective.

The younger of the two Merseysiders' contribution to that late winner was a particular joy. Clearly Thompson was in the traditional mould of vintage Reds such as Sammy Lee and Ray Houghton, a skilful and intelligent workaholic who punched his weight in physical challenges and embodied the timeless Liverpool pass-and-move philosophy.

Granted a lengthy loan stint at Swindon to broaden his experience that term, Thompson produced such outstanding form at the County Ground that Robins boss Steve McMahon was keen to buy him. But Roy Evans called him back and he impressed in each of a handful of senior outings in the spring, including that telling display against Palace.

Despite ferocious competition for places in 1998/99, he continued to make strides, and it was a pity that the instant precision of his through-pass for Michael Owen to open the scoring against Celta Vigo in Spain was ultimately submerged by the gloom of a comprehensive defeat.

The seemingly inevitable Thompson climb towards eminence gathered even more promising momentum in 1999/2000 when he made 27 senior appearances, featuring a goal of stunning quality against Sheffield Wednesday at Anfield in December when he mesmerised poor Lee Briscoe before netting with a perfectly curled left-footer.

However, his season was marred by disciplinary difficulties which resulted in Gerard Houllier dispatching him to train at the youth academy. Perhaps he failed to listen when sage advice was offered, and the unsatisfactory upshot was a £3 million move to Coventry in August 2000.

At Highfield Road, Thompson appeared to mature, giving Kopites a glimpse of what they had lost with a fulminating 25-yarder at Anfield that November, then his career stepped up a further gear under Graeme Souness at Blackburn. During 2002/03 he was called into the England squad, and the scale of Liverpool's potential loss took on significant proportions, only for further injuries to limit his progress drastically.

DAVID ANTHONY THOMPSON				
BORN	Birkenhead, Merseyside, 12 September 1977.		GAMES	31 (25)
OTHER CLUBS	Swindon Town on loan 97/8 (10, 0); Coventry City 00/01-02/03 (66, 15); Blackburn Rovers 02/03-05/06 (64, 5); Wigan Athletic 05/06 (10, 2); Portsmouth 06/07 (12, 0); Bolton Wanderers 06/07 (8, 0).		GOALS	5

SANDER WESTERVELD

1999/2000 → 2001/02

Sander Westerveld looked the part of a top goalkeeper, and sometimes he played it, but not consistently enough for Liverpool. The tall, imposing, immaculately groomed custodian positively oozed self-belief, and the Premiership boasted no more athletic shot-stopper. Indeed, he was capable of stunning feats of agility, painting in the mind's eye an obviously exaggerated but still vivid impression of soaring horizontally from one post to another, a genuine flying Dutchman.

With the ball at his feet, too, Westerveld was peerless on the domestic scene, the crispest of strikers who could transform defence into attack with raking, devastatingly accurate left-foot dispatches which travelled three-quarters of the pitch's length to send Michael Owen, Robbie Fowler or Emile Heskey on their merry way.

As for physical courage, he possessed it in spades, plunging his 6ft 3in frame into many a maelstrom of flailing feet, and his methods of dealing with one-on-one confrontations were as clever as they were brave. As a lone attacker bore down, Westerveld would advance boldly to meet him, standing tall until the optimum moment for decisive action, then spreading himself to present a formidable barrier.

Thus far, then, Sander takes on the aspect of a goalkeeping paragon but, alas, there was a flaw. When the ball was high in the air, when steepling crosses arrived from either flank, he was not always a commanding figure, being known to flap and fumble gruesomely when a clean take would have relieved the pressure instantly.

Though outwardly he continued to exude his characteristic confidence even as the evidence of aerial frailty piled up against him, a steadily mounting barrage of criticism must have had its effect, making the crucial decision-making process – when to leave his line and when to remain rooted – all the more agonising.

Yet despite the travail which ultimately undermined his position as the Reds' number-one, he remained popular with many Liverpool fans, who honoured him for his plentiful attributes and for the resolution with which he worked to eradicate mistakes.

Expectations had been considerable when Gerard Houllier ended David James' Anfield aspirations by paying Vitesse Arnhem £4 million to make Sander Westerveld Britain's most expensive goalkeeper in the summer of 1999. After all, he had been courted by Lazio, among others, and was seen as the heir apparent to Edwin van der Sar as Holland's top 'keeper, a stature underlined by his full international debut against Brazil that June.

Early indications were excellent as, overall, the lithely muscular 24-year-old cut an impressive dash with his new club. Admittedly there was some uncertainty at gathering crosses, but it was dismissed as mere teething trouble of the type endured by Peter Schmeichel during his acclimatisation with Manchester United, a reasonable reaction at that stage.

Saving a penalty by Davor Suker in a 2-0 Anfield triumph over Arsenal in August helped his cause, and he appeared to settle. Thereafter for two seasons Westerveld became a fixture between Liverpool's posts, and despite all the flak destined eventually to fly in his direction, it would be grotesquely unfair to overlook either the tremendous part he played in ensuring that Liverpool's defence was the Premiership's tightest in 1999/2000, with only 30 goals conceded, or his integral contribution to the fabulous cup treble of 2000/01. For instance, his late, gravity-defying spring to repel a 30-yard chip from Birmingham City's Andy Johnson in the League Cup Final will not be forgotten, and nor will his coolness to deny the same opponent at the decisive moment of the subsequent penalty shoot-out.

That said, the UEFA Cup Final against Alaves highlighted both sides of the Westerveld coin. First, after Liverpool had seized the early initiative, he rescued stretched defenders with several brilliant stops, but as the pressure mounted he appeared increasingly shaky, and failed to claim the corner from which Jordi Cruyff levelled at 4-4 with only a minute of normal time remaining.

Now Gerard Houllier was worried, stressing at the outset of 2001/02 that his goalkeeper needed to improve, and when Westerveld was guilty of a grievous error at Burnden Park in August, allowing a weak shot from Dean Holdsworth to squirm beneath his body for the winner, the manager's patience ran out. Jerzy Dudek and Chris Kirkland were signed without delay, and the Dutchman never played another senior game for Liverpool.

That December Westerveld joined Real Sociedad, then coached by John Toshack, for £3.4 million and set his sights on retrieving his fortune in Spain. It was a desperately poignant exit for an ambitious young man who believed himself the victim of chronically rough justice.

SANDER WESTERVELD	
BORN	Enschede, Holland, 23 October 1974.
HONOURS	UEFA Cup 00/01. FA Cup 00/01. League Cup 00/01. 6 Holland caps (99-04).
OTHER CLUBS	Twente Enschede, Holland, 94/5-95/6 (14, 0); Vitesse Arnhem, Holland, 96/7-98/9 (100, 0); Real Sociedad, Spain, 01/02-04/05 (77, 0); Real Mallorca on loan 04/05 (6, 0); Portsmouth 05/06 (6, 0); Everton on loan 05/06 (2, 0); Almeria, Spain, 06/07 (33, 0); Sparta Rotterdam, Holland, 07/08 (29, 0).

GAMES	103
GOALS	0

GARY McALLISTER

2000/01 → 2001/02

Gary McAllister was hardly the obvious transfer target in the summer of 2000. Though a proven play-maker of ravishing quality with more than 50 Scotland caps to his credit, he was halfway through his 36th year and, with all due respects to Coventry City, whose teams he had graced for four seasons, it seemed that he had retreated from the trophy-hunting frontline when he had left Leeds United in 1996.

As it turned out, McAllister was an inspirational acquisition, surely the key ingredient in Liverpool's momentous cup treble as he set a supreme example to Steven Gerrard and company with his imperiously imaginative, endlessly artful promptings. Thus Gerard Houllier, who is to be congratulated for harvesting the last of McAllister's summer wine, was left to reflect that he might have tasted an even more potent vintage had the Reds moved for the veteran a couple of years earlier.

Though some commentators saw the Frenchman as taking a gamble on the balding maestro, despite the fact that he was signed on a Bosman-style free transfer, closer examination of the circumstances tell a different story. After all, with Jamie Redknapp enduring yet more injury heartache, a new general was essential, and the Scot fitted the bill on practically every count.

He remained superbly fit, having missed only 56 minutes of 1999/2000 for the Sky Blues while contributing 13 goals from midfield and, apparently, although most minds might boggle at such a minutely detailed statistic, only Manchester United's Roy Keane had exceeded his total of 1,820 passes.

More relevant still were McAllister's vast experience, including a League Championship triumph with Leeds in 1992, his natural air of authority and composure, and an impeccably professional attitude which offered a clear explanation of his remarkable longevity.

From the moment of his arrival – when he joked that he could not indulge his long-time fixation with the number-ten shirt because some Anfield kid had bagged it! – Gary demonstrated a natural affinity with the Reds, revelling in their trademark pass-and-move creed and relentless ambition.

The last thing he desired was a gentle swansong and in 2000/01, despite the immeasurable distress of his wife's ultimately fatal illness, he emerged as the creative guru Liverpool had been lacking. Here was a man who could dictate the pace and flow of a contest, majestically enhancing the fluency of the side as he flighted and threaded his penetrative dispatches with immaculate precision, weight and timing, his deft touch making mincemeat of carefully constructed offside traps.

McAllister was lethal at dead-ball situations, too, whether arcing deliveries with wicked whip and velocity towards the head of Sami Hyypia and the rest, or going directly for goal. His skills, essentially natural but honed conscientiously over nearly two decades with Motherwell, Leicester, Leeds and Coventry, were well-nigh faultless, a transport of delight for the connoisseur.

Typically, when it mattered most, the McAllister magic was at its most deadly. As Liverpool closed in on three trophies and a precious Champions League place in the spring, he scored in five successive games, beginning with the most astonishing of all his strikes for the Reds, a free-kick from 44 yards which claimed a sensational Premiership victory at Goodison Park. Catching Everton 'keeper Paul Gerrard momentarily out of position, it was a stunning monument to technique, awareness and audacity.

The prolific sequence continued with a decisive penalty in the UEFA Cup semi-final against Barcelona at Anfield, another strike from the spot in a home win over Spurs and two more pinpoint free-kicks as maximum points were garnered at Coventry and Bradford.

So sorely was McAllister's nous missed in the FA Cup Final against Arsenal that he was called on to replace Dietmar Hamann, and he helped to steady the rocking Reds ship, but even that was merely a prelude to his starring role in the climax of the campaign, the 5-4 triumph over Alaves in the UEFA Cup Final.

On that searingly dramatic night in Dortmund, he supplied the delivery for Markus Babbel to score, converted a penalty, made the pass to Robbie Fowler which led to another goal and struck the late free-kick from which the hapless Geli glanced past his own 'keeper to complete the scoring.

Having scaled such a pinnacle at the age of 36, many men would have retired, but such was Gary's stamina and unquenchable appetite for football that he gave Liverpool another season, making 38 appearances in 2001/02 before leaving to begin a managerial career (while continuing to play, of course) in the familiar surroundings of Highfield Road.

Back in 1993, Kenny Dalglish had attempted in vain to recruit his gifted countryman for Blackburn but had been turned down by Leeds. What if Anfield boss Graeme Souness had entertained a similar thought, and made a successful bid for Gary McAllister in his prime? If only . . .

GARY McALLISTER	
BORN	Motherwell, Lanarkshire, 25 December 1964.
HONOURS	UEFA Cup 00/01. FA Cup 00/01. League Cup 00/01. 57 Scotland caps (90-99).
OTHER CLUBS	Motherwell 81/2-85/6 (59, 6); Leicester City 85/6-89/90 (201, 47); Leeds United 90/1-95/6 (231, 31); Coventry City 96/7-99/00 (119, 20) and 02/03-03/04 (55, 10).
MANAGER	Coventry City (02-04); Leeds United (08).

GAMES	52 (35)
GOALS	9

TITI CAMARA

1999/2000

Titi Camara was a loose cannon of a striker, but an engaging one. The Premiership's first Guinea international brought a dash of fantasy to the Anfield party, intermittently illuminating even the darkest game with his characteristic panache, and scoring a handful of fine goals.

Accordingly he was cherished by plenty of regular Reds-watchers, who were upset when Gerard Houllier sold him to West Ham for £1.5 million in December 2000. They had gloried in his swashbuckling runs laced with outrageously extravagant dummies, and marvelled at his scintillating technique. They loved the way the pacy, muscular, elastic-limbed raider would spin off a defender, then carry the ball enthrallingly before firing at goal or dispatching a deliciously unexpected pass.

Against that, Aboubacar Sidiki Camara might make a mess of the simplest of tasks, like finding a colleague ten yards away. Undeniably he blew hot and cold and Houllier, who bought him for £2.6 million from Marseille in July 1999, clearly demanded more consistency.

Despite such reservations, Camara played in all but six senior games in his first Liverpool term, netting on opening day at Sheffield Wednesday, caressing the imagination with his scissors-kick in the FA Cup triumph at Huddersfield, and striking ten times in all.

But with Heskey added to the strike-force of Owen and Fowler, there was no place for Titi in 2000/01. Soon he became disaffected and he departed, leaving one disgruntled Kopite to groan: 'He was unpredictable, so what? What's wrong with unpredictable?'

ABOUBACAR SIDIKI CAMARA
BORN Conakry, Guinea, 17 November 1972.
HONOURS 38 Guinea caps.
OTHER CLUBS St Etienne, France, 90/1-94/5 (94, 16); Lens, France, 95/6-96/7 (63, 14); Marseille, France, 97/8-98/9 (61, 8); West Ham United 00/01-(11, 0); Al-Ittihad, Saudi Arabia, on loan 02/03; Al-Sailiya, Qatar, 03/04 (20, 14); Amiens, France, 05/06 (26, 9).
MANAGER Guinea (09-).

GAMES	24 (13)
GOALS	10

ERIK MEIJER

1999/2000 → 2000/01

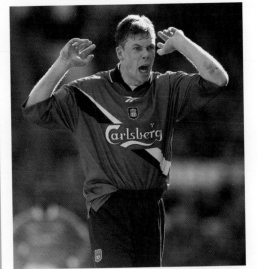

No Liverpool footballer since Joey Jones has enjoyed a more uproarious rapport with the Anfield crowd than Erik Meijer. The towering Dutch spearhead, a boyhood Reds fanatic signed on a Bosman-style free transfer from Bayer Leverkusen in the summer of 1999, had no pretensions to grandeur as a player, but he could wind the Kop around his little finger, conducting anthems and exchanging banter with all the earthy spontaneity of any Merseyside-born comedian.

It's fair to say that as a Dutch international marksman, Erik had precious little in common with the likes of van Basten, Kluivert or van Nistelrooy. Acquired to offer the Reds an aerial option which would complement nippy fellow strikers Michael Owen, Robbie Fowler and Titi Camara, he worked ferociously and selflessly, and occasionally produced an unexpectedly delicate touch, but mostly he was ponderous, his vast expenditure of energy sadly unproductive.

Indeed, for all his spirit, Meijer failed to net once in 24 Premiership outings – admittedly 17 of them were made as a substitute – and while the universal affection of the supporters bathed him in a glory of sorts, it was not enough to preserve his place in the squad.

Duly the much-travelled six-footer was loaned to Preston North End in October 2000 and, after registering nine blanks for the Deepdale club, he was freed to join Hamburg. Back at Anfield, though, the legend of 'Mad Erik' lives on.

ERIK MEIJER
BORN Meersen, Holland, 2 August 1969.
HONOURS 1 Holland cap (93).
OTHER CLUBS Fortuna Sittard, Holland, 88/9-90/1 (36, 6); Maastricht, Belgium, 91/2-92/3 (66, 34); PSV Eindhoven, Holland, 93/4-94/5 (39, 13); Uerdingen, Holland, 95/6 (32, 11); Bayer Leverkusen, Germany, 96/7-98/9 (84, 16); Preston North End on loan 00/01 (9, 0); Hamburg, Germany, 00/01-01/02 (45, 8); Alemania Aachen, Germany, 03/04-05/06 (92, 19).

GAMES	10 (17)
GOALS	2

NICK BARMBY

2000/01 → 2001/02

For a footballer once lauded as the classiest young English-born talent of his generation, Nick Barmby has endured a perplexing career.

Not that he has been a failure, or anything like it, having served five of England's most eminent clubs and accumulated nearly a quarter of a century of international caps while still in his twenties. Yet somehow the unrelenting excellence of which he was deemed capable since his schooldays, when scouts from desperate would-be employers laid siege to his home, remained bafflingly elusive.

At Liverpool, though he made dynamic contributions to the cup treble of 2000/01, the goal-scoring midfielder cum deep-lying striker did not enjoy the best of fortune after his £6 million transfer from Everton in July 2000.

The Blues' player of the season for 1999/2000 understood that he would face hysterical accusations of treachery when he became the first man to make a direct beeline from Goodison Park to Anfield since Dave Hickson back in 1959, and he wasn't wrong, but initial impressions were that for Nick Barmby, Liverpool were the right club at the right time.

He was 26, on the threshold of his prime and ready to translate his boundless quality into solid achievement; the Reds, whom he had idolised as a boy, seemed poised for the stratosphere under a visionary manager with money to spend.

Though naturally right-footed, the chunky Humbersider settled enterprisingly on the left side of midfield, his brightness and invention on the ball complemented by tenacity and non-stop industry. Virtually untrackable when drifting intelligently from his starting position, he could unhinge any defence with an unexpected, obliquely angled pass, and he was a capable finisher.

Few goals can have afforded Barmby more intense pleasure than his first Premiership strike for Liverpool, a header which combined power and placement in a 3-1 home victory over Everton that October, but in the context of the unfolding season, a succession of UEFA Cup strikes could be judged more precious still.

In Bucharest he lashed the winner into the roof of Rapid's net, there was an equaliser in the Czech Republic against Slovan Liberec, then crucial away and home efforts in the Olympiakos tie, the Anfield goal involving a nimble skip around the 'keeper and a slide-rule slot that would have done credit to Michael Owen.

So far, so good, but early in the New Year Nick suffered an ankle injury, after which the old Barmby sparkle was sadly missing. Though returning intermittently, he missed the climax of the treble campaign; two operations limited his total of 2001/02 starts to a paltry seven, and in the subsequent August he was sold to Leeds United for £2.75 million.

The Liverpool crowd, having embraced Barmby from the outset, stood by him to the last, sharing his frustration but recognising a gifted performer who was trying his heart out as his Anfield ambitions slipped agonisingly beyond reach.

NICHOLAS JONATHAN BARMBY

BORN	Hull, Humberside, 11 February 1974.
HONOURS	League Cup 00/01. 23 England caps (95-01).
OTHER CLUBS	Tottenham Hotspur 92/3-94/5 (87, 20); Middlesbrough 95/6-96/7 (42, 8); Everton 96/7-99/00 (116, 18); Leeds United 02/03-03/04 (25, 4); Nottingham Forest on loan 03/04 (6, 1); Hull City 04/05- (121, 20).

GAMES	38 (20)
GOALS	8

STEPHEN WRIGHT

2000/01 → 2001/02

Dismay vied with disbelief as the prevailing emotion among legions of Liverpool fans when 22-year-old Stephen Wright was sold to Sunderland for £3 million in August 2002.

Having relished the advances made by the ultra-competitive, home-grown right-back during the previous campaign, they believed he was brimming with the vim and the quality to make the position his own.

Six-footer Wright was athletic, skilful and abrasively courageous when the Reds were on the back foot, but it was when he stormed forward on aggressive overlaps that he riveted the eye most thrillingly, his spirit of adventure and overwhelming eagerness striking a welcome chord among Anfield regulars.

His admirers admitted that the England under-21 international had plenty to learn defensively, recognising his occasional positional lapses, but they believed that such rawness would be eradicated through experience, that patience would have paid rich dividends.

Wright entered the senior reckoning as an 18-year-old in autumn 1998, impressing newcomer Gerard Houllier so much that he was promoted instantly to train with the first team. He benefited from a loan stint at Crewe, he was Liverpool's young player of the season for 2000/01, then the following term he boosted his cause with 14 starts as deputy for the indisposed Markus Babbel.

The defining images of Stephen Wright are of his perfectly timed dash to turn home a cross from Patrik Berger at home to Borussia Dortmund that October, and the ecstatic grin with which he met the Kop's acclamation. At that deliriously joyous moment, he seemed a stone-cold certainty to become an Anfield stalwart; yet less than a year later, he was gone.

STEPHEN JOHN WRIGHT
BORN   Liverpool, 8 February 1980.
OTHER CLUBS   Crewe Alexandra on loan 99/00 (23, 0); Sunderland 02/03-07/08 (92, 2); Stoke City on loan 07/08 (16, 0); Coventry City 08/09- (17, 0).

GAMES **15 (6)**
GOALS **1**

GREGORY VIGNAL

2000/01 → 2002/03

If Gregory Vignal could have been granted that rarest of luxuries for any Premiership youngster, a lengthy settled first-team stint without his place coming under minute public scrutiny every time he made the slightest mistake, his early accomplishment suggested that he might mature into a left-back of the highest quality.

Certainly the French under-21 international, a £500,000 acquisition from Montpellier in September 2000, lacked none of the skill or courage needed for the job, as he demonstrated in brief spells during the spring and autumn of 2001.

Vignal was assured in possession, a neat passer and a natural timer of tackles, and he earned the approval of the fans by his willingness to overlap in attack, looking especially effective when John Arne Riise was operating directly ahead of him.

He took the eye against Everton at Goodison in April 2001, embarking on several exhilarating sorties and earning the late free-kick from which Gary McCallister won the match.

Vignal began shakily when brought on as a substitute for Riise at home to Aston Villa in September 2001, conceding possession repeatedly, but he recovered impressively and was rewarded with seven successive starts before injury halted his impetus.

True, there were occasions when he was caught on the wrong side of an opponent, prompting critics to raise doubts over his stamina and outright pace, though inexperienced positioning might have been to blame.

Overall, Gregory Vignal sketched the picture of a classy but unfinished performer who deserved further opportunities to cement a role in Gerard Houllier's Liverpool of the future, but he was allowed to drift inexorably out of contention, later featuring for Rangers and Portsmouth.

GREGORY VIGNAL
BORN   Montpellier, France, 19 July 1981.
OTHER CLUBS   Bastia, Italy, on loan 02/03 (15, 0); Rennes, France, on loan 03/04; Espanyol, Spain, 03/04 (8, 1); Rangers 04/05 (30, 3); Portsmouth 05/06 (14,0); Lens, France, 06/07- (22, 0); Kaiserslautern, Germany, on loan 06/07 (9, 1); Southampton on loan 07/08 (20, 3); Birmingham City on loan 09/10.

GAMES **14 (6)**
GOALS **0**

CHRISTIAN ZIEGE

· ·

2000/01

There were few finer attacking flank defenders-cum-midfielders in the world than Christian Ziege at the time of his controversial £6 million move from Middlesbrough to Liverpool in August 2000.

Yet the Reds never managed to get the best out of the lean, left-sided, vastly experienced Berliner, a star of Germany's triumph in Euro '96 and now fresh from a brilliant first season in the English game.

Within months of his arrival at Anfield, Ziege's relationship with the club appeared to be going sour, and after he discovered that his first-team berth was not sacrosanct, his springtime declaration that he hadn't moved to Merseyside merely to improve his English signalled that his tempestuous tenure would be a brief one.

The Ziege appeal, as demonstrated by his efforts on Teeside and for his country, was mightily persuasive. A born winner, he was unremittingly hard, he covered ground far more quickly than his loping stride might suggest, he was capable in aerial combat and his raking throw-in was a potent weapon anywhere in the opposition's half.

Most impressive of all, though, was his accomplishment on the ball, whether unloosing devious through-passes or arcing beautiful crosses, tantalising outswingers from the left flank and venomous inswingers from the right.

Yet surprisingly, for all his assured command, when Ziege was granted ample time to bring the ball forward, too frequently for comfort he would squander it with an apparently casual delivery, as he did when Liverpool were 2-0 up shortly before the interval at Elland Road in November 2001. One careless dispatch later, Leeds were back in contention and Liverpool were on their way to a debilitating and unnecessary 4-3 reverse. In the circumstances it scarcely registered that the German had contributed the Reds' second goal, his first strike for the club, with a close-range header from a Gary McAllister centre.

Perhaps Ziege was better suited to a wing-back role than a conventional left-back slot; arguably he appeared most comfortable and effective when deployed as a wide midfielder; and it was a pity that his settling-in period was disrupted by a hamstring problem.

Whatever, his acid response when Gerard Houllier experimented with other options in the spring of 2001 was disappointing, and though he entered the League Cup Final action as a substitute, contributing a penalty in the decisive shoot-out, he didn't even make the bench for the FA and UEFA Cup Finals.

Clearly a parting of the ways was inevitable, and the following summer Ziege joined Tottenham Hotspur in a £4 million deal, eventually going on to justify the prediction of White Hart Lane boss Glenn Hoddle that he would revive his flagging international career, before further fitness problems prompted early retirement.

However, it was sadly ironic that, after Liverpool had made such strenuous efforts to sign the famous German that they were accused of making an illegal approach, he should make his Anfield exit so soon and so acrimoniously.

CHRISTIAN ZIEGE
BORN Berlin, Germany, 1 February 1972.
HONOURS League Cup 00/01. 72 Germany caps (93-04).
OTHER CLUBS Bayern Munich 90/1-96/7 (172, 41); AC Milan 97/8-98/9 (39, 4); Middlesbrough 99/00-00/01 (29, 6); Tottenham Hotspur 01/02-03/04 (47, 7); Borussia Moenchengladbach, Germany, 04/05.

GAMES **20 (12)**
GOALS 2

VLADIMIR SMICER

1999/2000 → 2004/05

Could the delectably gifted but infuriatingly ethereal Vladimir Smicer make the crucial step from dangerous floater to big-match contributor? Would he ever make nonsense of irreverent jibes about disappearing from centre-stage so often that he should join the Magic Circle? In the late spring of 2005, with his Anfield days drawing to an unfulfilled close, the popular answer to both questions was in the negative . . . and then came Istanbul.

Some 11 minutes into the second half of the European Cup Final against AC Milan, the Reds were trailing 3-1 but hope had just been revived by a mighty Steven Gerrard header. Then, with the Italians still absorbing the reality that they faced a genuine contest rather than a formality, Dietmar Hamann slipped a square pass to Smicer, who had joined the action as a first-half substitute for Harry Kewell.

There seemed little imminent danger to Milan's formidable rearguard, but the little Czech unleashed a 25-yard snap-shot which bounced just inside 'keeper Dida's far post and suddenly the force was with Rafa Benitez's men. Later, amid the euphoria of the unlikeliest victory in the history of the grand old competition, Kenny Dalglish dubbed it the goal of the season.

For the author of the strike which transformed Liverpool's biggest match in two decades, and who further massaged his credibility by netting in the subsequent penalty shoot-out, it did not secure an extension to his Anfield career, but at least he could leave for his new club, Bordeaux, on the highest note imaginable.

To those who prized pure skill above all other footballing attributes, there was always something gloriously heartening about the rise to prominence, and continued survival on the fearsomely physical Premiership battlefield, of Vladimir Smicer. Lauded as world-class by no less a judge than Sir Alex Ferguson and the subject of frequent lavish eulogies by Gerard Houllier, the slender utility attacker knew no Anfield equal in the deftness of his touch, or in the subtlety with which he could drop a shoulder and leave an opponent tackling thin air.

But if none could reasonably deny his technical brilliance, there were plenty who questioned the value of such a refined and delicate bloom. Though they didn't doubt his courage, which he demonstrated in ample measure, Smicer's critics demanded more robustness, as well as more shots, more crosses, more through-passes; in short, they craved more end-product for all that smooth approach play.

With Steve McManaman having decamped recently for the Bernabeu, the multi-capped newcomer was seen as a natural replacement when he was acquired for £3.75 million in the summer of 1999 from Lens, where he was feted as a hero, having helped to win the French League title a year earlier.

But after spurning the advances of Paris St Germain, Smicer got off to a sticky start on Merseyside, his first-term progress hampered by a nagging ankle injury and a debilitating viral infection. Accordingly when he did feature he was not at his best and finished his first English campaign being derided cruelly in some quarters as the Premiership's most lightweight performer.

Certainly Smicer, his face habitually clouded by anxiety, could offer the impression of a wounded antelope when going to earth under tackles which appeared less than ferocious, but he admitted his shortcoming with disarming self-deprecation – 'I know I am not the strongest man in the world' – and he strove manfully to improve his stamina and resilience.

Meanwhile, admittedly in infuriatingly fleeting flashes, it became evident why he was held in such lofty esteem by Ferguson and Houllier. Whether operating on the right or the left flank, at the vanguard of a 'diamond' midfield, or as an auxiliary striker, he was a ball manipulator of the highest order, an incisive, beautifully balanced raider whose football brain was a match for his quicksilver feet.

He managed only one goal during that traumatic first term, but even though he was never sure of a regular place, he returned a worthy seven in 2000/01, including one which furnished a maddeningly short-lived lead against Leeds at Elland Road. Involving a nimble sidestep and a clinical finish, it was precisely the type of opportunistic effort which an elusive, darting forward of his ability might be expected to deliver on a frequent basis.

Thereafter, though, Smicer continued to flicker tantalisingly rather than assemble a consistent body of work, and it was sadly typical when his most convincing spell – partnering Gerrard in central midfield early in 2003/04 – should be halted by one of his many injuries.

After he entered his thirties, the uncertainty about his worth remained, but all who believed that there should be a place, amid the frenzy of the modern football scene, for a 'nice' player still hoped that Vladimir Smicer would earn redemption. And, one mild spring evening on the western shore of the Bosporus, he did just that.

	VLADIMIR SMICER
BORN	Degin, Czechoslovakia, 24 May 1973.
HONOURS	European Cup 04/05. UEFA Cup 00/01. FA Cup 00/01. League Cup 00/01, 02/03. 1 Czechoslovakia cap (93). 83 Czech Republic caps (93-06).
OTHER CLUBS	Slavia Prague, Czech Republic, 92/3-95/6 (81, 26); Lens, France, 96/7-98/9 (91, 16); Bordeaux, France, 05/06-06/07 (28, 3); Slavia Prague 07/08- (28, 5).

GAMES	110 (74)
GOALS	19

MARKUS BABBEL

2000/01 → 2002/03

The ups and downs of football life, the triumphs and so-called tragedies, were thrown into stark perspective by the horrifying trauma which engulfed Markus Babbel during his second season at Anfield.

Having played a majestically imposing part in Liverpool's historic cup treble of 2000/01, the thoroughbred German international defender was struck down by a rare and potentially fatal illness, and his fight back from death's door to resume his illustrious career ranks as a titanic achievement.

Only Markus and his family can gauge the human cost of his ordeal, but purely in sporting terms – obviously not of paramount importance in such a harrowing context – the Liverpool cause suffered grievously from the prolonged absence of such a world-class operator as they sought to step up their challenge to the Premiership domination of Arsenal and Manchester United.

A League title has long been the Reds' most cherished ambition and the tall, intelligent Bavarian knew all about lifting them from his tenure with his home-town club, Bayern Munich, with whom he pocketed medals in 1997, 1999 and 2000. In addition he had been a UEFA Cup winner in 1996, the year in which he had starred in Germany's European Championship victory, and he had been within three minutes of tasting Champions League glory in 1999, only to be foiled by the Mancunians' almost surreal recovery.

Ironically Babbel might have started that season at Old Trafford, but he rejected a proposed move and in January 2000 accepted terms offered by Liverpool, completing his Bosman-style free transfer during the following summer. In truth it had long been his heart's desire to enlist at Anfield, and not even a tantalisingly alluring invitation from Real Madrid could deter him, a circumstance which endeared him instantly to his new fans on Merseyside.

Soon they were warming to him even more enthusiastically. After coming to terms with the initial disappointment that he was not to be deployed in his favoured location of central defence, where Sami Hyypia and Stephane Henchoz continued to hold sway, Babbel buckled down to shine at right-back.

He emerged as a cultured, ultra-competent performer, the epitome of cool resolve at the back, a dashingly resourceful outlet on the right flank of attack and a lovely passer in every area of the pitch. At first, some observers were unnerved by his easy grace on the ball, mistaking it for a dangerous casualness, but quickly they came to appreciate that this was merely the polished Babbel style, and that he could be trusted.

In fact, for all that measured assurance, and while his preferred method might have been to read the action and tidy up accordingly rather than commit himself to neck-or-nothing challenges, Babbel was nothing loth to shrug aside that almost aristocratic air, tackling like a mobile mantrap when the need arose.

His strength and stamina were prodigious, particularly evident on his frequent forward sorties, such as the lung-stretching sprint to hammer home a cross from Robbie Fowler at Goodison Park in April 2001, after starting the move deep inside his own half.

As might be expected of a man who had spent much of his working life as a central defender, Babbel proved formidable in the air, too, his forceful headwork contributing tellingly in two finals. In the FA Cup against Arsenal he rose above Tony Adams to nod into the path of Michael Owen, who rifled a sensational equaliser. Then only three minutes into the UEFA Cup showdown with Alaves he opened Liverpool's account with a firm far-post header from a Gary McAllister floater.

As he shared in the uproarious celebrations which followed the treble and the clinching of a Champions League place, the future beckoned enticingly for a 28-year-old barely embarked on his prime. But a savage downturn in the Babbel fortunes was imminent.

After helping to beat Manchester United in the Charity Shield, he felt unnaturally drained and though he struggled through five more games, soon it became clear he was seriously ill. At first a virus was diagnosed, then the infinitely more serious Guillain-Barre syndrome which attacks the nervous system. Paralysis began to set in, he was confined to a wheelchair and the terrifying realisation dawned that far more than a football career was at risk.

Now Markus showed unquenchable courage and resilience and, with Liverpool standing by him, he clawed his gradual way back to health, returning to the Anfield reckoning for 2002/03.

Inevitably, though, his affliction had exacted a toll. Despite several decent displays in late autumn, he was far from his magisterial best, and it was sad to see his unhappiness at being substituted in the enthralling League Cup quarter-final win at Villa Park.

Thereafter he appeared to become increasingly frustrated with life on the Anfield periphery, being sent off twice while playing for the reserves, and his attitude was criticised by Gerard Houllier, who loaned him to Blackburn for 2003/04, then freed him to join Stuttgart. It was a shame that the German's hitherto inspirational tale of recovery from dire misfortune should be tarnished with acrimony in its final chapter.

MARKUS BABBEL

BORN	Munich, Germany, 8 September 1972.
HONOURS	UEFA Cup 00/01. FA Cup 00/01. League Cup 00/01. 51 Germany caps (95-00).
OTHER CLUBS	Bayern Munich, Germany, 91/2 (12, 0); Hamburg, Germany, 92/3-93/4 (60, 1); Bayern Munich 94/5-99/00 (170, 9); Blackburn Rovers on loan 03/04 (25, 3); VfB Stuttgart, Germany, 04/05-06/07 (46, 2).

GAMES	71 (2)
GOALS	6

DIETMAR HAMANN

1999/2000 → 2005/06

Dietmar Hamann could bring a crowd to its feet with a sudden pulverising strike, or thread the most delicate of first-time passes through the merest chink in an unwary rearguard, but Anfield regulars knew better than to hold their breath in anticipation of either occurrence.

What marked out the lean, whippily resilient German international as an exceptional performer, one linked regularly with the cream of Europe's clubs during his prime, was his relentless laying down of the law in front of his own back four, disrupting the supply lines to opposing strikers, anchoring the midfield with a daunting, vice-like certainty which brooked no argument.

The ultimate example of that oft-underrated authority proved the key to Liverpool's most astonishing achievement of modern times, when he was introduced for the second half of the 2005 European Cup Final, with the woebegone Reds trailing 3-0 to AC Milan. It's no exaggeration to state that Hamann's arrival changed the course of the contest, filling the yawning void in front of Sami Hyypia and Jamie Carragher, shackling the hitherto rampant Kaka and freeing Steven Gerrard to range forward so destructively. Had the German been in place from the outset, it's difficult to imagine the Italians running riot in the first 45 minutes.

The Hamann reputation for rigorous efficiency was forged initially in his homeland as he helped Bayern Munich to claim two Bundesliga titles, the UEFA Cup and the German Cup, then it was burnished during a single season with Newcastle United. The Geordie fans feted him as their player of 1998/99, only for a reported rift with manager Ruud Gullit to prompt an unexpectedly hasty departure from St James' Park.

At one point it seemed that Hamann was Highbury-bound, then a variety of continental destinations were mooted before Gerard Houllier, who was seeking a direct replacement for Paul Ince and had been turned down by Marc-Vivien Foe, stepped in with a successful £8 million offer which made the lanky enforcer Liverpool's second most expensive acquisition after Stan Collymore.

The prospect of introducing a central midfielder of such proven pedigree alongside either Jamie Redknapp or the exciting rookie Gerrard fuelled avid anticipation among travelling Reds as they settled in their seats for the new season's opener at Hillsborough, but 25 minutes later their immediate aspirations were in shreds as Hamann limped off with what proved to be serious damage to ankle ligaments.

He made a fleeting return in September, but he broke down again and it was November before he could make a meaningful beginning to his Liverpool career. Even then he was no overnight sensation; that was never the Hamann way.

Instead the undemonstrative Didi took to his new job gradually, unspectacularly, and received a degree of rough justice from critics who appeared not to grasp the nature of the beast, describing him as static, hesitant, even unobtrusive to the point of anonymity.

That they were mistaken became steadily more evident as he tightened his grip on the holding role, emerging as a ruthlessly effective shield for his defence, organising quietly, intercepting intelligently and tackling with a crushing force which belied the spareness of his frame.

It should be stressed, too, that patrolling his customary deep-lying beat, and earning the freedom for more expansive individuals to express themselves, did not preclude more creative contributions. When the opportunity arose, Hamann moved forward to devastating effect, distributing the ball with smooth subtlety, occasionally with a delicious outside-of-the-boot flourish, and while his goals were hardly plentiful, they tended to be memorable. Certainly Newcastle would not forget the imperious manner in which their former employee burst past two challenges to score at Anfield during the 2-2 draw in September 2002, and the stunning 30-yarder which was still rising as it tore into the top corner of Edwin van der Sar's net at Fulham two months later deserved a grander context than mere consolation in defeat. Then there was the swerving right-foot volley at home to Portsmouth which was voted Liverpool's goal of the 2003/04 campaign.

Naturally, for all his characteristic consistency, Hamann experienced peaks and troughs like every other footballer on the planet, for instance his dominant display against Birmingham City in the 2001 League Cup Final being following by a disappointing personal showing against Arsenal in the FA Cup triumph.

But, as a rule, the team looked far more vulnerable when its faithful policeman was not on the prowl, and there remain mystified supporters who will never forgive the manager for removing him from the action after an hour of the 2002 Champions League quarter-final second leg in Leverkusen. At the time Liverpool led 2-1 on aggregate, but then the roof fell in as Bayer netted twice in quick succession and went on to scupper the Reds' European dream. Testimony to the value of Hamann could hardly have been more eloquent, or more painful.

Come 2005/06, his opportunities were being limited by the effervescent input of Momo Sissoko, but the metronomically consistent 32-year-old's presence in the squad, if not in the starting eleven, remained vastly reassuring. However, his summer move to Manchester City, via a momentary non-playing diversion to Bolton, was not unexpected.

DIETMAR HAMANN

BORN   Waldasson, Germany, 27 August 1973.

HONOURS   European Cup 04/05. UEFA Cup 00/01. FA Cup 00/01, 05/06. League Cup 00/01, 02/03. 59 Germany caps (97-05).

OTHER CLUBS   Bayern Munich, Germany, 93/4-97/8 (105, 6); Newcastle United 98/9 (23, 4); Manchester City 06/07-08/09 (54, 0).

GAMES	253 (30)
GOALS	11

SAMI HYYPIA

1999/2000 → 2008/09

The jokes, like the old chestnut about Dracula being more partial to crosses than Liverpool's defence, were beginning to hurt. The perception among Kopites was that since the late prime of Alan Hansen at the end of the 1980s, there had been an aerial weakness at the heart of the Reds' rearguard, and it was a failing which upset them more than most of their serial disappointments during the ensuing decade. Enter Sami Hyypia, out of the unknown, to restore order and to take his place among Anfield's most revered central defenders of modern times.

In truth, it would have been a rare Liverpool fan who knew much, if anything, about the 6ft 4in Finn when he was signed for £2.6 million from the Dutch club, Willem II, in the summer of 1999. It was encouraging, however, to learn that he had been vetted by the likes of Ron Yeats and Phil Thompson, both stalwart stoppers during so many of the Reds' finest hours. Sami, it emerged, had made a gargantuan impression with a courageous display for his country against Germany, shackling the dangerous Oliver Bierhoff and refusing to leave the battleground prematurely despite sustaining a head injury, marching off at the final whistle bloodied and bandaged but defiantly unbowed.

Thus there was never the slightest doubt about Hyypia's warrior-like qualities. Though markedly slim – that lean frame and lantern jaw conjuring the very image of an old-time cowboy hero – he was as resilient as whipcord, towering over most opponents like some stately pine in the forests of his homeland. Sami wasn't the bullying type, didn't bristle with comic-strip menace, but he exuded a quiet authority which communicated itself tellingly to his team-mates, and his commanding physical prowess was evident in the crushing certainty of his challenges both in the air and on the ground.

Equally important, he emerged as a superbly accomplished all-round footballer who read the game with keen intelligence, snuffing out attacks through inspired anticipation, and if his pace was not of the blistering variety, that exceptional positional sense made light of it. Hyypia could control a ball plummeting from the clouds, then pass it accurately and intelligently. In addition he was cool and decisive, with an admirable attitude to adversity, being more prone to rueful smile than unseemly snarl. He was rarely booked and was an imperious leader, too, eventually distinguishing himself as the natural long-term choice to succeed Jamie Redknapp as Liverpool captain.

Yet all that talent might have been denied to the game as the teenage Hyypia had considered following his parents into top-level ice-hockey. Then, even after opting for football, he might have changed his mind after Kevin Keegan and Mark Lawrenson sent him home from a week's trial with Newcastle United without asking for his signature.

Undaunted, he built a solid reputation with MyPa in Finland, then made huge strides with Willem II, benefiting from the Dutch emphasis on ball-playing technique. Hyypia shone as the Tilburg club finished as runners-up in the race for Holland's domestic title in 1998/99 and a Champions League campaign beckoned, but he passed it up in favour of the Anfield move. Understandably there followed a brief stutter as he bedded into the Premiership, but soon he adjusted to the frenetic tempo and formed a reassuringly convincing central defensive partnership with fellow newcomer Stephane Henchoz.

In gratifyingly short order, Hyypia emerged as the talismanic marshal of Liverpool's reforged back line, invariably swallowing up straight through-balls and crosses from wide positions, if occasionally looking slightly less certain when tested by raking diagonal deliveries. He was key to the treble triumph of 2000/01, proving particularly steadfast on the road to European glory and defying Arsenal almost single-handedly at various points of the FA Cup Final with three goal-line clearances.

Hyypia became noted for his attacking enterprise, too. As might be expected, there were plenty of thunderous headers, but even more eye-catching was his winner in Auxerre in February 2003, when he wrong-footed the French defence with a clever first touch and slotted home as nervelessly as any specialist predator. For sheer importance, though, nothing matched his far-post volley which set Liverpool on the way to Anfield victory over Juventus in the European Cup quarter-final first leg in April 2005.

By then the Finnish colossus, who had been replaced as skipper by Steven Gerrard in October 2003, was in his 32nd year and exhibiting intimations of footballing mortality. There was a perception that as his pace continued to erode with age, he was on a slippery slope to imminent oblivion. Indeed, recently he had been ousted for several games by Mauricio Pellegrino.

Sami's reaction was awesome, reclaiming his place alongside Jamie Carragher, returning to his mighty best, and by the time he strode from the Istanbul pitch as a European champion, he was the only Red to have played throughout every minute of that tumultuous continental campaign.

Having thus made light of the gauntlet hurled down by Pellegrino, later Hyypia faced the more youthful challenges of Daniel Agger, then Martin Skrtel. Inevitably he gave ground, but when injuries bit his rookie rivals he was not found wanting, making 44 appearances in 2007/08. Even beyond that he endured, as unyielding as granite, a linchpin of one of the most clamlike defences in the world, his slips rare, his experience and determination compensating for the passing years. His status as a lasting Anfield icon was categorically assured, and when finally he was freed to join Bayer Leverkusen in 2009, tears of pure affection were shed both by Sami Hyypia and the grateful multitude who had come to love him.

SAMI TUOMAS HYYPIA

BORN   Porvoo, Finland, 7 October 1973.

HONOURS   European Cup 04/05. UEFA Cup 00/01. FA Cup 00/01, 05/06.
League Cup 00/01, 02/03. 97 Finland caps (92-).

OTHER CLUBS   MyPa 47, Finland, 93-95 (63, 3); Willem II, Holland, 95/6-98/9 (100, 3);
Bayer Leverkusen, Germany, 09/10-.

GAMES   **455 (9)**

GOALS   33

STEPHANE HENCHOZ

1999/2000 → 2004/05

For some seven weeks in the autumn of 2002, Stephane Henchoz never kicked a ball in anger, being laid low with a calf injury suffered in the home victory over Chelsea . . . and yet his popularity rating with Liverpool supporters positively soared.

The reason? The realisation dawned, gradually but inescapably as the Reds' rearguard looked alarmingly vulnerable in his absence, that the unobtrusive, redoubtably disciplined Swiss international stopper was a key constituent of the team's bedrock, every bit as crucial to its solidity as his more celebrated central defensive partner, Sami Hyypia.

Praise has been lavished liberally on the influential Finn's head, and rightly so because he has been a top performer down the years, but the fact remains that often he wasn't quite the same formidable force without the trusty Henchoz at his side.

Stephane patrolled his back-line beat with the minimum of fuss, like some calm, old-fashioned village bobby keeping a shrewd eye on the neighbourhood's potential trouble-makers. Situations were read coolly, then defused quietly; crosses cleared, interceptions completed, simple percentage passes dispatched.

But when mere firmness and composure were not sufficient to keep the peace, then the blond, rosy-cheeked six-footer erupted into action with a vengeance, hurling himself into challenges with a combination of expert timing and blood-curdling courage that made him, arguably, the most effective shot-blocker in the Premiership.

In the last ditch, the path to goal was barred by every inch of the Henchoz anatomy, as Arsenal's Thierry Henry discovered to his chagrin during the 2001 FA Cup Final, when two goal-bound efforts were repelled by a Swiss hand and arm . . . accidentally, of course!

Henchoz stood as one of Gerard Houllier's most triumphant excursions into the transfer market, all the more so since he did not seem an obvious target – at least, not to most Liverpool fans – when he was recruited for £3.75 million from Blackburn Rovers in July 1999.

The Ewood Park club had just been relegated from the top flight, and there was no shortage of critics on Merseyside who questioned whether such a debilitating experience offered the best recommendation for a much-needed defensive reinforcement at Anfield. However, it was telling that Rovers supporters had voted him their player of the season, and their former boss Roy Hodgson, who had worked with the teenage Henchoz at Neuchatel Xamax and later as manager of the Swiss international side, maintained emphatically that he hailed from the top drawer.

Frustratingly, he arrived at Liverpool in need of a hernia operation, and irritated some observers by playing for his country before starting for the Reds, but when finally he made his Premiership entrance, at Villa Park in October, he dovetailed encouragingly with Hyypia, another summer acquisition.

The partnership flourished apace, and though Henchoz encountered a few jittery moments during 2000/01, when Jamie Carragher was given a brief opportunity in a central berth, he proved the ideal foil for Hyypia, his work more assured as each season passed.

Some chided him for not sallying forward into attack more frequently in the enterprising manner of his cohort, and pointed to his lack of a successful strike after more than two centuries of Reds outings, but that was a fallacy. Scoring goals was not his responsibility, stopping them was; the Henchoz mandate was to be the last line of outfield defence, and he fulfilled it to the letter.

He excelled against some of the world's leading performers in European competition, notably Barcelona's Patrick Kluivert and Ronaldo in the UEFA Cup semi-final; he negated both Ruud van Nistelrooy of Manchester United and Arsenal's Henry in domestic clashes; and he was likened by no less a judge than Sir Bobby Robson to 'a bloody oak tree, you just can't get past him.'

Still only 28 in the spring of 2003, the unassuming Swiss appeared to be entering his prime, still magnificently athletic and with his capacity for sensing and snuffing out danger ever more acute. But then ankle, knee and groin injuries ruled him out for most of the ensuing term, and on his return, initially at right-back, he appeared perceptibly sluggish. There followed the 'Rafa revolution' and the continued development of the splendid Carragher, which left Henchoz on the margins, and in January 2005 he was loaned to Celtic, never to represent the Reds again.

Still, Stephane's part in a dramatic period of Liverpool history should be honoured in full. Perhaps, one day, he will receive the universal acclaim his unswervingly steadfast and increasingly polished contributions deserved. Perhaps not. Whatever, his stock could not have been higher where it was most meaningful – inside the game, where it was generally acknowledged that Gerard Houllier rarely struck a cannier bargain than the day he bought Stephane Henchoz.

STEPHANE HENCHOZ	
BORN	Billens, Switzerland, 7 September 1974.
HONOURS	UEFA Cup 00/01. FA Cup 00/01. League Cup 00/01, 02/03. 72 Switzerland caps (93-05).
OTHER CLUBS	Neuchatel Xamax, Switzerland, 92/3-94/5 (91, 1); Hamburg, Germany, 95/6-96/7 (49, 2); Blackburn Rovers 97/8-98/9 (70, 0); Celtic 04/05 (6, 0); Wigan Athletic 05/06 (26, 0); Blackburn Rovers 06/07 (12, 0).

GAMES	201 (4)
GOALS	0

EMILE HESKEY

1999/2000 → 2003/04

Emile Heskey was an Anfield enigma, sometimes electrifying, occasionally excruciating, unfailingly expending prodigious physical effort on behalf of his team. At his best, when he turned and ran with the ball, he seemed an unstoppable force of nature, with defenders no more relevant than sagging fenceposts in the path of a turbo-charged bulldozer. At his worst, apparently bereft of confidence, it was the hulking Midlander who resembled an inanimate object.

To many fans the bottom line was that, for a centre-forward – albeit one deployed periodically and curiously on the left side of midfield – Heskey did not score enough goals after plundering an admirable 22 in his first full season as a Red, during which Liverpool won three cups. That said, it is undeniable that Michael Owen's phenomenal tallies owed plenty to his strike partner's selflessness, persistence and Herculean work-rate, and though Heskey was savaged frequently by critics, his team-mates never doubted him.

When Gerard Houllier agreed an £11 million deal with Leicester City in March 2000, making Emile the third most expensive signing in British football history, he was investing in an alluring blend of youth and experience. Still only 22 at the time of the transfer, the mountainously-built marksman had already compiled more than a century and a half of League appearances and won five full England caps, statistics which suggested record-breaking potential.

Duly Heskey made a positive start, winning a penalty in the third minute of his Liverpool debut, at home to Sunderland, when his right-wing dash on to a pass from Rigobert Song was ended by a rash tackle by Darren Williams. Patrik Berger converted the spot-kick and Anfielders rejoiced at such telling early evidence of the newcomer's formidable pace and power.

When his form for the remainder of that spring proved distinctly tentative, allowances were made for an engagingly unassuming youngster settling in at one of the world's top clubs, but Kopites were beginning to voice anxiety after Heskey had spent the first hour of the 2000/01 opener, at home to Bradford City, lurking forlornly on the fringe of the action.

Then, suddenly, the mounting disillusionment was wiped away by a pulsating intervention which summed up the Heskey capabilities with vivid eloquence. Spinning off his immediate marker and accelerating away from the covering defender, he surged into the City box and drilled a savage rising drive into the far top corner of Matt Clarke's net from an improbably narrow angle. Anfield exploded in joyous salute, obvious glee at what turned out to be the match-winner equalled by a measure of relief at such sensational proof of their new spearhead's quality.

However, although Heskey always carried the threat of the destructively spectacular, such a moment did not define his worth in Liverpool's playing system. Rather it was his imposing strength as a target man who invariably received the ball with his back to goal and took horrendous punishment in protecting it; then there was his willingness to toil from first whistle to last, turning wild clearances into pinpoint passes, chasing balls which seemed hopelessly beyond his reach but which frequently he retrieved, hustling opponents to near distraction.

Such strenuous emphasis on the physical should not imply that Heskey lacked skill on the ball. Far from it. His touch could be delightfully assured, as he demonstrated with a measured chip to score in the 4-1 home victory over Coventry in November 2000, and his swerve around Nigel Martyn before volleying into the Elland Road net during the drubbing of Leeds in February 2002 lacked nothing in subtlety or balance. He was an accomplished crosser from either flank, too, though he was manifestly uncomfortable when starting in a withdrawn position near the left touchline, not possessing the trickery required in that role.

Regrettably, having stressed Heskey's essential ability to command the behaviour of a football, it must be noted that there were days when it appeared quite beyond him. Similarly, though he could finish like a god, he could be infuriatingly profligate with the net at his mercy, especially during one of his periodic goal famines; and while the Heskey distribution was customarily neat enough, it could be unnervingly wayward.

Overall he was a noble competitor who helped to capture four major trophies in the space of three seasons, who resisted challenges for his position from a variety of international stars, who was ever willing to sacrifice himself for the good of the team, and who never hid when the going became unremittingly rough.

Yet the feeling persisted that, with his awesome natural attributes, Emile Heskey never quite punched his weight. Was he ruthless enough? How strong was his self-belief? In the end, the Anfield jury answered in the negative, and in July 2004, still on the verge of his prime at 26, he was sold to Birmingham City for £3.5 million. Later, in the shirt of Wigan Athletic, maturity brought extra assurance and his return to England duty was well merited.

EMILE WILLIAM IVANHOE HESKEY

BORN Leicester, 11 January 1978.
HONOURS UEFA Cup 00/01. FA Cup 00/01. League Cup 00/01, 02/03. 53 England caps (99-).
OTHER CLUBS Leicester City 94/5-99/00 (154, 40); Birmingham City 04/05-05/06 (68, 14); Wigan Athletic 06/07-08/09 (82, 16); Aston Villa 08/09- (14, 2).

GAMES 176 (47)
GOALS 60

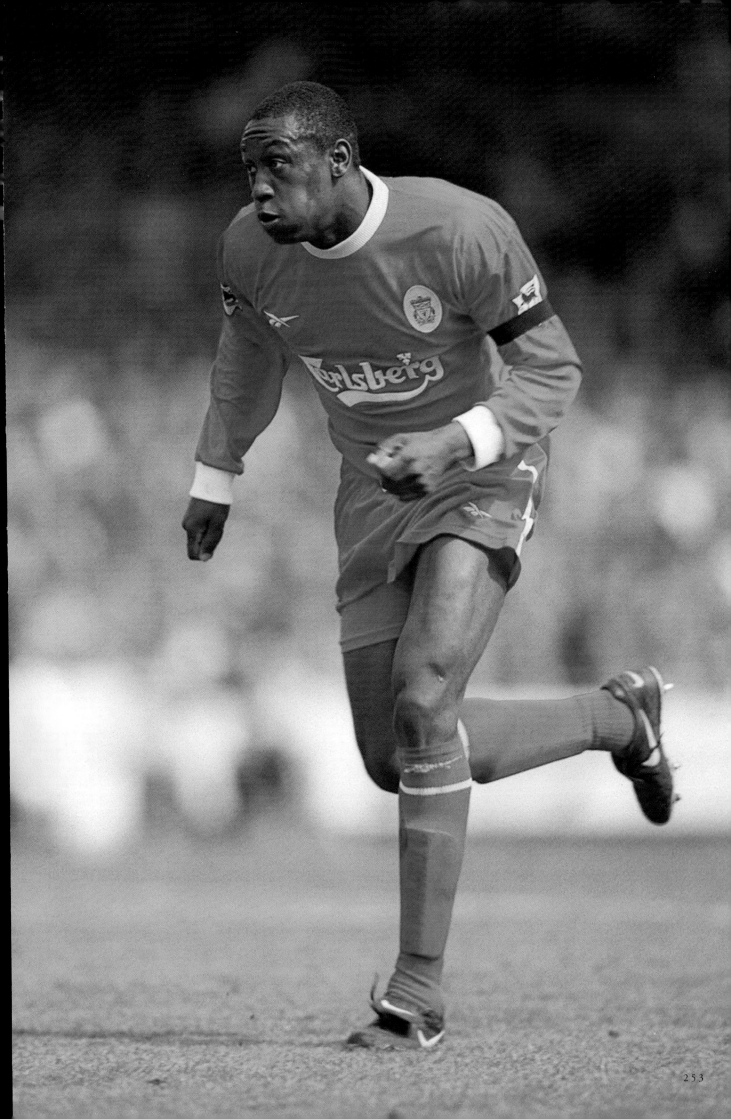

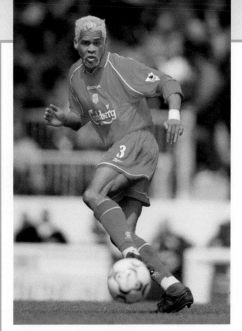

ABEL XAVIER

2001/02 → 2002/03

When Gerard Houllier welcomed 'Neptune' up the Anfield gangplank in January 2002, he appeared to have pulled off a transfer coup of major proportions. After all Abel Xavier, who had attracted that nickname together with a few less printable ones through his distinctive coiffure, was an experienced and respected Portuguese international utility defender, surely a shrewd addition to the Liverpool squad.

Duly the surprise £800,000 acquisition from Everton, who had performed splendidly in the Goodison rearguard but now found the lure of Champions League football irresistible, slotted in smoothly as the Reds' right-back and scored on his debut in a 6-0 victory at Ipswich.

With Markus Babbel ill and Jamie Carragher employed on the left, that spring Xavier was picked regularly and impressed with his decisive tackling and composed distribution, though the effect of his second goal – a headed equaliser in Leverkusen – was rather negated by his second-half struggles against the Brazilian winger Ze Roberto as the Reds bowed out of the Champions League.

Come 2002/03 he retained his place, but a chasing by Damien Duff at Ewood Park in August, admittedly mitigated by a lovely interchange with Danny Murphy which enabled the midfielder to score, did not augur well.

There followed illness and injury before Xavier was loaned to Galatasaray in January, but he didn't settle in Turkey. After being released by Liverpool in the summer of 2003 he made several more moves, suffered a drugs ban (he denied wrongdoing), then returned to the Premiership with Middlesbrough.

ABEL LUIS DA SILVA COSTA XAVIER
BORN Nampula, Mozambique, 30 November 1972.
HONOURS 20 Portugal caps (93-02).
OTHER CLUBS Amadora, Portugal, 90/1-91/2 (43, 0); Benfica, Portugal, 93/4-94/5 (46, 4); Bari, Italy, 95/6 (8, 0); Real Oviedo, Spain, 96/7-97/8 (58, 0); PSV Eindhoven, Holland, 98/9 (19, 2); Everton 99/00-01/02 (43, 0); Galatasaray, Turkey, on loan 02/03 (11, 0); Hannover, Germany, 03/04 (5, 0); Roma, Italy, 04/05 (3, 0); Middlesbrough 05/06-06/07 (18, 1); LA Galaxy, USA, 07-08 (21, 0).

GAMES 20 (1)
GOALS 2

NICOLAS ANELKA

2001/02

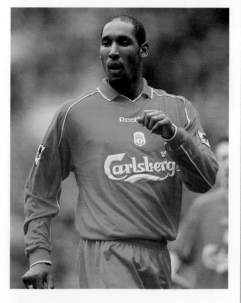

Nicolas Anelka was the most intriguing Anfield recruit of modern times when he was taken on loan from Paris St Germain in December 2001.

The deal, conceived by Gerard Houllier as he lay in hospital following his heart operation, then closed while he convalesced in Corsica, bore the hallmark of potential inspiration.

Though Anelka carried a worrying amount of unwelcome baggage, having passed stormy sojourns with both Arsenal and Real Madrid, he was a 22-year-old international marksman of awesome natural ability, with an English League and FA Cup double and a European Cup winner's medal among his credits. Furthermore, the happy thought persisted that if anyone could harness that prodigious talent then it might be Houllier, who had nurtured his early development in France.

The arrangement seemed ideal for both parties: Liverpool were in urgent need of a striker, with Fowler gone and Owen injured; and for Anelka, with his options dwindling, it was a gilded opportunity of a fresh start with a top club.

The newcomer made a tentative beginning, but soon he was parading his spellbinding pace, supple power and clever control to compelling effect, and the goals began to come, not exactly in a flood but in sufficient quantity to fuel heady optimism about a future long-term Owen-Anelka tandem.

But a proposed permanent deal – involving little more than half the £22 million once shelled out by Real – fell through amid acrimonious confusion, Anelka joined Manchester City, and Reds fans were left to sigh for what might have been.

NICOLAS SEBASTIEN ANELKA
BORN Versailles, France, 14 March 1979.
HONOURS 55 France caps (98-).
OTHER CLUBS Paris St Germain, France, 95/6-96/7 (10, 1); Arsenal 96/7-98/9 (65, 23); Real Madrid, Spain, 99/00 (19, 2); Paris St Germain 00/01-01/02 (39, 10); Manchester City 02/03-04/05 (89, 37); Fenerbahce, Turkey, 04/05-05/06 (39, 14); Bolton Wanderers 06/07-07/08 (53, 21); Chelsea 07/08- (51, 20).

GAMES 15 (7)
GOALS 5

JARI LITMANEN

2000/01 → 2001/02

The question will forever torment fans enchanted by the sophistication, the incisive flair, the unselfish mastery of Jari Litmanen: might the visionary Finn have become to Liverpool what Eric Cantona was to Manchester United, the catalyst for a return to greatness?

To their enduring frustration, the answer can be a matter only for agonised conjecture. After tracking Litmanen for two years, and finally capturing him on a free transfer from Barcelona in January 2001, Gerard Houllier never found a regular place for the man who had shone as both creative fulcrum and prolific scorer as Ajax won the European Cup in 1995, standing out even in such company as Kluivert, Davids, Seedorf and the De Boers.

So some 20 months after his Anfield arrival, having entered his thirties and feeling desperate for first-team football, Litmanen slipped back to Amsterdam, where he was revered practically as a god. Like the admirers he left behind him, he was sorely perplexed by his lack of fulfilment with Liverpool, a club he had idolised since childhood.

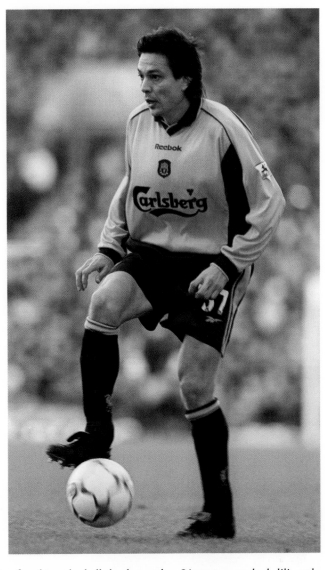

For all his career-long acclamation – he remains a national institution in Finland, immortalised by his appearance on a postage stamp – Litmanen did not cut a flamboyant figure, his off-pitch demeanour quiet and serious, his football infused with wit and subtlety rather than obvious pyrotechnics.

Capable of playing at the front or as a conventional midfielder, but maybe at his best drifting dangerously in the 'hole', he was a consummate linker of play through sublimely precise first-time passing, often recognising angles of attack to which colleagues remained blind, and inevitably they were bemused occasionally by the quickness of his thinking.

Though he wasn't pacy – his craft offered an inspiring example of making the ball do the work – Litmanen worked diligently in the common cause, even when balls were dispatched unimaginatively over his head, and his dedication to the team ethic was never in doubt.

Reds fans loved him from the off and still treasure examples of his audacity and control, such as his shattering of a stalemate at home to Spurs in September 2001 by netting with a sudden 30-yarder when no shot appeared to be on, or his instant subduing of an awkward rebound before rifling past the Dynamo Kiev 'keeper at Anfield four days later.

At this distance it is tantalising to ponder on the scale of his potential influence had his starts not been outnumbered by his introductions from the bench; had his role been central, like Cantona's, rather than peripheral.

A fellow artist of an earlier Reds vintage, Peter Beardsley, once said of Jari Litmanen: 'He is probably the best foreign player I've ever seen . . . he could be as successful in England as Bergkamp or Zola . . . eventually he might be compared to Dalglish.' It was an opinion shared unequivocally by a multitude of mystified Merseyside Reds.

JARI OLAVI LITMANEN

BORN   Lahti, Finland, 20 February 1971.
HONOURS   122 Finland caps (89-).
OTHER CLUBS   Reipas Lahti, Finland, 87-90 (86, 28); HJK Helsinki, Finland, 91 (27, 16); MyPa 47, Finland, 92 (18, 7); Ajax, Holland, 92/3-98/9 (159, 90); Barcelona, Spain, 99/00-00/01 (21, 3); Ajax 02/03-03/4 (20, 5); FC Lahti, Finland, 04 (11, 3); Hansa Rostock, Germany, 04/05 (13, 1); Malmo, Sweden, 05/06-06/07 (10, 3); FC Lahti 08- (10, 3).

GAMES	**19 (24)**
GOALS	9

IGOR BISCAN

2000/01 → 2004/05

He commenced his Liverpool days as the so-called Croatian Zidane but all too soon he became the Anfield Eeyore. In truth, both labels were memorably daft. Igor Biscan was never another Zinedine in the making, and certainly he was no hapless donkey, despite invariably presenting to the world a lugubrious expression that would have done full justice to Winnie the Pooh's miserable mate.

In fact, he was a talented all-rounder, at his most influential as a holding midfielder but also capable of sterling stints in central defence. Sadly for Biscan – capable of surprisingly dainty footwork for such a rangy beanpole yet who sometimes contrived to resemble a forlorn novice – he was not quite up to claiming either role on a regular basis.

After a bright beginning, he receded to the Anfield periphery, an enigmatic figure desperate to demonstrate his worth but struggling to make the most of sporadic opportunities. Expectations had been immense in December 2000 when Liverpool announced the £5.5 million signing of the tall, steely midfielder who, at 22, had already won full caps for Croatia, skippered Dinamo Zagreb, and been courted by Barcelona, Juventus and AC Milan.

Soon he had asserted himself in an Old Trafford victory over Manchester United, but thereafter he began to founder in the face of stern competition for a berth. Still Gerard Houllier retained faith, trying him in central defence where he excelled at times during 2003/04.

However, it was back in midfield during the 2004/05 European Cup campaign that he displayed his most commanding form, particularly during the key 1-0 win in Coruna and the heroic goalless draw with Juventus in Turin. Inevitably, though, when Gerrard and Hamann were available, Biscan was no longer required, and that summer he joined Panathinaikos.

IGOR BISCAN
BORN Zagreb, Croatia, 4 May 1978.
HONOURS League Cup 00/01, 02/03. 15 Croatia caps (99-).
OTHER CLUBS Samobor, Croatia, 97/8 (12, 1); Dinamo Zagreb, Croatia, 97/8-00/01 (67, 11); Panathinaikos, Greece, 05/06-07/08 (36, 3); Dinamo Zagreb 07/08- (28, 0).

GAMES **81 (37)**
GOALS **3**

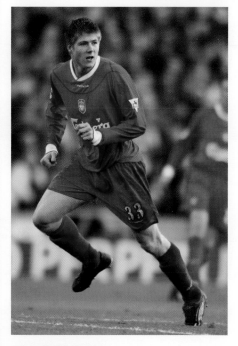

NEIL ANDREW MELLOR
BORN Sheffield, 4 November 1982.
OTHER CLUBS West Ham United on loan 03/04 (16, 2); Wigan Athletic on loan 05/06 (3, 1); Preston North End 06/07- (74, 20).

GAMES **15 (7)**
GOALS **6**

NEIL MELLOR

2002/03 → 2004/05

No matter what Neil Mellor ultimately achieves – and though at the time of writing he was still young enough to tilt for the stars, his injury record was not reassuring – it seems unlikely that he will taste a single more euphoric moment than fell to him in front of the Kop one Sunday teatime in November 2004.

Liverpool were holding Arsenal at 1-1, with time nearly up, when a loose ball bounced towards the hard-working, rumbustious marksman some 25 yards from goal. Mellor swung his right boot and lashed a perfect arcing volley beyond Jens Lehmann into the far corner of the net, claiming victory with virtually the last kick of the contest. It was a heavenly hit and soon it was followed by further strikes against Olympiakos and Newcastle, but then poor Mellor was sidelined by injury, after which he never regained full impetus.

Neil had been rejected by Manchester City as a teenager, but manfully he set about rebuilding his dream with Liverpool. The big, honest front-man, whose father Ian played for City in the 1970s and early 1980s, scored heavily for the reserves, then stepped up to the first-team ranks in 2002/03. There followed a loan stint at West Ham and that glorious interlude back at Liverpool before most of 2005 was lost to knee trouble.

Though strong and eager on the deck, and deft in the air, he could appear ponderous against nippy defenders, and few pundits credited him with the class required to unseat costly stars on a regular basis. But whatever awaited Neil Mellor following his £500,000 switch to Preston in August 2006, nothing would dim the memory of the day he spiked the Gunners so sensationally.

DJIMI TRAORE

1999/2000 → 2005/06

A young Marcel Desailly or Bambi on ice? Djimi Traore was likened to the majestic French star by Gerard Houllier when the Liverpool boss recruited him from Laval for £550,000 in February 1999, the judgement buttressed by interest in the tall, willowy teenager from the likes of AC Milan and Lazio.

But somehow, despite revealing vast potential, both in his preferred position as a centre-half and at left-back, the Mali international never wholly convinced during more than half a decade at Anfield, prompting the derisive Disney reference from disillusioned fans.

Traore's 2004/05 campaign offered a telling microcosm of his Anfield experience. There were lengthy spells on the rearguard's left flank in which his speed, composure, ball control and aerial prowess were a delight, particularly during the latter stages of the European Cup campaign against Juventus and Chelsea.

However, he appeared piteously vulnerable during the first-half shambles against AC Milan in the final before improving after the break, playing his part in that unforgettable comeback and making a crucial goal-line save from Shevchenko.

As far as raw ability was concerned, it seemed the superbly athletic Traore was well endowed, but maybe self-belief was an issue. If so he must have suffered horribly following one palsied moment against Burnley in that term's FA Cup, when he dallied instead of making a routine clearance, then backheeled bizarrely into his own net for the only goal of the Turf Moor tie.

When the Reds made their original investment in Traore, they understood that he would need honing in the reserves, whom he duly skippered to their league title in his first full English campaign. That season, too, he briefly tasted senior competition, impressing sufficiently to start 2000/01 as first-choice left-back pending the arrival of Christian Ziege.

There followed a return to the second string, then a year on loan at Lens, after which it seemed Traore might be on his way out of Anfield when Blackburn and Bordeaux both made substantial bids. But Houllier believed implicitly in his callow protege, whom he drafted back into his side at left-back at the outset of 2002/03.

Still, despite Traore's all-round prowess, there remained a worrying tendency to be sucked out of position, and a handful of unforced, fish-out-of-water errors spawned further qualms. However, he appeared in a more advantageous light when injury to Stephane Henchoz necessitated a move to the centre to partner Sami Hyypia. Now invariably facing play, the long-legged youngster was more assured, and his explosive acceleration rescued his side from serial scrapes.

For part of 2003/04 he was preferred to John Arne Riise on the left, but almost departed during the following summer after Everton and Liverpool had agreed a £1.5 million fee. That deal was scrapped by new manager Rafa Benitez and Traore appeared reborn under the Spaniard, more confident than ever before. But still he couldn't nail down a regular first-team slot, and in summer 2006 he joined Charlton Athletic for £2 million.

	DJIMI TRAORE
BORN	Saint-Ouen, France, 1 March 1980.
HONOURS	European Cup 04/05. 5 Mali caps (04-).
OTHER CLUBS	Laval, France, 98/9; Lens, France, on loan 01/02 (19, 0); Charlton Athletic 06/07 (11, 0); Portsmouth 06/07-07/08 (13, 0); Rennes, France, on loan 07/08 (15, 0); Birmingham City on loan 08/09 (3, 0); Monaco, France, 09/10-.

GAMES	120 (21)
GOALS	1

STEVEN GERRARD

1998/99 →

Steven Gerrard is the heart of the modern Reds, the living embodiment of Liverpool's rage for a lasting return to the mountaintops of English and European football. He is the club's best and most influential player since Kenny Dalglish, his all-encompassing talent screaming for fulfilment, asserting eloquently and urgently that the remarkable Champions League triumph was merely the first step.

To yearning Anfielders, eager to forgive and forget his unsettling dalliances with Chelsea in the summers of 2004 and 2005, Gerrard the rampant leviathan offers a compelling reason to believe. Unquestionably he is bounteously endowed with every quality demanded of a leader on the field, his galvanic natural gifts matched by the ruthless mentality of a born winner, and as indicated by his 2009 Footballer of the Year status, he was in the form of his life as he entered his 30th year. As Sir Alex Ferguson once remarked with undisguised envy: 'Gerrard is fantastic. Everywhere the ball is, he is there.' The Manchester United boss has never been a man to fawn over his rivals, but on that occasion he was voicing a fundamental truth.

Mammoth expectations, and the responsibility which rides with them, have been Gerrard's constant companions since he emerged into the public domain in December 1998. Progressing meteorically thereafter, he has matured into the finished article, versatile enough to operate at right-back or on the right of midfield or, most frequently, as a central colossus.

But with the end of the new millennium's first decade fast approaching, debate about his most effective position had become redundant, at least in this quarter. It was not as a controlling midfielder, admittedly a role in which he has proved majestic often enough but also one in which his passion has run away with him, leading him to dash ungovernably to all corners of the pitch, sometimes leaving alarming gaps in his wake.

Surely he is more gainfully employed as support striker to Fernando Torres, with whom he forged such a scintillating, instinctive alliance in 2007/08 that between them they notched 54 goals, of which Gerrard's share was a princely 21. Yet even that did not represent the pinnacle, as he demonstrated with 24 strikes in 40 starts during 2008/09, when Liverpool went so agonisingly close to ending their excruciating title famine. With Xabi Alonso and Javier Mascherano so steadfast behind him, still he enjoyed license to roam, to maraud, to create, but now with a more defined remit and more chance of a profitable outcome.

Gerrard's attributes are myriad. For a tall fellow, he is a devastating runner with or without the ball, possessing the guile to embarrass high-quality defenders with the nimblest of body-swerves and the explosive acceleration to make nonsense of careful positioning by would-be markers. He is a glorious passer, too, specialising in audacious, high-velocity, long-range dispatches which instantly transform defence into attack.

Crucially, the impeccable technique required for such ambitious deliveries is usually underpinned by an instinct for releasing them at the optimum moment, a priceless combination equalled by his facility for bending crosses with the wicked ease of a David Beckham. Gerrard relishes a thunderous tackle more than his England colleague, though, usually making the big challenges cleanly, just occasionally lunging in with rash abandon.

Because of the intense rivalry between the two clubs, images of Gerrard at his imperious best often involve Manchester United as victims, notably during Liverpool's emphatic win at Anfield in March 2001, when he left Fabien Barthez groping thin air with a sudden 30-yarder of pulverising power. Then there was the knife-through-butter pass to Danny Murphy for the late decider at Old Trafford in January 2002, and the fulminating League Cup Final opener at the Millennium Stadium just over a year later. Okay, so that one took a sizable deflection off Beckham, but it can be taken as overdue repayment for the outrageous deviation which furnished Jimmy Greenhoff with an FA Cup winner in 1977 (Liverpool fans have long memories).

More defining, still, were Gerrard's totemic contributions to the lifting of the European crown in 2005. Most vivid were his tracer-bullet strike to seal one comeback, against Olympiakos at Anfield, then the twisting header to launch another, in the final against AC Milan. Both times he dragged the Reds, whom he has skippered since October 2003, back from the abyss of imminent defeat, lifting his comrades by supreme personal example, a feat he repeated with a typical two-goal show in the 2006 FA Cup Final against West Ham.

If all this makes Gerrard sound like perfection on legs, it is not intended to; for all the panoramic grandeur of his game, sometimes he promises more than he delivers, maybe getting carried away and conceding possession needlessly with over-extravagant flourishes. On such days of flawed tactical discipline, and on increasingly rare ones of comparative anonymity, he appears to smoulder languidly instead of bending the contest more characteristically to his will.

Further, it's fair to say that his progress has not been uniformly devoid of tribulation. Gerard Houllier once dropped him briefly after questioning his work-rate, an anxiety which now seems risible. Then there was the Chelsea question, which did not reflect him in the most flattering of lights, especially in the emotional wake of Istanbul; and although he was cleared of assault at a Southport bar on a night out following a fabulous personal display at Newcastle in December 2008, it was a spot of turbulence which might have been avoided.

Through it all, though, Steven Gerrard remained Liverpool's most priceless asset, a man who bestrode the football fields of the world like some irresistible force of nature, one of the most beloved of all Anfield heroes.

STEVEN GEORGE GERRARD	
BORN	Huyton, Merseyside, 30 May 1980.
HONOURS	European Cup 04/05. UEFA Cup 00/01. FA Cup 00/01, 05/06. League Cup 00/01, 02/03. 72 England caps (00-). PFA Footballer of the Year 06. FWA Footballer of the Year 09.

GAMES	441 (42)
GOALS	120

JOHN ARNE RIISE

2001/02 → 2007/08

Even if John Arne Riise had never kicked another ball for Liverpool after the 39th minute of a tumultuous Saturday lunchtime encounter with Manchester United at Anfield in November 2001, his niche in Reds folklore would have been set in stone.

That much was assured when Dietmar Hamann touched a free-kick to the tigerish Norwegian redhead, who launched a 30-yard left-foot piledriver of such volcanic power that, had its trajectory been a yard or so to the right, it might have decaptitated his former Monaco team-mate, Fabien Barthez.

As it was, the Frenchman's shining topknot was spared, the hurtling leather merely singeing the underside of his crossbar on its high-velocity journey to the top corner of his net. It was a remarkable strike, especially given its context of a crushing victory over the old enemy, and Riise's trademark shirt-off celebration, a ritual revealing a ferocious flamboyance unusual among Scandinavians, offered a stirring symbol of Liverpool renaissance.

At this point, in fairness to John's tremendous all-round attributes, it should be stressed that he was no one-trick wonder. Indeed, long before boot met ball so memorably against the Mancunians, it had become abundantly clear that Gerard Houllier's £4 million summer swoop to secure the prodigiously promising 20-year-old represented a considerable coup. Certainly new Fulham boss Jean Tigana was grievously disappointed, having expected to persuade his former Monaco charge to follow in his own footsteps from the Mediterranean to the Thames, and there had been persistent rumours linking the Norwegian to Leeds United.

Slotting into Houllier's team initially as a marauding left-back, though soon he would prove arguably more potent still on the left flank of midfield, Riise lost no time in signalling his voracious attacking ambition with a goal in the Reds' European Super Cup victory over Bayern Munich. Liverpool supporters who believed their side had become too cautious were enthused by Riise's indomitable brio, his combination of swashbuckling enterprise and pugnacious conviction, all underpinned by skill, pace, stamina and a blazing work ethic.

In fact, he had been obsessed by training since his boyhood, and before he joined Monaco – with whom he earned a French title medal at 18 – he had adopted a punishing fitness regime encompassing 24 sessions per week. Even Bill Shankly might have deemed that sufficient!

Not surprisingly, unlike many overseas recruits, Riise had little trouble in acclimatising to English football's rigorous physical demands; indeed, it was Premiership opponents who had to make rapid adjustments, as Everton discovered to their chagrin at Goodison Park in September when the newcomer marked his first Merseyside derby with a slaloming left-wing rampage which culminated in a low cross-shot past 'keeper Paul Gerrard, the final goal in a 3-1 triumph.

Crucially, that exhilarating flair was not limited to solo bursts but could be integrated devastatingly in team play, as at Highbury in January 2002 when he took a pass from Hamann midway inside his own half, then gave the ball to Patrik Berger before sprinting down the left touchline; the Czech found Steven Gerrard who unloosed an instant 50-yard dispatch into the path of the charging full-back, enabling Riise to gull Oleg Luzhny before netting with a coolness and precision that was positively Owenesque.

Arcing crosses, aerial expertise and one of the League's longest throws offered further attacking dimensions, though it became clear as the season wore on that he lost his defensive bearings at times. Still, no one was complaining at the end of a debut term which he finished as the Reds' only Premiership ever-present and their joint-third highest scorer with eight goals in senior competitions.

After such a fabulous introduction, it was predictable that Riise's progress might suffer a short-term setback as opponents wised up to him, and so it proved over the next two seasons. Though he continued to thrill when going forward, there were shaky moments at the back, a few occasions when he was caught in possession.

When Houllier gave him a rest, he reacted positively, acknowledging that he had plenty to learn, returning as a more effective contributor to the rearguard. However, it was not until the arrival of Rafa Benitez in 2004 that Riise truly flourished afresh, responding eagerly to the Spaniard's shrewd tuition on positioning and the timing of runs. Pushed forward in October to replace the labouring Harry Kewell, he returned to his best, finishing the campaign with eight goals, including the fizzing volley which stung Chelsea in the opening sequence of the League Cup Final.

Still, though, it was not wholly clear which was his best position, and gradually, alongside that uncertainty, there became apparent a creeping loss of impetus, a feeling that for all his natural fire and resolution a decline had set in. True, there remained occasional gems to applaud from that mortar of a left foot, such as the rasper past Chelsea's Carlo Cudicini which capped an 80-yard run in the 2006 FA Community Shield, but his overall game became parlously patchy.

Amid stories of off-the-pitch problems, his form reached a new low in 2007/08, culminating in the nightmarish stoppage-time own goal – an almost surreally botched header from an innocuous Salomon Kalou cross – in the Anfield leg of the Champions League semi-final against Chelsea.

Duly no one was surprised when he accepted a £4 million move to Roma in the following June. Most fans agreed that his Anfield career had run its course, but they were mortified that he had departed on such a dismal note. John Arne Riise had contributed mightily to the Liverpool cause and deserved a far more uplifting finale.

JOHN ARNE SEMUNDSETH RIISE

BORN	Molde, Norway, 24 September 1980.
HONOURS	European Cup 04/05. FA Cup 05/06. League Cup 02/03. 68 Norway caps (00–).
OTHER CLUBS	Aalesunds FK, Norway, 97/8 (25, 5); Monaco, France, 98/9-00/01 (44, 4); Roma, Italy, 08/09- (30, 2).

GAMES **296 (52)**
GOALS **31**

JERZY DUDEK

2001/02 → 2006/07

The crazy switchback of footballing fortune ridden by Jerzy Dudek following his arrival at Anfield as a replacement for the discarded Sander Westerveld revealed two essential truths about the engagingly unfussy Pole: that on his day he was one of the finest goalkeepers in the world; and that he was resilient to the core.

Consider Dudek's experiences in merely his first 20 months on Merseyside: a brilliant, rapturously acclaimed debut campaign between Liverpool's posts; World Cup misery as mistakes in South Korea cost him his international place; a subsequent autumn of uncertainty climaxed by a grotesque, match-turning error against Manchester United; being dropped by the Reds in favour of the formidably promising Chris Kirkland; League Cup Final redemption against the Mancunians, and a triumphant return to top form.

There followed two more seasons during which Dudek clangers were not unknown and in both he was ousted by Kirkland, only regaining his place through injuries to his ill-fated rival. By the spring of 2005 his Liverpool future was being questioned ever more insistently – and then came Istanbul.

For much of the European Cup Final against AC Milan, the Pole hardly radiated confidence, appearing unsure and fretful as the Reds fell three behind. But when his inspired team-mates had defied logic to level the scores, the real Jerzy Dudek stepped up to the plate.

As the end of extra-time loomed, Andriy Shevchenko thought he had shattered the Liverpool dream with a precise downward header, and even when Dudek plunged alertly to repel the awkwardly bouncing ball, netting the rebound seemed to be a formality for the predatory Ukrainian. Duly Shevchenko shot from point-blank range, but somehow, perhaps involuntarily, Jerzy raised an arm to parry the missile to safety and the crisis was past.

After that minor miracle, nothing seemed impossible for the Reds and, sure enough, when the outwardly nonchalant custodian had saved two penalties in the ensuing shoot-out, they lifted the prize with which his name would now be associated forever.

Though the highs of his Anfield sojourn were euphoric, the lows might have been terminally demoralising, but no one who had charted the Dudek progress since his teenage semi-professional days as a 'keeper-cum-groundsman in the Polish Third Division could be surprised by his unwavering resolution.

At that point Jerzy's prime concern had been to avoid following his father and grandfather into the coalmines of Silesia, which would have been his grim destiny but for his sporting prowess, and his providential escape furnished him with commendable perspective when confronted by adversity later in life.

In 1995 Dudek joined a bigger club, Sokol Tychy, before attracting the attention of the Dutch giants Feyenoord, with whom he blossomed, attaining full international status in 1998. Despite being linked repeatedly with a move to Arsenal, Dudek was recruited for £4.85 million in August 2001 by Gerard Houllier, whose simmering dissatisfaction with Westerveld had finally boiled over, the damning finality of his verdict on the unfortunate Dutchman being underlined by the simultaneous signing of Kirkland.

Standing a little over 6ft but of slighter build than the majority of modern 'keepers, Dudek did not exude authority at first glance, but he emerged as a tremendous calming influence. There was never the slightest suggestion of panic and team-mates were reassured by a combination of lightning footwork and sensible decision-making which made him a positional master.

Magnificently agile and blessed with hair-trigger reflexes, he made staggering mid-air adjustments to reach goal-bound deflections and he was significantly more reliable at claiming crosses than his predecessor. At need he was willing to risk life and limb, and the picture of all-round excellence was completed by left-footed distribution which was invariably intelligent and cool under pressure.

Dudek returned no fewer than 26 clean sheets in his first 50 outings, a Liverpool record which outstripped even those of Ray Clemence and Bruce Grobbelaar, and it seemed that the 2002 World Cup could not be better timed for the continued enhancement of his reputation. But a mortifying letdown was in store: Poland struggled, Dudek did not shine and he was axed.

On resuming duty with the Reds, initially it appeared that the trauma was firmly behind him, as he was competent during the early autumn. But then came a succession of costly incidents – an unlucky spill at Middlesbrough, a blunder in Basle, a fumble at Fulham – culminating with that momentous Anfield howler against Manchester United, when he failed to gather a routine nod from Jamie Carragher and gifted a goal to Diego Forlan.

The manager had shown commendable loyalty to Jerzy during this time of trial but now, understandably, he promised Kirkland a spell in the side and when the rookie responded splendidly, Dudek's future was shrouded in doubt. But then the Englishman suffered serious injury, the Pole was recalled, and soon he exorcised his United demons with a man-of-the-match display as Sir Alex Ferguson's men were defeated at the Millennium Stadium.

Thereafter, the Dudek rollercoaster continued to lurch up and down in time with Kirkland's misfortunes until the arrival of Jose Reina in 2005 finally ended, conclusively but with due honours, his colourful days as Anfield's number-one.

	JERZY DUDEK		
BORN	Ribnek, Poland, 23 March 1973.		
HONOURS	European Cup 04/05. League Cup 02/03. 56 Poland caps (98-).		
OTHER CLUBS	Concordia Knurow, Poland; Sokol Tychy, Poland, 95/6 (15, 0); Feyenoord, Holland, 97/8-00/01 (136, 0); Real Madrid, Spain, 07/08- (1, 0).	GAMES	184 (2)
		GOALS	0

SALIF DIAO

. . . .

2002/03 → 2004/05

When Salif Diao emerged as one of the most commanding defensive midfielders of the 2002 World Cup finals, Gerard Houllier was jubilant. Shortly before the tournament, he had tied up a £4.3 million deal to sign the tall, superbly athletic Senegalese from his French club, Sedan, and the Reds boss reckoned that the price would have mushroomed had negotiations been delayed until Diao's excellence in the Far East had registered with potential purchasers all over Europe.

Certainly Salif, who came with a glowing recommendation from Michel Platini, made an impressive mark in South Korea and Japan, displaying authority as a ball-winner, breaking up attacks in front of his back line and then feeding intelligent passes forward. He scored a fine goal against Denmark, too, and if comparisons with Arsenal's Patrick Vieira seemed a trifle effusive, at least it was clear what prompted them.

For all that, and despite making a decent early impression, Diao was destined to flounder as a long-term Liverpool investment, being part of an horrendous summer's business which also included the acquisition of El-Hadji Diouf and Bruno Cheyrou.

The Anfield arrival of the experienced 25-year-old, who contributed to a French title triumph with Monaco after growing up at the club's academy in Senegal, was rather overshadowed by that of his callow compatriot Diouf, but it was the older of the pair who settled first.

After demonstrating his versatility by appearing in central defence alongside Sami Hyypia in the September defeat in Valencia, he delivered several eye-catching displays in his specialist midfield role as the autumn progressed.

At Leeds in October he timed his run perfectly to meet a Diouf cross, then stretched elastically to beat Ian Harte and score the game's only goal with a delicate flick. Then in November he played a colossal part in the Reds' recovery of a three-goal deficit in Basle, having been called on to replace the off-colour Steven Gerrard.

Yet while Diao's ability and commitment were beyond question, he was inclined to be impetuous, occasionally hurling himself into rash challenges with such apparent abandon that it was hard to tell whether he was making a tackle or attempting to dig a tunnel with his leading foot. Also, there were moments when he drifted out of position inexplicably, as he did repeatedly when confronted by the elusive Sean Davis at Fulham in November.

Still it seemed that Salif Diao had brought high-quality depth to the Liverpool squad, especially when he revealed expertise in a third role, excelling as an emergency right-back at Goodison Park in April. Indeed, some pundits opined that he was capable of escaping from the shadow of Dietmar Hamann to become the Reds' anchorman-in-chief, but such a scenario became nonsensical during 2003/04 and the first half of 2004/05 as a combination of nagging injuries and dismal form removed him from first-team contention. Inevitable loan spells followed as the term of his costly contract dragged on, until he joined Stoke in October 2006.

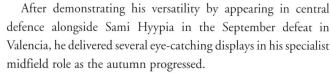

SALIF ALASSANE DIAO
BORN Kedougou, Senegal, 10 February 1977.
HONOURS 39 Senegal caps (00-).
OTHER CLUBS Monaco 96/7-99/00 (29, 0); Epinal on loan; Sedan 00/01-01/02 (48, 0), all France; Birmingham City on loan 04/05 (2, 0); Portsmouth on loan 05/06 (11, 0); Stoke City 06/07- (58, 0).

GAMES 35 (26)
GOALS 3

BRUNO CHEYROU

2002/03 → 2003/04

The French attacking midfielder Bruno Cheyrou was a subtly expressive talent who withered on the Anfield vine with bewildering rapidity, seemingly too fragile a bloom for the rumbustious Premiership jungle.

Yet the fanfares which heralded his £4 million arrival on Merseyside in the summer of 2002 had been no less than tumultuous. His international coach Jacques Santini dubbed him the new Jean Tigana, journalists wrote of the French answer to David Beckham, and Gerard Houllier – never averse to voicing a newsworthy comparison and apparently unconcerned about delivering a hostage to fortune – went even further, identifying echoes of Zinedine Zidane in the style of the tall, slender 24-year-old.

In the event, such frenzied fuelling of expectations did Cheyrou no favours. Though clearly a sophisticated performer, brimming with skill and vision, only rarely in his two English campaigns did he appear attuned to the hectic action raging around him.

Yet in fairness to those who had waxed so lyrical, anyone who had witnessed his boldly imaginative input for Lille would have verified the essential Cheyrou quality. Ask Manchester United, whom he tormented in two Champions League clashes in the autumn of 2001, linking play with a beguiling smoothness and presenting a potent goal threat with a succession of crisp shots.

Left-sided Bruno, equally at home on either flank or as a support striker, offered a captivating spectacle in full flow, all pace, grace and trickery. A quick-footed purveyor of dummies, a perceptive and accurate crosser and a beautiful passer, he helped Lille to the French Second Division championship, then became increasingly influential as they recorded two successive top-six finishes among the elite.

His purchase by Houllier was viewed widely as a veritable coup, especially when a sparkily impressive full League debut in a 3-2 victory at Bolton was followed by a smartly dispatched goal at home to Spartak Moscow.

Now Kopites waited confidently for Cheyrou to kick on. Instead he encountered injury problems, after which his self-belief appeared to evaporate. He admitted as such, speaking of feeling immense pressure every time he played, performing hesitantly as if the Sword of Damocles was poised above his close-cropped head.

Still salvation was anticipated even after Cheyrou lost the first half of his second season to foot and back injuries, and in January he offered a broad hint of riches in store, shooting a brilliant winner against Chelsea at Stamford Bridge after conducting a sweet exchange of passes with Emile Heskey.

There followed in quick order another goal against Wolves and a smartly taken brace – including a courageous header – to knock Newcastle out of the FA Cup. Suddenly Cheyrou appeared confident where previously he had been tentative and it seemed that Liverpool were about to be repaid for their patience as the elegant Frenchman began purring smoothly in a central role behind the main marksman.

Thus it was profoundly frustrating when his impact decreased dramatically as the spring wore on, as if playing on the grand stage for Liverpool was simply too daunting for him. By season's end Cheyrou was back on the periphery, his long-term Anfield prospects in ruins, and in 2006 he was transferred to Rennes.

BRUNO CHEYROU
BORN   Suresnes, France, 10 May 1978.
HONOURS   3 France caps (02-).
OTHER CLUBS   Lens; Racing Paris; Lille 95/6-01/02 (95, 28); Marseille on loan 04/05 (19, 1); Bordeaux on loan 05/06 (26, 1); Rennes 06/07- (102, 9), all France.

GAMES   27 (21)
GOALS   5

EL-HADJI DIOUF

2002/03 → 2003/04

Fresh, hungry and audacious to the point of insolence, El-Hadji Diouf terrorised the lionised French rearguard on the opening day of the 2002 World Cup, emerging convincingly as the tournament's most exciting and talked-about new star.

Here, surely, was a player any club would covet, and Liverpool fans desperate for an icon, a man to lead and inspire a long-awaited rampage back to the pinnacle of the English game, were euphoric at the Reds' projected acquisition of the strutting Senegalese swashbuckler, whose £10 million transfer from Lens would be completed later that summer.

Duly Gerard Houllier clinched the deal – and less than two years later the would-be messiah, who aspired to be the best footballer in the world, was being damned by Kopites as the most shameful waste of money in the club's history and was shunted off to Bolton on loan.

In truth, even in his first Anfield campaign any notion that Diouf would make a difference to the Premiership balance of power proved deflatingly illusory, an assessment which makes due allowance for his understandable need to settle in the remorselessly demanding climate of English football. True, he rallied commendably in the spring after a lacklustre beginning, but it was clear that his football education was far from complete, that he could be ludicrously selfish, and that his temperament was volatile, to put it mildly.

Given his turbulent upbringing in a West African ghetto and a variety of colourful incidents in his past – once he upset his employers at Lens by arriving back late from international duty because he had been consulting a witch doctor – it was always unlikely that the ascent of El-Hadji Diouf to superstardom would be either smooth or predictable.

Having had to fight for everything in life, he was a spiky individual, yet those same barbed edges which rendered him hard to handle were exactly what, when melded with a lustrous all-round talent, made him a target for many of Europe's leading clubs.

Clearly elated at pipping Valencia and other eminent suitors for the 21-year-old African Footballer of the Year's signature, Houllier had declared that if Diouf played with a Brazil shirt on his back, then he'd be feted the world over, a claim supported by his performances in Japan and South Korea.

In that tournament, operating principally as a lone marksman, he had laid bare a succession of international defences with a combination of destructive acceleration, glorious guile and an utter disrespect for reputation. Intimidatingly strong and difficult to dispossess, he had roamed enterprisingly to both flanks, invariably leaving chaos in his wake, and the prospect of such a wildly ebullient foil for Michael Owen and company had Reds fans counting the hours to the start of the new domestic campaign.

Diouf's ultra-competitive outlook was readily apparent on his senior debut in the Community Shield clash with Arsenal, though theatrical gestures and perplexed grimaces were more in evidence than telling contributions with the ball, a pattern which would become familiar during his first English autumn.

After marking his League entrance at Anfield with two goals against Southampton, Diouf struggled to make an impact. Often he appeared to be on a different wavelength to his colleagues, dwelling on the ball when he might have passed, and he looked unsure about his role. Potentially penetrative forays would peter out tamely when he ran out of ground, goals proved elusive, and there seemed to be an ebbing away of his characteristic confidence.

Like some exotic sun-loving bird of passage in an alien northerly clime, Diouf was ill at ease, out of his element, and his manager reacted wisely, maintaining faith in his extravagant ability but withdrawing him periodically from the heat of combat, giving him time to attune to his new environment.

In fairness, when deployed regularly on the right side of midfield in the New Year, he made positive strides. Occasionally he was the side's most penetrative attacker, and he supplemented his value by tracking back tirelessly. Indeed, that spring Phil Thompson was spot on in asserting that El-Hadji was not getting the praise his efforts deserved, and it was a shame when his gathering impetus was jolted by a spitting incident involving Celtic fans at Parkhead.

However, in 2003/04 he was a continuing disappointment to manager, team-mates and supporters alike, his flashy pyrotechnics on the right flank usually ending unproductively, his failure to release the ball intelligently disrupting the team's fluency.

Not surprisingly, when Houllier departed that summer Diouf soon followed him to the exit door, and many observers predicted that he would flop as comprehensively at the Reebok as he had at Anfield. To his credit, El-Hadji proved them wrong, emerging as a key component in the improvement of his new club, whom he joined on a permanent basis in June 2005 for a fee which was not disclosed officially but which was believed to be around £3 million. For Liverpool it amounted to a massive cash loss, and a miserable bonfire of so much hope.

EL-HADJI OUSSEYNOU DIOUF

BORN   Dakar, Senegal, 15 January 1981.

HONOURS   League Cup 02/03. 41 Senegal caps (00-). African Player of the Year 01, 03.

OTHER CLUBS   Sochaux 98/9 (16, 0); Rennes 99/00 (28, 1); Lens 00/01-01/02 (54, 18), all France; Bolton Wanderers, at first on loan 04/05-07/08 (114, 21); Sunderland 08/09 (14, 0); Blackburn Rovers 08/09- (14, 1).

GAMES	60 (19)
GOALS	6

MILAN BAROS

2001/02 → 2005/06

The relationship between Milan Baros and Liverpool, once the source of unbridled optimism in Kop circles, was to end in the anti-climax of a move to Aston Villa in August 2005 before the dashing, but arguably blinkered, young marksman had entered his prime.

That represented a vivid contrast to the situation only a year earlier when the recently sacked Gerard Houllier, widely vilified for wasting more than £18 million on the under-achievers Diouf, Diao and Cheyrou, could at least take a retrospective bow on the subject of the Czech Republic's leading light.

Baros had just massaged an already excellent international scoring record by topping the European Championship goal charts with five strikes in Portugal, and many of the world's most respected football judges were marvelling at Houllier's acumen in recruiting the 22-year-old sharp-shooter three years earlier for a relatively modest £3.6 million.

In truth, when Gerard waxed lyrical over the *wunderkind* after thrilling to his efforts in an under-21 international, not every member of his Anfield staff was overwhelmed by enthusiasm. But the boss stuck to his guns, beat off brisk competition from Juventus, Internazionale and Borussia Dortmund to land his quarry, and by the end of 2002/03, there were few rookie front-men in the British game whose potential matched that of the boy revered in his homeland as the Ostravan Maradona.

Baros' progress was a tribute not only to managerial insight, but also to his own strength of purpose, for nothing about his early association with Liverpool was easy. After the deal to sign him from his local club, Banik Ostrava, was struck in the summer of 2001, work-permit difficulty delayed his move for six months.

Eventually he arrived on the same day as Nicolas Anelka and, with Michael Owen, Emile Heskey and Jari Litmanen already *in situ*, he found himself languishing at the rear of a daunting queue. At first, unsurprisingly, he strove unavailingly to assert himself, but Houllier never lost faith, and neither did Baros.

Duly, when Milan was granted his first senior start for the Reds at Bolton in September, the fruits of his labours became gratifyingly apparent as he decided the contest with two memorably contrasting strikes, a fierce rising drive and an adroit close-range volley. Now the fans understood Houllier's enthusiasm for his pacy protege and before the month was out they were cheering further Baros hits against West Bromwich Albion and Basle.

Equally as significant as Milan's goals was his capacity to transform the atmosphere of a game. Rising from the bench to enter what had become an arid stalemate at home to Chelsea in October, he roused the crowd with a series of driving runs at the Londoners' defence, introducing sudden uncertainty among Marcel Desailly and company where there had been virtual tranquillity, and Liverpool went on to snatch the points with a late Owen winner.

There followed more games in which his enterprising incursions into hostile territory, often without support, proved invaluable in relieving pressure, his strength, directness and fearlessness supplemented by occasional clever touches.

Baros made a considerable impact at full international level, too, netting six times in his first dozen outings, yet for all that he was far from the finished article. There were times when he conceded possession too easily through rash distribution, more experienced opponents proved adept at ushering him into unproductive areas, and improvement was needed in the timing of his runs.

Still, Baros emerged as a major Anfield asset during the often troubled 2002/03 term, fully deserving his late-season selection ahead of Emile Heskey, but clouds loomed on his horizon. Early in 2003/04, during which he had been expected to establish himself as Owen's premier partner, his momentum was jolted by a broken ankle and never fully regained.

Come the following campaign, with both Heskey and Owen gone, he might have shone but after a bright start he faded, finishing as top scorer, in the absence through injury of newcomer Djibril Cisse, but with only 13 goals.

Why so flat? Well, though Baros worked prodigiously, never lost heart and was thrillingly direct, there were questions about his awareness, his capacity to hold the ball up and a perceived inability to bring others into the game.

With Fernando Morientes and Peter Crouch competing for places in 2005/06, it was no real surprise when he departed to Villa in exchange for £6.5 million in early autumn. Some fans weren't sorry, others believed he might have achieved as productive a link with the lanky Crouch as he had with the giant Jan Koller for his country. Who was right? We'll never know.

MILAN BAROS

BORN	Valassake Mezirici, Czechoslovakia, 28 October 1981.
HONOURS	European Cup 04/05. League Cup 02/03. 73 Czech Republic caps (01-).
OTHER CLUBS	Banik Ostrava, Czech Republic, 98/9-00/01 (61, 11); Aston Villa 05/06-06/07 (42, 9); Lyon, France, 06/07-07/08 (24, 7); Portsmouth on loan 07/08 (12, 0); Galatasaray, Turkey, 08/09- (31, 20).

GAMES	66 (42)
GOALS	27

SEAN DUNDEE

1998/99

In the summer of 1998, with Robbie Fowler injured, Liverpool paid Karlsruhe £2 million for the African-born striker, who had forced his way into the German national squad. He flopped at Anfield and joined Stuttgart a year later for half his original fee

SEAN WILLIAM DUNDEE
BORN: Durban, South Africa, 7 December 1972.
OTHER CLUBS: Karlsruhe, Germany, (85, 36); VfB Stuttgart, Germany, 99/00-02/03 (21, 11); Austria Vienna 03/04 (18, 0); Karlsruhe 04/05-05/06 (52, 14); Kickers Offenbach 06/07; Stuttgart Kickers, Germany, 06/07; AmaZulu, South Africa, 08/09-.

GAMES **0 (5)**
GOALS **0**

JON NEWBY

1999/2000

A fleet-footed, industrious frontman, Newby shone as the Reds reserves lifted their title in 1999/2000. After failing to progress further, he joined Bury for £100,000 in February 2001, earning club awards from players and fans in his first Gigg Lane term.

JONATHAN PHILIP NEWBY
BORN: Warrington, Lancashire, 28 November 1978.
OTHER CLUBS: Crewe Alexandra on loan 99/00 (6, 0); Sheffield United on loan 00/01 (13, 0); Bury 00/01-02/03 (109, 21); Huddersfield Town 03/04 (14, 0); York City on loan 03/04 (7, 0); Bury 04/05-05/06 (46, 5); Wrexham 06/07 (11, 0); Morecambe 07/08 (32, 6); Morton 08/09 (4, 1).

GAMES **0 (4)**
GOALS **0**

JEAN-MICHEL FERRI

1998/99

An experienced French midfield anchorman well known to Gerard Houllier, Ferri cost £1.5 million when he arrived from Turkey in December 1998. Six injury-plagued months later, he returned to his homeland for a similar amount.

JEAN-MICHEL FERRI
BORN: Lyon, France, 7 February 1969.
OTHER CLUBS: Nantes, France, (290, 21); Istanbulspor, Turkey; Sochaux, France, 99/00-02/03.

GAMES **0 (2)**
GOALS **0**

BERNARD DIOMEDE

2000/01 → 2001/02

Two years on from helping France to win the World Cup, the left-sided midfielder cost £3 million from Auxerre. But he suffered injuries, then never found form at Anfield, remaining a mystery man until he left for Ajaccio in January 2003.

BERNARD DIOMEDE
BORN: Bourges, France, 23 January 1974.
HONOURS: 8 France caps (98).
OTHER CLUBS: Auxerre 92/3-99/00 (176, 30); Ajaccio 02/03-03/04 (47, 9); Creteil 04/05 (12, 4); Clermont Foot 05/06 (11, 1), all France.

GAMES **4 (1)**
GOALS **0**

LAYTON MAXWELL

1999/2000

The hard-working Welsh under-21 midfielder scored on his sole senior Reds outing, a League Cup win over Hull, but in 2001 he was freed to join Cardiff, going on to help the Bluebirds reach the Second Division play-offs in successive seasons.

LAYTON JONATHAN MAXWELL
BORN: Rhyl, Denbighshire, 3 October 1979.
OTHER CLUBS: Stockport County on loan 00/01 (20, 2); Cardiff City 01/02-03/04 (34, 1); Swansea City 03/04 (3, 0); Mansfield Town 04/05 (1, 0).

GAMES **1**
GOALS **1**

PEGGUY ARPHEXAD

2000/01 → 2001/02

Having proved himself a fine shot-stopper with the Foxes, Arphexad was signed on a free transfer as cover for Sander Westerveld in July 2000, then descended further in the pecking order when Jerzy Dudek and Chris Kirkland arrived.

PEGGUY MICHEL ARPHEXAD
BORN: Abymes, Guadeloupe, 18 May 1973.
OTHER CLUBS: Lens, France, 95/6 (3, 0); Leicester City 97/8-99/00 (21, 0); Stockport County on loan 01/02 (3, 0); Coventry City 03/04 (5, 0); Notts County on loan 03/04 (3, 0).

GAMES **5**
GOALS **0**

FRODE KIPPE

1999/2000 → 2001/02

Fitness problems marred the Anfield prospects of the towering Norway under-21 central defender, a £700,000 capture from Lillestrom of whom much was expected. He returned to the same club on a free transfer in summer 2002.

FRODE KIPPE
BORN: Oslo, Norway, 17 January 1978.
HONOURS: 6 Norway caps (03-).
OTHER CLUBS: Lillestrom, Norway, 97-98 (34, 2); Stoke City on loan 99/00 (15, 1) and 00/01 (19, 0); Lillestrom 01/02- (62, 8).

GAMES **0 (2)**
GOALS **0**

RICHIE PARTRIDGE

2000/01 → 2004/05

Partridge was a lively winger, a Republic of Ireland under-21 international and a thriller on his day. He made his senior entrance in an 8-0 League Cup win at Stoke, then learned plenty on loan, especially under Gary McAllister at Coventry, but an Anfield breakthrough proved beyond him.

RICHARD JOSEPH PARTRIDGE
BORN: Dublin, 12 September 1980.
OTHER CLUBS: Bristol Rovers on loan 00/01 (6, 1); Coventry City on loan 02/03 (27, 4); Sheffield Wednesday 05/06 (18, 0); Rotherham United 06/07 (33, 3); Chester City 07/08- (64, 5).

GAMES **1 (2)**
GOALS **0**

PAUL JONES

2003/04

Jones was a hugely experienced international custodian who turned down a long-term deal with Portsmouth to join the Reds for a month as emergency cover. Composed, steady and deliriously happy with the opportunity, he never let his childhood favourites down.

PAUL STEVEN JONES
BORN: Chirk, Denbighshire, 18 April 1967. HONOURS: 50 Wales caps (97-06).
OTHER CLUBS: Wolverhampton Wanderers 92/3-95/6 (33, 0); Stockport County 96/7 (46, 0); Southampton 97/8-03/04 (193, 1); Wolverhampton Wanderers 03/04-04/05 (26, 0); Watford on loan 04/05 (9, 0); Millwall on loan 05/06; Queen's Park Rangers 05/06-06/07 (26, 0).

| GAMES | 2 |
| GOALS | 0 |

PATRICE LUZI

2003/04

Luzi performed admirably on his sole senior outing as a substitute for the injured Dudek, preserving a 1-0 lead against Chelsea for some 15 minutes at Stamford Bridge. However, he was not deemed likely to emerge as the Reds' number-one and was freed in 2005.

PATRICE LUZI-BERNARDI
BORN: Ajaccio, France, 8 July 1980.
OTHER CLUBS: Monaco, France, 01/02; Excelsior Mouscron, Belgium, 05/06 (26, 0); Charleroi, Belgium, 06/07 (28, 0); Rennes, France, 07/08- (25, 0).

| GAMES | 0 (1) |
| GOALS | 0 |

MARK SMYTH

2004/05

Smyth was a busy midfielder who rose through the ranks of the Reds' academy and made his senior entrance against Spurs in the League Cup at White Hart Lane on the same night as Raven. At season's end, though, he was released without another chance.

MARK MICHAEL SMYTH
BORN: Liverpool, 9 January 1985.

| GAMES | 0 (1) |
| GOALS | 0 |

ANTONIO BARRAGAN

2005/06

Barragan is a polished attacking right-back or midfielder, and it was regarded as a coup when he was signed from Sevilla for £250,000 as an 18-year-old in July 2005. But a year later he was sold to Deportivo La Coruna for £680,000 with a buy-back clause.

BORN: Pontedeume, Spain, 12 June 1987.
OTHER CLUBS: Sevilla; Deportivo La Coruna 06/07-08/09 (26, 2); Real Valladolid 09/10-, all Spain.

| GAMES | 0 (1) |
| GOALS | 0 |

DAVID RAVEN

2004/05 → 2005/06

An England youth international central defender cum full-back, Raven thought about becoming a rock guitarist before opting for football. He impressed on his senior debut against Spurs in the League Cup, but was released to join Carlisle in 2006.

DAVID HAYDN RAVEN
BORN: Birkenhead, Cheshire, 10 March 1985.
OTHER CLUBS: Tranmere Rovers on loan 05/06 (11, 0); Carlisle United 06/07- (120, 1).

| GAMES | 3 (1) |
| GOALS | 0 |

JON OTSEMOBOR

2002/03 → 2003/04

Quick, skilful and versatile enough to fill any defensive slot, England under-19 international 'Semmy' was cool, confident and classy going forward during most of his senior outings. Arguably he deserved further chances, but was discarded in 2005.

JON OTSEMOBOR
BORN: Liverpool, 23 March 1983.
OTHER CLUBS: Hull City on loan 02/03 (9, 3); Bolton Wanderers on loan 03/04 (1, 0); Crewe Alexandra on loan 04/05 (14, 1); Rotherham United 05/06 (10, 0); Crewe Alexandra 05/06-06/07 (43, 0); Norwich City 07/08- (80, 1).

| GAMES | 6 |
| GOALS | 0 |

ZAK WHITBREAD

2004/05 → 2005/06

The blond, gangly, eager-to-learn USA under-21 central stopper appeared unlikely to be offered terms at the end of his Liverpool academy stint, but he was given a brief senior chance before being transferred to Millwall.

ZAK BENJAMIN WHITBREAD
BORN: Houston, USA, 4 March 1984.
OTHER CLUBS: Millwall 05/06- (100, 3).

| GAMES | 6 (1) |
| GOALS | 0 |

JOHN WELSH

2002/03 → 2004/05

An all-purpose midfielder gratifyingly reminiscent of Steven Gerrard in style, Welsh was at the club from the age of ten, and played for England at every level up to the under-21s. Some observers were perplexed when he joined Hull in exchange for Paul Anderson.

JOHN JOSEPH WELSH
BORN: Liverpool, 10 January 1984.
OTHER CLUBS: Hull City 05/06-08/09 (50, 3); Chester City on loan 07/08 (6, 0); Carlisle United on loan 08/09 (4, 0); Bury on loan 08/09 (5, 0); Tranmere Rovers 09/10-.

| GAMES | 3 (7) |
| GOALS | 0 |

CHRIS KIRKLAND

2001/02 → 2004/05

Fortune doesn't always favour the brave. Take Chris Kirkland, for example. Midway through 2002/03, the sandy-haired, 21-year-old beanpole was being hailed as one of the most complete goalkeepers in the land, despite having played only a handful of games for Liverpool. An England call-up was in the offing, but then he suffered a serious knee injury which ruled him out for the remainder of that term.

Having fought back from that mishap, during 2003/04 he regained his club place from Jerzy Dudek and returned to the international reckoning. This time his prospects were blighted first by a broken finger, then a damaged wrist.

Come 2004/05, once again he established himself ahead of the Pole, but now fell prey to back problems which required surgery, cutting short yet another season which had been redolent with promise. Meanwhile the Reds had recruited another promising custodian in Scott Carson, and soon the rising Spanish star Jose Reina would be added to an ominously imposing goalkeeping roster.

Where did all that leave poor Kirkland, who had striven successfully to regain fitness, demonstrating immense courage and fortitude along the way? The short answer was on loan to West Bromwich Albion for 2005/06; the long-term one, inevitably but painfully, was bidding a permanent farewell to the Anfield club he had supported all his life as he joined Wigan Athletic in July 2006.

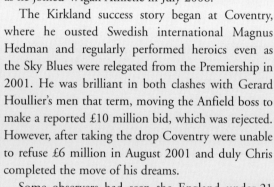

The Kirkland success story began at Coventry, where he ousted Swedish international Magnus Hedman and regularly performed heroics even as the Sky Blues were relegated from the Premiership in 2001. He was brilliant in both clashes with Gerard Houllier's men that term, moving the Anfield boss to make a reported £10 million bid, which was rejected. However, after taking the drop Coventry were unable to refuse £6 million in August 2001 and duly Chris completed the move of his dreams.

Some observers had seen the England under-21 man as an instant replacement for the outgoing Sander Westerveld, but such notions were dispelled when the signing of Dudek was unveiled on the same day. Kirkland understood that initially he would be exchanging regular top-flight football for a second-string role, but he was ready for the challenge and slaved single-mindedly to improve his game, turning heads at Melwood with his almost demonic eagerness to learn.

After impressing on occasional outings, in December 2002 he was promised a settled first-team run. The rookie responded with the assurance of a veteran, returning a succession of majestic personal performances while Liverpool were floundering collectively, offering a beacon of hope at a time of travail for the club.

Standing 6ft 6in and growing steadily more muscular under an intensive training regime, he proved immeasurably brave and a supremely athletic shot-stopper. Also, prior to that debilitating run of setbacks, he was a reassuringly reliable claimer of crosses and a positive decision-maker whose positional instinct was rarely flawed. Understandably in the circumstances, some of that certainty appeared to have deserted him halfway through 2004/05, yet the basics of an exceptional performer remained, somewhat poignantly, in place, and it was hardly surprising that he was awarded his first full cap shortly after his Anfield exit.

Back in 2002, someone had remarked that all Chris Kirkland lacked was experience. They were wrong. All he lacked was luck.

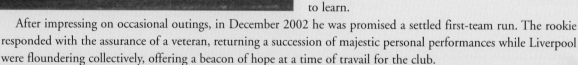

CHRISTOPHER KIRKLAND

		GAMES	45
BORN	Leicester, 2 May 1981.		
HONOURS	1 England cap (06-).		
OTHER CLUBS	Coventry City 00/01-01/02 (24, 0); West Bromwich Albion on loan 05/06 (10, 0); Wigan Athletic 06/07- (95, 0).	GOALS	0

FLORENT SINAMA-PONGOLLE

2003/04 → 2006/07

When Gerard Houllier announced the acquisition of Florent Sinama-Pongolle and Anthony Le Tallec from Le Havre in the summer of 2002, Europe's top coaches, pretty well without exception, turned an unbecoming shade of green.

The naked envy of those wise football men was easy to understand. The multi-gifted pair of teenage attackers had not long since inspired France to triumph in the World Under-17 Championships in Trinidad, and there wasn't a leading continental club that wouldn't have parted with a small fortune to secure their services.

Though it was Le Tallec whose sumptuous talent elicited marginally the more excitement, it was Sinama-Pongolle, 'The Little Bomb', who had emerged from that international tournament most heavily laden with prizes, having bagged the golden ball as best player and the golden shoe as top scorer with nine goals.

The pair – who had grown up together in France after Florent had left his home on Reunion Island, a tropical paradise in the Indian Ocean, as an 11-year-old to further his football education – spent a season loaned back to Le Havre before switching to Anfield in time for the 2003/04 campaign.

Arguably neither of the rookies was quite ready for the white-hot intensity of Premiership competition but, with his resources stretched by injuries, Houllier was forced to pitch them in and, contrary to many expectations, it was the diminutive Sinama-Pongolle who made the more marked initial impact.

Used mainly as a substitute, the scurrying raider startled more than a few experienced defenders with his blistering pace and insatiable eagerness, and he was boosted in October by a terrific goal against Leeds United at Anfield, pouncing to convert with an adroit volley across 'keeper Paul Robinson from ten yards.

The following term, when his chum Le Tallec opted to return to France on loan, the determined Sinama-Pongolle elected to stay and fight for his place, and he was rewarded by a senior run from October to January before a knee injury suffered against Watford in the League Cup semi-final sidelined him until season's end.

Undoubtedly the highlight was his second-half contribution after rising from the bench against Olympiakos at Anfield. To Steven Gerrard have gone most of the plaudits for the Reds' rousing three-goal comeback which earned them a place in the knockout stages of the European Cup they were destined to win, and rightly so.

But it was little Flo who was the catalyst, poaching an early goal from a Harry Kewell cross, then tormenting the Greek rearguard with his effervescent probing, helping to create their raggedness when Gerrard struck decisively.

Fit again for 2005/06, he was given a brief run on the right flank, but maybe needed more stamina to supplement his pace in that demanding role. That January he was loaned to Blackburn Rovers, raising questions about his long-term future. A loan to Recreativo preceded a permanent £2.7 million transfer in May 2007, then later he shone as a striker for Atletico Madrid.

FLORENT SINAMA-PONGOLLE		
BORN	Saint Pierre, Reunion Island, 20 October 1984.	
HONOURS	1 France cap (08-).	
OTHER CLUBS	Le Havre, France, 01/02-02/03 (11, 2); Blackburn Rovers on loan 05/06 (10, 1); Recreativo de Huelva, Spain, 06/07-07/08 (68, 22); Atletico Madrid 08/09- (30, 5).	GAMES **21 (45)** GOALS **9**

STEVE FINNAN

2003/04 → 2007/08

As Steve Finnan entered his 30th year in the spring of 2006, the unassuming, deceptively unobtrusive Republic of Ireland international found himself the subject of a quietly mushrooming mountain of praise.

Alan Hansen reckoned he was the best right-back in the Premiership; John Aldridge dubbed him the most improved player in the country, and Alan Kennedy described his progress as phenomenal. Meanwhile the most demanding judges of all, the paying customers at Anfield, were increasingly of the opinion that steady Steve was Liverpool's most consistently excellent flank defender since Phil Neal completed his extraordinary medal collection way back in the mid-1980s.

Given that Finnan had been required to operate behind some dozen and a half different right-sided midfielders since his £3.5 million arrival from Fulham in June 2003 – and sometimes was pushed into the advanced position himself – it spoke volumes for both his professionalism and his all-round ability that he had attained such lofty standards.

His position within the Anfield hierarchy appeared to become even more secure when the fans voted him their player of the year for 2006/07, after which he signed a new contract. But then, unexpectedly, his form dipped and he lost ground to newcomer Alvaro Arbeloa. Soon Philipp Degen was added to the squad and in the autumn of 2008 the Irishman was gone, sold to Espanyol for around £2 million.

Like Neal before him, Finnan had received his Football League grounding in the lower divisions. In truth, there were junctures when he might not even have progressed that far, having been rejected as a teenager by both Wimbledon and Crystal Palace. However, he refused to be undermined and revived his prospects with non-League Welling United, whence he was rescued by that canny talent-spotter Barry Fry, then manager of Birmingham City, in 1995.

Thereafter he progressed through Notts County, with whom he won a Third Division title medal in 1998, then Fulham, where he picked up championship gongs in both the Second Division (1999) and the First (2001), which left him needing only the Premiership to complete a remarkable collection.

It was at Craven Cottage that the Finnan career truly blossomed, first under the tutelage of Kevin Keegan, who was delighted by his versatility and deployed him variously at wing-back, central midfield and even as an emergency striker. Under the next Fulham boss, Jean Tigana, he made further colossal strides, specialising at right-back and consolidating his international status, impressing in the 2002 World Cup Finals.

After that Steve became a target for Manchester United, and Gerard Houllier was relieved to win the battle for his signature early in a busy Anfield summer which also saw the high-profile arrival of Harry Kewell, who attracted the lion's share of attention.

Typically unperturbed by the media's priorities, the modest Finnan set about regaining full fitness following a recent hernia operation, but then struggled to do justice to himself as calf and shoulder injuries sabotaged his impetus during a disappointing first season as a Red.

He came under fire during a series of shaky springtime displays in which he failed either to impose his defensive authority or to reveal his characteristic attacking zest, and even though Houllier stood by him, an early exit was being predicted freely, especially after the man who had bought him was sacked. Certainly when one of Rafa Benitez's first acts as the new Liverpool boss was to invest in a new right-back, his Spanish countryman Josemi, the 28-year-old Irishman must have feared the worst.

At this point, some established internationals might have caused toys to part company with pram, but Finnan reacted with calm common sense, demonstrating his quality on the training ground and taking advantage of injuries to Vladimir Smicer and Antonio Nunez to earn an early opportunity on the right of midfield.

Seasoned Finnan-watchers were hardly dumbfounded by his meticulous efficiency in the role, nor were eyebrows raised in November when, with Josemi beginning to wilt in the searing heat of Premiership competition, Steve was restored to his preferred right-back berth. Duly he thrived, proving sound at the back and exhilaratingly enterprising on the offensive.

In the spring he played in two cup finals, earning commendation as the Reds' man of the match in the League Cup defeat by Chelsea, but being substituted at half-time after an uncomfortable first 45 minutes against AC Milan in Istanbul.

Typically unaffected by what more temperamental peformers might have perceived as a mortal slight, Finnan took his game up yet another notch in 2005/06. Throughout that term he was a model of consistency, despite being distracted for several months by the inquest into the death of a pensioner in a road accident in which he had been involved. In the end he faced no charges but his handling of a deeply harrowing situation offered a telling illustration of his mental strength.

On the pitch, while facing competition from January onwards from the newly acquired Jan Kromkamp, Finnan soared ever higher in the estimation of the football community. Spending plenty of time on the overlap as Liverpool built their attacks, invariably he eschewed over-elaboration, passing reliably but often imaginatively and crossing menacingly with either foot. As a defender he was agile, neat and composed, more a reader of situations and jockier of opponents than a forceful tackler, but rarely bested by anyone.

By 2006/07 Steve Finnan seemed to be at the peak of his powers, admirably equipped to finish off an enviable sequence of championship medals – but then came that perplexing departure.

STEPHEN JOHN FINNAN

BORN   Limerick, Republic of Ireland, 20 April 1976.

HONOURS   European Cup 04/05. FA Cup 05/06. 53 Republic of Ireland caps (00-).

OTHER CLUBS   Birmingham City 95/6-96/7 (15, 1); Notts County on loan 95/6 (17, 2); Notts County 96/7-98/9 (80, 5); Fulham 98/9-02/03 (172, 6); Espanyol, Spain, 08/09- (4, 0).

	GAMES	200 (15)
	GOALS	1

HARRY KEWELL

2003/04 → 2007/08

Harry Kewell endured a long, dark night of his footballing soul after arriving at Anfield in the summer of 2003 with the reputation of a match-winner supreme.

The Australian swashbuckler had been recruited to inject sorely needed attacking flair and adventure into what had become a worryingly prosaic side. But after flattering to deceive for half a season, what he delivered was nearly two years of injury-ravaged wretchedness during which he forfeited the faith of many fans before inching a little way along the road to redemption with a run of devastating form in 2005/06. Alas, that uplifting mini-renaissance was to prove nothing more than a cruel illusion.

When Kewell's misery was at its deepest, when he was playing through pain to groin, back, hamstring or ankle, he was unable to perform anywhere near his peak, having to do the best he could in front of an Anfield audience which seemed frequently on the point of exploding with rage and frustration at his below-par efforts.

He was perceived widely as a tantalising enigma, potentially too brilliant to ditch, actually too shaky to trust, a star hiding behind an endless cloud but insulated by his vast wages. It must have felt like hell.

Earlier in his career, there had seemed no limits to Kewell's possibilities as he emerged as the most scintillating of Leeds United's new generation, a group which appeared capable of aspiring to club football's ultimate mountain-tops until being wiped out by a financial fiasco of monumental proportions.

Thus, with the Elland Road club desperate for cash and Kewell's contract running down, the Reds recruited the sumptuously gifted 'Socceroo' for a comparatively modest £5 million, his capture rendered all the sweeter by the fact that he had spurned Manchester United. Harry was handed the sacred number-seven shirt, once the preserve of Kevin Keegan and Kenny Dalglish, and there were sober observers who reckoned he had the capacity to match even such illustrious predecessors.

And why not? The Kewell game encompassed pace and strength, wit and audacity. He possessed the flinty edge of ambition which characterises so many of his nation's sportsmen, but also he was a thrilling entertainer, a purveyor of the explosively unexpected, truly a Wizard of Oz.

At first, there was no reason to doubt Gerard Houllier's acclamation of the newcomer as a key to future glory. Instantly he added more width, flow and creativity to the attack, with the priceless bonus of variety.

Whether operating on his natural left flank, or cutting in from the right, or as roaming support striker, Kewell was a nightmare to mark. When he received the ball opponents had no idea whether he was going to run at them, unloose an early cross or fire a sudden pulverising howitzer goalwards. He was ready to drop deep and forage for possession, he embarrassed defenders with extravagant dummies and he could turn any game on its head.

In that initial term he contributed 11 goals, none more typical than an incendiary pair within the space of three February days, the first at home to Levski Sofia, the second, ironically, at Elland Road. Both were exquisite 20-yard curlers dispatched with his left foot from the right-hand corner of the box, and both were unstoppable.

But then came the onset of ankle pain and an attendant slump in productivity, which was greeted with sympathy at first but, when it extended into 2004/05, became the subject of steadily more vitriolic criticism.

His physical travail mounted, but because he continued to play through autumn and early winter, striving to do himself justice but often to dismal effect, his difficulties appeared vague to the paying customers, who vilified him for complaining about injuries no one could remember him sustaining.

Sometimes his body language suggested, misleadingly but vividly, a lack of courage and commitment, something Kopites could never tolerate. There were moments when his concentration drifted, even incidents when he appeared to give up the race after an opponent had darted past him, and he appeared to be so low on confidence that almost everything he attempted went wrong.

Consequently he was subjected to a flood of bile and ridicule, and many who didn't perceive his agony held him up as a symbol of waste. There was even a stage when Rafa Benitez, who had always supported him loyally, appeared to be running out of patience.

Perhaps Kewell's personal nadir was wandering disconsolately from the Istanbul pitch shortly after the start of the European Cup Final, tortured by pain in his groin, his Liverpool career apparently in ruins.

But after an operation he worked manically to regain full fitness, returned to action in October, and gradually began to win back the sceptics who had damned him prematurely. It wasn't instant, but by the New Year often he was the Reds' most eye-catching performer, his ingenuity giving the side a new dimension, and he confirmed his professional rebirth with a sensational volleyed winner against Spurs in front of the Kop.

There followed another masterpiece at Goodison, a fulminating dipper out of nothing, and although he hadn't regained the extreme pace of his Leeds days, he was a major contributor once more. At last Kewell was looking like a Liverpool player again.

But there was to be no happy ending. Ankle trouble kept him out for almost all of 2006/07; then, after reappearing as a woefully wan contributor in 2007/08, he was offloaded to Galatasaray during the following summer. Harry Kewell had arrived on Merseyside bursting with infinite possibilities; he left as one of the saddest footnotes in Anfield history.

HAROLD KEWELL

BORN	Sydney, Australia, 22 September 1978.
HONOURS	European Cup 04/05. FA Cup 05/06. 41 Australia caps (96-).
OTHER CLUBS	Leeds United 95/6-02/03 (181, 45); Galatasaray, Turkey, 08/09- (26, 8).

GAMES	109 (30)
GOALS	16

ANTHONY LE TALLEC

2003/04 → 2005/06

The opulence of Anthony Le Tallec's talent was never in doubt, and his achievements at French junior levels were glittering, indeed. But did the French prodigy possess the footballing street-wisdom to be plunged into the Premiership maelstrom as an 18-year-old in autumn 2003? For all his flair, artistry and versatility as an attacking midfielder or support striker, was he tough and quick-thinking enough to thrive?

With the benefit of hindsight, and while acknowledging that Gerard Houllier was in extreme need of inspirational contributors at the time of Le Tallec's debut, the answers appear to be in the negative. Thus he flitted in and out of contention during his first campaign as a Red before falling prey to an ankle injury.

A more sustained breakthrough might have been possible in 2004/05, but Anthony mystified most observers by accepting a loan transfer to St Etienne after new boss Rafa Benitez had refused to guarantee him a first-team berth.

Given his fabulous natural ability, maybe if Le Tallec had shown more allegiance to the red shirt, and maintained his Anfield impetus, he might have been a Liverpool regular in his early twenties.

As it was he was recalled from Paris in the spring, set up a lovely goal for Luis Garcia at home to Juventus and generally troubled the 'Old Lady' with his fluid movement and clever passing, but still couldn't pin down a place.

Next Le Tallec spent 2005/06 on loan with doomed Sunderland, making an unremarkable impact, before further loans presaged a permanent £1 million move to Le Mans in 2008. It all begged a burning question: was his earlier decision to take leave of absence from Anfield at a crucial stage of his development a mistake of epic proportions?

MAURICIO PELLEGRINO

2004/05

In different circumstances Mauricio Pellegrino might have been the right man, and Anfield might even have been an ideal place for him to shine, but unquestionably the two did not converge at a favourable time, either for Liverpool or the ageing Argentinian international defender.

He was drafted in by Rafa Benitez in January 2005 as central defensive cover following the departure of Stephane Henchoz and, having helped the Spaniard to lift two domestic titles and the UEFA Cup during their time together at Valencia, he was scarcely an unknown quantity to the Reds' boss. But despite displacing Sami Hyypia for a handful of games – which seems unthinkable in retrospect – Pellegrino was a dismal disappointment.

He arrived with a reputation for being shrewd and, at need, crudely aggressive, yet the lanky South American – the club's first recruit from that continent – proved to be a relatively weak reed, being easily brushed aside by lusty Premiership muscle-men. More noticeably still, he appeared woefully ponderous, and if there was one addition Liverpool did not need it was another big defender lacking in pace.

In fairness, Pellegrino was commanding in aerial combat, but despite glowing reports to the contrary his passing was variable, in terms of both quality and ambition, and derisive Kopites began greeting his clearances with the contemptuous chant of 'Hoooof!' Few observers could fathom why the former Velez Sarsfield and Barcelona stopper should be preferred to Henchoz, and soon Valencia's 'Long Pork Sausage' was the recipient of rather less printable nicknames on Merseyside. Unsurprisingly he was not offered a new contract in the summer of 2005, and joined Alaves.

Happily Pellegrino made a more positive impression at Anfield after returning as first-team coach three years later.

ANTHONY LE TALLEC
BORN Hennebont, France, 3 October 1984.
OTHER CLUBS Le Havre, France, 01/02-02/03 (54, 7); St Etienne, France, on loan 04/05 (7, 1); Sunderland on loan 05/06 (27, 3); Sochaux, France, on loan 06/07 (25, 4); Le Mans, France, 07/08- (58, 10).

GAMES 13 (19)
GOALS 1

MAURICIO ANDRES PELLEGRINO
BORN Leones, Argentina, 5 October 1971.
HONOURS 3 Argentina caps (97).
OTHER CLUBS Velez Sarsfield, Argentina, 92-98 (172, 10); Barcelona, Spain, 98/9 (23, 0); Velez Sarsfield 99 (3, 0); Valencia, Spain, 99/00-04/05 (139, 5); Alaves, Spain, 05/06 (14, 0).

GAMES 12 (1)
GOALS 0

JOSEMI

2004/05 → 2005/06

When Josemi was voted man of the match on his Premiership debut against Spurs in August 2004, it seemed inconceivable that within 18 months he would have returned to Spain having made precious little impact as a Red, but so it turned out.

That afternoon at White Hart Lane, the 24-year-old – touted as the possible long-term successor to Michel Salgado as Spain's right-back – had looked a bargain at the £2 million Rafa Benitez had just paid Malaga to make his first signing as Liverpool boss.

Josemi won virtually every tackle, passed accurately (a rare occurrence, as it transpired) and was unflappable under pressure, and pretty soon the fans were chanting: 'He comes from Ma-la-ga, he plays like Ca-rra-gher.' Not for long, unfortunately.

Gradually, as he settled into the side with Steve Finnan being pushed forward into midfield, flaws began to appear. Though he was tough, accomplished in the air and relished surging forward on attacking sorties, he tended to be caught out of position and the timing of his challenges was frequently erratic.

There were torrid examinations by Chelsea's Damien Duff and Cristiano Ronaldo of Manchester United, but it was Josemi's aimless distribution which was the biggest bugbear to supporters reared on quality. By November he had lost his place to Finnan, and shortly afterwards suffered a knee injury which sidelined him for five months.

The Spaniard hoped to rebuild his reputation in 2005/06, but in January he returned to his homeland in a transaction which saw Villarreal's Jan Kromkamp travel in the opposite direction.

Josemi's main contribution to the Anfield cause? Undoubtedly that his brief presence appeared to produce a marked improvement in the redoubtable Steve Finnan.

JOSE MIGUEL GONZALEZ
BORN   Malaga, Spain, 15 November 1979.
OTHER CLUBS   Malaga 00/01-03/04 (93, 0); Villarreal 05/06-07/08 (26, 0); Real Mallorca 08/09- (25, 1), all Spain.

GAMES **28 (7)**
GOALS 0

ANTONIO NUNEZ

2004/05

Nothing much went right for Antonio Nunez during a fleeting and unproductive sojourn on Merseyside.

Tony, as he was dubbed instantly by the Kop, was recruited from Real Madrid in August 2004 as a makeweight in the transaction that took Michael Owen to the Bernabeu, though Rafa Benitez was at pains to point out that he had planned to buy the right-sided midfielder even if the Owen deal had fallen through.

It seemed no reflection on his ability that Nunez had been squeezed out of contention in Madrid by the likes of Luis Figo and David Beckham. Now he had the chance of a fresh start, with his brief to address the lack of width and unpredictability so conspicuous in Gerard Houllier's recent teams.

However, the Spaniard's Liverpool prospects took an immediate dive when he suffered a serious knee injury in his first training session as a Red, which delayed his senior entrance until November.

Sadly, the quietly spoken graduate in international law made little impact when he did taste first-team action. He wasn't a disaster, exhibiting commendable stamina and industry, and he could deliver crosses from the right touchline which curved tantalisingly away from the goalkeeper.

But the majority of his input was frankly mundane, and Benitez did not persist with his countryman, allowing him to sign a three-year contract with Celta Vigo at the end of his sole Anfield term.

Nunez will be best remembered for heading a late consolation goal against Chelsea in the League Cup Final defeat at the Millennium Stadium, a scrappy effort which, it might be argued, summed up his Liverpool experience.

ANTONIO NUNEZ
BORN   Madrid, Spain, 15 January 1979.
OTHER CLUBS   Real Madrid B 01/02-02/03 (57, 11); Real Madrid 03/04 (11, 1); Celta Vigo 05/06-07/08 (79, 4); Real Murcia 08/09-, all Spain.

GAMES **13 (14)**
GOALS 1

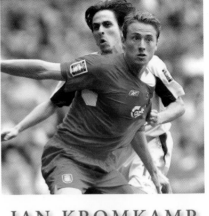

SCOTT CARSON

2004/05 → 2005/06

It's staggering to reflect that 20-year-old Scott Carson had made a mere six Premiership starts when Sven-Goran Eriksson put him on standby, as England's fourth-choice goalkeeper, for the 2006 World Cup Finals. To even enter the frame for international recognition at such an early stage of his development offered vivid validation of Rafa Benitez's decision to pay Leeds United £750,000, plus top-ups linked to future appearances, for the under-21 custodian in January 2005.

After Leeds' financial plight had forced them to sell, Carson might have anticipated gradual progress as a Red. But by early March injuries to Chris Kirkland and Jerzy Dudek had plunged the 6ft 3in Cumbrian into the Premiership maelstrom, and soon he was minding Liverpool's net against Juventus in a European Cup quarter-final at Anfield.

It was now that Carson learned the cruellest lesson of goalkeeping life – that no matter how brilliantly you perform for most of a match, one slip can shatter your world. After dealing masterfully with everything the Italians could throw at him for an hour, he allowed a gentle header from Fabio Cannavaro to squirm through his hands, thus conceding what might have been a crucial away goal.

The young man might have wilted, but he didn't, displaying further fine form in Liverpool's cause before starring during a loan stint at Sheffield Wednesday, then widening his experience further in season-long spells with Charlton and Aston Villa. It spoke volumes for his character, too, that he refused to be cowed by a traumatic full competitive debut for England in 2007.

However, given the enduring excellence of Jose Reina, in July 2008 the Reds were ready to accept a cheque for £3.25 million, and the still-promising Carson joined West Bromwich Albion.

SCOTT PAUL CARSON
BORN Whitehaven, Cumbria, 3 September 1985.
HONOURS 3 England caps (07-).
OTHER CLUBS Leeds United 03/4 (3, 0); Sheffield Wednesday on loan 05/06 (9, 0); Charlton Athletic on loan 06/07 (36, 0); Aston Villa on loan 07/08 (35, 0); West Bromwich Albion 08/09- (35, 0).

GAMES	9
GOALS	0

DARREN POTTER

2004/05 → 2005/06

With foreign imports flooding the English game during the Premiership era, much has been made of the difficulties faced by talented British youngsters in forging careers at the top level of professional football. A compelling example of this trend is offered by Darren Potter, a former captain of Liverpool Schoolboys and a subtly gifted, creative central midfielder.

After signing as a trainee in 2002, Potter, who was once on Everton's books, continued to develop apace. He proved himself an imaginative passer, he was acutely aware of team responsibilities and the callow six-footer tackled with a briskness which belied his slim build.

Though never summoned for first-team duty by Gerard Houllier, he leapt up the pecking order under Rafa Benitez and was given his first senior opportunities on the right of midfield in the European Cup qualifiers against AK Graz in August 2004.

In senior company Potter looked bright and inventive, almost claiming an assist on his debut but Djibril Cisse failed to capitalise on the rookie's clever dink. However, he remained in Rafa's reckoning, and that autumn he showcased his potential by splitting two defenders with a beautifully weighted dispatch to set up a League Cup goal for Milan Baros against Millwall.

A year later, having overcome injuries, the Republic of Ireland under-21 international signed a new three-year deal. But with Alonso, Sissoko, Garcia, Hamann and Gerrard to contend with, his long-term prospects with Liverpool were limited and, after a mooted New Year switch to Hearts fell through, he was loaned to Southampton.

After thriving on the south coast, Potter was sold to Wolves for £250,000 in August 2006 and ascended to full international status the following year. What might have achieved in a red shirt given further chances? We'll never know.

DARREN MICHAEL POTTER
BORN Liverpool, 21 December 1984.
HONOURS 5 Republic of Ireland caps (07-).
OTHER CLUBS Southampton on loan 05/06 (10, 0); Wolverhampton Wanderers 06/07- (56, 0); Sheffield Wednesday 08/09- (17, 2).

GAMES	10 (7)
GOALS	0

JAN KROMKAMP

2005/06 → 2006/07

Jan Kromkamp was a smoothly efficient exponent of the 'total football' pioneered by his famous forerunners in the Dutch national team, but he never became integrated into the Liverpool set-up and departed only a few months after his arrival.

Composed and confident, he was a polished right-back or wide midfielder who could fill in comfortably as a conventional winger. In addition, he boasted the height and authority to deputise at need in central defence, and he could point to teenage success as a striker with his local club, Makkinga.

After joining Villarreal from AZ67 Alkmaar in August 2005, Kromkamp did not expect another transfer during the following January, but he had struggled to settle in Spain and was keen for first-team football with the World Cup finals looming. Thus when Josemi was ready to return to his native land a straight swap deal suited all parties, and Kromkamp eagerly accepted the move to English football, which is rather more similar to the Dutch variety than the Spanish.

He made his Liverpool entrance as a substitute for Peter Crouch, thus necessitating a reshuffle, in the enthralling FA Cup encounter with Luton Town at Kenilworth Road, and when subsequently offered a handful of starts, he demonstrated both his defensive quality and his zest for driving forward.

When he completed the Kromkamp signing, Rafa Benitez stressed that Jan was not being recruited merely as cover, but to provide a genuine challenge to Steve Finnan. With further new recruits also pressing for recognition, the contest for the Reds' right-back berth over the next few seasons seemed certain to be intense, and it's possible that the Dutchman didn't relish the prospect of such a scrap. Whatever, on transfer deadline day in August 2006 Kromkamp joined PSV Eindhoven for an undisclosed fee.

JAN KROMKAMP
BORN Makkinga, Holland, 17 August 1980.
HONOURS 11 Holland caps (04-).
OTHER CLUBS Go Ahead Eagles 98; AZ67 Alkmaar, both Holland; Villarreal, Spain, 05/06; PSV Eindhoven, Holland 06/07- (70, 1).

GAMES	8 (10)
GOALS	0

STEPHEN WARNOCK

2004/05 → 2006/07

A lesser man than Stephen Warnock might have surrendered to the serial pain and uncertainty strewn in his path as he fought with every last shred of his being to forge a first-team future at Anfield.

The gutsy Lancastrian left-back cum midfielder broke a leg on three occasions as a teenager while toiling towards a possible top-level career alongside legions of fellow rookie Reds.

Many lads, perhaps even most, would have let their dream die, and no one could have blamed him if he had. But although the possibility of a future outside the game must have crossed Warnock's mind, he refused to yield to the unkind fates and, bolstered by the faith of academy chief Steve Heighway, he undertook three plodding fights back into contention.

And that was only the beginning of the epic struggle facing the stout-hearted Warnock. Next he had to prove that he was good enough as a footballer to make the grade at one of the world's leading clubs.

Having celebrated his 20th birthday and with lost time to make up, he spent a brief spell on loan with Bradford City, then passed the whole of 2003/04 under the benevolent eye of Gary McAllister at Coventry City, shining so insistently that he was voted supporters' player of the year.

The Sky Blues were keen to sign him permanently but Warnock's ambition to play his football for Liverpool still blazed unquenchably, and after impressing on a summer tour of the United States and Canada he was given his senior debut in a European Cup qualifier against AK Graz in Austria that August.

New boss Rafa Benitez liked what he saw and that term Warnock made 30 senior appearances, splitting his duties between left-back and left midfield, and being horribly unlucky to miss a place on the bench in Istanbul.

He invited attention with his single-minded commitment in the tackle and a disregard for personal safety all the more remarkable for his earlier trauma, but there was more to Warnock than the merely physical. He passed and crossed accurately with his left foot, he was eager to join in neat attacking triangles and he loved to run at opponents. Against that, there was a tendency to be caught out of position, his naivety resulting in occasional substitutions, but Benitez was sufficiently enamoured of his talents to give him a new two-year deal in August 2005.

Most Kopites were delighted by this apparent show of faith, then accordingly dismayed when he was sold to Blackburn for £1.5 million in January 2007. They saw him as the latest of a succession of locally produced players who had impressed before being shown the door with unwarranted haste, and they were not surprised when he earned his first full cap in 2008. Even today two questions are asked repeatedly by his disgruntled admirers. Firstly, what was wrong with Stephen Warnock? And secondly, have the Reds ever found a better left-back?

	STEPHEN WARNOCK		
BORN	Ormskirk, Lancashire, 12 December 1981.		
HONOURS	1 England cap (08-).		
OTHER CLUBS	Bradford City on loan 02/03 (12, 1); Coventry City on loan 03/04 (44, 3); Blackburn Rovers 06/07-09/10 (88, 5);	GAMES	46 (21)
	Aston Villa 09/10-.	GOALS	1

LUIS GARCIA

2004/05 → 2006/07

Luis Garcia was Liverpool's butterfly, but the bewitchingly audacious little Spaniard was no mere delicate adornment to Rafa Benitez's enterprising new team. Although he could be infuriatingly profligate with the ball, squandering hard-won possession with an insouciance which left manager and team-mates grinding their teeth in barely suppressed rage, so he could shatter the most rigid of stalemates with a moment of sensational, often disarmingly beautiful inspiration.

Garcia's sudden, arcing volley against Juventus at Anfield in the first leg of the European Cup quarter-final at Anfield in April 2005, and a similar strike a year later to scupper Chelsea in an Old Trafford FA Cup semi-final, were perfect illustrations of a lusciously unpredictable talent.

The mercurial properties of the versatile raider – who could thrive in any attacking role, but usually operated on the right of midfield or in the 'hole' – were well known to Benitez when he paid Barcelona £6 million to sign him in August 2004.

Garcia had played under Rafa at Tenerife, helping to gain promotion to *La Liga* in 2001 and impressing that exacting taskmaster with his combination of flair, boundless energy and the little matter of 16 goals. Thereafter the 5ft 7in individualist spent a season each with Real Valladolid and Atletico Madrid before returning to Barca, his hometown club where he had risen through the junior ranks at the outset of his career. Having tasted the atmosphere at the Nou Camp, Garcia was not overawed by the outpouring of passion at Anfield, where he wasted no time in laying his footballing character bare.

Immediately he was ensconced in the first team, alternately provoking delighted gasps and outraged profanities as he veered between sublime artistic expression and casual wastage of opportunities which bordered on the crass.

First, let's accentuate the positive which, in fairness to the Reds' diminutive D'Artagnan, far outweighed the rest. An engaging bundle of creative energy, Garcia flitted capriciously to all attacking areas, scrambling the brains of would-be markers with his combination of pace and eccentricity.

His cute first-time distribution, which evoked comparisons with a Dalglish or a Beardsley, was a joy to behold – at least, when it came off – and his deft feet could make fools of opponents on characteristic darting dribbles. He took up dangerous positions near goal instinctively, seeming to read his colleagues' intentions more accurately than most of his fellow strikers, Robbie Fowler being an honourable exception; and when he found himself in space he tended to exploit it joyously.

Garcia was terrific in the air for such a small fellow, being reminiscent of Kevin Keegan in his prodigious spring and the timing of his leaps, and he could protect the ball assiduously, being far stronger than he looked.

Then there were his goals, of which the aforementioned pair against Juventus and Chelsea were merely this observer's personal favourites. Others might go for the sumptuous 25-yarder at home to Charlton Athletic in October 2004, when the ball seemed to drop to Garcia as if in slow motion before he deposited it regally past shocked 'keeper Dean Kiely, or the superb left-foot curler following a slick turn against Tottenham at Anfield in April 2005. And what about the priceless trio over the two legs against Bayer Leverkusen on the road to Istanbul, the controversial scrambled effort which ejected Jose Mourinho's Chelsea from that term's Champions League, or the opportunistic dink at Goodison Park in the spring of 2006?

Considerations of space preclude more details, but suffice it to say that Garcia's trademark thumb-sucking celebration, a tribute to his baby son, became a gratifying regular occurrence, his tally of 29 hits over two and a half campaigns compensating amply for the instances of sloppiness which were an unavoidable constituent of the Garcia cocktail.

Supporters had to remember all that when they felt like exploding with frustration as another pass went astray, or Luis wandered naively down his latest blind alley, or spoiled a flowing move by drifting offside like some absent-minded schoolboy who hadn't listened to a word his long-suffering games master had been saying.

Rafa Benitez understood that Garcia was what he was and was unlikely to change. So did his international boss, who was grateful for the Spanish sprite's hat-trick against Slovenia on his first competitive start for his country, which was instrumental in claiming a place in the 2006 World Cup finals.

Evidence of his increasing status during his Liverpool pomp was his selection on the right of midfield for UEFA's team of 2005, thus depriving the likes of David Beckham and Cristiano Ronaldo of a berth. It was a richly deserved accolade for an enchanting entertainer.

Sadly his Anfield days ended with a damaged cruciate ligament suffered during the horrendous 6-3 League Cup humiliation at the hands of Arsenal in January 2007. When Garcia was fit again, Benitez was bent on integrating new men with flair, the likes of Ryan Babel and Yossi Benayoun, so that summer the manager sold his skilful countryman to Atletico Madrid for £5 million.

Typically, he left in good humour, expressing warm regard for Liverpool, the club and the city – and the feeling was mutual. For all his occasional fripperies, he had lit up many a contest and left behind some joyous memories. When there is no place in football for the likes of Luis Garcia, it is time for all of us who love the game to pack up and go home.

LUIS JAVIER GARCIA SANZ

BORN Barcelona, 24 June 1978.
HONOURS European Cup 04/05. 18 Spain caps (05-).
OTHER CLUBS Barcelona B 97/8-98/9 (72, 25); Real Valladolid 99/00 (6, 0); Toledo 99/00 (17, 4); Tenerife 00/01 (40, 16); Real Valladolid 01/02 (25, 6); Atletico Madrid 02/03 (30, 9); Barcelona 03/04 (25, 4); Atletico Madrid 07/08- (47, 2), all Spain.

GAMES 85 (36)
GOALS 29

XABI ALONSO

2004/05 → 2008/09

Just how much would Liverpool miss Xabi Alonso following his £30 million sale to Real Madrid in August 2009? That would be known only when the honours were handed out at the end of the new campaign, and when his replacement, Alberto Aquilani, had been given time to bed in.

Wise men had dubbed Alonso the brains of the best Liverpool side since the pomp of Barnes and Beardsley; adoring Kopites came up with the irreverent 'Molby without pies.' But whatever the preferred label, none could reasonably deny that Xabi was one of the most delectably gifted play-makers to grace English football in the last quarter of a century.

It was hardly surprising, then, that the tiresomely drawn-out exit of the visionary Basque with the stupendous passing range was mourned profoundly by his Merseyside legion of admirers, who so wanted to believe that he had found his spiritual home at Anfield.

Not that Alonso's Liverpool sojourn was unremittingly serene. Two seasons of untramelled excellence after his £10.5 million purchase in August 2004 were followed by two more of comparative mediocrity, and in the summer of 2008 Rafael Benitez attempted to offload him – apparently hawking him repeatedly, and unsuccessfully, around some of Europe's leading clubs – in a bid to raise enough cash to buy Aston Villa's Gareth Barry.

Alonso's supporters were enraged at what they saw as the crazy notion of swapping their favourite – whose progress had been slowed by injuries and, perhaps, a consequent loss of confidence – for a player they deemed to be relatively prosaic. As for Xabi himself, he must have felt fearfully insecure, as well as unwanted and unloved by the fellow Spaniard who had invited him to Anfield. How remarkable, then, that after the Barry deal failed to materialise, Alonso struck the form of his life, excelling alongside Javier Mascherano as the pair provided a durable midfield shield in front of the back four and an effective attacking springboard as the Reds launched their most convincing title challenge for many years.

Back in 2004 it had appeared an act of inspiration when Benitez had recruited the creative 22-year-old from Real Sociedad. The distressing lack of inventiveness during the dying embers of the Gerard Houllier regime had been widely criticised, and the new manager could not have addressed the issue more eloquently.

Likened by some to a quarterback in American football, Alonso operated as the Reds' central intelligence agency. He was not a marauder like Steven Gerrard but a deep-lying orchestrator, a linker of play who kept the team ticking, giving it coherence by stitching moves together.

Much was made, rightly, of Alonso's ability to sweep breathtaking 60-yard dispatches with unerring accuracy, but equally significant was his mastery of the game's nuts and bolts. Constantly he instigated quickfire passing interchanges, his clarity of thought under intense pressure and his capacity for one-touch distribution creating extra time and space both for himself and his team-mates. If there was a midfield mix-up, usually Alonso could resolve it. He gloried in hard work, he made his wiry six-foot stature count in the air and, for all the delicacy of his most extravagant flourishes, those who felt the bite of his tackle were wary of second encounters.

Crucially, too, his presence released Gerrard, allowing the skipper freedom to embark on rip-roaring forward runs, into the path of which Alonso was capable of spearing missives with incisive precision. Conversely, one quibble was that the former Sociedad schemer didn't play enough killer through-balls, but surely a long-term link with the swift and deadly Fernando Torres would have proved to be, given the particular attributes of these international team-mates, a collaboration to cherish.

The Anfield love affair with Alonso began with his flawless full home debut in the 2-0 win over Monaco in September 2004, and soon conviction grew that this was no transient infatuation. There was a standing ovation when he was substituted near the end of a scintillating display at home to Norwich, gasps for a sensational free-kick which put the Reds in front after falling two behind at Fulham, and ecstatic acclamation for an immaculately controlled 18-yard rasper in the 2-1 defeat of Arsenal on Merseyside.

But just as Alonso's star was beginning to soar, his momentum was halted by a broken ankle suffered in a challenge with Chelsea's Frank Lampard on New Year's Day. It was a cruel setback to a side which missed him horribly but which welcomed him back rapturously when he shone against Juventus in Turin on his first start for three months.

Six weeks later he confirmed his eternal niche in Liverpool folklore by tying the score at 3-3 against AC Milan in Istanbul – his penalty was saved by Dida but he reacted sharply by slamming home the loose ball – and then, after a steady rather than spectacular start to 2005/06, he hit top gear again.

Especially memorable was his contribution to another rousing comeback, from 3-1 down to a 5-3 triumph at Luton in the FA Cup in January. The first of his two goals, a 35-yard right-footer, was merely magnificent; his second, driven all of 65 yards from inside his own half with his unfavoured left peg, was downright miraculous.

True, Hatters custodian Marlon Beresford had left his goal vacant by sallying upfield for an injury-time corner, but the midfielder's poise in sidestepping the retreating 'keeper, his confidence in ignoring Gerrard's impassioned plea for a simple five-yard pass, and his technique in firing the Beckhamesque missile all spoke of a wondrous individual talent. And that – despite those two lacklustre terms, his uneasy relationship with Benitez and his ultimately insatiable yen for the Bernabeu – summed up Xabi Alonso to perfection.

XABIER ALONSO OLANO	
BORN	Tolosa, Spain, 25 November 1981.
HONOURS	European Cup 04/05. FA Cup 05/06. 56 Spain caps (03-).
OTHER CLUBS	Eibar 00/01 (14, 0); Real Sociedad 00/01-03/04 (115, 9); Real Madrid 09/10-; all Spain.

GAMES	181 (29)
GOALS	18

DJIBRIL CISSE

2004/05 → 2005/06

He became Lord of the Manor at Frodsham, the small Cheshire market town where he made friends and influenced people by banning fox-hunters from his land, but Djibril Cisse failed to claim full sovereignty over an Anfield kingdom which had been his for the taking.

Indeed, had he come even close to replicating his ratio of significantly better than a goal every two games in French football following his club-record £14.5 million acquisition from Le Havre in the summer of 2004, the big, occasionally blond, invariably flamboyant centre-forward would have been the monarch of all he surveyed.

Cisse's name first appeared on the Liverpool radar some two years before he completed his move. Gerard Houllier had long coveted his prolific countryman, but was frustrated by the reluctance of Auxerre boss Guy Roux to part. Thus it was ironic that by the time the Reds had beaten off competition from Barcelona to seal the Cisse signature, Houllier had gone.

So had Michael Owen, and the disappearance of both the manager who rated Djibril so highly and the striker with whom he had hoped to form a dream partnership was hardly conducive to peace of mind for the imposing newcomer.

However, the 'Blue Panther', as he was dubbed in his homeland, did not appear to be short of confidence despite the vast expectations, and when he registered on his Premiership debut on the season's opening day at White Hart Lane, pouncing to tuck home assuredly from a Jamie Carragher knockdown, his future appeared cloudless.

Reports of his awesome pace and power were soon borne out, but quickly, too, it became worryingly apparent that those potentially fearsome assets were not always applied productively. Though Cisse packed a tumultuous shot and appeared capable of showing a clean pair of heels to virtually any opponent, it became apparent that he might not be the ideal team player.

Understandable though it was that he might need an acclimatisation period, the first furrows had begun to appear on the brows of perplexed Kopites when, suddenly in late October, mere footballing considerations were pushed to one side by a sickening accident at Ewood Park.

Cisse suffered a double fracture of his left leg in an innocent tangle with young defender Jay McEveley, and there were initial fears that he might lose the limb. Even when that dire threat was lifted, the prognosis was that his season was over, but the phenomenally determined Frenchman defied medical logic to return in the spring and he played his part in the European Cup Final, being summoned from the bench to replace Milan Baros and converting a penalty in the decisive shoot-out.

That seemed a perfect platform for the exuberant Cisse to justify his former reputation as one of the world's most exciting young marksmen, and when he netted in four of Liverpool's opening five Champions League qualifiers, the fans dared to dream again.

But as the season wore on, despite the two late strikes which effectively secured the European Super Cup against CSKA Moscow in Monaco, the old doubts began to reappear. For all his vaunted physical prowess, the Reds' wild card appeared one-dimensional, divorced from the team pattern, lacking in finesse and seemingly as unable to strike up an effective link with either Peter Crouch or Fernando Morientes as he had been with Baros during the previous term.

At times his head-down-and-chase style and his obvious preference for the swaggeringly sensational over the sensible option seemed more akin to a kid in the playground than an international performer; meanwhile at others he upset supporters with petulant gestures towards team-mates when he might have been fighting to regain possession.

Clearly the negative body language stemmed from desperate frustration rather than lack of commitment but it did nothing to massage his declining popularity, especially when allied to several awful misses, including a gruesome punt over a gaping net during a 1-0 defeat at Old Trafford.

That's not to say Cisse did not produce moments to savour, notably his goal at Goodison Park in December 2005 when, fed by Harry Kewell, he thundered down the left flank, then cut inside and skipped a Davie Weir challenge before slotting past Nigel Martyn with all the cool precision of an Owen or a Fowler.

In fact, often Cisse looked at his most convincing when deployed wide, usually on the right, where his speed could leave most markers in a heap and he was capable of creating chances with fiercely driven crosses as well as grabbing goals of his own.

For all the brickbats heaved in his direction, Cisse was Liverpool's only striker possessing extreme pace during 2005/06, and he did manage 19 goals, including a sweet volley in the FA Cup Final against West Ham.

In theory he remained unstoppable, if only his singular gifts could be harnessed, and at 25 he would be on the verge of his prime when the new campaign kicked off. Should Liverpool offload Cisse in favour of new blood, or should they gamble on his return to the gold standard of his youth? Benitez opted for the former, dispatching the Frenchman – nursing another broken leg, suffered in a World Cup warm-up clash with China – to Marseille on a season-long loan, with a view to a more long-lasting arrangement, which duly came to pass with a reported £6 million changing hands.

DJIBRIL CISSE		
BORN	Arles, France, 12 August 1981.	
HONOURS	European Cup 04/05. FA Cup 05/06. 37 France caps (02-).	
OTHER CLUBS	Auxerre, France, 98/9-03/04 (128, 70); Marseille 06/07-08/09 (58, 24); Sunderland on loan 08/09 (35, 10); Panathinaikos, Greece, 09/10-.	

GAMES	43 (36)
GOALS	24

FERNANDO MORIENTES

2004/05 → 2005/06

In theory Liverpool had acquired a rare gem when they paid Real Madrid £6.5 million to sign an honour-laden, free-scoring 'galactico' in January 2005, but the cold light of reality revealed a less palatable truth.

Though Fernando Morientes was dripping in quality, he was parlously short on goals, his painfully stilted season and a half at Anfield making a nonsense of his billing as one of the most feared sharpshooters in Europe.

Yet there is no doubt that the 6ft 3in Spaniard amply justified that gilded reputation at the time of his transfer. Apparently in his prime at 28, he had plundered some quarter of a century of goals in 40 internationals, and during his scintillating sojourn at the Bernabeu his marksmanship had been instrumental in the lifting of three European crowns and as many domestic titles.

It wasn't even as though Morientes was not able to flourish away from his fellow superstars in Madrid. When on loan to Monaco in 2003/04, having been squeezed out of the Real reckoning by the likes of Raul and Ronaldo, he finished as the Champions League's top scorer with nine goals and his all-round game developed significantly under the shrewd aegis of French coach Didier Deschamps.

Clearly, at his best, Morientes was a beautifully fluent footballer and a seemingly perfect fit for Liverpool. A lethal finisher with his head and both feet, he possessed an astute soccer brain, he was adept at slick touches and adroit turns, and he was endlessly industrious. Though never particularly pacy, he made up for that by breaking his runs, then surging in a different direction, testing defenders' balance and concentration to the limit.

Thus there were no dissenting voices, not even the faintest suggestion that Rafael Benitez was gambling with his employers' money, when he pipped Newcastle United for Morientes' signature. The Liverpool boss knew exactly what to expect for his investment; it was just that by the end of 2005/06, the promised dividend had failed to materialise.

At first generous allowances were made for the newcomer's rustiness, which was blamed on his lack of recent first-team action in Spain. Certainly he was little more than a forlorn bystander on debut in a home defeat by Manchester United, when his work lacked either enterprise or bite and he was caught in possession repeatedly.

Judgement continued to be suspended throughout January, and when Fernando opened his scoring account with a peach of an effort at Charlton in February – sidestepping a challenge and drilling in a low drive from the edge of the box – the accepted wisdom was that now the Morientes bandwagon would begin to roll with its customary smoothness.

At Anfield in March there was a snapshot of the Spaniard's verve and technique when he unloosed a sudden, awkwardly arcing volley which brought a fumble from startled Everton 'keeper Nigel Martyn and a resultant goal for Luis Garcia.

Still, Morientes returned a disappointing end-of-term tally of three strikes in 15 outings, his settling-in process perhaps not helped by being shuttled in and out of the side as a consequence of being cup-tied for Champions League games. However, now he faced a definitive test of his usefulness to the Reds' cause in 2005/06.

Come that crunch campaign and Morientes' confidence appeared still to be dredging the bottom of a numbingly gruesome trough. Maybe he sensed the impatience of Kopites who had never seen him at his regal best, and several niggling injuries disrupted his impetus, but despite excelling in training, matches usually found him sluggish, anonymous and serially out of sorts in front of goal.

Typical of his experience were two misses at Blackburn in October which verged on the grotesque and a trio of limp efforts at home to Arsenal in February when he appeared desperate and peripheral.

The most frustrating aspect was that Morientes remained essentially a top-notch performer, but one encased in some invisible straitjacket which prevented him from fulfilling his prime professional purpose. Even when he did hit the target occasionally, it failed to lift him from the mire of under-achievement.

For a time attention was deflected from his plight by Peter Crouch's even more pronounced shortage of goals, but the difference was that the Englishman's overall contribution was exemplary and when *his* drought ended then Morientes, who managed only four Premiership hits all season, was left cruelly exposed.

As the spring of 2006 wore on he became the regular butt of the supporters' ire, and when they were polled fewer than one per-cent believed he should make up half of the Reds' first-choice strike-force.

Only just 30 and with two years left on his contract, Fernando Morientes still had time to prove himself at Anfield. But after the jury had been out for an inordinately lengthy period, the preliminary verdict was distinctly ominous, and few were surprised when he accepted a £3 million move to Valencia at season's end.

FERNANDO MORIENTES SANCHEZ

BORN   Caceres, Spain, 5 April 1976.
HONOURS   FA Cup 05/06. 47 Spain caps (98-).
OTHER CLUBS   Albacete 93/4-94/5 (22, 5); Real Zaragoza 95/6-96/7 (66, 28); Real Madrid 97/8-04/05 (178, 72); all Spain;
Monaco, France, on loan 03/04 (28, 10); Valencia, Spain, 06/07-08/09 (60, 19); Marseille, France, 09/10-.

GAMES	47 (14)
GOALS	12

MOMO SISSOKO

2005/06 → 2007/08

Descriptions of Momo Sissoko as the new Patrick Vieira, or even a nascent Roy Keane, were always likely to prove fanciful. Yet although clearly an exuberant work in progress rather than the finished article, his edges not so much rough as veritably jagged during his first campaign in English football, there seemed virtually no limit to what the spidery Mali international might achieve in the red shirt of Liverpool. Barring mishaps, that is, an apt and chilling proviso in the light of his terrifying brush with blindness early in 2006.

In the event he bounced back from that, and from another major injury, but his hitherto runaway progress stalled disappointingly, and when he was allowed to join Juventus for £8 million in June 2008, the prevailing feeling around Anfield was of delight at the size of the fee rather than regret at losing a possible future star.

At first Sissoko had appeared to be the personification of the ideal modern holding midfielder – tall, athletic, powerful, aggressive, demonically energetic and with no shortage of natural ability on the ball, although that last-named attribute remained in need of assiduous polishing.

One of a family of 15 children, he always had to battle for his place in the world, and soon recognised that football was his likeliest passport to success. He pursued it with single-minded dedication, being accepted into the Auxerre youth academy, where he thrived and was spotted by a Valencia scout during Rafa Benitez's reign at the Mestalla.

The willowy but whipcord-tough rookie did not settle to a specific role in his learning years, and he relished operating as both a striker and an attacking midfield marauder. But it was at right-back that he made many of his initial appearances for Valencia before Benitez decided that his remarkable capacity for non-stop work would suit him best for a deep-lying midfield role.

Momo took to the position as if born to it and when he was ready for a move to England in the summer of 2005 there was no shortage of eager suitors. Chelsea, for all the vast midfield resources already at their disposal, were intensely interested in the steely 20-year-old, but it was Everton who seized poll position in the race for the Sissoko signature, and he was on the verge of putting pen to paper at Goodison Park when Liverpool pounced.

To the mortification of David Moyes, Momo was overjoyed at renewing his link with Benitez, a man whom he trusted and respected following their time together in Spain, and a £5.6 million deal was swiftly concluded.

With household names such as Steven Gerrard, Xabi Alonso and Didi Hamann already *in situ*, most observers believed that Sissoko would hold a watching brief during 2005/06, gaining further experience in the reserves, but the manager pressed the newcomer into first-team duty practically from the off.

Just a little time spent watching Sissoko in action revealed why Benitez was so keen to unleash his prodigy at the top level. Though exceedingly raw and coltish, he hit the ground running and he never flagged, barely even paused for breath. Opposing play-makers were hunted down and tackled ruthlessly, or their creativity was suffocated by the limpet-like attentions of their lanky attendant as he swarmed all over them like an uncontrollable rash.

So strong was he in possession that it was well-nigh impossible to shrug him off the ball and he never hid from responsibility, his eager acceptance of the donkey work freeing his eminent colleagues to make mayhem elsewhere. Thus Sissoko made such a telling impact on the spine of the team that he moved ahead of Hamann in the midfield pecking order, a scenario which few would have predicted at the outset of the campaign.

Still, understandably, he was not yet the complete performer. He needed to work on his distribution – so often did he give the ball away in the FA Cup semi-final against Chelsea that one seasoned observer noted that he might as well have been wearing a blue shirt – and it was crucial that he curbed the rashness of some of his challenges if he was to avoid unnecessary yellow cards and a black reputation with referees. But it was felt that such refinements would come in time, and that when they did Sissoko might even be worthy of the currently premature Vieira comparisons.

Yet there was one perilous moment when it seemed that all that awesome potential might count for nothing. After touching new heights with dominant displays against Arsenal and Manchester United in February 2006, he received an accidental kick in the eye from Beto of Benfica and, fleetingly but all too traumatically, his career seemed in jeopardy. There were even fears that he might lose his sight. Initially he was written off for the remainder of the season at least, but he would have none of it, returning after only a month to face Birmingham City wearing a protective mask, which he rapidly cast off when it steamed up, a robust reaction to adversity which summed up the man perfectly.

There was disbelief at Anfield when he was not nominated in that term's PFA young player of the year category, but faith in his future remained buoyant. However he became increasingly eclipsed by newcomer Javier Mascherano, he lost several months of 2006/07 to a dislocated shoulder, his form continued to decline and then came the move to Italy.

It may still be that Momo Sissoko will not be short of top prizes when the time finally comes, in a decade or so, for the Mali marathon man to stop running, but what once seemed a sure thing now appears to be just a little less bankable.

MOHAMED LAMINE SISSOKO

BORN   Rouen, France, 22 January 1985.
HONOURS   FA Cup 05/06. 14 Mali caps (04-).
OTHER CLUBS   Valencia, Spain, 03/04-04/05 (45, 0); Juventus, Italy, 07/08- (37, 3) .

GAMES   **72 (15)**
GOALS   **1**

BOLO ZENDEN

2005/06 → 2006/07

The fledgling Liverpool career of Bolo Zenden was beginning to bubble promisingly when the versatile Dutch flier was halted in his tracks by a serious knee injury which he didn't even know he had sustained.

The former Barcelona star snapped a cruciate ligament in an innocuous challenge with a Real Betis opponent ten minutes before the end of a Champions League clash at Anfield in November 2005.

Astonishingly he felt only slight discomfort and finished the match, only for subsequent tests to reveal the extent of his problem, which was to sideline him for the rest of the season.

It was a chronic blow to Zenden, who had joined the Reds on a Bosman-style free transfer from Middlesbrough in the summer of 2005 as Rafa Benitez had sought to bolster the squad's quality, experience and adaptability.

Certainly Liverpool weren't taking any risk when they targeted the man who was dubbed 'the new Marc Overmars' during his early days with PSV Eindhoven, with whom he won a title medal as a tearaway left winger in 1996/97.

There was another League gong in his first season with Barcelona before Chelsea paid £7.5 million to take Zenden to Stamford Bridge, where he was edged out by Damien Duff *et al* despite his capability of doubling effectively as a wing-back.

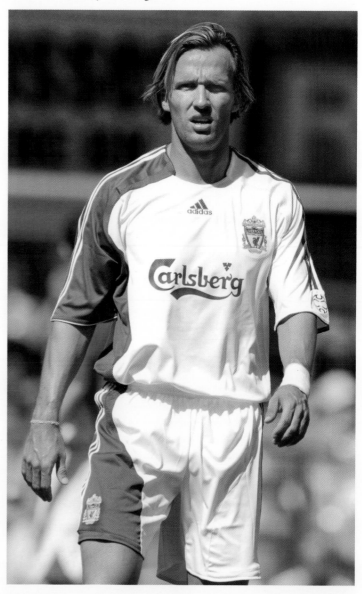

There followed a loan to Middlesbrough, whom he helped to win the League Cup in 2004, then a full transfer to the Riverside, where he blossomed in 2004/05 as a dynamic presence in central midfield and was voted player of the year by the fans.

On arrival at Anfield, aged 29 and with more than half a century of international caps to his credit, Zenden was reckoned to be in his prime, and after a cautious start he began to reveal the full range of his capabilities.

Neat in possession and a thrilling sprinter at defences from his left-flank beat, he carried a savage shot and his power was also in evidence in his tackling back, a task which some wingers abhor but which he could be trusted not to neglect.

In October he put himself on the scoresheet for the first time with a screamer in front of the Kop which clinched a 2-0 victory over West Ham, then three weeks later he struck again in the home triumph over Portsmouth.

With Zenden increasingly on song and Harry Kewell returning to form after injury, an intriguing rivalry which could only benefit the Reds was taking shape. Then came that fateful snap inside the Dutchman's knee, and suddenly he was looking at 2006/07 as the term in which he would seek to earn his Liverpool spurs. However, despite a succession of steady displays, many of them in central midfield, he was freed to join Marseille in July 2007.

BOUDEWIJN ZENDEN

BORN	Maastricht, Holland, 15 August 1976.
HONOURS	54 Holland caps (97-04).
OTHER CLUBS	PSV Eindhoven, Holland, 94/5-97/8 (111, 23); Barcelona, Spain, 98/9-00/01 (64, 3); Chelsea 01/02-03/04 (43, 4); Middlesbrough 03/04-04/05 (67, 9); Marseille, France, 07/08-08/09 (54, 6); Sunderland 09/10-.

GAMES	30 (17)
GOALS	2

MARK GONZALEZ

2006/07

Trumpeted blithely as one of the most sought-after footballing talents of the day, Mark Gonzalez scored a neat goal to claim a dramatic late European victory only three minutes into his Liverpool career, and then netted on his first League start for the Reds. At this point in the autumn of 2006, hopes for a scintillating Anfield future could hardly have been more buoyant, but all too soon they fizzled out in limp anti-climax and the dashing Chilean international left winger was gone.

Initially Gonzalez had been scheduled to arrive from the Spanish club Albacete in the summer of 2005 but then he suffered a serious knee injury and the move was put on ice for a year. Having completed his recovery by the spring of 2006, he rehabilitated on loan with Real Sociedad, for whom he shone in a successful relegation battle.

Thus expectations had been massaged to colossal proportions when he finally arrived at Anfield for a £4 million fee in July 2006, and Gonzalez wasted no time in impressing his new admirers.

At home to Maccabi Haifa in August, called on as an 88th-minute substitute with the Israelis closing in on a morale-boosting draw at Anfield in the first leg of a Champions League qualifier, Mark popped up to convert a lofted pass from Xabi Alonso, poking the ball with cool adroitness beyond the charging goalkeeper and high into the net.

Soon there followed another strike, this time as Tottenham were dispatched 3-0 at Anfield, and it seemed possible that the Reds might have solved a long-standing problem on the left flank of their attack.

Sadly, it was all an illusion. Though Gonzalez had pace to burn, his game was woefully lacking in variety. There seemed to be little else in his mind other than pushing the ball beyond his marker and sprinting after it, a manoeuvre which the classier of his opponents countered by astute positioning.

At Old Trafford in October he threatened briefly as a counter-attacker, but appeared to be a tad overawed by the occasion, proving gruesomely wasteful in his distribution.

Gonzalez suffered a hamstring injury in November, bouncing back to net with a wickedly curving 25-yard free-kick as Fulham were crushed at Anfield a month later, but then descended into virtual anonymity as the season wore on.

Thus there was a feeling of grim inevitability about his £3.5 million transfer to Real Betis in the summer. Liverpool's single-minded persistence in pursuing Mark Gonzalez throughout his earlier injury difficulties had proved to be not worth the effort.

MARK DENNIS GONZALEZ HOFFMAN

BORN Durban, South Africa, 10 July 1984.

HONOURS 35 Chile caps (03-).

OTHER CLUBS Universidad Catolica, Chile, 02-04 (42, 10); Albacete 04/05 (26, 5), Real Sociedad on loan 05/06 (12, 5), Real Betis 07/08- (43, 10), all Spain.

GAMES	20 (16)
GOALS	3

PETER CROUCH

2005/06 → 2007/08

The descriptions of Peter Crouch were invariably colourful but they came with contrasting degrees of affection and derision. David O'Leary's 'lovely big bag of bones' was warm and full of respect; Arsene Wenger's 'more like a basketball player' smacked of unbecoming disdain. From others, meanwhile, issued a flood of glib and casual cruelty, with 'head on a stick' and 'ungainly beanpole' two of the printable examples, and a newspaper account of the 6ft 7ins centre-forward 'collapsing in a heap under challenge like a puppet whose strings had been cut' one of the more imaginative.

But the obsession with Crouch's elongated build, though inevitable and occasionally entertaining, was merely a sideshow. What it failed signally to address was that, even at the height of his initial scoring drought at Liverpool, when he went more than a thousand minutes of playing time without finding the net, he was creating a stream of opportunities for his colleagues, thus contributing significantly to a team that was winning the majority of its matches.

To his eternal credit, Crouch emerged from that distressing period of tribulation as a player with heart and deceptive talent who rose triumphantly above a cacophony of cheap sneers. In the long run the dignified manner in which he handled the situation raised him in the estimation of all fair-finded supporters, and as Rafa Benitez declared pointedly at the time, those who ridiculed him were merely revealing their own ignorance about the game. Gratifyingly, by the time he departed to Portsmouth for £11 million in July 2008, searching for the regular football denied him on Merseyside by the potent presence of Fernando Torres, he was appreciated enthusiastically by most Anfield regulars, even revered by quite a few.

The former Tottenham trainee had joined the Reds from Southampton for £7 million in July 2005. In truth his career had meandered before his stint as a Saint, and there were plenty who pondered the wisdom of parting with such a hefty sum for a front-runner who was not a prolific goal-scorer and who had gone through six professional clubs by the age of 24.

But as he went to work with top-quality team-mates for the first time, Peter began to show exactly what the canny Spaniard had seen in him. Though he possessed no outright pace, so there was no point in hoofing long balls for him to chase, he was a skilled target man with a deceptively deft touch who didn't waste possession like Baros or Cisse, and was clever at linking with his advancing midfielders. His bony, angular frame made him difficult for defenders to get close enough to rob him, and although he was not the strongest, he displayed bags of courage.

In the air, of course, Crouch was an unmissable beacon, providing an outlet that was unique in the Premiership, particularly valuable in away games when the team was under pressure. He got his head to almost everything fired in his direction, provoking the thought that if he was provided with a nippy and intelligent partner, he might prove virtually unstoppable.

Yet despite his physical advantage, Crouch was no natural at aerial combat. So often he was static when he headed the ball, thus failing to generate power. His flicks and deflections could cause havoc, but with more bite and aggression he might have proved a truly fearsome proposition. However, there wasn't a smidgeon of malice in Anfield's gentle giant, and it can be noted, too, that sometimes he appeared to lack the killer instinct in front of goal, even when the ball was on the ground. When Harry Kewell or Steven Gerrard bent in inviting crosses, the likes of Robbie Fowler knew exactly where to run, whereas Crouch might stretch vainly for a connection, having made his move slightly too late.

Not that he was maladroit when chances presented themselves, as he demonstrated with his long-awaited first goals in a red shirt, at home to Wigan in December 2005. After registering with a deflected shot which entered the net via Arjan de Zeeuw and Mike Pollitt and which niggardly critics reckoned was an own goal – no way! – Crouch dispatched a perfectly weighted lob with consummate elan.

There were memorable strikes, too, at Everton later that month when he latched on to a diving header from Steven Gerrard before rounding Nigel Martyn, and at home to Manchester United in February, when his precise nod ended the old enemy's 85-year FA Cup hoodoo over Liverpool.

Throughout his first term as a Red, Crouch steadily introduced more variation to his play, bearing testimony to supreme dedication in training and a mature, intelligent approach. His immediate reward was an FA Cup winner's medal and a place in England's World Cup party. But it was in 2006/07 that he truly blossomed, netting 18 times, including twice with stupendous telescopic scissors-kicks at home to Galatasaray and Bolton. Unforgettable, too, was a smartly executed hat-trick in the springtime drubbing of Arsenal – employing right foot, head and left foot – and there was the little matter of 11 goals for his country during 2006, a record for England in a calendar year.

But even as those who had mocked Benitez for his towering blunder were being forced to acknowledge that the purchase had proved, in fact, a colossal coup, Torres arrived and the unfortunate Crouch receded to the fringe. There were sound judges who reckoned the Englishman might have dovetailed sublimely with the Spaniard, but he was offered only minimal opportunities to forge a partnership and duly returned to the south coast. Thus was a folk idol spurned.

PETER JAMES CROUCH

BORN   Macclesfield, Cheshire, 30 January 1981.

HONOURS   FA Cup 05/06. 33 England caps (05-).

OTHER CLUBS   Queen's Park Rangers 00/01 (42, 10); Portsmouth 01/02 (37, 18); Aston Villa 01/02-03/04 (37, 6); Norwich City on loan 03/04 (15, 4); Southampton 04/05 (27, 12); Portsmouth 08/09 (38, 10); Tottenham Hotspur 09/10-.

GAMES	93 (41)
GOALS	42

CRAIG BELLAMY

2006/07

The serial whining of Craig Bellamy blinded many observers to his immense talent. To his legion of critics he was a tediously posturing pain in the posterior, no sort of adornment to the beautiful game. Indeed, there was a widespread chorus of approval when the Newcastle coach and former Liverpool hero Terry McDermott dismissed him as a little upstart following an unseemly altercation after the Reds had beaten the Magpies, one of the Welsh international striker's former clubs, at Anfield in September 2006.

For all that, there was never the remotest doubt that when Bellamy's mind was wholly on the business of scoring and creating goals rather than snarling complaints at officials, opponents or even team-mates, he was a thrilling performer. That his footballing intelligence was dwarfed so often by petty belligerence can be viewed, therefore, as a minor sporting tragedy.

There was considerable scepticism among supporters when Rafael Benitez signed Bellamy from Blackburn in the summer of 2006 for £6 million, the worry being that Liverpool were gambling on a temperamental individual with a messy disciplinary record. However, the Reds boss reckoned his new acquisition had matured and was a reformed character both on and off the pitch, though at that point the probable reality was that Bellamy was all he could afford.

The newcomer's playing credentials were impressive. To lacerating pace, deft control and unquenchable zest and courage were added an instinct for making awkward angled runs which frequently wrong-footed opposing defenders, and the versatility to operate at the front or on the left of midfield. Endlessly game, he was a waspishly potent counter-attacker and, at his best, he could finish with admirable efficiency.

Bellamy was expected to provide the Reds with a cutting edge following the loss of Morientes and Cisse, and on paper he appeared to be an ideal partner for the unselfish Crouch, but the pairing never truly gelled.

His progress hindered by injuries, the Welshman made a slow start, not scoring his first Premiership goal until October, but his Liverpool career appeared finally to burst into life at Wigan in December when he showcased his enviable ability with two typical darting runs capped by precise shots and slick work to set up a goal for Dirk Kuyt. More strikes followed but it seemed the impulse to press the self-destruct button was irresistible when, allegedly, he attacked John Arne Riise with a golf club at a training session ahead of the Reds' visit to the Nou Camp.

Crazy enough, it might have seemed, but then after scoring the equaliser in Barcelona he celebrated with a golf swing, an action some might have viewed as perkily defiant but rather more condemned as crassly objectionable. If that was Bellamy at his worst, there soon followed Bellamy at his best as he completed a bizarre interlude with a visionary pull-back to set up the winning goal for . . . Riise.

Unsurprisingly his Liverpool day was almost done. That summer, with Benitez's patience plainly at an end, Bellamy was dispatched to West Ham for £7.5 million, his Anfield exit widely unmourned.

CRAIG DOUGLAS BELLAMY

BORN   Cardiff, 13 July 1979.
HONOURS   56 Wales caps (98-).
OTHER CLUBS   Norwich City 96/7-00/01 (84, 32); Coventry City 00/01 (34, 6); Newcastle United 01/02-04/05 (93, 27); Celtic on loan 04/05 (12, 7); Blackburn Rovers 05/06 (27, 13); West Ham United 07/08-08/09 (24, 7); Manchester City 08/09- (8, 3).

GAMES   33 (9)
GOALS   9

LEE PELTIER

2006/07

An energetic, enthusiastic ball-playing right-back who can double as a midfielder, Peltier made his Reds debut at home to Reading in the League Cup. Successful loans to Hull and Yeovil followed before he moved to Huish Park for a nominal fee in January 2008.

LEE ANTHONY PELTIER

BORN Liverpool, 11 December 1986.
OTHER CLUBS Hull City on loan 06/07 (7, 0); Yeovil Town 07/08- (69, 1).

GAMES	4
GOALS	0

DANNY GUTHRIE

2006/07

Guthrie was a dynamically industrious, pleasingly skilful central midfielder who captained Liverpool's reserves but didn't quite make the first-team grade. He went on to prove his Premiership pedigree on loan at Bolton, and then at Newcastle, whom he joined for £2.5 million in July 2008.

DANIEL SEAN GUTHRIE

BORN Shrewsbury, Shropshire, 18 April 1987.
OTHER CLUBS Southampton on loan 06/07 (10, 0); Bolton Wanderers on loan 07/08 (25, 0); Newcastle United 08/09- (24, 2).

GAMES	2 (5)
GOALS	0

GABRIEL PALETTA

2006/07

Liverpool invested £2 million to sign Paletta, a strapping young central defender, from Atletico Banfield in July 2006. He scored on debut in front of the Kop, a header in a League Cup clash with Reading, but later proved ponderous against nippy forwards and returned to his homeland in 2007.

GABRIEL ALEJANDRO PALETTA

BORN Buenos Aires, Argentina, 15 February 1986.
OTHER CLUBS Atletico Banfield 04-06 (42, 5), Boca Juniors 07-, both Argentina.

GAMES	6 (2)
GOALS	1

MIKI ROQUE

2006/07

Big Roque is a versatile young Spaniard with a formidable physical presence who usually plays in central defence but can also perform in midfield, where he passes the ball fluently. However, his substantial succession of loan stints suggests that his future lies away from Anfield.

MIGUEL ROQUE FARRERO

BORN Lleida, Spain, 8 July 1988.
OTHER CLUBS Lleida, Spain; Oldham Athletic on loan 06/07 (4, 0); Xerez on loan 07/08, Cartagena on loan 08/09, Real Betis 09/10-, all Spain.

GAMES	0 (1)
GOALS	0

CHARLES ITANDJE

2007/08 →

A France under-21 goalkeeper, Itandje was trialled and rejected by Gerard Houllier, then flourished at Lens before returning to Anfield in August 2007 as a stand-in for Pepe Reina. His form fluctuated between brilliant and uncertain in his first term, after which he fell behind Diego Cavalieri. Itandje was suspended by Liverpool for inappropriate behaviour during the Hillsborough memorial service in 2009. Later he apologised.

CHARLES-HUBERT ITANDJE

BORN Bobigny, France, 2 November 1982
OTHER CLUBS Red Star 93, Cameroon, 00/01 (9, 0); Lens, France, 02/03-06/07 (170, 0).

GAMES	7
GOALS	0

JAMES SMITH

2006/07

A vigorous utility defender, comfortable in possession, Smith enjoyed only a few first-team minutes as a Red, rising from the bench in a League Cup encounter with Reading. He joined Stockport in January 2008, following a loan stint, and helped the Hatters gain promotion to League One.

JAMES SMITH

BORN Liverpool, 17 October 1985.
OTHER CLUBS Ross County on loan 06/07 (8, 0); Stockport County 07/08 (26, 0).

GAMES	0 (1)
GOALS	0

SEBASTIAN LETO

2007/08

Liverpool paid £1.85 million to enlist Leto, a flying left winger, from Atletico Lanus in August 2007, only for the Argentinian to be beset by work-permit problems. In his few outings for the Reds before being loaned out, he revealed flashes of quality but also a tendency to drift into blind alleys. He joined Panathinaikos for £3 million in July 2009.

SEBASTIAN EDUARDO LETO

BORN Buenos Aires, Argentina, 30 August 1986.
OTHER CLUBS Atletico Lanus, Argentina, 05-07 (52, 8); Olympiakos on loan 08/09 (22, 1); Panathinaikos 09/10-, both Greece.

GAMES	4
GOALS	0

ANDRIY VORONIN

2007/08 →

Andriy Voronin fell in love with the Kop when he walked out at Anfield wearing the colours of Bayer Leverkusen in February 2005. Unfortunately for the blond, pony-tailed marksman, the feeling was never quite reciprocated after he joined Liverpool on a Bosman-style free transfer a little more than two years later.

Not that the extremely game Ukrainian has proved an unmitigated failure. Far from it. He has toiled faithfully for the team and has enjoyed his moments of inspiration. But he has been comprehensively overshadowed by Fernando Torres, who arrived at Anfield in that same summer of 2007, and, sad to relate, there have been times when he has been unjustly pummelled as a scapegoat by demanding fans frustrated that he cannot emulate the deeds of the remarkable Spaniard.

Voronin had been courted by leading clubs in Spain, Italy and France, and had also been linked strongly to Celtic, when he arrived on a four-year deal to replace the departed Robbie Fowler on Rafael Benitez's roster of strikers.

He made a bright, incisive beginning and soon the manager was hailing him as a revelation. Certainly if his first goal for his new club was anything to judge by, then Rafa's reasoning could hardly be faulted. Facing Toulouse in France in the first leg of a Champions League qualifier, Voronin controlled a flicked dispatch from Peter Crouch on his chest, then swivelled to net with a glorious rising drive from 25 yards. It won the game and convinced travelling Kopites that they had found a new hero.

He followed that up with several more workmanlike contributions, then in November he produced arguably his finest all-round performance as a Red in the 8-0 Anfield annihilation of Besiktas. On that unforgettable night he ran incessantly and intelligently, his touch was invariably assured, and the slick flick with the inside of a heel to set up a goal for Steven Gerrard was nothing short of sensational.

He left the pitch to a deserved ovation, but that looked likely to be as good as it got at Liverpool for Andriy Voronin. Despite his commendable work ethic and invaluable versatility – he could play as an orthodox front-man, in the 'hole' or on the right flank of midfield – he was not a prolific scorer and, for the most part, his virtues were perceived as solid rather than spectacular.

With Liverpool well adrift in the Championship race, and with Voronin clearly mundane in comparison to the scintillating Torres, soon a faction of disillusioned supporters began to carp. He missed much of the spring with an ankle injury and despite a couple of goals towards the end of that term, his stock in the stands never recovered.

Following Robbie Keane's arrival, it was hardly a shock on the last day of August 2008 when he joined Hertha Berlin on a season-long loan. After that Voronin still had two years left on his Liverpool contract, but an Anfield return was deemed unlikely. Surprise, surprise! With Keane gone and the club coffers distressed, he was back in the squad at the outset of 2009/10.

ANDRIY VIKTOROVYCH VORONIN

BORN   Odessa, Ukraine, 21 July 1979.

HONOURS   58 Ukraine caps (02-).

OTHER CLUBS   Borussia Moenchengladbach 97/8-99/00 (9, 1), Mainz 00/01-02/03 (75, 29), Cologne 03/04 (19, 4), Bayer Leverkusen 04/05-06/07 (92, 32), Hertha Berlin on loan 08/09, all Germany.

GAMES   **18 (10)**

GOALS   6

JERMAINE PENNANT

2006/07 → 2008/09

Jermaine Pennant presented a perplexing case. On one hand he was loaded with as much natural ability as any Liverpool footballer of the Rafael Benitez era, and it was overwhelmingly frustrating, some might say infuriating, that he failed so palpably to make the most of his sumptuous gifts.

On the other he came from a tumultuously troubled background, the product of a fractured family, the son of a convicted crack dealer, the author of various misdemeanours himself, including a drink-drive offence which landed him in jail. In such harrowing circumstances, it might be said that he had achieved some sort of miracle by playing for two of the world's premier clubs, Arsenal as well as the Reds, while still in his early twenties.

Plucked from one of Nottingham's meaner streets, where poverty and crime walked hand in hand, Pennant served a fleeting apprenticeship with Notts County before Arsenal paid £2 million to sign him at the age of 16, with Arsene Wenger hailing 'the greatest English talent of his generation.'

Early evidence to support that lavish claim was furnished by a hat-trick on his top-flight debut, but the effervescent Midlander's problems proved too deep-seated for Arsenal and a series of loans was followed by a transfer to Birmingham City.

At St Andrews under the canny Steve Bruce, Pennant re-established sufficient credibility for Benitez to hazard £6.7 million to acquire his potentially dazzling right-flank services in the summer of 2006.

Thus offered a golden chance for redemption at the highest level, he appeared to knuckle down and soon he was producing some fine displays, albeit not on a regular basis, which raised the possibility that Benitez might have pulled off a considerable coup.

With his lively pace, his knack of leaving confused markers in his wake and his capability of dispatching delightfully measured crosses, Pennant appeared to be a match-winner in the making. He was magnificent, for instance, at home to Galatasaray in September, and his first goal for Liverpool, an unstoppable looping 25-yard volley against Chelsea at Anfield in January, was memorable.

For all his acknowledged inconsistency and the ongoing need to massage his self-belief, he took the field 52 times during 2006/07, more than any of his team-mates, culminating in a tantalising performance which initially threatened much but ultimately delivered little in the Champions League Final against Milan.

However, after a bright resumption, Pennant's form became wayward in the following autumn, his contributions sometimes appearing to lack either thought or diligence. Then a shin injury demanded surgery, and soon he found himself languishing on the margins, even though the Reds were crying out for creativity and width.

Thereafter it seemed that the manager had run out of patience with his unreliable charge, who barely played in 2008/09 before he was loaned to Portsmouth in January. Even then Jermaine Pennant maintained stoutly that he wanted to remain a Red, but that seemed likely to be a miracle too far and so it proved, as he was freed to join Real Zaragoza in July.

JERMAINE LLOYD PENNANT

BORN Nottingham, 15 January 1983.

OTHER CLUBS Notts County 98/9 (0, 0); Arsenal 98/9-04/05 (12, 3); Watford on loan 01/02 (9, 2); Watford on loan 02/03 (12, 0); Leeds United on loan 03/04 (36, 2); Birmingham City 04/05-05/06 (59, 2); Portsmouth on loan 08/09 (13, 0); Real Zaragoza, Spain, 09/10-.

GAMES **54 (27)**

GOALS **3**

PEPE REINA

2005/06 →

It won't be music to the ears of Bruce Grobbelaar, but while reflecting on four seasons of Pepe Reina's calm and imposing presence between the Reds' posts, Kopites of a certain age have been queueing to declare that not since the golden days of Ray Clemence have they been so consistently content with the efforts of a Liverpool goalkeeper.

Certainly in the spring of 2009, as Rafael Benitez's men gathered themselves for a spirited tilt at the club game's two most coveted prizes, Reina represented a trusty beacon of solidity, one sure thing in a team unsettled periodically that term by a perplexing catalogue of injuries, inadequacies and political intrigue.

That rock-like reliability was illustrated in one telling cameo, only three minutes into the Reds' home encounter with Sunderland in early March. Kenwyne Jones had managed to escape the joint attentions of Martin Skrtel and Jamie Carragher, who was gesturing urgently for Reina to charge from his line as the Wearsiders' dauntingly muscular marksman bore down unhindered on the Liverpool goal.

Reina didn't panic, merely taking a couple of purposeful strides, refusing to commit himself with undue haste, then seemingly suckering the giant Trinidadian into a miserably ineffectual shot which was gathered with authoritative ease. For the remainder of the evening, the hitherto on-form Jones appeared to have been separated from his self-belief and the hosts ran out comfortable winners, but how different it might have been had the Spaniard dithered.

It was a typically decisive contribution from the man from Madrid, whose near-comprehensive list of attributes has earned him the right to be regarded as one of the top net-minders in Europe.

Reina projects a commanding, composed presence as he directs his defenders and instils them with confidence. He is strong, agile and brave, prerequisites for any top-level custodian. Beyond that, his positioning is almost invariably impeccable, his reading of the game and accurate distribution makes him the launchpad for countless attacks, and he rarely succumbs to injury.

This is not to say that Pepe is perfect. There have been a handful of uncharacteristically palsied moments provoked by steepling crosses into the penalty box, and there are plenty of observers who maintain that he remains too eager to punch the ball, instead of pouching it safely, when not under severe pressure. But any perceived vulnerability in that area is not a major issue. He has his own method and, taken in the round, it works magnificently.

Dubbed the best 'keeper in Spain by Rafa Benitez following his £6 million summer 2005 move from Villarreal – for whom he had repelled seven penalties while helping to secure third place in *La Liga* in his farewell season at El Madrigal – Reina, who was still only 22 on his arrival, was soon showing his mettle.

In the away leg of the Champions League clash with Real Betis in September, he pulled off four spellbinding saves to see the Reds through to a telling 2-1 victory, yet in many ways that was not a typical Reina performance.

Operating behind a superlatively steady back line with which he enjoyed an increasingly impressive understanding, he tended to be unobtrusive, reducing the necessity for full-blooded interventions by canny anticipation of the unfolding action and by remarkable lightness of foot for such a hefty fellow. Not for Reina the flashy swallow dive, though clearly he could get down athletically to low shots at need. Rather he aimed to dominate his area, turning his goal into a citadel, all the while radiating that trademark coolness which almost borders on serenity.

Like all the Reds' sweeper-keepers since Tommy Lawrence in the 1960s, he spent much of his time on the edge of his box, particularly important when liaising with centre-backs whose prime asset was not searing pace, and his concentration was of a supremely high order.

Though he wouldn't claim all the credit, Reina was hugely instrumental in creating a new club record of 11 successive games without conceding a goal during his first Merseyside midwinter and yet, given his youth, it seemed likely that his best was to come. That view was endorsed by his performances over the next few campaigns, including three in a row in which he earned the Premiership's golden gloves accolade for the most clean sheets. There was a fleeting suggestion of second-season syndrome in 2006/07 but he worked his way through that in typically professional manner, with a highlight being his two penalty saves in the Champions League semi-final shoot-out against Chelsea.

By the outset of 2008/09 Reina was in the most imperious form of his life, as demonstrated by at least six fabulous stops, including one from the spot, against Standard Liege at the European competition's preliminary stage. Liverpool prevailed by a single goal in that tie, and must surely have suffered a costly and embarrassing early exit but for the Spaniard, who rightly was not pilloried for his rare near-post fumble which arguably proved the turning point in the tumultuous Champions League quarter-final with Chelsea.

A former Barcelona starlet who was beaten only by Gary McCallister's penalty in a UEFA Cup semi-final at Anfield in April 2001, Pepe has goalkeeping in his blood, his father Miguel having played for Atletico Madrid against Bayern Munich in the 1974 European Cup Final, picking up a loser's medal after a replay. One day, maybe, Reina Junior will go one better with the Reds.

JOSE MANUEL REINA	
BORN	Madrid, Spain, 31 August 1982.
HONOURS	FA Cup 05/06. 13 Spain caps (05-).
OTHER CLUBS	Barcelona 99/00-01/02 (30, 0); Villarreal 02/03-04/05 (109, 0); both Spain.

GAMES	207
GOALS	0

DIRK KUYT

2006/07 →

In his own engagingly uncomplicated manner, Dirk Kuyt is pure gold. True, he did not turn out to be the deadly sharpshooter envisaged by hyper-expectant Kopites, their dreams fuelled by the blond Dutchman's exceptional return of 71 strikes in 101 *Eredivisie* outings ahead of his £9 million purchase from Feyenoord in August 2006 – although having accepted that qualification, it would be churlish not to stress that he does weigh in with his share. Certainly, a 15-goal contribution in 2008/09 was by no means negligible for a fellow who spent most of the campaign scurrying up and down the right flank.

But no, it is not for his goals that most Liverpool fans have learned to love him. It is for his remarkable work ethic. No matter how daunting the task placed before him, Kuyt will dredge the very depths of body and soul for the good of his team, and he appears to positively relish hard labour. Indeed, show him a deckchair and probably he would tackle it forcibly before closing down the attendant.

A fisherman's son who would have followed his father to sea but for his knack of placing footballs into nets, Kuyt was recruited by Rafael Benitez after a lengthy pursuit in the belief that he could form a potent dual-spearhead with fellow newcomer Craig Bellamy, or perhaps Peter Crouch, but during his first season that never quite came to pass.

As he sought to settle at Anfield in the autumn of 2006 Kuyt looked sporadically dangerous without getting much luck, peppering the woodwork and receiving scant material reward for all that eager bustling. His ability to unsettle defenders through honest combativeness, his capacity to hold the ball under ferocious challenge before turning adroitly away from markers like some muscular eel, drew comparisons from some fanciful quarters with the likes of Alan Shearer and Mark Hughes. Though he demonstrated that he could finish with venom on occasion, and that his all-round technique was sound, it became obvious as the term wore on that if Kuyt nursed aspirations to attain such an illustrious plane, he was still some way off it.

The lasting impression left by the Dutchman in 2006/07 was of an overwhelming willingness to toil and a defiant refusal to give up any cause, as exemplified by his too-late header in the Champions League Final against AC Milan, though in fairness there were moments, too, of sheer quality. For instance, when Chelsea were dispatched in January, the Dutchman enraptured the Kop when his cushioned header from a Crouch knock-on hopelessly wrong-footed Paulo Ferreira to set up an exquisite dink past Peter Cech.

Kuyt's second season as a Red produced contrasting fortunes in the two principal competitions. Now paired most frequently with the immeasurably more classy Fernando Torres, Dirk managed only three goals in 32 Premiership outings, including a pair of penalties in an eventful Mersyside derby during which he enraged Everton supporters with an uncharacteristic two-footed lunge at Phil Neville which somehow didn't earn him a red card.

In the Champions League, however, he hit the target seven times in a dozen appearances, including the equaliser in Porto, the late ice-breaker against Internazionale at Anfield, the precious quarter-final strike at the Emirates and the semi-final opener against Chelsea. In general they weren't pretty, a few being scrappy affairs from close range, but they proved that the predatory instinct which had served him so well in his homeland had not deserted him.

Perhaps the defining decision of Kuyt's Liverpool career arrived that spring, when Benitez switched him to the right of midfield, allowing Steven Gerrard to forge his sumptuous frontline link with Torres. In his new role the prodigiously industrious Dirk took the eye through his tireless harrying of dangerous attacking left-backs such as Patrice Evra of Manchester United and Arsenal's Gael Clichy, while invariably he was on hand to support his front two.

On the debit side, for all his drive, he lacked the cuteness to leave defenders for dead in the manner of a traditional flankman. But having paid his money, Benitez made his choice, surely realising it would have been asking too much even of his faithful workhorse to be both *Duracell* bunny and wizard of the wing.

By 2008/09, Kuyt had truly come into his own. Though still deployed occasionally as a striker when the need arose, and looking more at home in his former position than either the hapless Robbie Keane or the inexperienced David Ngog – witness his accomplished two-goal show in the home victory over Wigan in October and the savage acute-angled slash in the undeserved defeat at White Hart Lane in November – now his specialist beat was along the right touchline.

Yes, there remained Anfield regulars who maintained that the sensational Torres-Gerrard combo would inflict even more damage if fed by a more penetrative dribbler than the ex-skipper of Feyenoord could ever aspire to be. But the feeling here, one shared by a sizeable proportion of the legions who watch him play his heart out for the Reds every time he runs on to the field, is that the loyal, likeable Kuyt had become an integral part of a very fine team. He has earned the right to see out his best days with Liverpool.

	DIRK KUYT		
BORN	Katwijk, Holland, 22 July 1980.		
HONOURS	51 Holland caps (04-).	GAMES	122 (25)
OTHER CLUBS	Utrecht 98/9-02/03 (160, 51), Feyenoord 03/04-05/06 (101, 71), both Holland.	GOALS	40

FABIO AURELIO

2006/07 →

When Fabio Aurelio curled a veritable boomerang of a free-kick into Edwin van der Sar's net at Old Trafford in March 2009, he set the seal on three mightily significant achievements. The first two, clinching an overwhelming victory against Manchester United and keeping alive the race for the Premiership crown, were grounds enough for an ecstatic communal celebration among travelling Kopites, but the third called for a little more reflection.

What the first Brazilian to play for the Reds had done was finally to step over the line separating worthy but merely competent performers from those recognised by the Liverpool cognoscenti as bona fide high-quality members of their beloved team.

If further confirmation were needed, it arrived a month later at Stamford Bridge when he opened the scoring in the epic Champions League quarter-final showdown with Chelsea through an inspired piece of improvisation, netting at the near post with a low drilled shot which utterly befuddled 'keeper Peter Cech, who had been expecting a conventional floater.

It had taken the versatile left-back cum midfielder the best part of three seasons to earn his acceptance, but if some sceptics were surprised at his successful negotiation of his rites of passage, certainly his manager wasn't. After all, when Rafael Benitez had taken over as boss of Valencia, one of the first signatures he had sought was that of Fabio Aurelio, who proceeded to play a mammoth part in lifting the *La Liga* title in only his second season at the Mestalla.

Thus it was no surprise in July 2006 when Benitez took advantage of freedom-of-contract rules to acquire the services of his former protégé, but equally it was hardly a shock when, like so many South American imports to the Premiership, he looked a tad stunned at first by the rampant power and pace of the English game.

After creating a favourable impression with his cultured passing, easy ball control and aura of composure in the Community Shield clash with Chelsea, soon he found himself ousted from the left-back berth by the vigorous John Arne Riise.

Thereafter that term he struggled to regain his place, though periodically he issued telling reminders of his class, mostly by means of his beautifully measured left-foot crosses. Peter Crouch was the beneficiary against Galatasaray at Anfield in September and again at home to Arsenal in March, when Daniel Agger also cashed in on the Aurelio service.

Against that, he suffered like most of his colleagues in the 3-6 League Cup humiliation handed out by the Gunners in front of the Kop on a night when he was tried as a holding midfielder. It didn't work, and when called up again he resumed his back-line role, only for his season to be ended by a ruptured Achilles tendon in Eindhoven in April.

Aurelio returned to contention in the autumn, but still didn't quite convince. There was a feeling that his defensive work was no better than average and going forward, for all that he could join in attractively with smooth passing movements, there were too many 'Hollywood' dispatches, and still precious little had been seen of the much-trailed shooting ability which had characterised his spell in Valencia.

At last that was revealed at the Reebok in March 2008 when he left Bolton 'keeper Jussi Jaaskelainen helpless with a fizzing volley. Nine days later it seemed that Fabio had finally turned the corner when his smart interception and perfectly weighted delivery set up Fernando Torres for the only goal against Internazionale on an unforgettable night at the San Siro. But the Brazilian was about to be ambushed by another cruel setback, suffering a severely torn thigh muscle while facing Chelsea in the Champions League semi-final. He didn't play again that term and when 2008/09 began, although Riise had gone, Aurelio was now faced by a daunting double challenge for the left-back slot, from newly purchased Italian international Andrea Dossena and the hugely promising Argentinian tyro Emiliano Insua.

It was a critical crossroads in the 29-year-old's Anfield development. If he didn't consolidate now, it seemed likely that, despite his affinity with Benitez, it couldn't be too long before he was discarded. Two things happened. Dossena, the biggest immediate threat to his place, under-performed chronically in the first half of the season, and when Aurelio was given another chance, he began to shine. Shrugging off a minor mid-season injury, he married defensive rigour to attacking flair and suddenly he looked the natural choice to fill what had been becoming a problem position at left-back.

His keen eye for an incisive pass was demonstrated in November when he sent in Robbie Keane for a lovely goal at home to West Bromwich Albion, then a week later Dirk Kuyt converted his curling cross at Bolton. He set up Torres for the crucial breakthrough strike against Chelsea at Anfield in February, notched a bullet of an equaliser at Portsmouth, admittedly while putting in a midfield stint, and then entered the purplest patch of his Merseyside tenure to date.

It was Aurelio's devilish inswinger from the right flank which enabled Yossi Benayoun to head a late winner at the Bernabeu, and then came that delicious Old Trafford moment. Better still, in each of those marquee contests he effectively shackled one of the world's most dangerous opponents, shutting Real Madrid's Arjen Robben out of the first game and reducing Cristiano Ronaldo of Manchester United to a state of petulant impotence in the second. Truly Fabio Aurelio had arrived.

It didn't change him, though. He remained the same unassuming, softly spoken individual he had always been, though his enjoyment of walking anonymously on the streets of Liverpool did seem set to be compromised.

FABIO AURELIO RODRIGUES		
BORN Sao Carlos, Brazil, 24 September 1979.	GAMES	64 (23)
OTHER CLUBS Sao Paulo, Brazil, 97-00 (53, 3); Valencia, Spain, 00/01-05/06 (95, 11).	GOALS	4

ALVARO ARBELOA

2006/07 → 2008/09

For a season and a half, perhaps even a little longer, the majority of Liverpool fans took a neutral attitude to Alvaro Arbeloa. They felt there was not a lot to like or dislike about the dark, dapper right-back signed from Deportivo La Coruna for £2.6 million in January 2007. But as the 2008/09 campaign progressed, and the Reds' focus on regaining the League Championship for the first time in 19 years took on an ever-sharper focus, Anfield's connoisseurs, who know a thing or two about classy defenders, began to change their tune.

Just as the ultra-efficient but similarly unobtrusive Phil Neal captured hearts and earned respect in the 1970s and '80s, so Arbeloa's stock began to rise steadily as he settled into a winning team. Like his immediate predecessor, Steve Finnan, he did not push himself forward for recognition but, also like the unassuming Irishman, gradually the chirpily irrepressible Spaniard took on the aspect of an unsung hero.

Understandably in the early going of his Merseyside tenure, Arbeloa took time to adjust to the frenetic tempo of the Premiership, and the settling process was hardly aided by positional switches. Being able to step in as a central defender or at left-back provides the manager with enviable extra options, but such versatility is not always calculated to benefit the individual's integration into the team.

Even in the first half of 2008/09, Arbeloa's Anfield critics, while conceding that he was generally competent in his work at the back, cast envious eyes on the overlapping likes of Ashley Cole, Patrice Evra and Gael Clichy, coveting the attacking verve they offered to Chelsea, Manchester United and Arsenal, and finding their man wanting in comparison.

They felt he didn't get forward often enough, and that when he did his crossing was unreliable, but almost imperceptibly his influence began to grow, perhaps along with his confidence, and gradually his popularity rating started to improve.

In fairness Arbeloa, who as a youngster had been coached by Rafael Benitez at Real Madrid, made a more than tolerably auspicious start to his Liverpool career. Only a week after a tidy entrance as a substitute in a 2-1 defeat at Newcastle in February 2007, he was granted a start at left-back in the Nou Camp, where he was not found wanting when confronted by Lionel Messi and company, playing his part admirably in the rousing 2-1 triumph.

A few weeks on, his intelligent near-post dispatch facilitated Peter Crouch's first goal on his way to a hat-trick against Arsenal, then a week later he was on the mark himself in memorable fashion. Against Reading at the Madejski Stadium, he chased his own clearing header out of the Reds' box and executed a neat one-two interchange with Crouch, then strode on to bend a shot precisely inside goalkeeper Marcus Hahnemann's far post.

The Spaniard started 2007/08 at left-back in preference to John Arne Riise, then unseated Finnan on the right and thereafter vied for supremacy with the former Fulham man as the season wore on.

That summer Finnan departed and by the time the nights closed in Arbeloa was appearing ever more consistent. His marking was intelligent, his tackling brisk and usually well-timed, and his excursions as an accessory attacker were becoming increasingly incisive, his growing self-belief illustrated aptly by the exquisite 15-yarder he curled into the West Bromwich Albion net in November.

Admittedly there were a couple of palsied moments in the spring of 2009: the dithering which led to one of Andrey Arshavin's quartet of Anfield strikes, and a marking lapse at West Bromwich which earned a sharp rebuke from the indefatigable Jamie Carragher.

Fuelled by these, rumours persisted that Benitez would seek a new right-back during the summer, and sure enough Portsmouth's Glen Johnson was recruited for £18 million in June. After that it was always unlikely that the Spaniard would stay and fight for his place rather than return to his homeland to take up a challenge with the world's most glamorous club.

Duly a £3.5 million fee took him back to the Bernabeu, where he could be expected to prove himself once again as a solid citizen of the type needed by every successful team.

ALVARO ARBELOA COCA
BORN   Salamanca, Spain, 17 January 1983.
HONOURS   5 Spain caps (08-).
OTHER CLUBS   Real Madrid 04/05 (2, 0), Real Castilla 05/06 (34, 0), Deportivo La Coruna 06/07 (21, 0), Real Madrid 09/10-, all Spain.

GAMES   93 (5)
GOALS   2

DANIEL AGGER

2005/06 →

Rafael Benitez was never a man given to rash predictions, but when he clinched the £5.8 million signing of Daniel Agger from Brondby in January 2006, the customarily understated Liverpool manager observed that the 21-year-old Dane might become the best centre-half in England for the next ten years.

Yet with approximately a third of that span behind him, Agger was a study in frustration, unable to hold down a first-team berth, plagued by serial injuries, embroiled in a tortuous contract saga and linked with a move to various eminent Italian and Spanish clubs.

The fact was that although unquestionably he was the Reds' most cultured and naturally gifted central stopper, he did not project the indomitable, ruthless certainty exhibited in the work of Jamie Carragher, Martin Skrtel or Sami Hyypia, and his Anfield prospects suffered accordingly.

For those who had not monitored Agger's early career, Benitez's extravagant prophecy had veered uncomfortably close to the reckless and unnecessary offering of a hostage to fortune, but the shrewd Spaniard had plenty of firm evidence on which to base his optimism.

While seeking a long-term replacement for the ageing, though not yet superannuated Hyypia, Liverpool's scouts had placed Agger under prolonged and microscopic scrutiny before concluding that here was excellence in the making.

Certainly anyone who witnessed the rookie international's calm command when confronted by England's formidable strike partnership of Michael Owen and Wayne Rooney in August 2005 could have little doubt of his quality as he played an integral role in his country's 4-1 victory.

That night in Copenhagen there appeared to be no discernible weakness in the Agger game. Strong, athletic and radiating confidence, he read the action intelligently, his distribution was unusually imaginative and ambitious for a big defender, and he carried the ball forward with a majestic assurance which awoke echoes of a young Alan Hansen.

Consumed with the hunger to succeed, he is fiercely competitive on the field – contrasting vividly with his modest demeanour at the press conference which welcomed him to Anfield – and in earlier years that aggressive streak had landed him in trouble, earning a succession of red cards.

But after leaving his home-town club, Rosenhoj BK, for the powerful Brondby in 2004, Agger matured rapidly, understanding that he was no longer playing for fun while contemplating a career in business, and adopting an impeccably professional approach.

His progress from Rosenhoj to the Reds encompassed a mere 34 outings for Brondby, an 18-month magic-carpet ride which might have left many a callow hopeful in a spin, but the lanky, left-sided Agger appeared to possess unshakeable self-belief.

True, there were signs of nerves on his Liverpool debut at home to Birmingham City in February 2006, when he was given a searching examination by Chris Sutton and Emile Heskey, but although there were a couple of slips in concentration he also showcased his skill, pace, composure and positional instinct.

At that point, maybe he wasn't quite ready for the Premiership battle zone, but it should be remembered that he was ring-rusty on his arrival on Merseyside, having been injured for several months before completing his transfer.

Agger started the following campaign by scoring one of Liverpool's goals of the season, striding forward magisterially to net with a searing 25-yard bender at home to West Ham, then throughout the remainder of that term he established a richly promising partnership with Carragher.

At this point he was not quite the polished gem, as evidenced in the Champions League semi-final first leg at Stamford Bridge in April when he was outmuscled and outpaced as Didier Drogba set up the winning goal for Joe Cole. A week later at Anfield, however, he demonstrated there was nothing wrong with either his spirit or his quality when he swept home a Steven Gerrard free-kick from 16 yards to level the tie.

Though Pippo Inzaghi proved a taxing handful in the final defeat by AC Milan, Agger began 2007/08 with assurance, only for his gathering momentum to be mangled by a potentially career-shattering metatarsal break in Porto in September.

He was out of the side for nearly a year, and on his return in August 2008 he was confronted by a high-quality competitor for his place in the form of the flinty Skrtel. Though Agger looked smoother than ever with the ball at his feet, witness a sensational run to set up a goal for Dirk Kuyt against Wigan at Anfield in October, he seemed more tentative in his defensive tasks, both in the air and on the deck, and he couldn't quite capitalise when Skrtel's absence through injury offered him a chance to regain lost ground.

Duly the Slovak reclaimed the berth and Agger's future became open to question. Clinging to the ancient adage that class is permanent, though, most Anfield regulars remained sanguine that the talented Dane could yet forge a lasting niche with the Reds, and his signature on a new long-term contract in spring 2009 gave substance to that view.

DANIEL MUNTHE AGGER

BORN	Hvidovre, Denmark, 12 December 1984.	GAMES	71 (7)
HONOURS	26 Denmark caps (05-).	GOALS	6
OTHER CLUBS	Rosenhoj; Brondby 04/05-05/06 (34, 5), both Denmark.		

JAVIER MASCHERANO

2006/07 →

Some footballers, globally idolised individuals such as Fernando Torres and Steven Gerrard, are born to be heroes. They operate on a grand scale, bestriding the world's great arenas like sleek young supermen, their talent blazing unquenchably as they infuse their comrades with inspiration and belief. When they win, they are engulfed in clouds of glory, and understandably so. But there is another type of contributor in any successful team. He is the unobtrusive labourer, the skivvy who does the dirty work to build the platform on which the golden ones parade their dazzling wares – and such a man is Javier Mascherano.

In the view of this humble onlooker, the sheer intensity of the spiky little Argentinian midfielder as he scuttles like some miniature tank in front of Liverpool's back-line is a colossal factor in the Reds' invigorating progress towards attaining their heart's desire, namely regaining the League title after the excruciating hiatus of 20 years.

Mascherano wears his remorselessly competitive heart on his sleeve as he breaks up attack after attack, pressing and tackling with inextinguishable energy and bite, swooping venomously on any opponents unwise enough to dwell on the ball in his vicinity, invariably dispossessing them with the implacable will of a particularly mean and single-minded bailiff.

Admittedly his passing doesn't match the vision and accuracy of, say, Xabi Alonso's, at least not on a consistent basis. Indeed, he endures spells when it is downright haphazard, though when he is on his game, which is most of the time, the scope of his distribution is hardly negligible. And even when the Mascherano radar is out of kilter, and dispatches go infuriatingly astray, his innate positional sense and undying watchfulness make him a crucial presence, ever ready to succour a colleague on the ball.

Above all else, Javier Mascherano has proven himself a winner. He has helped to lift League titles with River Plate in his homeland and with Corinthians in Brazil; he is Argentina's first ever Olympic double gold-medallist in any sport, triumphing in Athens in 2004 and Beijing in 2008, and although his country perished on penalties at the quarter-final stage of the 2006 World Cup, unquestionably he was one of the tournament's brightest stars.

How inappropriate, then, that such a thoroughbred should enter English football encumbered by murky, confusing and controversial contract arrangements, which involved his commercial rights being owned by an investment group rather than a club. Along with fellow Argentine Carlos Tevez, he joined West Ham United in August 2006, but did not adapt to life at Upton Park, where he was offered only a handful of senior outings and felt distinctly miserable.

This sorry plight of a 22-year-old world-class performer prompted Rafa Benitez to knock on the door of the midfielder's Docklands home unannounced, offering an escape route which Mascherano accepted with alacrity, agreeing to join Liverpool, initially on loan, in January 2007.

At Anfield, made to feel welcome by a dressing-room packed with Spanish-speakers, and utilised intelligently by a manager who believed in him, the wiry newcomer flourished almost immediately, a stark contrast with his east London experience. Attuning himself instinctively to the Reds' style, he accepted major responsibility from the outset, quickly establishing superiority over Momo Sissoko and ousting the Mali international for the closing stages of the Champions League campaign.

Mascherano proved immensely influential in both legs of the semi-final victory over Chelsea, and he was quietly but firmly magnificent against AC Milan in Athens, virtually neutralising the quicksilver wiles of Kaka, simply by never allowing the Brazilian play-maker the space to justify his billing as the best footballer on the planet.

In 2007/08 Mascherano consolidated his Anfield niche, emerging as a fans' favourite in the process, and in February Liverpool made his transfer permanent by writing a cheque for £18.6 million to the businessmen in control of his destiny. In March he celebrated with his first goal, a fulminating 25-yard drive at home to Reading, but a week later garnered a black mark for being sent off at Old Trafford, where he lost the plot in absurd fashion, ranting pointlessly at the referee and initially refusing to leave the pitch.

Perhaps a tad debilitated by his summer heroics in China, he struck a vein of uncharacteristically flaky form in the subsequent autumn, but he recovered quickly enough to become a moving force as the Reds bore down on the League crown in the spring.

Mascherano's status was underlined when new Argentina coach Diego Maradona selected him to captain his country. At first the diminutive enforcer, a shy fellow away from the game, was reluctant to assume such a high-profile position, but Maradona convinced him, saying: 'He is a monster of a player. Argentina is Mascherano and ten others.' Rafa Benitez might not put it quite so emphatically, but the enormous value of Liverpool's little big man to the Anfield cause is not in doubt.

Worryingly for the Liverpool manager's piece of mind, it was obvious in the Nou Camp, too, with Barcelona's interest in Mascherano becoming evident in the summer of 2009.

JAVIER ALEJANDRO MASCHERANO

BORN	San Lorenzo, Argentina, 8 June 1984.		
HONOURS	48 Argentina caps (03-).	GAMES	83 (3)
OTHER CLUBS	River Plate, Argentina, 03-05 (46, 0); Corinthians, Brazil, 05 (7, 0); West Ham United 06/07 (5, 0).	GOALS	1

YOSSI BENAYOUN

2007/08 →

Yossi Benayoun is a lovely footballer, a delight to the sporting senses as he shimmies ingeniously through a seemingly impenetrable thicket of defenders before dispatching one of his waspish shots towards goal. But how long will the angular Israeli be content to remain a relative minnow in the Anfield pond, instead of moving on to become a veritable monster in a more modest pool?

Indisputably Benayoun is a major player, but on Merseyside he appears to be faced with an insoluble difficulty. His favoured positions, and ones which he might argue his handsome ability merits, are in central midfield or in the slot slightly behind the main striker.

At most clubs this would pose no problem, but Liverpool have been blessed with a cornucopia of talents in those key areas, so almost invariably Benayoun has been pushed to the wing, usually the right, occasionally the left; once or twice he has even put in stints on both flanks in the same match.

Often enough he has dazzled when raiding from a wide berth despite an apparently irresistible tendency to drift inside, which has resulted in some sensational goals but which has been equally as likely to cause unhelpful congestion in the middle of the pitch.

But even that is not the extent of the Benayoun dilemma. The fact is that, with the Reds, he has been by no means guaranteed a start in any role. In 2008/09, for instance, he began only 26 of their 55 matches in all competitions. For a fellow endowed so lavishly with footballing talent, clearly that is not enough.

Yossi's quality was recognised at an early age by Ajax of Amsterdam, for whom he signed as a 15-year-old. But he couldn't settle in the Netherlands, returning quickly to his homeland where his fledgling career picked up rapid momentum as he helped Maccabi Haifa to two domestic championships. There followed service with Santander and West Ham, with whom the Israeli international, certainly a man who knows his own worth, suffered irreconcilable differences, which were concluded by his £5 million transfer to Liverpool in July 2007.

About Benayoun's ability to torment opponents with his enchanting range of dummies, swerves and flicks there was never the slightest doubt, but he appeared a tad lightweight in his early outings for the Reds and, right from the off, he failed to command a regular place.

Reportedly he was both displeased and surprised by this development, and soon there were murmurs of discontent from the Benayoun camp, even rumours of an early Anfield exit. This irritated many fans, though they could hardly be other than impressed by some of his sumptuous first-term contributions: the sinuous wriggle past two defenders capped by a scorching cross-shot into the roof of Reading's net in the League Cup; the audacious turn, outrageous feint and threaded ten-yard finish at Wigan; the hat-trick and glorious all-round display in the 8-0 Anfield obliteration of Besiktas; and the typical swaying run to send in Fernando Torres to score at Chelsea in the Champions League semi-final.

The 2008/09 campaign brought similar frustrations for Benayoun, who intimated in the autumn that he might consider leaving if he continued to be consigned so frequently to the substitutes' bench, perhaps reflecting that as a right-flank option he was immeasurably more creative than either Dirk Kuyt or Ryan Babel.

Happily for Liverpool, this nagging discontent did not preclude further flashes of brilliance, notably precise narrow-angle finishes at Wigan and Blackburn, and as the season progressed Benayoun became increasingly influential, especially during Gerrard's absences through injury. Indeed, his customary invention, enhanced by a commendable passion which seemed ever more evident, had erstwhile critics warming to him at last.

In February he left the Bernabeu a hero thanks to his late headed winner against Real Madrid; he emphasised his worth yet further by netting in stoppage time to claim all three points at Fulham as the title race hotted up in April, then he struck twice to salvage a defiant point when the Andrey Arshavin wonder-show blew into town later that month.

But still there was the unchanging reality that the scope of his game was potentially far greater than he had the opportunity to express on a consistent basis with Liverpool. If his need to be the fulcrum of an attack rather than an optional extra could not be suppressed, if the practically guaranteed annual quest for silverware with the Reds was not enough to satisfy his ambition, then the likelihood appeared to be that eventually Yossi Benayoun would seek his fulfilment elsewhere. That was an impression that not even a contract extension, signed in July 2009 and ostensibly guaranteeing his presence until 2013, could wholly dispel.

YOSEF SHAI BENAYOUN
BORN   Dimona, Israel, 5 May 1980.
HONOURS   72 Israel caps (98-).
OTHER CLUBS   Hapoel Be'er Sheva 97/8 (25, 15), Maccabi Haifa 98/9-01/02 (130, 55), both Israel; Racing Santander, Spain, 02/03-04/05 (101, 21); West Ham United 05/06-06/07 (63, 8).

GAMES   52 (37)
GOALS   20

RYAN BABEL

· ·

2 0 0 7 / 0 8 →

Ever since Ryan Babel arrived at Anfield from Ajax as an extravagantly lauded 20-year-old in July 2007, Liverpool fans have been told endlessly of his vast potential. But come the spring of 2009, most of them had run out of patience. Priced at £11.5 million and supposedly sprinkled liberally with stardust, Babel had yet truly to convince. What his would-be admirers had witnessed was a tantalising enigma, a mercurial performer who had glittered and faded again and again, revealing only glimpses of the top quality they longed to applaud.

As to the presence of exceptional ability, there can be no reasonable doubt. The Dutchman, who can operate on either flank or in his preferred position of support striker, is a scything, high-velocity runner who packs an explosive shot, and in theory he should be able to terrorise any defence. But there is a troubling question to which he has never quite managed to supply a satisfactory answer during his Anfield sojourn. Has he the necessary fire in his belly?

Maybe it's natural and wholly misleading, but much of the time there is about Babel a languid look which suggests he is not wholly engaged in the task before him. True, not everyone wears their heart on their sleeve, and that is fine as long as a footballer is producing the goods. But the people who pay hard cash to watch him week after week need a modicum of reassurance that, at the every least, they are being offered spirit and desire, a certain passion that affords some degree of redemption even when form and confidence are at a low ebb.

Prior to his Liverpool move, Babel's career trajectory had been steep, as he made his senior entrance for Ajax at 17, then for Holland at 18, netting on his international debut. That renowned admirer of youthful football talent, Arsène Wenger, placed him under the microscope and there was talk of a switch to Arsenal in the January 2007 transfer window, but the Gunners' boss withdrew, maybe not quite convinced that the rookie justified the hefty price tag.

Not unnaturally, perhaps, Ajax coach Marco van Basten begged to differ, reckoning that Babel's possibilities were boundless, an opinion evidently shared by Rafael Benitez when he stepped in during the following summer. The newcomer was tall and slender, with a hint of Bambi legs, but clearly he was built for speed and the hope was that the Reds had acquired their most potent wing threat in years, a player who would offer a different attacking dimension.

Early impressions were largely positive. Indeed, his first goal, plundered during the 6-0 demolition of Derby County at Anfield on the first day of September, was a classic. Having taking possession on the edge of the box, he feinted to shoot with his left foot, sending two defenders flailing helplessly in the wrong direction, then duped goalkeeper Steve Bywater with a venomous right-foot placement just inside a post.

As the season wore on, with his inconsistency deemed understandable in a youngster adjusting to life in a foreign country, Babel offered further lively contributions. He scored with a cute backheeled flick as Besiktas were put to the sword to the tune of 8-0 at Anfield, there was a sweet exchange of passes with Steven Gerrard prior to netting at Newcastle, he earned a penalty and sealed victory with a late goal against Arsenal in the Champions League quarter-final and he netted with a sudden 30-yard screamer, admittedly only a consolation, as the Reds were ousted by Chelsea in the last four.

But promise can be maintained only for so long before it is backed up by solid regular achievement, and although he stabbed the goal that secured home triumph over Manchester United in September 2008, Babel's was an indeterminate presence as the term progressed and he was granted only six Premiership starts. Perhaps he was not helped by being utilised mainly on the left flank, which meant that often he had to check back on to his favoured right side, thus disrupting the momentum of attacks. However, he was hardly on fire when given a chance on the right either, and when employed as supplementary striker at Portsmouth, he could only wander ineffectually.

Babel admitted that the manager had urged him to improve on his defensive contribution, but was aggrieved that after he had worked hard on that aspect of his game, he was still selected only rarely. Too often he had looked potentially – that word again! – dangerous but the Dutchman had never truly imposed himself on a contest, had never shaped it or bent it to his will.

It might be seen as mitigation that he has scored more goals as a Liverpool substitute than anyone except David Fairclough, but clearly that does not justify his erstwhile exalted reputation. In 2009/10, during which he will celebrate his 23rd birthday, Ryan Babel can no longer afford to be one for the future. It is time to deliver.

RYAN MIGUEL GUNO BABEL

BORN Amsterdam, Holland, 19 December 1986.
HONOURS 31 Holland caps (05-).
OTHER CLUBS Ajax, Holland, 04/05-06/07 (73, 14).

GAMES **42 (49)**
GOALS **14**

FERNANDO TORRES

2007/08 →

Fernando Torres is the man who has catapulted Liverpool into a different dimension. It's not just the pace, the power and the precision that produces goal after goal, no matter how imposing the opposition. Most important of all is the confidence he brings to the rest of a team which had so long been desperate for a marksman to convert an acceptable percentage of the countless scoring chances they created. Now, with the prolific young Spaniard as their spearhead, banished is the ineffable frustration that overtook them so routinely as precious points drained away in contests they had dominated. At last the Reds know that no game is beyond them while El Nino strides the turf, and from that sublime certainty flows priceless belief.

Torres is a beautiful footballer, and we are not talking here about the fresh-faced good looks, the golden locks and the lithe yet deceptively resilient frame. He appears to glide over the grass with an ungovernable freedom which intimidates the most vaunted of foes.

Consider what he did to two of the most celebrated defenders on the planet in the space of four days in the spring of 2009. When Real Madrid were the visitors to Anfield, his sumptuous touch and quicksilver turn took him past Fabio Cannavaro in the blink of an eye, leaving the revered Italian stopper dithering, as one scribe put it so deliciously, like a pensioner on a pelican crossing when the lights have changed.

On that occasion his shot was saved, but there was no such reprieve for the 'monster' at the heart of the Manchester United rearguard, Nemanja Vidic, at Old Trafford. The brawny Serbian hesitated under Martin Skrtel's ballooning punt out of defence, and in a flash he was toast. Torres first robbed him, then outpaced him, before slipping the ball beyond Edwin van der Sar with characteristically nerveless composure.

From the moment of Vidic's fleeting indecision, there was a profound inevitability about the outcome. The implacable Spaniard might have been an executioner, and with United's head on the block, and maybe even a shift in the balance of Premiership sovereignty in the offing, there was simply no way he was going to miss.

So is Torres truly a paragon? Are there really no weaknesses in his make-up, either on or off the pitch? Well, if there are, they have not been discerned in this quarter. Among his peers there is no one quicker, or cuter with his off-the-ball darts; no one with a slicker facility for switching the position of the ball in the last split-second before hitting it; no one with a sweeter, more accurate shot; in aerial combat he is a force both courageous and deft. He is willowy but as tough as whipcord, he is no bruiser but is ready to fight, he is preternaturally calm in the moments that matter, and has always been mature for his age, so much so that he was handed the captaincy of Atletico Madrid while still in his teens. And then there is his passion for the Reds, his regard for the fans and his adoptive city, all of which seem engagingly genuine.

The springtime totting up at the end of his first campaign on Merseyside revealed that Torres had made 41 starts and scored 33 goals in major competition, then in the summer he took himself off to Austria where he starred for Spain in the European Championships, contributing Spain's winner in the final with a delectable chip that would not have disgraced the boot of Dalglish.

After all that, unsurprisingly, there was a hint of fatigue at the outset of 2008/09, then just as he was picking up speed with a pair of predatory two-goal displays at Everton and Manchester City in the autumn, he was struck down with an ominous succession of hamstring maladies. Now fears surfaced that the long-awaited shooting star might be brought down to earth by a physical flaw, but he was handled wisely by his manager, who refused to rush him back ahead of schedule, and when he did return in midwinter he was soon back to his scintillating best, particularly when operating in front-line tandem with Steven Gerrard.

The catalogue of Torres' finest goals is wondrous to behold, and although lack of space precludes any comprehensive list, mention must be made of at least a handful. He announced himself on his Anfield debut in August 2007 with a pearler against Chelsea, racing down the left flank to accept a perfectly weighted through-ball from Gerrard before skimming past Tal Ben Haim and delivering a pinpoint right-foot caress into the far corner of Peter Cech's net.

At home to Arsenal in the Champions League quarter-final in April he controlled a high ball, swivelled away from a mesmerised Philippe Senderos and crashed in a fizzing cross-shot from 15 yards. He had made space where there had seemed to be none, the goal a product of a fabulous fusion of skill, power and icy self-possession, the very ingredients which facilitated yet another sublime strike, the audacious volley against Blackburn at Anfield in April 2009.

Finally, late in an otherwise unremarkable display at Sunderland the previous August, he found himself suddenly with room to turn and unleashed an unstoppable 25-yard tracer-bullet which won the game out of nothing. That was a definitive demonstration of the Spanish talisman representing the difference between a team that could push for the title, and one likely to subside tamely as the race hotted up.

When Benitez signed Fernando Torres for £26.5 million from Atletico in July 2007 he shattered the Liverpool transfer record. But by paying top money he got top, top quality . . . and an Anfield hero for the ages.

FERNANDO JOSE TORRES SANZ

BORN	Madrid, Spain, 20 March 1984.	
HONOURS	61 Spain caps (03-).	
OTHER CLUBS	Atletico Madrid, Spain, 01/02-06/07 (214, 82).	

GAMES **73 (11)**
GOALS **50**

MARTIN SKRTEL

· ·

2007/08 →

Martin Skrtel is a beast of a centre-half. Glowering, shaven-headed, tattooed and exceedingly large, he offers a fearsomely intimidating prospect to opposition strikers charged with the unenviable task of getting past him to score goals against Liverpool.

Indeed, with all due respect to the formidable Sami Hyypia, equally mountainous and resolute but somehow less menacing of mien, Skrtel is arguably the Reds' most physically imposing stopper since the pomp of Ron Yeats and Tommy Smith.

Okay, Larry Lloyd was a big lad, too, and certainly he knew how to dish out the punishment, but there is something in the Slovakian's steely glare that is downright chilling. Perhaps it stems from his ferocious determination, or desperation as he has referred to it himself, to escape from the grim coal-mining village in his homeland where he grew up.

To put it politely, Skrtel is the type of old-fashioned operator appreciated by fans who warm to back-four bulwarks of the rough-edged variety, into which category he could be placed instantly when Liverpool signed the 24-year-old from the Russian champions, Zenit St Petersburg, in the January 2008 transfer window.

His £6.5 million capture, an Anfield record for a defender, was rendered crucial by a long-term injury to Daniel Agger, the cultured Dane whose smooth style contrasted so vividly with that of the newcomer.

However, no one should run away with the notion that Skrtel, who gave up the chance of an ice-hockey career to major in football, is a mere clogger. In fact, though he has plenty to learn – and was doing so rapidly and avidly, with Jamie Carragher as his principal instructor, during his first full season as a Red – Skrtel is comfortable with the ball at his feet, is capable of passing it accurately and reads the game with considerable acumen.

Meanwhile there are his more obvious assets to applaud. He is prodigiously strong and unfailingly brave, ready in Carragher-like manner to throw his body in the way of anything that threatens the Liverpool goal; he is immensely pacy, invariably closing on the ball like a speeding mantrap; he possesses exceptional ability in the air; and when he yields to an occasional urge to storm forward into enemy territory, he is capable of unloosing a savage shot.

As for his faults, they are diminishing with experience. Initially he tended to commit himself to challenges too early, diving in clumsily when it would have been preferable to have remained on his feet, jockeying his opponent away from the area of maximum danger.

Certainly Skrtel appeared crude when making his first Anfield start, being embarrassed on a couple of occasions in the FA Cup encounter with Havant and Waterlooville. Not unnaturally, anxious Kopites shuddered, fearing that if the 6ft 4in Slovakian could look so shaky against gallant but hardly demanding non-League opposition, then calamity must surely ensue when he was exposed to top-class international centre-forwards.

Not so. Within a couple of weeks he had shone against Chelsea's Didier Drogba, as hard and fast an opponent as could be imagined, and by season's end he had excelled, too, when confronted by Zlatan Ibrahimovic of Internazionale and Arsenal's Emmanuel Adebayor. By then, no less respected a judge than Kenny Dalglish was hailing the rugged stopper as the best young defender in Europe, and barely a voice was raised in disagreement.

Thus Skrtel, who had already endeared himself to the Liverpool faithful by spurning an offer from Goodison Park to enlist at Anfield, was riding a heady wave of popularity in the early weeks of 2008/09 as he continued to show encouraging signs of forming a profitable partnership with his mentor Carragher.

But then his burgeoning momentum was cruelly shattered when he severely damaged knee ligaments at Manchester City, the shock of the injury so sharp that medics administered oxygen on the pitch.

This was a crushing blow, not least because it offered a heaven-sent opening to his direct rival for a first-team berth, the worthy Agger, whom he had been keeping out of the side. With such a talented performer *in situ*, lesser men might have wilted, but once again Skrtel summoned that same grit which had eradicated the possibility of a life spent labouring in a Slovakian pit.

He battled back to fitness ahead of schedule and in early January he was restored to the team, wasting no time in regaining impressive form as Liverpool tilted at both Champions League and Premiership crowns. Understandably for a craftsman still learning his trade, he made the occasional mistake, notably allowing Chelsea's Branislav Ivanovic to invade his space and nod a goal direct from a corner in the Anfield leg of the European quarter-final, although blaming Martin for that might be a tad harsh, with many observers making Rafael Benitez's zonal marking system the villain of the piece.

Far more significant in the long term, Skrtel looked certain to become an Anfield stalwart, perhaps even eventually inheriting the mantle of the redoubtable Carragher. Emphatically, the Slovakian coal industry's loss had been Liverpool's colossal gain.

	MARTIN SKRTEL		
BORN	Handlova, Slovakia, 15 December 1984.		
HONOURS	32 Slovakia caps (04-).		
OTHER CLUBS	AS Trencin, Slovakia, 01/02-03/04 (45, 8); Zenit St Petersburg, Russia, 04/05-07/08 (74, 3).	GAMES	48 (2)
		GOALS	0

ALBERT RIERA

2008/09 →

Albert Riera enjoyed one priceless advantage when he arrived from Espanyol for £8 million in August 2008 – he was greeted by minimal expectations.

Thanks to the tall Spanish left-winger spending the second half of 2005/06 on loan in a distinctly lacklustre Manchester City side, and then not signing a permanent deal, widespread perceptions of him, certainly among most Liverpool fans, were hardly of the complimentary variety.

In truth, that was doing Rieira a grave injustice. He had proved a popular figure during his Eastlands stint, and it's fair to suggest that if the majority of his City team-mates had equalled his liveliness then the Mancunians would not have endured such an uninspiring campaign.

Still, the fact was that Kopites were markedly underwhelmed by his arrival, which removed the pressure which often weighs heavily on the shoulders of newcomers at top clubs. Just ask Robbie Keane.

Happily for the Reds, Rafael Benitez had done his homework on Rieira rather more thoroughly than the doubters in the stands. Having pointed out the benefits of his countryman already being attuned to the unique rigours of the English game, the manager drew attention to Albert's myriad footballing attributes.

He was, said Benitez as he confirmed the acquisition just before the transfer window expired, strong, eager to work hard, a lovely crosser, capable of beating his markers by both speed and trickery, and excellent in the air, which would help immensely in defensive situations. In addition, he wanted to play for Liverpool, having favoured a move to Anfield even though a reportedly higher offer had emanated from Goodison Park.

It sounded like a terrific package, an impression borne out by his debut in September at home to Manchester United. On that sunny Saturday lunchtime, as Liverpool gave credence to the notion of harbouring realistic title ambitions by coming from behind to beat the reigning champions, Riera made a gratifyingly promising start, harassing Wes Brown to distraction and meshing effectively both with his fellow attackers and left-back Fabio Aurelio.

Over subsequent weeks it seemed that Liverpool just might have unearthed a consistently menacing left winger for the first time since John Barnes withdrew to central midfield. Riera was a waft of invigorating air in that clearly he relished powering his way to the byline and dispatching a centre without dallying. It was a bonus that all that welcome drive was married to a capacity for subtle touches, delightful body-swerves, the occasional extravagant backheel. Above all, he brought much-needed balance to the side and gradually he began to emerge as an unlikely symbol of Benitez's more adventurous approach in 2008/09.

At Stamford Bridge in October, Riera was especially outstanding as another key victory was claimed, not only putting Chelsea's defensive right flank under sustained pressure, but also grafting to limit the menace of the dangerous overlapper Jose Boswinga.

There were goals to applaud, too, not exactly in profusion, but when the Spanish international did find the net it tended to be on the grand scale. For instance, there was the awesome arrow unleashed from 30 yards following a Lucas Leiva lay-off against PSV in Eindhoven in December, and the savage cross-shot which ripped into the Preston North End net after he doubled back and dashed wide of a disoriented marker during the FA Cup clash at Deepdale in January.

There followed a somewhat quieter spell in the spring, but the feeling was that Albert Riera remained a practical left-flank option, a pleasingly down-to-earth performer with plenty still to offer the Reds over the next few seasons. The potential of, say, Ryan Babel might be immeasurably richer, but with the amiable Spaniard, you get what you see, a reassuring proposition for any manager.

ALBERTO RIERA

BORN   Mallorca, Spain, 15 April 1982.
HONOURS   8 Spain caps (07-).
OTHER CLUBS   Real Mallorca, Spain, 00/01-02/03 (44, 6); Bordeaux, France, 03/04-04/05 (53, 4); Espanyol, Spain, 05/06-07/08 (71, 8); Manchester City on loan 05/06 (15, 1).

GAMES   **33 (7)**
GOALS   5

PHILIPP DEGEN

2008/09 →

When Rafael Benitez recruited Philipp Degen on a free transfer from Borussia Dortmund in the summer of 2008, he was acquiring a fellow who knew a thing or two about winning championships. The Swiss international full-back had helped Basel to lift three League titles, but hopes that he might replicate such glories in his debut term with Liverpool were still-born.

All too soon Degen, a classy operator of whom so much was expected, became Anfield's invisible man as he suffered an extraordinary sequence of injuries which limited him to only two senior starts.

Having missed much of the previous Bundesliga campaign with fitness problems, Degen began his Merseyside tenure with a knock in pre-season which ruled him out of contention for the Premiership's opening day.

Then, after showing up brightly in the early going of a League Cup encounter with Crewe in September, he broke two ribs in a collision with Sami Hyypia. Back again in November, he took the field against Spurs in the same competition before withdrawing with a metatarsal malady, then suffered a similar setback in January.

It was a shame for a skilful performer who might have offered a more adventurous attacking option to Alvaro Arbeloa. Only 26 at the outset of 2009/10, he still had time to make an Anfield impact, but it's unlikely that Benitez was holding his breath.

PHILIPP DEGEN
BORN Holstein, Switzerland, 15 February 1983.
HONOURS 30 Switzerland caps (05-).
OTHER CLUBS Basel, Switzerland, 01/02-04/05 (82, 4); Aarau, Switzerland, on loan 02/03 (16, 0); Borussia Dortmund, Germany, 05/06-07/08 (68, 1).

GAMES 2
GOALS 0

DAMIEN PLESSIS

2007/08 →

When Damien Plessis strode unexpectedly into the Liverpool first-team picture, the occasion and venue no less daunting than a key Premiership clash at Arsenal's Emirates Stadium in April 2008, the Reds' travelling fans were distinctly impressed by the cut of his jib.

Pitched into the midfield fray against the likes of the precocious Cesc Fabregas and the vastly experienced Gilberto, the 6ft 4in French under-21 international conducted himself with unhurried aplomb. Playing just in front of the back four, he controlled the ball with assurance, passed it with composure and his shrewd positioning did much to limit the Gunners' threat.

True, he lacked the pace and physical presence of, say, Momo Sissoko, a recently departed would-be rival for the holding role, but he was brave enough and far more polished than the Mali man. It mattered not that with his gangly frame he appeared a tad awkward, and it seemed clear that he was a prospect worth nurturing.

Since then Plessis, signed on a three-year deal from Lyons in August 2007, has been granted only a handful of senior outings, during which he has not quite replicated the impression made at the Emirates.

Still, he scored with a cushioned header from a Ryan Babel corner to reduce the Reds' arrears in a League Cup reverse at White Hart Lane in November 2008, and although his progress with the reserves has not been exceptional, it would be perplexing if a lad with so much natural talent did not come again.

DAMIEN PLESSIS
BORN Neuville-aux-Bois, France, 5 March 1988.
OTHER CLUBS Lyons, France.

GAMES 6
GOALS 1

EMILIANO INSUA

2006/07 →

With every respect for the increasingly consistent and productive Fabio Aurelio, and with a brief nod of acknowledgement that Andrea Dossena had yet to produce the best of himself ar Anfield, there was a theory gaining currency among Liverpool fans towards the end of 2008/09 that, in the long term, Emiliano Insua was the man to occupy the Reds' often troublesome left-back slot.

As is commonly the case in this era of recruiting rookie footballers from all corners of the globe, barely a soul on Merseyside had heard of the 18-year-old Argentinian when he commenced a loan period with the Reds from his home-town club, Boca Juniors, in January 2007.

But he settled so quickly, and performed with such class and industry for the reserves, that he was given his senior debut in a Premiership defeat at Portsmouth that April, then figured in another reverse at Fulham a week later.

In truth the newcomer looked a touch tentative in both outings, but his promise was such that in August his loan was upgraded to a full contract as part of an arrangement which took Gabriel Paletta to Buenos Aires.

Returning to the reserves to continue his football education, Insua showed exceptional form as Gary Ablett's team captured their own version of the Premiership crown in 2007/08, and such was his progress that he was promoted to the senior side for the last two games of the season.

Though still by no means the finished article, by now he had matured impressively, and duly he excelled in victories against Manchester City and Spurs. Quick and tenacious, he proved cool, resourceful and solid at the back and thrillingly adventurous going forward. His combination of pace and slickness on the ball made him a thoroughly modern full-back, and when he had eluded a marker he was capable of capitalising with a testing cross.

Insua displayed a capacity to do the simple things well, a prerequisite of any successful defender, but lifted himself into an altogether more exciting category by doing more difficult things brilliantly, such as executing inch-perfect passes while sprinting at high speed.

However, the advent of Dossena for 2008/09, added to the presence of Aurelio, appeared to limit his immediate opportunities, but with the Italian ill and the Brazilian injured he stepped up to deliver an outstanding performance in the 1-1 draw with Arsenal at the Emirates in December 2008.

Thereafter he continued to thrive, retaining his berth for four successive games, only for his gathering momentum to be interrupted by a call-up for the South American under-20 international championship in January.

Liverpool supporters who were not entirely enamoured of Aurelio, and the many more who thought even less of Dossena, were upset to lose him at such a crucial juncture in the title race.

For Insua, too, for all his genuine patriotic fervour, it must have been a frustrating situation, but he returned to make another half-dozen senior appearances before season's end, and was seen as the coming man as the Reds prepared for a massive Premier League push in 2009/10.

EMILIANO ADRIAN INSUA ZAPATA		GAMES	15 (3)
BORN	Buenos Aires, Argentina, 7 January 1989.	GOALS	0
OTHER CLUBS	Boca Juniors, Argentina.		

ROBBIE KEANE

2008/09

When Robbie Keane moved from Tottenham Hotspur to Liverpool for £20.3 million in the summer of 2008 he was in the pomp of a productive career which had seen him score goals – and plenty of them – for Wolves, Coventry, Leeds and Spurs. True, there were always sceptics who had shaken their heads in disbelief at that colossal fee, but even they could not have envisaged how rapidly the diminutive Dubliner's star would plummet after his arrival at Anfield.

For Keane it must have been the stuff of dreams to join the club he had idolised as a boy, but then to be summarily labelled as a flop and a misfit for his record of seven goals in six months as a Red would have been supremely difficult to bear. Even so, while some of his clumsiness in front of goal did verge on pantomime-horse proportions, there were also moments of sublime opportunism – most memorably a searing half-volley at Arsenal in December – which indicated that he might, after all, have had plenty to offer the Liverpool cause.

Thus when he returned to White Hart Lane in January 2009, with the Reds taking a loss reported widely as £8 million, possibly descending to £4 million with add-ons, it begged two questions. Was Robbie Keane given a fair crack of the whip on Merseyside? And if not, why not?

First it can be established that the Irishman, incidentally the top marksman in the Republic's history by a vast margin, was an impeccable professional who based his game on a prodigious work ethic which never flagged. At all times he bristled with desire to chase and to challenge for every ball, roaming all across the pitch in the process.

But his premier position had always been as support striker. At Tottenham he had been the perfect foil for Dimitar Berbatov; now the idea was that he should link in a similar fashion with Fernando Torres. However, injuries to the Spanish spearhead meant that, after early autumn, the pair started only two matches together. Instead Keane tended to be employed either as a lone front-runner or as a wide midfielder, and in neither role did he excel.

Thus by the time Torres was fit enough for a sustained run in the team, the newcomer had already created the impression of a performer slightly out of his depth, and Benitez clearly preferred Steven Gerrard in the key berth just off the front-man.

Despite the non-stop effort, there was a haunting uncertainty about so much of Keane's work. Too often he seemed like a bystander scurrying after shadows as the action raged around him, snatching desperately at fleeting opportunities to score, his characteristic exuberance draining away as he appeared to sense the increasing doubts of the fans.

Not surprisingly given his plight, frequently Keane was the sacrificial lamb hooked by his manager and he looked ever more demoralised at each new substitution, each killing outburst of sympathetic applause as he trudged towards the dugout.

It was all such a dismal contrast to the buoyant expectations he carried in the immediate aftermath of his arrival. Despite the doubts of some shrewd observers, Keane fired the imaginations of most Liverpool supporters far more than many expensive acquisitions of recent years. He was a known quantity, already hardened to the Premiership fray, and there was an impish eagerness about his demeanour which they found irresistible. It didn't half help, too, that he made no secret of his lifelong love of the club.

Bright displays in pre-season whetted appetites still more tantalisingly, and even when he made a disappointing impact as the serious competition got under way, generous allowances were made for his need to settle.

Roars of relief greeted his first goal, at home to PSV Eindhoven during his 11th senior appearance, and when he broke his League duck with a beautifully taken brace in the Anfield defeat of West Bromwich Albion in November, the assumption was that now the goals would begin to flow.

Six weeks later came that spectacularly drilled equaliser from the edge of the box after racing on to a long ball at the Emirates, and another two in the next match against Bolton at Anfield smoothed the hitherto corrugated brows of anxious Kopites.

But that was as good as it got. At Preston in the FA Cup in January, he was embarrassingly inaccurate, first falling over his own feet with the goal gaping, then shooting lamely when well placed. After that, for all his industry and unselfishness, the clock was ticking down loudly on Keane's Liverpool career.

In the next round he was not even on the bench for the visit of Everton, but even when Spurs made their move it seemed unlikely that Benitez would allow the second most expensive purchase in the club's history to depart unfulfilled after half a season. However, his thinking became a little more transparent when he hinted that the Irishman's purchase had not been his top personal priority, thus fuelling the widely-held theory that the player had become a victim of internecine strife about transfer policy.

Keane appeared baffled by his banishment, seemingly failing to grasp exactly why his dream had turned sour. A bizarre Anfield interlude had ended with unanswered questions hanging in the air.

ROBERT DAVID KEANE

BORN	Dublin, 8 July 1980.
HONOURS	88 Republic of Ireland caps (98-).
OTHER CLUBS	Wolverhampton Wanderers 97/8-99/00 (73, 24); Coventry City 99/00 (31, 12); Internazionale, Italy, 00/01 (6, 0); Leeds United 00/01-02/03 (46, 13); Tottenham Hotspur 02/03-07/08 (197, 80) and 08/09- (14, 5).

GAMES **23 (5)**

GOALS **7**

ANDREA DOSSENA

2008/09 →

Andrea Dossena was a man of mystery at Anfield for most of 2008/09, his debut campaign as a Red. Unfortunately, the main question being posed was far from complimentary, running along the lines of: 'How can such a ponderous, periodically inept, occasionally confused individual possibly be in contention to be Italy's first-choice left-back?'

Dossena, who might have joined Spurs in the January 2008 transfer window, was signed from Udinese during the following summer for £7 million, which made him the most expensive full-back in Liverpool's history to that point, and the first Italian to pull on the red shirt.

Early indications were not promising as he struggled to become accustomed to the unrelenting pace and generally frenetic nature of the English game. Dossena proved parlously vulnerable to both pace and trickery, either committing himself rashly and being left for dead or standing off too long, thus allowing the delivery of menacing crosses.

The initial alarm signals were triggered by the elusive Wilfried Dalmat of Standard Liege, who tormented the Italian in the first leg of the Champions League qualifier in August. That the game finished goalless was not down to Dossena, and while allowances were made for his need to settle, the omens were not propitious.

In fairness, the newcomer was not devoid of quality. He was hardy and unstinting in his effort, and possessed an attacking instinct which would have earned far more plaudits had the fans been confident of his defensive capabilities. Clearly Dossena relished an overlap, and when he found himself in a position to threaten the opposition goal he could deliver devilishly bending crosses in a manner reminiscent of Stig-Inge Bjornebye, who occupied the Reds' left-back slot during the mid-1990s.

But trying times were ahead as the newcomer fought what seemed increasingly likely to be a losing battle for his place with Fabio Aurelio. He looked tentative and nervous during his Merseyside derby debut at Goodison in September, he was troubled distressingly by Wigan's Antonio Valencia – who turned him inside out at Anfield in October before setting up a sensational goal for Amr Zaki – and he was embarrassed by both Aaron Lennon of Spurs and Marseille's Ben Arfa in November.

Worst of all, poor Dossena was figuratively undressed by Hull's Bernard Mendy in the 2-2 draw at Anfield shortly before Christmas. Rafa Benitez sought mitigation in the Italian's enterprise when going forward, a point which might have carried more weight had Mendy not appeared several times more effective when motoring in any direction.

Yet after appearing to recede to the fringes of the squad as young Emiliano Insua continued his promising emergence, Dossena achieved a startling springtime renaissance as a midfield substitute, contributing wonderful goals in vital matches against Real Madrid and Manchester United in the space of four days. After sweeping home emphatically to round off a flowing move against the stricken Spaniards at Anfield, he netted at Old Trafford with the sweetest of lobs to complete the comprehensive annihilation of the champions.

However, with Dossena third in the left-back pecking order behind Insua and Aurelio, his future as a Red was clouded with uncertainty as the 2009/10 campaign loomed.

ANDREA DOSSENA

BORN   Lodi, Italy, 11 September 1981.
HONOURS   7 Italy caps (07-).
OTHER CLUBS   Hellas Verona 01/02-04/05 (99, 3); Udinese 05/06-07/08 (63, 2); Treviso on loan 05/06 (21, 0); all Italy.

GAMES   **19 (7)**
GOALS   **2**

LUCAS LEIVA

2007/08 →

Rafa Benitez loves him, the majority of Liverpool fans don't rate him – that was one veteran Kopite's crude, simplistic, but really rather persuasive take on the situation of Lucas Leiva after the Brazilian international had spent two seasons in and out of the Liverpool team.

The extent of the manager's faith can be gauged by his employment of Lucas in no fewer than 70 games over the course of 2007/08 and 2008/09, a significant total even though the blond midfielder joined the action from the bench on 30 of those occasions.

Such irrefutable evidence of his status both perplexed and infuriated the legion of Anfield sceptics who maintained that the man voted the best player in the *Campeanato*, the Brazilian League, in 2006 had proved an uninspiring deputy for the likes of Xabi Alonso and Javier Mascherano.

Reportedly Liverpool beat Atletico Madrid and Internazionale of Milan in the race to sign Lucas for £6 million from Gremio in the summer of 2007, which seemed like a considerable coup, touted as he was as a dynamic box-to-box performer who could fill any midfield berth but who preferred to operate centrally.

But even making due allowance for a young South American's need to settle in England and assimilate a new culture while fulfilling his potential on the pitch, Lucas' early progress was not convincing. He appeared tentative, none too swift a mover and not even particularly accurate with his distribution, which was said to be one of his prime assets.

His role seemed indeterminate, neither acting as an anchor in front of the back four nor pushing forward to support the front men, and his tackling tended towards the awkward, often conceding free-kicks unnecessarily in dangerous locations. Occasionally there would be flashes of delightful skill and cool deliberation, offering an explanation, or at least a clue, concerning his exalted status in his homeland, but there was little to suggest the presence or the overall influence which might be expected of a top-quality midfield man.

Particularly galling to supporters were instances when Benitez preferred him to one of their favourites, such as Steven Gerrard, Alonso or Mascherano. For example, when Gerrard's passion was perceived by the manager to be excessive at Goodison Park in October 2007, Lucas was sent on in his place, and even though it was his shot which was palmed off the line by Phil Neville, thus earning the penalty that won the match, he accrued precious little public credit for that.

Indeed, it has often been the case that the Brazilian has being singled out as a convenient scapegoat even before he has kicked a ball, such as when he was selected ahead of Alonso at home to Internazionale in February 2008, and that is as unproductive as it is unjust.

Unable to curry favour by weight of his goals – the beautifully curled 20-yard equaliser against Havant and Waterlooville at Anfield in January 2008 was his sole strike of that campaign – Lucas needed to express himself more vividly, and there were some encouraging signs during his second term. Indeed, the sumptuous 40-yard through-ball which split the Newcastle rearguard to send in Gerrard at St James' Park in December 2008 would have done credit to Jan Molby.

But as 2009/10 dawned, Lucas Leiva was still engaged in a battle for acceptance. For him, a make-or-break campaign was surely in prospect.

LUCAS PEZZINI LEIVA

BORN	Dourados, Brazil, 9 January 1987.	GAMES	40 (30)
HONOURS	3 Brazil caps (07-).	GOALS	4
OTHER CLUBS	Gremio, Brazil, 05-07 (38, 5).		

NABIL EL ZHAR

2006/07 →

Sparky little French-born Moroccan international raider Nabil El Zhar proved a potent good-luck charm for the Reds in August 2008. In three consecutive matches he rose from the bench with Liverpool drawing or losing, and each time they won, seeing off Sunderland at the Stadium of Light, then Middlesbrough and Standard Liege at Anfield.

Constantly busy and capable of operating on either flank or through the middle, he exudes an irrepressible appetite for the action which can prove infectious, moving some supporters to compare him favourably, if acidly, with Ryan Babel. In truth El Zhar is yet to exhibit the natural talent of the Dutchman, and would benefit from a little more composure, even if his dash, directness and determination can clearly unsettle unwary defenders.

Whisper it softly, as he might be expected to despise the tag as much as David Fairclough did in his day, but he might be best employed as an impact player to be summoned from the dugout.

Signed by Rafael Benitez from St Etienne as a 19-year-old in August 2005, El Zhar waited until November 2006 for his senior entrance, as a substitute in the goalless home draw with Portsmouth, and contributed his first strike a year later in front of the Kop, a 25-yard swerver against Cardiff City in the League Cup.

In 2008/09 he made progress, along with 19 senior appearances, and was not expected to seek a move despite the Moroccan coach warning that he would jeopardise his international prospects by not playing more frequently at club level.

NABIL EL ZHAR
BORN   Ales, France, 27 August 1986.
HONOURS 8 Morocco caps (08-).
OTHER CLUBS Ales, Nimes, St Etienne, all France.

GAMES **4 (21)**
GOALS 1

DAVID NGOG

2008/09 →

He's tall, he's quick and he's French, so it was inevitable that someone would describe Liverpool's youthful striker David Ngog, imaginatively if supremely unhelpfully, as the new Thierry Henry.

Of course, he's nothing of the kind. In fact, he's a coltish, hard-working, engagingly eager-to-please hopeful who clearly has plenty to learn if he's going to make the Premiership grade, either with the Reds or at a slightly less rarefied level.

By the summer of 2008, when Rafael Benitez signed Ngog for £1.5 million from Paris St Germain, with whom the boy had been developing since the age of 12, he had scored goals for France at all junior grades, including under-21. Some sceptical observers, however, were more concerned with his senior club record of a single goal in 18 outings.

After being plunged into top-flight action for an hour at Aston Villa in August due to Fernando Torres' injury, Ngog made his full debut against Crewe at Anfield in the League Cup and made scant impact.

Subsequent brief run-outs confirmed the need of more experience, which began to be granted to him following the January sale, without replacement, of Robbie Keane. He scored in Eindhoven in December, looked horribly out of his depth when making his full Premiership entrance in February, but had improved markedly by the time Sunderland visited Anfield in March, celebrating with his first League strike.

Clearly it would be both unfair and unwise to attempt a definitive judgement on David Ngog at this stage of his career, but early indications are that he has a long road to travel if he is going to enjoy prolonged success in a Liverpool shirt.

DAVID NGOG
BORN   Gennevilliers, France, 1 April 1989.
OTHER CLUBS Paris St Germain, France, 06/07-07/08 (18, 1).

GAMES **5 (14)**
GOALS 3

DANIELE PADELLI

2006/07

Italy under-21 international Padelli was seen as a high-quality understudy to Pepe Reina when he was acquired on a half-season loan from Sampdoria in January 2007. His only senior outing was in the 2-2 home draw with Charlton in May, after which the Reds rejected the option of a permanent deal.

DANIELE PADELLI
BORN Lecco, Italy, 25 October 1985.
OTHER CLUBS Sampdoria 04/05-05/06 (0, 0); Pizzighettone on loan 05/06 (33, 0); Crotone on loan 06/07 (1, 0); Pisa on loan 07/08 (7, 0); Avellino on loan 08/08, all Italy.

GAMES	1
GOALS	0

STEPHEN DARBY

2008/09 →

The rookie right-back is a proven winner, having been part of the FA Youth Cup wins of 2006 and 2007, and the reserves' title triumph of 2007/08. He filled in efficiently for Alvaro Arbeloa when summoned from the bench in Eindhoven in November 2008, and is one to watch.

STEPHEN DARBY
BORN Liverpool, 6 October 1988.

GAMES	0 (2)
GOALS	0

JACK HOBBS

2007/08

After making his League entrance for Lincoln, aged 16, Hobbs joined Liverpool for £750,000 in August 2005. The young central defender was made skipper of the reserves and looked assured when offered senior opportunities. After earning a League One title gong while on loan at Leicester in 2008/09, he signed permanently for the Foxes.

JACK HOBBS
BORN Portsmouth, Hampshire, 18 August 1988.
OTHER CLUBS Lincoln City 04/05 (1, 0); Scunthorpe United on loan 07/08 (9, 1); Leicester City on loan 08/09 (44, 1).

GAMES	3 (2)
GOALS	0

MARTIN KELLY

2008/09 →

Kelly is a tall, elegant central defender whose early progress was hampered by back problems. However, he was integral to the reserves' clinching of their championship in 2007/08, and the well-built, level-headed Lancastrian is viewed as genuine first-team material at Anfield.

MARTIN KELLY
BORN Bolton, Lancashire, 27 April 1990.
OTHER CLUBS Huddersfield Town on loan 08/09 (7, 1).

GAMES	0 (1)
GOALS	0

DIEGO CAVALIERI

2008/09 →

Liverpool paid £3.5 million for Palmeiras' second-string 'keeper in summer 2008, since when he has progressed apace. At Preston in January he read the play shrewdly, was confident at claiming crosses and distributed the ball accurately. Cavalieri is the most promising of Reina's understudies to date.

DIEGO CAVALIERI
BORN Sao Paulo, Brazil, 1 December 1982.
OTHER CLUBS Palmeiras, Brazil.

GAMES	4
GOALS	0

JAY SPEARING

2008/09 →

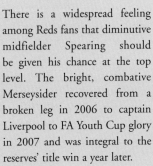

There is a widespread feeling among Reds fans that diminutive midfielder Spearing should be given his chance at the top level. The bright, combative Merseysider recovered from a broken leg in 2006 to captain Liverpool to FA Youth Cup glory in 2007 and was integral to the reserves' title win a year later.

JAY SPEARING
BORN Wirral, 25 November 1988.

GAMES	0 (2)
GOALS	0

NEWCOMERS

SUMMER 2009

As Liverpool girded their loins for a renewed assault on domestic and European glory in 2009/10, the ever-changing cast of Anfield characters was tweaked again by manager Rafael Benitez. Once more he spent heavily as he prepared for his latest challenge, but sought also to nurture promising young talent. Here is a picture gallery of the latest Reds at the time of going to press. It is hoped to feature their achievements fully in future editions of *Liverpool Player by Player*.

Left: Glen Johnson, £18 million from Portsmouth in June 2009.
Right: Alberto Aquilani, £20 million from Roma in August 2009.
Below: Sotirios Kyrgiakis, £2 million from AEK Athens in August 2009.
Left (inset): Daniel Ayala, signed from Sevilla Atletico in September 2007.

PLAYERS' STATISTICS

DECEMBER 1959 → MAY 2009

Player	Season	League App (Sub) GI			FA Cup App (Sub) GI			League Cup App (Sub) GI			Europe App (Sub) GI			Others App (Sub) GI			Total App (Sub) GI		
Ablett G	86–91	103 [6]	1		16 [2]	0		10 [1]	0		6 [0]	0		2 [0]	0		137 [9]	1
A'Court A	52–64	355 [0]	61		24 [0]	2		2 [0]	0		1 [0]	0		0 [0]	0		382 [0]	63
Agger D	05–	46 [7]	3		2 [0]	0		4 [0]	2		18 [0]	1		1 [0]	0		71 [7]	6
Aldridge J	86–89	69 [14]	50		12 [0]	8		7 [1]	3		0 [0]	0		1 [0]	2		89 [15]	63
Alonso X	04–08	121 [22]	14		12 [0]	2		1 [3]	0		44 [3]	2		3 [1]	0		181 [29]	18
Anelka N	2001	13 [7]	4		2 [0]	1		0 [0]	0		0 [0]	0		0 [0]	0		15 [7]	5
Arbeloa A	06–08	63 [3]	2		3 [0]	0		3 [0]	0		24 [2]	0		0 [0]	0		93 [5]	2
Arnell A	53–60	69 [0]	33		6 [0]	2		0 [0]	0		0 [0]	0		0 [0]	0		75 [0]	35
Arnold S	1970	1 [0]	0		0 [0]	0		0 [0]	0		0 [0]	0		0 [0]	0		1 [0]	0
Arphexad P	00–01	1 [0]	0		0 [0]	0		2 [0]	0		2 [0]	0		0 [0]	0		5 [0]	0
Arrowsmith A	61–67	43 [4]	20		6 [0]	4		0 [0]	0		1 [0]	0		1 [0]	0		51 [4]	24
Aurelio F	06–	42 [15]	3		0 [3]	0		4 [0]	0		18 [4]	1		0 [1]	0		64 [23]	4
Babb P	94–98	124 [4]	1		12 [0]	0		16 [0]	0		12 [2]	0		0 [0]	0		164 [6]	1
Babbel M	00–02	42 [0]	3		5 [0]	1		7 [0]	1		15 [1]	1		2 [1]	0		71 [2]	6
Babel R	07–	21 [36]	7		6 [1]	1		4 [0]	0		11 [12]	6		0 [0]	0		42 [49]	14
Banks A	58–60	8 [0]	6		0 [0]	0		0 [0]	0		0 [0]	0		0 [0]	0		8 [0]	6
Barmby N	00–01	23 [9]	2		2 [3]	1		3 [4]	1		9 [4]	4		1 [0]	0		38 [20]	8
Barnes J	87–96	310 [4]	84		51 [0]	16		22 [6]	3		2 [0]	3		3 [0]	1		402 [4]	107
Baros M	01–05	45 [23]	19		0 [3]	0		3 [5]	4		18 [10]	4		0 [1]	0		66 [42]	27
Barragan A	2005	0 [0]	0		0 [0]	0		0 [0]	0		0 [1]	0		0 [0]	0		0 [1]	0
Beardsley P	87–90	120 [11]	46		22 [3]	11		13 [1]	1		0 [0]	0		3 [0]	1		158 [15]	59
Beglin J	84–87	64 [0]	2		10 [0]	0		13 [0]	0		3 [0]	1		1 [0]	0		91 [0]	3
Bellamy C	2006	23 [4]	7		0 [0]	0		2 [0]	0		8 [4]	2		0 [1]	0		33 [9]	9
Benayoun Y	07–	36 [26]	12		3 [1]	3		1 [2]	1		12 [8]	4		0 [0]	0		52 [37]	20
Berger P	96–02	106 [42]	28		4 [4]	0		9 [2]	3		17 [11]	4		0 [1]	0		136 [60]	35
Biscan I	00–04	50 [22]	2		5 [2]	0		12 [3]	1		14 [8]	0		0 [2]	0		81 [37]	3
Bjornebye S	92–98	132 [7]	2		11 [2]	0		16 [0]	0		16 [0]	2		0 [0]	0		175 [9]	4
Boersma P	69–75	73 [9]	17		7 [3]	1		5 [3]	3		13 [6]	8		1 [0]	1		99 [21]	30
Brownbill D	1973	1 [0]	0		0 [0]	0		0 [0]	0		0 [0]	0		0 [0]	0		1 [0]	0
Burrows D	88–93	135 [11]	3		16 [1]	0		16 [0]	0		11 [0]	0		3 [0]	0		181 [12]	3
Byrne G	57–68	273 [1]	2		29 [0]	0		5 [0]	0		22 [0]	1		3 [0]	1		332 [1]	4
Callaghan I	59–77	637 [3]	50		77 [1]	2		42 [0]	7		87 [1]	10		8 [0]	0		851 [5]	69
Camara T	1999	22 [11]	9		2 [0]	1		0 [2]	0		0 [0]	0		0 [0]	0		24 [13]	10
Campbell R	59–60	14 [0]	1		0 [0]	0		0 [0]	0		0 [0]	0		0 [0]	0		14 [0]	1
Carragher J	96–	384 [14]	3		31 [1]	0		22 [5]	0		114 [0]	1		5 [1]	0		556 [21]	4
Carson S	04–05	4 [0]	0		1 [0]	0		1 [0]	0		3 [0]	0		0 [0]	0		9 [0]	0
Carter J	90–91	2 [3]	0		2 [0]	0		0 [0]	0		0 [1]	0		0 [0]	0		4 [4]	0
Case J	74–80	170 [16]	23		20 [2]	7		21 [1]	3		25 [6]	12		8 [0]	1		244 [25]	46
Cavalieri D	08–	0 [0]	0		1 [0]	0		2 [0]	0		1 [0]	0		0 [0]	0		4 [0]	0
Charnock P	1992	0 [0]	0		0 [0]	0		1 [0]	0		0 [1]	0		0 [0]	0		1 [1]	0
Cheyrou B	02–03	17 [14]	2		5 [1]	2		1 [1]	0		4 [4]	1		0 [1]	0		27 [21]	5
Chisnall P	64–65	6 [0]	1		0 [0]	0		0 [0]	0		2 [0]	1		0 [1]	0		8 [1]	2
Cisse D	04–05	29 [20]	13		3 [3]	2		0 [0]	0		10 [12]	7		1 [1]	2		43 [36]	24
Clemence R	68–80	470 [0]	0		54 [0]	0		55 [0]	0		77 [0]	0		9 [0]	0		665 [0]	0
Clough N	93–95	29 [10]	7		2 [0]	0		3 [0]	2		0 [0]	0		0 [0]	0		34 [10]	9
Cohen A	79–80	16 [2]	1		1 [0]	0		1 [0]	0		2 [1]	0		0 [0]	0		20 [3]	1
Collymore S	95–96	55 [6]	26		9 [0]	7		2 [2]	0		5 [2]	2		0 [0]	0		71 [10]	35
Cormack P	72–75	119 [6]	21		14 [0]	2		20 [0]	1		15 [3]	2		1 [0]	0		169 [9]	26
Crouch P	05–07	55 [30]	22		10 [1]	5		5 [0]	1		21 [9]	11		2 [1]	3		93 [41]	42
Dalglish K	77–89	342 [13]	118		36 [0]	13		57 [2]	27		46 [1]	10		12 [1]	2		493 [17]	170
Darby S	08–	0 [0]	0		0 [0]	0		0 [1]	0		0 [1]	0		0 [0]	0		0 [2]	0
Degen P	08–	0 [0]	0		0 [0]	0		2 [0]	0		0 [0]	0		0 [0]	0		2 [0]	0
Diao S	02–04	19 [18]	1		1 [1]	0		7 [1]	1		8 [6]	1		0 [0]	0		35 [26]	3

Player	Season	League App	(Sub)	GI	FA Cup App	(Sub)	GI	League Cup App	(Sub)	GI	Europe App	(Sub)	GI	Others App	(Sub)	GI	Total App	(Sub)	GI
Dicks J	1993	24	[0]	3	1	[0]	0	3	[0]	0	0	[0]	0	0	[0]	0	28	[0]	3
Diomede B	00–01	1	[1]	0	0	[0]	0	0	[0]	0	3	[0]	0	0	[0]	0	4	[1]	0
Diouf EH	02–03	41	[14]	3	4	[0]	0	7	[0]	3	8	[5]	0	1	[0]	0	60	[19]	6
Dossena A	08–	12	[4]	1	2	[0]	0	1	[0]	0	4	[3]	1	0	[0]	0	19	[7]	2
Dudek J	01–06	126	[1]	0	8	[1]	0	11	[0]	0	38	[0]	0	1	[0]	0	184	[2]	0
Dundee S	1998	0	[3]	0	0	[0]	0	0	[1]	0	0	[1]	0	0	[0]	0	0	[5]	0
Durnin J	86–88	0	[0]	0	0	[0]	0	1	[1]	0	0	[0]	0	0	[0]	0	1	[1]	0
El Zhar N	06–	1	[17]	0	0	[1]	0	3	[1]	1	0	[2]	0	0	[0]	0	4	[21]	1
Evans A	68–71	77	[2]	21	9	[2]	3	7	[0]	2	11	[2]	7	1	[0]	0	105	[6]	33
Evans R	69–73	9	[0]	0	0	[0]	0	1	[0]	0	1	[0]	0	0	[0]	0	11	[0]	0
Fagan C	1970	1	[0]	0	0	[0]	0	0	[0]	0	0	[0]	0	0	[0]	0	1	[0]	0
Fairclough D	75–82	64	[36]	34	10	[4]	4	7	[13]	10	7	[9]	4	4	[0]	3	92	[62]	55
Ferns P	62–64	27	[0]	1	1	[0]	0	0	[0]	0	0	[0]	0	0	[0]	0	28	[0]	1
Ferri J	1998	0	[2]	0	0	[0]	0	0	[0]	0	0	[0]	0	0	[0]	0	0	[2]	0
Finnan S	03–07	134	[11]	1	12	[1]	0	5	[1]	0	46	[4]	0	3	[0]	0	200	[15]	1
Fowler R	93-01 & 05-06	225	[41]	128	21	[3]	12	35	[0]	29	28	[15]	4	0	[1]	0	309	[60]	183
Friedel B	97–99	25	[0]	0	0	[0]	0	4	[0]	0	1	[1]	0	0	[0]	0	30	[1]	0
Furnell J	61–63	28	[0]	0	0	[0]	0	0	[0]	0	0	[0]	0	0	[0]	0	28	[0]	0
Garcia L	04–06	52	[25]	18	3	[1]	1	2	[3]	0	25	[6]	9	3	[1]	1	85	[36]	29
Gayle H	1980	3	[1]	1	0	[0]	0	0	[0]	0	0	[1]	0	0	[0]	0	3	[2]	1
Gerrard S	98–	308	[25]	71	22	[4]	9	17	[2]	7	90	[10]	32	4	[1]	1	441	[42]	120
Gillespie G	83–90	152	[4]	14	21	[2]	0	22	[0]	2	2	[1]	0	2	[1]	0	199	[8]	6
Gonzalez M	2006	14	[11]	2	0	[0]	0	2	[0]	0	3	[5]	1	1	[0]	0	20	[16]	3
Graham R	64–71	96	[5]	31	7	[2]	4	7	[1]	2	13	[0]	5	1	[0]	0	124	[8]	42
Grobbelaar B	81–93	440	[0]	0	62	[0]	0	70	[0]	0	37	[0]	0	11	[0]	0	620	[0]	0
Guthrie D	2006	0	[3]	0	0	[0]	0	1	[2]	0	1	[0]	0	0	[0]	0	2	[5]	0
Hall B	68–75	140	[13]	15	17	[2]	3	12	[1]	1	27	[8]	2	2	[0]	0	198	[24]	21
Hamann D	99–05	174	[17]	8	15	[1]	1	8	[4]	0	52	[7]	2	4	[1]	0	253	[30]	11
Hansen A	77–89	435	[2]	7	59	[1]	2	68	[0]	1	42	[1]	3	12	[0]	0	616	[4]	13
Harkness S	91–98	90	[12]	3	5	[1]	0	11	[2]	3	13	[3]	0	0	[0]	0	119	[18]	6
Harrower J	57–60	96	[0]	21	6	[0]	1	3	[0]	0	0	[0]	0	0	[0]	0	105	[0]	22
Hateley A	67–68	42	[0]	17	7	[0]	8	2	[0]	0	5	[0]	3	0	[0]	0	56	[0]	28
Heggem V	98–00	38	[16]	3	1	[0]	0	2	[2]	0	5	[1]	0	0	[0]	0	46	[19]	3
Heighway S	70–80	312	[17]	50	33	[3]	8	38	[0]	7	61	[3]	11	5	[1]	0	449	[24]	76
Henchoz S	99–04	132	[3]	0	15	[0]	0	16	[0]	0	35	[1]	0	3	[0]	0	201	[4]	0
Heskey E	99–03	118	[32]	39	9	[5]	6	7	[5]	2	39	[5]	12	3	[0]	1	176	[47]	60
Hickson D	59–60	60	[0]	37	4	[0]	0	3	[0]	1	0	[0]	0	0	[0]	0	67	[0]	38
Hignett A	1964	1	[0]	0	0	[0]	0	0	[0]	0	0	[0]	0	0	[0]	0	1	[0]	0
Hobbs J	2007	1	[1]	0	0	[0]	0	2	[1]	0	0	[0]	0	0	[0]	0	3	[2]	0
Hodgson D	82–83	21	[7]	4	3	[0]	1	6	[3]	3	3	[4]	2	0	[2]	0	33	[16]	10
Hooper M	86–92	50	[1]	0	5	[0]	0	10	[0]	0	4	[0]	0	0	[1]	0	69	[2]	0
Houghton R	87–91	147	[6]	28	26	[1]	0	4	[0]	3	4	[0]	2	2	[0]	0	193	[7]	37
Hughes E	66–78	474	[0]	35	62	[0]	1	46	[0]	3	75	[0]	9	8	[0]	1	665	[0]	49
Hutchison D	91–93	33	[12]	7	1	[2]	0	7	[1]	2	3	[0]	1	0	[1]	0	44	[16]	10
Hunt R	59–69	401	[3]	245	44	[0]	18	10	[0]	5	29	[2]	17	3	[0]	1	487	[5]	286
Hysen G	89–91	70	[2]	2	13	[0]	0	6	[0]	1	0	[0]	0	2	[0]	0	91	[2]	3
Hyypia S	99–08	310	[8]	22	29	[0]	1	19	[0]	2	91	[1]	8	6	[0]	0	455	[9]	33
Ince P	97–98	65	[0]	14	3	[0]	1	6	[0]	1	7	[0]	1	0	[0]	0	81	[0]	17
Insua E	06–	13	[2]	0	1	[0]	0	1	[0]	0	0	[0]	0	0	[0]	0	15	[3]	0
Irvine A	86–87	0	[2]	0	0	[1]	0	0	[1]	0	0	[0]	0	0	[0]	0	0	[4]	0
Irwin C	79–80	26	[3]	3	4	[0]	0	6	[0]	0	4	[1]	0	0	[0]	0	40	[4]	3
Itandje C	07-	0	[0]	0	4	[0]	0	3	[0]	0	0	[0]	0	0	[0]	0	7	[0]	0
James D	92–98	213	[1]	0	20	[0]	0	22	[0]	0	22	[0]	0	0	[0]	0	277	[1]	0
Johnson D	76–81	128	[20]	55	17	[2]	6	15	[3]	9	14	[5]	8	3	[3]	0	177	[33]	78
Johnston C	81–87	165	[25]	30	14	[4]	4	32	[3]	3	13	[4]	2	3	[1]	0	227	[37]	39
Jones A	59–62	5	[0]	0	0	[0]	0	0	[0]	0	0	[0]	0	0	[0]	0	5	[0]	0
Jones B	1991	0	[0]	0	0	[0]	0	0	[0]	0	0	[1]	0	0	[0]	0	0	[1]	0
Jones J	75–77	72	[0]	3	9	[0]	0	4	[0]	0	12	[0]	0	3	[0]	0	100	[0]	3
Jones L	94–96	0	[3]	0	0	[0]	0	0	[1]	0	0	[0]	0	0	[0]	0	0	[4]	0

Player	Season	League			FA Cup			League Cup			Europe			Others			Total		
		App	(Sub)	Gl	App	(Sub)	Gl	App	(Sub)	Gl	App	(Sub)	Gl	App	(Sub)	Gl	App	(Sub)	Gl
Jones P	2003	2	[0]	0	0	[0]	0	0	[0]	0	0	[0]	0	0	[0]	0	2	[0]	0
Jones R	91–97	182	[1]	0	27	[0]	0	21	[1]	0	11	[0]	0	0	[0]	0	241	[2]	0
Josemi	04–05	16	[5]	0	0	[0]	0	1	[0]	0	9	[2]	0	2	[0]	0	28	[7]	0
Keane R	2008	16	[3]	5	1	[0]	0	0	[1]	0	6	[1]	2	0	[0]	0	23	[5]	7
Keegan K	71–76	230	[0]	68	28	[0]	14	23	[0]	6	40	[0]	12	2	[0]	0	323	[0]	100
Kelly M	08–	0	[0]	0	0	[0]	0	0	[0]	0	0	[1]	0	0	[0]	0	0	[1]	0
Kennedy A	78–85	247	[2]	15	21	[0]	0	45	[0]	2	34	[0]	4	8	[0]	0	355	[2]	21
Kennedy M	94–97	5	[11]	0	0	[1]	0	0	[2]	0	0	[2]	0	0	[0]	0	5	[16]	0
Kennedy R	74–81	272	[3]	51	28	[0]	3	35	[0]	6	46	[0]	12	9	[0]	0	390	[3]	72
Kettle B	75–76	3	[0]	0	0	[0]	0	0	[0]	0	1	[0]	0	0	[0]	0	4	[0]	0
Kewell H	03–07	81	[12]	12	7	[3]	0	2	[3]	1	18	[12]	3	1	[0]	0	109	[30]	16
Kewley K	1977	0	[1]	0	0	[0]	0	0	[0]	0	0	[0]	0	0	[0]	0	0	[1]	0
Kippe F	99–01	0	[0]	0	0	[0]	0	0	[2]	0	0	[0]	0	0	[0]	0	0	[2]	0
Kirkland C	01–04	25	[0]	0	3	[0]	0	6	[0]	0	11	[0]	0	0	[0]	0	45	[0]	0
Kozma I	91–92	3	[3]	0	0	[2]	0	0	[1]	0	0	[0]	0	0	[1]	0	3	[7]	0
Kromkamp J	05–06	7	[7]	0	1	[3]	0	0	[0]	0	0	[0]	0	0	[0]	0	8	[10]	0
Kuyt D	06–	87	[17]	27	5	[2]	2	0	[2]	0	30	[4]	11	0	[0]	0	122	[25]	40
Kvarme B	96–98	39	[6]	0	2	[0]	0	2	[0]	0	5	[0]	0	0	[0]	0	48	[6]	0
Lane F	1972	1	[0]	0	0	[0]	0	1	[0]	0	0	[0]	0	0	[0]	0	2	[0]	0
Lawler C	62–75	406	[0]	41	47	[0]	4	27	[0]	5	66	[0]	11	3	[0]	0	549	[0]	61
Lawrence T	62–70	306	[0]	0	42	[0]	0	6	[0]	0	33	[0]	0	3	[0]	0	390	[0]	0
Lawrenson M	81–87	233	[8]	11	24	[0]	2	49	[0]	2	26	[1]	2	6	[0]	0	338	[9]	17
Lee S	77–85	190	[7]	13	17	[0]	0	39	[0]	2	33	[0]	4	4	[0]	0	283	[7]	19
Leishman T	59–62	107	[0]	6	9	[0]	0	3	[0]	1	0	[0]	0	0	[0]	0	119	[0]	7
Leonhardsen O	97–98	34	[3]	7	1	[0]	0	4	[2]	0	3	[2]	0	0	[0]	0	42	[7]	7
Le Tallec A	03–05	5	[12]	0	1	[3]	0	2	[0]	0	5	[4]	1	0	[0]	0	13	[19]	1
Leto S	2007	0	[0]	0	0	[0]	0	2	[0]	0	2	[0]	0	0	[0]	0	4	[0]	0
Lewis K	60–62	71	[0]	39	8	[0]	3	2	[0]	2	0	[0]	0	0	[0]	0	81	[0]	44
Liddell W	45–60	495	[0]	216	42	[0]	13	0	[0]	0	0	[0]	0	0	[0]	0	537	[0]	229
Lindsay A	69–76	168	[2]	12	22	[0]	1	23	[0]	1	31	[0]	4	2	[0]	0	246	[2]	18
Litmanen J	00–01	12	[14]	5	1	[2]	1	2	[1]	0	4	[7]	3	0	[0]	0	19	[24]	9
Livermore D	67–70	13	[3]	0	0	[0]	0	1	[0]	0	0	[0]	0	0	[0]	0	14	[3]	0
Lloyd L	69–73	150	[0]	4	16	[0]	0	20	[0]	0	31	[0]	1	1	[0]	0	218	[0]	5
Lowry T	1964	1	[0]	0	0	[0]	0	0	[0]	0	0	[0]	0	0	[0]	0	1	[0]	0
Lucas L	07–	25	[18]	1	4	[2]	1	5	[0]	1	6	[10]	1	0	[0]	0	40	[30]	4
Luzi P	2003	0	[1]	0	0	[0]	0	0	[0]	0	0	[0]	0	0	[0]	0	0	[1]	0
McAllister G	00–01	35	[20]	5	4	[1]	0	3	[3]	1	8	[11]	2	2	[0]	1	52	[35]	9
McAteer J	95–98	84	[16]	3	11	[1]	3	12	[1]	0	12	[2]	0	0	[0]	0	119	[20]	6
McDermott T	74–82	221	[11]	54	23	[0]	4	36	[0]	5	30	[1]	12	7	[0]	6	317	[12]	81
MacDonald K	84–88	29	[11]	1	9	[0]	1	1	[3]	1	3	[0]	0	2	[0]	0	44	[14]	3
McLaughlin J	69–74	38	[2]	2	4	[0]	1	3	[0]	0	8	[0]	0	0	[0]	0	53	[2]	3
McMahon S	85–91	202	[2]	29	30	[0]	7	27	[0]	13	5	[0]	0	4	[0]	0	268	[2]	49
McManaman S	90–98	258	[14]	45	28	[1]	5	32	[1]	10	30	[0]	5	0	[0]	0	348	[16]	65
Marsh M	88–93	42	[27]	2	6	[2]	0	10	[1]	3	11	[1]	1	1	[0]	0	70	[31]	6
Mascherano J	06–	59	[0]	1	3	[2]	0	0	[1]	0	25	[0]	0	0	[0]	0	83	[3]	1
Matteo D	93–99	112	[15]	1	6	[2]	1	9	[0]	0	10	[1]	0	0	[0]	0	137	[18]	2
Maxwell L	1999	0	[0]	0	0	[0]	0	1	[0]	1	0	[0]	0	0	[0]	0	1	[0]	1
Meijer E	99–00	7	[17]	0	0	[0]	0	3	[0]	2	0	[0]	0	0	[0]	0	10	[17]	2
Melia J	55–63	269	[0]	76	18	[0]	2	0	[0]	0	0	[0]	0	0	[0]	0	287	[0]	78
Mellor N	02–04	7	[5]	2	1	[1]	0	6	[0]	3	1	[1]	1	0	[0]	0	15	[7]	6
Milne G	60–66	234	[2]	18	27	[0]	1	0	[0]	0	16	[0]	0	2	[0]	0	279	[2]	19
Molby J	84–94	195	[23]	44	24	[4]	4	25	[3]	9	7	[0]	1	2	[0]	0	253	[30]	58
Molyneux J	55–61	229	[0]	2	17	[0]	1	3	[0]	0	0	[0]	0	0	[0]	0	249	[0]	3
Molyneux W	1964	1	[0]	0	0	[0]	0	0	[0]	0	0	[0]	0	0	[0]	0	1	[0]	0
Money R	1980	12	[2]	0	1	[0]	0	1	[0]	0	1	[0]	0	0	[0]	0	15	[2]	0
Mooney B	1986	0	[0]	0	0	[0]	0	0	[1]	0	0	[0]	0	0	[0]	0	0	[1]	0
Moran R	52–64	343	[0]	14	32	[0]	2	0	[0]	0	4	[0]	0	1	[0]	0	380	[0]	16
Morientes F	04–05	32	[9]	8	2	[3]	1	3	[0]	0	8	[2]	3	2	[0]	0	47	[14]	12
Morris F	58–59	47	[0]	14	1	[0]	0	0	[0]	0	0	[0]	0	0	[0]	0	48	[0]	14

Player	Season	League App	(Sub)	Gl	FA Cup App	(Sub)	Gl	League Cup App	(Sub)	Gl	Europe App	(Sub)	Gl	Others App	(Sub)	Gl	Total App	(Sub)	Gl
Morrissey J	57–60	36	[0]	6	1	[0]	0	0	[0]	0	0	[0]	0	0	[0]	0	37	[0]	6
Murphy D	97–03	114	[56]	25	11	[4]	3	15	[1]	11	37	[8]	5	1	[2]	0	178	[71]	44
Neal P	74–85	453	[2]	41	45	[0]	3	66	[0]	4	69	[0]	12	14	[0]	0	647	[2]	60
Newby J	1999	0	[1]	0	0	[2]	0	0	[1]	0	0	[0]	0	0	[0]	0	0	[4]	0
Ngog D	08–	2	[12]	2	0	[0]	0	2	[0]	0	1	[2]	1	0	[0]	0	5	[14]	3
Nicol S	82–94	328	[15]	36	50	[0]	3	42	[0]	4	17	[2]	2	4	[0]	0	441	[17]	45
Nunez A	2004	8	[10]	0	1	[0]	0	2	[1]	1	2	[3]	0	0	[0]	0	13	[14]	1
Ogrizovic S	77–80	4	[0]	0	0	[0]	0	0	[0]	0	0	[0]	0	1	[0]	0	5	[0]	0
Ogston J	1966	1	[0]	0	0	[0]	0	0	[0]	0	0	[0]	0	0	[0]	0	1	[0]	0
Otsemobor J	02–03	4	[0]	0	0	[0]	0	2	[0]	0	0	[0]	0	0	[0]	0	6	[0]	0
Owen M	96–03	193	[23]	118	14	[1]	8	12	[2]	9	45	[4]	21	3	[0]	2	267	[30]	158
Padelli D	2006	1	[0]	0	0	[0]	0	0	[0]	0	0	[0]	0	0	[0]	0	1	[0]	0
Paletta G	2006	2	[1]	0	0	[0]	0	3	[0]	1	1	[1]	0	0	[0]	0	6	[2]	1
Partridge R	00–04	0	[0]	0	0	[0]	0	1	[2]	0	0	[0]	0	0	[0]	0	1	[2]	0
Pellegrino M	2004	11	[1]	0	0	[0]	0	1	[0]	0	0	[0]	0	0	[0]	0	12	[1]	0
Peltier L	2006	0	[0]	0	0	[0]	0	3	[0]	0	1	[0]	0	0	[0]	0	4	[0]	0
Pennant J	06–08	36	[19]	3	3	[0]	0	3	[0]	0	11	[8]	0	1	[0]	0	54	[27]	3
Peplow S	1969	2	[0]	0	0	[0]	0	0	[0]	0	1	[0]	0	0	[0]	0	3	[0]	0
Piechnik T	92–93	16	[1]	0	2	[0]	0	5	[0]	0	0	[0]	0	0	[0]	0	23	[1]	0
Plessis D	07–	3	[0]	0	0	[0]	0	2	[0]	1	1	[0]	0	0	[0]	0	6	[0]	1
Potter D	04–05	0	[2]	0	1	[0]	0	4	[1]	0	5	[4]	0	0	[0]	0	10	[7]	0
Raven D	04–05	0	[1]	0	1	[0]	0	2	[0]	0	0	[0]	0	0	[0]	0	3	[1]	0
Redknapp J	91–01	207	[30]	31	17	[1]	2	26	[1]	5	20	[6]	4	0	[0]	0	270	[38]	42
Reina J	05–	144	[0]	0	7	[0]	0	1	[0]	0	51	[0]	0	4	[0]	0	207	[0]	0
Riedle K	97–99	34	[26]	11	2	[0]	0	3	[4]	2	3	[4]	2	0	[0]	0	42	[34]	15
Riera A	08–	24	[4]	3	2	[1]	1	0	[0]	0	7	[2]	1	0	[0]	0	33	[7]	5
Riise JA	01–07	196	[38]	21	16	[1]	3	9	[4]	2	69	[8]	3	6	[1]	2	296	[52]	31
Robinson M	83–84	26	[4]	6	2	[0]	1	11	[1]	4	6	[1]	2	1	[0]	0	46	[6]	13
Roque M	2006	0	[0]	0	0	[0]	0	0	[0]	0	0	[1]	0	0	[0]	0	0	[1]	0
Rosenthal R	89–93	32	[42]	21	5	[3]	0	2	[7]	1	1	[3]	0	1	[1]	0	41	[56]	22
Ross I	66–71	42	[6]	2	9	[1]	1	3	[0]	0	5	[2]	1	0	[0]	0	59	[9]	4
Ruddock N	93–97	111	[4]	11	11	[0]	0	19	[1]	1	5	[1]	0	0	[0]	0	146	[6]	12
Rush I	80-86 & 88-95	448	[22]	229	55	[6]	39	78	[0]	48	35	[2]	21	9	[0]	3	625	[30]	340
Russell C	1980	0	[1]	0	0	[0]	0	0	[0]	0	0	[0]	0	0	[0]	0	0	[1]	0
Rylands D	1973	0	[0]	0	1	[0]	0	0	[0]	0	0	[0]	0	0	[0]	0	1	[0]	0
St John I	61–70	334	[2]	95	48	[1]	12	6	[0]	1	30	[2]	10	2	[0]	0	420	[5]	118
Saunders D	91–92	42	[0]	11	8	[0]	2	5	[0]	2	5	[0]	9	1	[0]	1	61	[0]	25
Scales J	94–96	65	[0]	2	14	[0]	0	10	[0]	2	4	[1]	0	0	[0]	0	93	[1]	4
Seagraves M	1985	0	[0]	0	1	[0]	0	1	[0]	0	0	[0]	0	0	[0]	0	2	[0]	0
Sealey J	1964	1	[0]	1	0	[0]	0	0	[0]	0	0	[0]	0	0	[0]	0	1	[0]	1
Sheedy K	80–81	1	[2]	0	0	[0]	0	2	[0]	2	0	[0]	0	0	[0]	0	3	[2]	2
Sinama-Pongolle F	03–06	12	[26]	4	2	[3]	2	5	[3]	1	2	[9]	2	0	[4]	0	21	[45]	9
Sissoko M	05–07	42	[9]	1	6	[0]	0	4	[0]	0	17	[5]	0	3	[1]	0	72	[15]	1
Skrtel M	07–	33	[2]	0	3	[0]	0	0	[0]	0	12	[0]	0	0	[0]	0	48	[2]	0
Slater B	59–61	99	[0]	0	9	[0]	0	3	[0]	0	0	[0]	0	0	[0]	0	111	[0]	0
Smicer V	99–04	69	[52]	10	9	[1]	1	13	[2]	5	19	[18]	3	0	[1]	0	110	[74]	19
Smith J	2006	0	[0]	0	0	[0]	0	0	[1]	0	0	[0]	0	0	[0]	0	0	[1]	0
Smith T	62–77	467	[0]	36	52	[0]	2	30	[0]	2	83	[1]	8	5	[0]	0	637	[2]	48
Smyth M	2004	0	[0]	0	0	[0]	0	0	[1]	0	0	[0]	0	0	[0]	0	0	[1]	0
Song R	98–00	27	[7]	0	0	[1]	0	2	[0]	0	1	[0]	0	0	[0]	0	30	[8]	0
Souness G	77–83	246	[1]	38	24	[0]	2	45	[0]	9	35	[1]	7	7	[0]	0	357	[2]	56
Spackman N	86–88	39	[12]	0	5	[0]	0	6	[1]	0	0	[0]	0	0	[0]	0	50	[13]	0
Spearing J	08–	0	[0]	0	0	[0]	0	0	[0]	0	0	[2]	0	0	[0]	0	0	[2]	0
Speedie D	1990	8	[4]	6	1	[1]	0	0	[0]	0	0	[0]	0	0	[0]	0	9	[5]	6
Staunton S	88-90 & 98-00	93	[16]	0	16	[2]	1	11	[2]	5	5	[2]	0	0	[0]	0	125	[22]	6
Stevenson W	62–67	188	[0]	15	24	[0]	1	0	[0]	0	25	[1]	1	3	[0]	0	240	[1]	17
Stewart P	92–93	28	[4]	1	1	[0]	0	6	[0]	0	2	[0]	2	1	[0]	0	38	[4]	3
Storton T	72–73	5	[0]	0	1	[0]	0	4	[0]	0	1	[1]	0	0	[0]	0	11	[1]	0
Strong G	64–69	150	[5]	29	23	[0]	1	4	[0]	0	16	[0]	2	1	[0]	0	194	[5]	32

Player	Season	League App	(Sub)	Gl	FA Cup App	(Sub)	Gl	League Cup App	(Sub)	Gl	Europe App	(Sub)	Gl	Others App	(Sub)	Gl	Total App	(Sub)	Gl
Tanner N	89–92	36	[4]	1	2	[0]	0	6	[2]	0	6	[2]	0	1	[0]	0	51	[8]	1
Thomas M	91–97	96	[28]	9	15	[2]	2	7	[3]	1	10	[2]	0	0	[0]	0	128	[35]	12
Thompson D	96–99	24	[24]	5	0	[1]	0	5	[0]	0	2	[0]	0	0	[0]	0	31	[25]	5
Thompson M	73–75	1	[0]	0	0	[0]	0	0	[0]	0	0	[1]	0	0	[0]	0	1	[1]	0
Thompson Peter	63–71	318	[4]	41	37	[1]	5	9	[0]	2	40	[3]	6	2	[0]	0	406	[8]	54
Thompson Phil	71–82	337	[3]	7	36	[0]	0	42	[1]	1	44	[3]	4	11	[0]	1	470	[7]	13
Thomson R	62–63	6	[0]	0	1	[0]	0	0	[0]	0	0	[0]	0	0	[0]	0	7	[0]	0
Torres F	07–	49	[8]	38	3	[1]	1	2	[1]	3	19	[1]	8	0	[0]	0	73	[11]	50
Toshack J	70–77	169	[3]	74	24	[0]	8	13	[0]	3	30	[6]	10	1	[0]	1	237	[9]	96
Traore D	99–05	72	[16]	0	4	[1]	0	12	[2]	0	30	[2]	1	2	[0]	0	120	[21]	1
Venison B	86–91	103	[7]	1	16	[5]	0	14	[3]	0	0	[3]	1	4	[0]	0	137	[18]	2
Vignal G	00–02	7	[4]	0	0	[1]	0	3	[0]	0	4	[1]	0	0	[0]	0	14	[6]	0
Voronin A	07–	13	[6]	5	0	[1]	0	1	[0]	0	4	[3]	1	0	[0]	0	18	[10]	6
Waddle A	73–76	11	[5]	1	2	[0]	0	3	[0]	0	0	[1]	0	0	[0]	0	16	[6]	1
Wall P	67–69	31	[0]	0	6	[0]	0	2	[0]	0	3	[0]	0	0	[0]	0	42	[0]	0
Wallace G	62–66	19	[1]	3	0	[0]	0	0	[0]	0	1	[0]	2	1	[0]	1	21	[1]	6
Walsh P	84–87	63	[14]	25	6	[2]	3	10	[2]	4	6	[0]	3	1	[1]	0	86	[19]	35
Walters M	91–94	58	[36]	14	6	[3]	0	10	[2]	4	7	[1]	1	1	[0]	0	82	[42]	19
Wark J	83–87	64	[6]	28	11	[2]	6	6	[4]	3	9	[0]	5	3	[0]	0	93	[12]	42
Warnock S	04–06	27	[13]	1	2	[1]	0	7	[1]	0	9	[6]	0	1	[0]	0	46	[21]	1
Watson A	87–88	3	[1]	1	1	[1]	0	1	[1]	0	0	[0]	0	1	[0]	0	6	[3]	0
Welsh J	02–04	2	[2]	0	1	[0]	0	0	[3]	0	0	[2]	0	0	[0]	0	3	[7]	0
Westerveld S	99–01	75	[0]	0	8	[0]	0	5	[0]	0	13	[0]	0	2	[0]	0	103	[0]	0
Wheeler J	56–61	164	[0]	21	10	[0]	2	3	[0]	0	0	[0]	0	0	[0]	0	177	[0]	23
Whelan R	80–93	351	[11]	46	40	[1]	7	46	[4]	14	22	[1]	6	8	[1]	0	467	[18]	73
Whitbread Z	04–05	0	[0]	0	1	[0]	0	4	[0]	0	1	[1]	0	0	[0]	0	6	[1]	0
White R	55–61	203	[0]	0	10	[0]	1	3	[0]	0	0	[0]	0	0	[0]	0	216	[0]	1
Whitham J	70–71	15	[0]	7	0	[0]	0	1	[0]	0	0	[0]	0	0	[0]	0	16	[0]	7
Wilson D	1966	0	[1]	0	0	[0]	0	0	[0]	0	0	[0]	0	0	[0]	0	0	[1]	0
Wright M	91–97	156	[2]	5	18	[0]	0	14	[2]	1	17	[0]	2	1	[0]	0	206	[4]	8
Wright S	00–01	10	[4]	0	2	[0]	0	1	[1]	0	2	[1]	1	0	[0]	0	15	[6]	1
Xavier A	01–02	13	[1]	1	0	[0]	0	1	[0]	0	5	[0]	1	1	[0]	0	20	[1]	2
Yeats R	61–70	357	[1]	13	50	[0]	0	7	[0]	0	36	[0]	2	3	[0]	1	453	[1]	16
Zenden B	05–06	14	[9]	2	0	[0]	0	2	[0]	0	12	[8]	0	2	[0]	0	30	[17]	2
Ziege C	2000	11	[5]	1	2	[1]	0	1	[3]	1	6	[3]	0	0	[0]	0	20	[12]	2

Dates shown indicate the first year of each season. Thus 64–66 means 1964/65 to 1966/67. A single entry indicates one season only – eg 2002 refers to 2002/03.